The Work of the Negative

The Work of the Negative

André Green

Translated by Andrew Weller

FREE ASSOCIATION BOOKS / LONDON / NEW YORK

Published in 1999 by
FREE ASSOCIATION BOOKS
57 Warren Street
London W1P 5PA

A CIP catalogue record for this book is available
from the British Library.

ISBN 1 85343 470 1 pbk; 1 85343 460 4 hbk

Designed and produced for the publisher by
Chase Production Services, Chadlington OX7 3LN
Printed and bound by Antony Rowe Ltd, Eastbourne

Contents

Translator's Note

It was a great privilege, a year ago, to be asked to translate *Le travail du Négatif* into English. I had already read with interest André Green's *On Private Madness*. Both these titles attracted me. It is difficult to imagine how anyone could take on the task of translating a typescript of approximately 400 pages, renowned for its difficulty, if there was not some personal engagement involved. It is true that there is a real sense in which I can say that my subject has found me! I have long been interested in Keat's idea of 'negative capability' – which, incidentally, is the title of an article by André Green reviewing Bion's book *Attention and Interpretation*[1] – and my Christian upbringing, childhood experiences and later studies in theology resulted in a considerable struggle with what I would call the shadow side of things or negativity in both its creative and destructive aspects. Further, the creative struggle involved in this translation undoubtedly helped me cope with the loss of my much-loved father just as I was beginning this task.

This book is very demanding on the reader and it is likely that many will take encouragement, as I did, from the author's own acknowledgement at one point that 'all this is not easy to understand'! I have often felt I was climbing a mountain with limited oxygen supply. At times in fine weather, at others in thick fog, and always with the sense that there was yet another ridge to climb. But once on top and able to cast my eye over the scene below, I have begun to get a better sense of the lie of the land, even if I am still unable to make out all the details of the landscape. Perhaps, as is sometimes the case in analysis itself, deeper understanding will come after the event. But in spite of the difficulties, or perhaps because of them, this has been an extremely rewarding year. An additional pleasure was the discovery of Stefan Zweig's novella and Gérard de Nerval's writing in the chapter on sublimation.

In translating *Le Travail du Négatif* one is necessarily confronted with the influence of three languages, three philosophical traditions, German, French and English which all have, as it is known, a very different spirit. The term 'the work of the negative' was borrowed from Hegel, even if the way it is employed in psychoanalysis has little relation to Hegel's philosophy. But his thinking, along with others such as Kant, Husserl, Nietzsche and Heidegger forms a backdrop to André Green's argument in the early chapters, presenting the reader with a heady task from the outset! Then, of course, there is Freud's German and Lacan's re-interpretation of Freud's work to take into account. French psychoanalysis has a strong inclination for philosophy and linguistics and many analysts in France come to psychoanalysis from philosophy. It is often observed that French discourse is marked by a taste for abstraction and intellectualism. The English tradition, on the other hand – perhaps more wary of abstraction and intellectualism – is seen by some as more empirical, pragmatic, concerned with the facts of experience and 'theories are the human stammer towards grasping those facts'.[2] Such philosophical differences reflect the differences of language itself and as André Green says, French lends itself more than other languages to a conceptual treatment of the concept of the negative.

My sense is that it might be helpful to try and set the scene for the reader by making some general introductory remarks on the negative. These are simply some key ideas, brought together into a sort of collage, which I have gleaned from reading the book and speaking with the author; they are developed fully in the text. First a word on etymology. Latin: *negativus*, from *negare* = to say No, to *negate* a proposition. Hegel was the thinker *par excellence* in the nineteenth century of the negative and negativity. For him negativity was an essential property of consciousness, of thinking: 'the moment in the process of development in which positive determinations are suppressed represents a really creative "work". It destroys, maintains and preserves in one and the same movement. The positive moment and the negative moment are the two sides of Hegelian dialectics.'[3] Negativity in Hegel is thus 'the activity of negation' enriching itself from the term it negates. As the author has pointed out, Hegel's idea was not stillborn and is echoed, for example, by Sartre's statement that *'la conscience est ce qu'elle n'est pas'*.[4]

The first act of negation in psychoanalysis was the discovery of the unconscious and a latent structuring organisation. In this book the term 'the work of the negative' covers all the psychical operations of which repression is the prototype, i.e., denial, disavowal, negation and foreclosure. Thus it falls between the two extremes of repression, which is necessary and inevitable, and rejection which obstructs all positive investment. André Green emphasises that the word 'work' is important in psychoanalysis. We are familiar with dream work, the work of mourning, the work of elaboration, for example. It insists, he says, on a process which is destabilising, tormenting. One of the essential properties of the negative, then, is to *contest unity*. This occurs when the unconscious is activated by the return of the repressed confronting us with a part or parts of ourselves we tend to consider as trivial or unimportant. This implies the need to *mistrust appearances*, that is, what is manifest and conscious, what seems to be common sense, self-evident. The negative is thus characterised by the *logic of the shadow*. The positive contains the negative within it and vice versa. There is therefore always a potential for *reversal*. Negativity is a common feature of mankind but as the author argues there are *two basic kinds of negativity*: one which is potentially creative and structuring, when elaborated, and another which is disorganising and destructuring, when evacuated. In its extreme form the latter may develop into the radical refusal of all desire, 'except negative desire', found in the *negativism* of non-neurotic structures. This book is mainly about the second kind of negativity which colours the whole personality. The chapters on masochism, splitting and narcissism are central here.

Now some remarks on language. One feature of the text is the author's use of neologisms which may be stylistically congruent in French but are undoubtedly awkward in English. A major difficulty of translation has been the derivative forms of '*négatif*' such as *négativation, négativé, négativante* as well as their counterparts *positivation, positivisé* etc. Green emphasises that negation is concerned with language but that this is only one aspect of the process he is writing about which goes beyond language and affects different forms of psychic life including the affects and drives. I have therefore decided to retain the term *négativation* and its derivatives as technical terms in an anglicised form, and the first time they appear in the text I have put the French in italics immediately after. 'Negativising' or 'negativisation', then, refers to the process or act of denying, or negating the positive aspect of impulse or desire which results in negation. Positivising refers to the almost constant process by which we become aware of something, either directly (I want this, I am this) or indirectly (not just direct affirmation but by negating negation (Hegel)).

The reader should also be aware of some of the basic choices which have been made with regard to technical psychoanalytic terminology. First, all references to Freud's work follow the *Standard Edition*. However, in view of the fact that this translation has come in for a good deal of criticism, particularly in France and America, but also from some of the more hermeneutically-minded analysts in Britain, I have deviated from the *Standard Edition* with respect to certain terms. Where this is the case I have made an annotation the first time the word occurs in the text, giving the German, French and *Standard Edition* rendering. The main differences are:

Drive: Reflecting both French and increasingly American usage (Kernberg) and some British authors (Segal), I have translated Fr: *pulsion*; [G: *Trieb*] throughout by 'drive' with its wholly psychical meaning, rather than by 'instinct' with its biological connotations. I therefore refer to the life drive (*pulsion de vie/Lebenstrieb*) and death drive (*pulsion de mort/Todestrieb*) rather than life instinct and death instinct (*Standard Edition*). There are a number of derivatives of *pulsion* such as *pulsionnalité, pulsionnalisation* (which are neologisms) which do not have a straightforward equivalent in English. In these cases I have offered a translation and left the original French word in brackets immediately after.

Representation: The French word *représentation* (*Vorstellung*) (*Standard Edition*: idea or presentation) is rendered throughout as 'representation' and *représentation de mot et représentation de chose* (*Wortvorstellung* and *Sachvorstellung*) as word representation and thing representation. (*Standard Edition*: word and thing presentations) reflecting the author's wish to stress the re-evocation of mnemic traces. I have followed the *Standard Edition* in translating *figurabilité* (*Darstellbarkeit*) as representability.

Desire and wish (*désir, voeu; Begierde, Wunsch*): the *Standard Edition* translates Freud's '*Wunsch*' as 'wish'. Freud's French translators, however, have always used '*désir*' rather than '*voeu*'. The main distinction is that *Wunsch* and wish refer to isolated acts of wishing and *désir* to a continuous force. I have used both wish and desire depending on the context.

Investment: I have preferred investment/disinvestment to the Latinised terms cathexis/decathexis.

Finally, a brief word on two key terms coined by the author: *objectalisation* and *désobjectalisation*. Objectalising, Green says (personal communication) is the natural tendency to transform drive activity into an object. Functions thus become objects. The activity of painting or stamp collecting, for example, becomes more important than the work of art produced or the stamp collection itself. In *disobjectalising*, i.e., the process of withdrawing investment – in some cases radically – from objects, what makes an object unique vanishes and any substitute will do; the human aspect is lost. The fetishist, for example, does not care who wears the raincoat; it is the raincoat which excites him. I have also retained the term *subjectal*, created by the author and forming a symmetrical pair with the term *objectal* which already existed and was created to make a distinction with *objectif* (objective). Thus *relations objectales or relations d'objet* (object relations) refers particularly to internal fantasmatic objects rather than external, objectively perceived objects. The author created the term *subjectal* to gather together a number of terms in contemporary psychoanalysis such as ego, I, self, which have a common basis, i.e., pertaining to the subject.

A certain number of other French words which have no exact translation in English such as *méconnaissance, jouissance, réel* have been retained in French with an explanatory annotation the first time they appear. Where the French is particularly idiomatic or neologistic I have often left the French term in brackets immediately after the offered translation or in an annotation so that the reader can benefit from both.

Finally, I would like to make a few comments on style and readability. André Green's argument is highly metapsychological, compact, complex and subtle and his style somewhat literary and rhetorical. One of the principal difficulties I found was the sheer length and complexity of the sentences in French! As if the pressure and flow of thoughts somehow resisted simpler units. Such long sentences are not usual in English. On the whole I have tried to respect the nature and style of the French text. If the reader finds this irritating I apologise and can only recommend that he reads the original!

Whatever its shortcomings may be, this translation will make it possible for *The Work of the Negative* to be read in English for the first time and I am glad to have been able to participate in this exchange of experience and ideas.

Translator's Acknowledgements

It remains for me to express my sincere thanks to all those who have assisted in this task in many different ways: I would especially like to thank Gill Davies and Trevor Brown of Free Association Books for their confidence in entrusting me with this work in the first place and for the support I have received throughout.

André Green has also been very encouraging and has spent a good deal of time answering my questions, reading and revising the manuscript and I am particularly grateful for the series of conversations we had when the translation was completed which helped me to gain a better understanding of the book and to clarify outstanding issues.

Very warm thanks, too, to Monique Zerbib. This translation would have been much more onerous if she had not given me her generous collaboration throughout the year, helping me untangle the most difficult passages in French and reading through much of the translation with me in French and English simultaneously.

I am also indebted to Hilde Rapp for reading through the manuscript on behalf of Free Association Books in the final stages and reminding me that I had not quite finished yet! Her comments and feedback have enabled me to make many improvements and give the text more coherence generally.

There are a large number of other people who have contributed in some way or other by answering questions, in some cases by reading through a chapter(s) and giving me their comments, and by general encouragement and I would like to thank particularly: Ian Snowball, Des Sowerby and Clare Parkinson, Joël Dor and Marie-Dominique De Coulhac, Marie-Paule Berranger, Edwige Encaoua and my brother David. Of course, any errors and inadequacies which remain are my own.

Andrew Weller, Paris, April 1999

Author's Acknowledgements

I should like to thank Christelle Bécant and Florence Bruneau for their help in finalising the manuscript. The transcription of my seminar at Paris V11 on the work of the negative by C. Michaelidès was a considerable help to me as I was writing this book.

My gratitude also goes to John Jackson who was kind enough to have a final look at the text prior to its publication in French.

For Litza

Introduction

by Otto F. Kernberg, M.D.

The present volume is a major contribution to psychoanalytic theory, its implications for the treatment of patients with severe psychopathology, and its application to cultural and philosophical concerns. It represents the culmination of some thirty years of systematic work, some of the highlights of which have been published in English, while others, unfortunately, are still unavailable to the English language speaking psychoanalytic community.

Starting with his 1973 book *Le Discours Vivant* (presently being translated into English under the title 'The Fabric of Affect and the Psychoanalytic Discourse', to be published by Routledge), André Green offered a revision of the psychoanalytic theory of affect, and of the place of affect expression in psychoanalytic practice. In this context, he also undertook a systematic examination of the contributions of Lacan, Melanie Klein, Bion and Winnicott and the relevance and limitations of their theoretical formulations for contemporary psychoanalytic theory and technique.

His 1983 book *Narcissisme de vie, narcissisme de mort* (not translated into English) continued to explore severe psychopathologies, expanding on his clinical descriptions of cases in which radical destruction of the internalised world of object relations dominated the transference. 'Blank psychosis', 'the dead mother', 'negative hallucination' were major conditions he described, and linked, by the formulation of a malignant form of narcissism dominated by the death drive, to the radical elimination of object relations, and pervasive negation of the need for libidinal relationships.

On Private Madness, originally published in 1986, and available in an abbreviated edition in English, finally opened up to the Anglo-American psychoanalytic community the path-breaking contributions of André Green. It describes the application of his evolving theoretical frame to the treatment of patients with severe personality disorders and extreme forms of negative transferences and negative therapeutic reactions.

The present volume, originally published in French in 1993, presents the reader with an entirely original, comprehensive psychoanalytic model of the intrapsychic consequences of severe aggression, which André Green subsumes under Freud's concept of the death drive (in contrast to the life drive as representing libido in the broadest sense). He systematically explores the influence of the death drive, thus conceived, on psychic functioning along a broad spectrum from normality to the extremely ill, almost unapproachable patients for whom a psychoanalytic approach may still be indicated.

The 'negative', as formulated by André Green, refers to two closely related aspects of human psychology: the first one includes the consistent rejection of whatever is intolerable to the ego, exemplified by the mechanism of repression, the ongoing and unavoidable shadow of the need to control the drives that challenge all ego activities. The second aspect refers to the profound and pervasive destructiveness of the death drive, that operates as a radical refusal of satisfaction and pleasure, and becomes so dominant in some personalities that it effectively leads to a global destruction of object relations. The 'negative' thus exceeds by far the death drive, but also includes the expression of the death drive as an ever present, intrinsic and unavoidable aspect of all object relations. Its expression, in fact, emerges in ways that may have been observed clinically by many authors over the years, but were never captured in an integrated theoretical frame such as the one André Green presents in this volume. The 'negative' includes the utilisation of 'negative' derivatives of primitive aggression that are employed by the ego in the defensive operations of repression, negation, disavowal, and foreclosure; the elimination of aspects of reality in the process of defense against intolerable unconscious drive derivatives ('negative hallucination'); and primitive sadomasochistic transferences relentlessly attempting to destroy both the availability of the analyst as a good object and the patient's cognitive capacity to maintain a relationship in reality with him. In exploring all facets of the 'negative', André Green systematically points to the ways in which aggression can infiltrate a patient's intrapsychic and interpersonal life, and thus affect the development of the transference.

Green reaches the conclusion that the central difference between the life and the death drives is the 'objectalising function' of the life drive, and the 'disobjectalising function' of the death drive, that is, the corresponding drive to establish, maintain and develop object relations, in contrast to the drive to destroy and withdraw from object relations. A universal, unavoidable, consistent struggle between the objectalising function as the Positive and the disobjectalising function as the negative is an essential characteristic of all aspects of psychic functions and development. He convincingly points to circumstances in which the setting up of a bad internal and external object as a consequence of severe trauma or frustration does not constitute the worst of cases: a secondary elimination of the masochistic relation to a bad object, in the form of a total annihilation of that very relationship by a radical withdrawal and defensive elimination of all the traces of such a conflict (the only trace that remains is the corresponding elimination of all significant object relations in the transference) constitutes a most dangerous, malignant development in the psychoanalytic treatment. André Green thus differentiates the aggressive aspects of the death drive – directly expressed as attacks on self or others – from the destructive aspects of it. Destruction without aggression can be expressed in a radical withdrawal from objects, or in a tendency to eliminate the very self as an agency searching for satisfaction, as is the case in 'negative narcissism'.

The ego's complex defensive operations, such as the process and outcome of identification, the setting up of the ego ideal, and the super-ego's influence on processes of sublimation, all contain aspects of the negative, and may evolve in a variety of ways in which the negative may dominate over the protection of eroticism and sexuality. Thus, for example, identification may serve functions of primitive attachment and consolation, but may also foster detachment from objects. The drives, André Green stresses, create the need for an object, but when the object is excessively frustrating this strengthens the aggressive drive, thus intensifying the push in the direction of deobjectalisation. The aggressive component of the relation to an object may in turn be linked to libidinal needs in a compromise formation of sadomasochistic pleasure.

André Green explores in great detail the contributions of Melanie Klein to the paranoid-schizoid position and its dominant defences, particularly splitting and projective identification; he explores Bion's contribution to the study of the evasion of severely threatening situations by destroying the psychic apparatuses' capacity for elaborating reality, and even by eliminating perception altogether. He includes Lacan's stress on the mechanism of *forclusion* as a radical elimination of intolerable contents from psychic experience. André Green explores the processes in pathological mourning from the viewpoint of the multiple ways in which the negative operates in the direction of deobjectalisation, and the corresponding functions of negative therapeutic reaction typical for such patients.

While Green does not focus systematically on psychoanalytic technique *per se*, his rich references to particular clinical situations involving patients with severe psychopathology make this a major contribution for the psychoanalytic practitioner: for instance, the negative characteristically manifests itself in the 'negative hallucinations' in the transference, as when the patient does not remember or recognise what he himself just said to the analyst, or cannot make sense of what the analyst is saying because of being unable to think about it. André Green describes the many ways in which patients express fear of authentic involvement by symptoms of depersonalisation and diffuse anxiety, and tend to rationalise the fear of the encounter between their drive invested self and the analyst by attempting to transform him into a non-responsive object.

Green points out how an object's love for the patient is useless unless the analyst first helps him to develop a capacity for loving, that is, for risking an encounter. He describes the dynamics of moral masochism as expressed in destructive clinging in the transference, and in the intimate connection between (1) the denial of the oedipal situation as the ultimate reality of the intimate relations of two objects that are separate from the patient – and who confirm this very separateness in their mutual relationship, and (2) the patient's struggle to extricate himself from a primitive sadomasochistic, symbiotic relationship with a bad mother.

For the American reader, it may be surprising how much of André Green's formulations are expressed in a critical review and dialogue with Freud's work. This tendency to develop new formulations in the context of such a critical dialogue transcends, in Green's writing, this particular French cultural tradition. He points to fundamental contributions as well as to fundamental problems generated by Freud's writings that, in the light of today's knowledge, require a new reading as well as a new confrontation with Freud. In the process, André Green critically reviews psychoanalytic methodology as well as the application of psychoanalysis to the understanding of contemporary cultural conflicts. He points out how the ego's apparent adaptation to social and cultural requirements may express super-ego determined negativity, concealed in the subtle tendencies to dissociate sexuality from meaningful object investments, and to foster spurious narcissistic gratification in collusion with the negative. And he shows how the negative may expand destructively the frustrations related to trauma in setting up internal as well as external destructive object relations and self-destructive ego functions in the form of cognitive and affective disorganisation.

His analysis of sublimation as a process leading to desexualisation and, therefore, to the neutralisation of instinctual drive, as he points out, has as a consequence, the potential for an eventual recruitment of such 'neutralised energy' by the death drive, and an infiltration, under the frame of sublimation, of the destructive effects of the negative. At the same time, Green goes on, in so far as masochism can resexualise sublimation, it may be part of a general solution to the danger of the negative, capturing the death drive in life, binding it to the manifestations of the life drive, in an effort to construct convergent aims. This dynamic, André Green points out, operates even at the level of the oedipal couple, in the mother's unconscious idealisation of her own father, with an implicit devaluation of her mate's sexuality, leading indirectly to 'anti-Çros' demands in the infant's ego ideal.

At a cultural level, the development of ideologies that attempt a general improvement of mankind through either spirituality or social manipulation, from religious fundamentalism to Marxist theory, have produced such horrible consequences as Nazism and the Communist regimes. This illustrates the effects of the negative: the death drive, André Green stresses again and again, operates at the level of the individual as well as at the level of the social and cultural environment. He proposes original contributions to the conceptual and clinical relationship between sublimation and creativity, explores Winnicott's effort to explain cultural creativity by means of the transitional process, and ends up this impressive book with a critical exploration of the relation between reparation, sublimation, and creativity in Art, and their limitations as regarding the consequences of the death drive in the very life of the creative artist.

A note of warning: For the American reader, the intensive dialogue with philosophical thinking that characterises André Green – and French psychoanalysis in general – may come as a surprise; and, for the reader not specially interested in this interface, the early chapters on the relationship between the negative in Hegel and Freud may be disconcerting. Therefore, it would be perfectly reasonable to follow the reading of André Green's own introduction to this book and Chapter 1, by skipping to Chapter 3, and returning to the second chapter only after becoming familiar with Green's general psychoanalytic formulations. For the American reader familiar with this francophone tradition, or directly interested in philosophy, the first two chapters are a fascinating introduction to the philosophical implications of Freudian metapsychology, and a reflection of the original and creative mind of the author beyond the field of psychoanalysis proper.

In our science as in the others the problem is the same: behind the attributes (qualities) of the object under examination which are presented directly to our perception, we have to discover something else which is more independent of the particular receptive capacity of our sense-organs and which approximates more closely to what may be supposed to be the real state of affairs. We have no hope of being able to reach the latter itself, since it is evident that everything new that we have inferred must nevertheless be translated back into the language of our perceptions, from which it is simply impossible for us to free ourselves. But herein lies the very nature and limitation of our science.

Freud, *An Outline of Psycho-Analysis*
SE, **23**: 196

An Introduction to the Negative in Psychoanalysis

The work of the negative has been a subject of debate for some time now.[1] There are three questions which need to be taken into consideration in regard to it: What are its sources? How is it related to Freud's work? What aspects of contemporary clinical practice and theory lie behind it? I shall content myself for the time being with addressing the first question which deserves to be explored at some length, before going on to tackle the other two.

Hegel's name comes immediately to mind. The history of the relations between Hegelian thought and psychoanalysis still remains to be written. *Here, we shall have to confine ourselves to a study restricted to the Hegelian sources of a particular development of Freud's theory raised by Lacan's interpretation of it.* Readers may recall Jean Hippolyte's commentary on Freud's *Die Verneinung* ('Negation') given at Lacan's seminar and subsequently published in the first volume of *La Psychanalyse*.[2] A lot of ground has been covered since the inaugural positions associated with Lacan's name and my own contributions of which I will simply recall two stages here. The first, a recent one, is 'The Work of the Negative',[3] the other, more long-standing, is 'The Double Limit'.[4] Earlier texts contained numerous allusions to it without, however, exploring the question further.

Let us return to our point of departure: the Hippolyte–Lacan couple. This exchange between the philosopher who was an authority on Hegelian studies and the psychoanalyst who was cultivating an affinity with philosophy took place at the highest point of Hegel–Freud relations. For it followed upon numerous Hegelian references already present in Lacan's work. 'The mirror stage' (1949) and 'Remarks on Psychical Causality' (1946) testify to that.[5] After the dialogue with Hippolyte, Lacanian Hegelianism gave way to options which were more in tune with the times. Saussurian linguistics, followed by topography, pushed the dialectics of the philosopher from Jena into the

1

background. The link between these two periods of Lacanian theory has never been closely examined.

Post-Second World War French psychoanalysis developed in the mould of psychiatry and many analysts from this era were marked by their origins in this field. Now, as a result of the impetus given to it by Henry Ey, modern psychiatry was impregnated with phenomenology, apart from when it sought inspiration from Marxists who, in conformity with their political positions, believed in the sociogenesis of mental illnesses. But this trend, which was at the origin of an important institutional revival, always remained in the minority. Husserl and Heidegger – whose influence on Lacanian thought I will underline later – remained the major philosophical references in the psychiatry of that period, nourished as it was by existential analysis. Hegel, who was their ancestor, as well as Marx's, was enjoying a certain vogue via Alexandre Kojève. Through the combined influence of Ey and Lacan, psychiatrists were drawn to Hegel, seeing a possibility in his system of linking the dialectics of alienation with a hierarchical view of the psyche.

Lacan's adherence to the synchronism of Saussurian linguistics marked the end of his encounter with Hegel. But the Rome address on 'The function and field of speech and language in Psychoanalysis' still bears its trace with the memorable analysis which Lacan made of the *Fort-Da*.[6] It is indeed in these few paragraphs that the Hegelian inspiration of Lacan's thought finds its fullest expression, giving an account of the combined effects of childhood, the status of absence, the emergence of self-consciousness, alienation from one's own productions (sound, signifier and sign), the conflict between various aspects of the psyche in their relation to language and the subject's relationship to death. But this happy episode was not to last, for Lacan's thought was to respond to the siren calls of the signifier, and then to that of topography where references to language and history were gradually supplanted by other, more 'scientific' ones.

We should bear in mind here that the Lacanian interpretation of the cotton-reel game did not simply involve theorising about the game, as someone like Winnicott would have done, but was the *remake* of the Freudian interpretation, the initial description of which was reformulated in terms that allowed – and, up to a point, even called for – a new version steeped in the ink of Hegel. The true interlocutor of Lacan during the years when his work was taking shape was not another analyst, but Henry Ey. What was at stake in the intellectual debate was nothing less than the leadership of the young psychiatrists whom the psychoanalysts sought to convert. Ey's organo-dynamism was in line with the movement of the philosophies of nature (Spencer, through Jackson), while at the same time drawing on the modern phenomenological movement. Lacan opposed this with Hegel's thought. The debate at that time was centred on the causes of madness, leaving psychiatrists of diverse tendencies to fight it out:

organicists who nonetheless were phenomenologists; Marxist-inspired proponents of the sociogenesis of mental illnesses; psychoanalysts divided over their interpretation of Freud, etc. Lacan saw the advantage he could gain from taking an approach to alienation which allowed him to build a bridge between academic philosophical knowledge and a philosophical interpretation of Freud. His paper 'Remarks on Psychical Causality' came at a time when Hegel's influence on Lacan was at its strongest. It was his contribution at the Conference of Bonneval in 1946, before an audience of psychiatrists,[7] on the psychogenesis of the psychoses and neuroses. Lacan later freed himself from the polemical context within psychiatry in order to transfer the debate to the unconscious which was at the heart of the evolution of ideas in the fifties. Sartre and Merleau-Ponty were at that time the leading thinkers for many young French psychiatrists. However, while the latter took their bearings mainly from Husserl, the author of *Being and Nothingness* and later the *Critique of Dialectical Reason* was, without doubt, more influenced by Hegel than the other phenomenological philosophers (J. Wahl, P. Ricoeur, A. de Waehlens) read by the psychiatrists to make up for the poverty of medical psychiatric discourse. Lacan was vigorously opposed to Sartre's ideas, whose analyses he contested as well as those of Merleau-Ponty. Soon he established the bases of his own theoretical system. Lacan's first outlines, which formed the foundations of his later work, contained traces of Hegel's *Phenomenology of Spirit* and were contemporaneous with his first references to the Other and to desire. They were supplanted by the discovery of the signifier and were soon replaced by the tripartite orders Real–Imaginary–Symbolic, subject to the intertwining of Borromean knots.[8] This development was to last about twenty years.

Hegel's influence did little to foster a deeper study which might have put the two systems of thought – Hegel's and Freud's – into perspective and clarified their relations.[9] Any comparative study would need to make a distinction between direct and indirect connections: Lacan's procedure is based more on what is implicit than explicit, i.e., on the intuition that the psychoanalytic process might be resonant with Hegel's thought. But, what was the pathway from Hegel to Freud? It is difficult to see how the former who places Absolute Knowledge at the pinnacle of the human quest could dialogue with the latter who, in his meetings with Brentano, had declared that since his youth he had been an out-and-out materialist, a confirmed evolutionist.[10] In view of the most obvious differences which exist over central premises, is there any justification for an inquiry whose aim would be to bring to light a set of subtle pointers carrying more weight than was hitherto supposed? It looks as if the conceptual fringes work secretly on the central concepts, clarifying them in a way which makes them appear in a new light. They would thus reveal, through their potential for reversal, the measure of the negativity which they enclose.

Every Freud reader will have come across such instances while reflecting on the concepts of the founder of psychoanalysis. It remains to be seen whether the revelation of this shadow which is hinted at in the aura of the fundamental concepts justifies, for all that, the slightest connection with Hegel's thought. Is the article on 'Negation', with a commentary by one of his foremost exponents, sufficient argument?

Such an inquiry would have to determine whether the introduction of the notion of the work of the negative into psychoanalysis really owes something to Hegel, even though the debt to Lacan should be recognised.

This question can only be answered by studying the posterity of Hegel's work. Alongside the well-trodden path from Hegel to Freud, there is a derivative itinerary which it would be interesting to explore. Provided that we do not seek to remain absolutely faithful to Hegel's ideas – in which case we would not get very far – we could discover fruitful offshoots, in the same way that Bion made use of Kant, i.e., very freely. It can not be emphasised enough that Freud was an admirer of Feuerbach. We need to broaden the scope of Hegelian thought and not tie our hands too readily by perpetually recalling that which relates to the thesis of consciousness as opposed to any idea of unconsciousness. Let us turn, rather, towards the evolutionary movement or to the perspectives of reversal which are an essential feature of this movement, to the relation between the products of historicity and the historical subject, and examine the formative stages of a hierarchy of meaning. This would allow us to find in psychoanalysis many remote derivatives of this philosophy. Linking this somewhat syncretic procedure with the *Phenomenology of Spirit* will doubtless be contested as much by philosophers as by psychoanalysts. It may, however, not prove to be fruitless if we see things in the context of the history of ideas which itself owes something to the Hegelian concept of the development and creation of theoretical systems. Lacan's reading of Hegel[11] can perhaps only be explained in this way. Indeed it is through this reading that the idea of a work of the negative has taken root in psychoanalysis without our needing to feel bound by the heritage which it implies.

Nevertheless, during the course of its development, psychoanalytic thinking distanced itself from the Hegelian ideas which had influenced Lacan. Similarly, with time, the notion of the work of the negative freed itself from Lacanian thought. Is it not true that the latter had also distanced itself from its early allegiances? In short, the Hegelian wave died away on the beach and was covered by succeeding waves, its ebb remaining no more than a memory. Subsequently, the impetus which this notion had originally received from Lacan was subjected to the same fate by the intrinsic strength of psychoanalytic thought, that is, its internal questionings.

Psychoanalysis was burdened with its Hegelian antecedents which needed jettisoning. But borrowing terminology is not enough in itself to alienate a title of ownership. Anyone who has come across the work of the negative will have something different in mind from that which is spoken of in the *Phenomenology of Spirit*. It is possible for psychoanalysts to come to the work of the negative without ever having studied Hegel at all. The tradition which prevails in the British Psycho-Analytic Society is a case in point. It is there that I have come across the work of the negative in two authors whom, in many other respects, I have long considered to be major points of reference.

The first of these is Winnicott who only became aware of the work of the negative retrospectively, I would say. In fact, the germ of an idea leading to it can be found in *Playing and Reality* in the 'tail piece' which he wrote in 1969 after his article on objects and transitional phenomena, first published fifteen years earlier. This re-edition contains a commentary inspired by certain of his patients, and one in particular, for whom he was the umpteenth analyst following an initial experience, when she was a young woman, which bore all the marks of a passionate transference (clearly of a maternal type). This continued to interfere with her work with Winnicott in the form of suffering, accusations and grief which nothing would change. Hence his comment: 'The negative of him (the first analyst) was more important than the positive of me.' Winnicott cites the case as an example of a more general situation and speaks on this occasion of the psychoanalytic set-up which allows us to acknowledge the importance of 'the negative side of relationships'. This remark goes beyond what is generally said on the subject of negative therapeutic reaction. Winnicott suggests that the traumatic experiences which have tested the child's capacity to wait for the mother's longed-for response, lead, when this response is not forthcoming, to a state where only what is negative is felt to be real. What is more, the effect of these experiences is such that it spreads to the whole psychic structure and becomes autonomous, so to speak, from the future appearances and disappearances of the object. This means that the object's presence is not able to modify the negative model which has become characteristic of the subject's experience. The negative has imposed itself as an organised object relationship quite independent of the object's presence or absence.

These remarks have all the more import in that they constitute the heart of a later, deferred extension of an article on objects and transitional phenomena. We can interpret the situation as it is described in two ways: either as the reverse side (negative) of the positive and structuring experience of the creation of the transitional object and the resources which this constitutes for separation or – and this is the thesis which I adhere to – as a 'negativistic' vicissitude of a potentially creative negative which suffering, rage and impotence have distorted and transformed into psychical paralysis. But in the new internal situation created by the analytic setting it is not only the subject who is affected by impotence but the object also. This is what the term negative therapeutic reaction means. The relation between the two forms of negativity is more important than the sole consideration of its desperate and despairing form. It cannot be interpreted as a simple failure to create transitional objects.

It is better to set the two solutions in opposition. The first, which is creative, recognises through separation the potential anxiety of loss and deals with it by creating an object – to be more exact, by giving a different status to an existing object – making use both of the ego and the internal object representation[12] in the process. It is not that the psyche restricts itself thereby to giving shape to its production via the transitional object, nor that it is confined to a representative hyper-investment. It wards off the lack of reality from which the representation suffers by establishing a fictional reality which it displaces to another space than that of representation. So although we should not delude ourselves as to the replacement of the missing object and its creative power which risks letting it burn itself up with regret for its purely fictitious nature, this solution satisfies the psyche's need for an available object. The possibility which this provides of being perceived in this space and of procuring physical satisfactions, as well as psychical ones, prevents it from toppling over into hallucination. Besides, we know that this acquisition leads to numerous enrichments from the standpoint of logical mechanisms ('It is-and-is-not-the-breast').

On the contrary, the second solution – negativism – experiments with negativity by dealing with it in a reiterative way and shutting it in on itself. By investing the lack with all the bad attributes, the psyche hopes to make the positive appear by offering itself as a victim for the object. It burdens the latter with guilt which provokes its repentance and return, and, after killing it unwittingly, tries to provoke its resurrection, not in the area of reality, nor in the transitional area, nor in that of representation but in a 'surreal', exclusively affective, imaginary realm created by the strength of the complaint alone. It is highly probable that such functioning is based on an identification with the primary object expressing its dissatisfaction with the baby to whom it would only give assistance reluctantly. The negative of the negative, i.e., the lack in the absence, duplicated by the lack due to the presence of suffering which is more aggravating than putting an end to it, stimulates indefinitely the process of painful querulousness. As this state of affairs is ultimately designed to make the object 'emerge' from its absence, the demonstration of reciprocal mistreatment in this case gives rise to the fiction of a 'materialised' affect which takes the place of any sort of representation. In order to achieve this, it carries out a self-amputation of the ego which causes a feeling of emptiness or of a gap which is simply a double, a kind of whipping-boy, which has managed to imprison itself in a form which is not conveyed by a representation and is therefore not available for use; for the only use to which it could be put would be the non-representability of an object, devoured by its lack, whose fate it is to be merged and amalgamated with the sense of its own existence. It seems to me that what is involved here is not so much masochistic pleasure as conflict centred on the reactions provoked by the object's non-existence – a part of its own doing, an aspect of the ego's retaliatory treatment of it – which, beyond the suffering thus created, (in which the masochistic quality is overwhelmed) can only be resolved by seeking the disappearance of the ego itself. It is difficult to know whether this stems from its own destructiveness or from a kind of mimetic symmetry of the non-appearance of the object.

From another viewpoint, albeit within the same theoretical framework, Bion, embarking on his vast theoretical revision, particularly of Kleinian theory, since it played a major role in his training, introduced a conceptual distinction which, in my view, applies as much to Freud as it does to Melanie Klein. He underscored the need not to confuse the 'no-thing' and the 'nothing'. Bion, who generally speaking has leanings towards Kant, seems to me on this point to move further towards the negative and to come closer, unwittingly perhaps, to Hegel.[13] Here we come across an idea which is not fundamentally different from Winnicott's in that it endeavours to envisage different outcomes for a situation of lack. It shows the ways in which this lack is elaborated and is in conflict with, for example, the somewhat cut-and-dried 'positive' solution adopted by Melanie Klein in her description of the paranoid-schizoid position. Positive, not in the sense of its beneficial value, but as an expression of an idea of psychic space which for her is always full, having effaced for ever the traces of the loss it has suffered. It is not so much that Bion contests Klein's description as that he supplements it by making reference to the differentiated aspects of a non-presence with which it is unfamiliar.

Furthermore, in order to give an account of the psychical complexity of the issue, Bion proposes a paradigm which has the merit of providing us with a clear basis for discussion. He suggests that the whole problem of psychic structure resides in just two possible responses to frustration: modification or evasion. The double intervention of the negative should be noted here: the location of the referent with frustration, a psychic phenomenon arising from the negativity of the absence of expected satisfaction and the reduplication of the negative through the solution which consists in evading frustration, i.e., attempting to ignore its existence.

In keeping with its own development, psychoanalytic theory gave birth to a new idea which, of all those that have emerged in the recent past, comes closest to the work of the negative. It has always been acknowledged – even if it has been formulated in different ways – that love and hate have a position of the highest importance in the different theoretical developments which have succeeded each other in psychoanalysis. But Bion was the first to come up with the idea of adding another term, that of knowledge, the combination of the three forming a coherent and necessary whole. However, the introduction of a third term might lead one to think that its individualisation stems from the inadequacy of the other two to achieve the degree of refinement characteristic of knowledge, or even that their effect might inhibit its development. Thereafter, the fate of knowledge was conferred on an autonomous agency able to account for its function and ensure its full development. Broadly speaking, this is the solution adopted by philosophy. There might have been cause for apprehension, on the other hand, that this theoretical necessity be understood in terms of a preoccupation to create a psychical entity capable of dominating love and hate, a necessary condition for knowledge to guarantee its power of intellection.

It was doubtless to avoid such misunderstandings that Bion took care to attribute a double value, positive and negative (+K, –K) to knowledge. There are some who might think that such a duality simply reflects that of the pair love–hate. But this is not so, for Bion insists on distinguishing the two preceding terms, pointing out for example that the opposite of love (–L) is not hate (H), and vice versa. There is, therefore, a division specific to the symbol of knowledge which we would do well to notice since it reveals the power which characterises the negative. In introducing the idea of 'negative knowledge' Bion indeed bases himself on experiences which are common to all analyses but which, in certain cases, can become a matter for concern since the psychoanalytic field is invaded. He distinguishes the effects of not-understanding and mis-understanding, an opposition which brings out the essential difference between nothing and no thing. It will be immediately clear that *mis-understanding* contains an ambiguity which can have certain advantages such as enabling one to have a pleasant surprise at discovering another meaning, just as unexpected as unheard – whereas *not-understanding* puts an end to any process of comprehensive understanding. We do not need to lose time in showing how such thinking is sensitive to the negative. It is true that adopting a Hegelian standpoint allows one to cover an even wider field than the one I have just described if one considers that Hegel places considerable emphasis on *mé-connaissance*[14] (English has no equivalent: to recognise admits of no negative prefix), a concept which Lacan transposed to psychoanalysis.

Abstraction is an effect of knowledge. But it would be a mistake to locate it at the end of the process of knowledge, as an outcome of the drives. On the contrary, Bion shows that it is present in the earliest stages of knowledge and relates it to concrete thinking which he does not only see as a primitive state of mind but also as the result of an early contamination of the mind by the dysfunctioning characteristic of the child, or he sees its origin in the mother's dysfunctioning (excessive projective identification, inability to tolerate frustration and evacuation being dominant in the first case, a lack of maternal reverie in the second). This complicity results in an alteration in alpha function which Bion makes the pivotal point of his theoretical system.[15] He shows this in his seminal paper 'Attacks on Linking'.[16] –K is not content with qualifying the negative in terms of an insufficiency or deficit; it gives it status. Not-understanding is brought into play by the patient's psyche when it is in his interest to stop understanding. This is a widely encountered phenomenon. It is with psychotic patients, or in Bion's terminology, with the psychotic part of the personality, that the specific nature of this mechanism can be pinpointed. The analyst witnesses a sort of *coup de Jarnac*[17] which the patient carries out on his own discourse. It is as if he wants to impede the work of association from developing towards an eventual widening of consciousness which has been strikingly and silently anticipated. The analyst only understands this subsequently. Certainly, the symbol –K bears witness to the fact that the developmental stages of abstraction appear not to have taken place, but also that psychical activity is aiming at 'minus linking'. This image of a psyche which 'compresses' its component parts (by de-differentiating them) and prohibits or refuses any elaboration is similar to the ideas Freud put forward with regard to psychosis (word–thing confusion). But the devastating consequences of this fundamental intolerance of frustration are linked by Bion to the recognition of the structural attributes of the negative. Does he not commend the virtues of being without memory and desire, at times when the analyst's thinking seems to be getting bogged down, and did he not consider 'negative capability', the presence of which Keats had observed in Shakespeare, as the highest accomplishment of the psyche?[18]

It can be seen that Bion and I are agreed on the twin structuring and destructuring aspect of the negative. But there may have been other solutions which Bion neglected apart from the ones he described, such as the predominance of beta function – which favours the processes of evacuation by constant projective identification – over-elaboration, the specific attribute of alpha function. When the subject has escaped the temptation of sinking into the total refusal or impossibility of any displacement whatsoever, and even when he has succeeded in allaying suspicion concerning his willingness to live, there emerges, behind what Winnicott called the 'false self', a thought (which has largely gone unnoticed) which makes extremely cunning use of imaginary and speculative distortions such as games of hide and seek, strategies aimed at avoiding awareness or the exclusion of its own thought contents, and a desperate determination to avoid acknowledging the links between the preconscious and the unconscious which are suggestive of what is known as perversion in the domain of sexuality. If it were applied to the ego, the content of this notion would doubtless require a re-evaluation. The inversion contained in the formula 'neurosis is the negative of perversion' corresponds to the negative therapeutic reaction which does not only concern sexuality. The paradox is that 're-positivising' Freud's formula does implicate sexuality, and concerns, indirectly, not so much neurosis as what, today, are called borderline cases, many aspects of the psychic functioning of which still remain unclear to us. One is reminded of Freud's enigmatic proposition when he envisages the case where, to save itself from internal rupture, the ego manages to deform itself, sacrificing its unitary character, even to the extent of self-division or splitting. 'In this way the inconsistencies, eccentricities and follies of men would appear in a similar light to their sexual perversions, through the acceptance of which they spare themselves repressions.'[19] Freud was, it seems to me, opening up avenues of research which others after him would pursue by exploring the work of the negative. My book *On Private Madness*[20] was an attempt at this. If Winnicott and Bion came to conclusions which have a number of points in common, it is because they were interested in cases which were considered to be beyond the scope of classical treatment. Although I am not entirely certain – for here we are dealing much more with true negativism than with the elaboration of the negative which always implies the presence of complex attributes – it seems to me that some of Searles' writings, of which 'Driving the Other Person Crazy' is doubtless the most eloquent, could be included in the same descriptive frame of reference. But it is above all through a close analysis of the counter-transference that Searles opens up new and rich horizons, if only because he shows that the negative must be seen not only in terms of its relation with the other but also in terms of its attributes of diffusion, of soliciting the other who appears to be similar into changing his being, making himself change tack and allowing a reverse side of himself to appear, the existence of which he is not even aware of.[21] This possibility, with which anyone who has had an experience of analysis will be familiar, is the source of psychical happenings which are even more surprising when they are occasioned by another person who has assigned you the place of a transference object. The eclipse of the transference which should develop in the setting specially designed for it is projected into a blind spot in the analyst's understanding. On the other hand, it stimulates psychical manifestations which are reflected in his subjectivity and this in turn indirectly serves the purpose of blinding and suspending interpretative work.

I shall end with a radical negative form, i.e., 'extreme', which calls for special precautions to be taken. I am referring here to what can be observed in the psychosomatic field. Without going into the details of the debate ignited by the work of P. Marty,[22] it is clear that the majority of psychosomatic theories make implicit reference to a negativity affecting the psyche, the importance of which cannot be over-emphasised. I wish to underline two aspects.

The first concerns the 'normal' character of the psyche of the patient who, in the eyes of his fellow creatures, is afflicted with *psychosomatosis*. However, behind this formal normality – all the more convincing in that it seems so free of any element of 'normal' madness (of fantasy in common idiom) that it is more likely to pass for being too normal – the psychosomaticist uncovers a kind of sclerosis or psychic anaemia whose effects (as the terms 'operational thinking', 'essential depression' suggest) appear to have their root in psychic forces reduced to a level of minimal functioning. Now, what is striking is the link between this psychic reduction and the way the patient is endangering his life. In this case, it is not just psychic death which is at stake; nor is it the result of conflict between the conscious and unconscious spheres. It appears to occur as a consequence of an internal disorganisation, which seems likely to have psychic causes but these are difficult to define, i.e., they are unintelligible. Here, we are at the extreme limits of analysability. We are often reminded of how Freudian thought developed from 'neurosis as the negative of perversion' to the concept of negative therapeutic reaction. A corollary development, from hysterical conversion to psychosomatic illness, can be placed alongside this. Without wishing to be smugly metaphysical, it is only right to point out that death often intervenes in an untimely fashion. Far from criticising Freud for introducing a philosophical concept into psychoanalytic theory – the primary obligation of which is to address clinical issues, even if this is not its sole task – we can be satisfied that, alongside the existing meanings attributed to death (religious, metaphysical, philosophical), a place has been found for those which speak of the presence of death in life and of the realm where its different figures appear in constant conflict with life in all its physical and psychical diversity.

We shall see how the work of the negative seeks accomplishment by expressing itself in different ways depending on the circumstances: as a passage, a procession, a figure, a moment of transformation, the significance and extent of which will only become clear retrospectively, a moment in the process or, conversely, as obstruction, rigidity, blockage, the illusion of stopping the process as if trying ahead of time to appropriate an end which is beyond the object's reach. Henceforth, the entire activity of analysis aims to restore freedom of movement to the structure of the psyche, leaving the analysand responsible for his decisions, sometimes without any concern for the remains of his analysis which he lets the analyst deal with as he wishes, but without involving the 'I' who was at great pains to get rid of aspects of himself.

As it can be seen, the work of the negative has haunted psychoanalytic theory for the best part of forty years with different outcomes. Authors who once openly laid claim to it later abandoned it, tempted by other adventures. Others who have never referred to it explicitly have developed ideas reminiscent of it which can without the slightest difficulty figure alongside those claiming to be connected with it. In other words, if one looks into the matter more closely, one can see that there are many concepts which can be brought together whereas traditionally they remained apart. And it is not unsurprising that certain major themes in Freudian theory have been clarified by this interpretation.

Such dispersion does not make it any easier to group ideas according to orderly principles. It is possible, for example, by relying on an authoritative tradition which has stood the test of time, to start with negation from a logical and philosophical viewpoint – which means taking Freud's article on *Die Verneinung* as a point of departure – and to extend the discussion to include the field opened up by modern psychoanalysis. There would be a certain difficulty in this case of making thinking about negation co-exist with concepts which, according to psychoanalysis, are connected with it (repression and other defences); thereafter, the exposition would suffer. It is more legitimate to start with repression – which marks the birth of psychoanalysis – and to look for circumstances in which variations of it appear with which it has complex relations (foreclosure, negation, disavowal etc.). It seemed to me that there was a justification for gathering under the denomination of primary defences these mechanisms which, unlike others, all have a common denominator: the Yes or No treatment of psychic activity falling within its jurisdiction. This is without doubt the heart of what is meant by the work of the negative, viewed in particular from the angle of ego functioning. But it would be an error to confine the work of the negative to this body of defences, which I propose to call primary, because it would be forgotten that the avenue of research initiated by Freud with his article 'Negation' (1925) is concerned with establishing the relations between the psychoanalytic incidences of this linguistic phenomenon and other more fundamental psychic activities depending on the activity of primary drive motions (*SE*: 'instinctual impulses').[23] We therefore have to accept that the work of the negative extends well beyond the sphere of the ego. In a debate on the death drive[24] I proposed an interpretation of the latter in terms of its disobjectalising function[25] and of negative narcissism. The latter aspect makes it possible to build a bridge between ego activity and certain forms of drive activity if we follow Freud on the link between narcissism and the sphere of the drives.

Moreover, the work of the negative seems to shed light on some concepts even though they are not connected with defensive activity: I am thinking particularly of identification and sublimation. To conclude, let me say that I have decided to account for the work of the negative from two points of view:

– The first brings together aspects inherent to psychic activity in general, common to all human beings, which cannot avoid negativising (*la négativation*) excess (drive activity); among the principal vicissitudes met with are repression, identification and sublimation. The first of these will not concern us much here for it has already been the object of many studies and to return to it again would be tiresome – it is better to concentrate on studying its harmonics. On the contrary, the two others will be examined in more detail.

– The second will be central to our study and will aim to show how the work of the negative is used for different purposes, all of which, however, have a disorganising effect. We will discover the different modes by which negation turns into denial, thanks to which narcissism takes over from masochism to ensure the closure which makes it impermeable to change; and finally, how disavowal, the effects of which seem at first sight to be limited, can subject splitting to a withdrawal of investment causing the subject to experience extreme states of disengagement.

There is one phenomenon which appears to be at the cross-roads of many of the ideas elaborated, that is, negative hallucination. We can only appreciate its importance if it is seen as the reverse side of hallucinatory wish-fulfilment, basic to Freud's metapsychological model. As a central hypothesis, negative hallucination is seen as being indispensable to the constitution of psychic space, its perverse and alienating effects having been observed in clinical work. It is these issues which will be the focus of study in the following chapters. For practical reasons, the latter do not always follow the order of exposition found in this brief introduction. Nonetheless, I hope that their internal logic will not escape the reader.

1
Aspects of the Negative:
Semantic, Linguistic and Psychic

The proponents of the negative in psychoanalysis form a family whose members are not united by any organic link. But they are linked by a certain way of thinking which they share. In fact, a familiarity exists between them which enables them to recognise each other from the outset, not with respect to a defined doctrinal position but by a cast of mind which identifies them in their way of looking at problems or of seeking the most interesting means of resolving them. It is once again the resistance they show towards another group of opponents that allows us to discern more clearly what they stand for, for nothing would be less obvious than to maintain that they share a common point of view regarding the solutions to certain questions.

It is far from easy to make psychoanalysts themselves understand what the category of the negative refers to in psychoanalysis, although they are in an ideal position to observe it. When one employs current concepts to illustrate the way they refer to a patent or allusive negativity, there is a serious risk of increasing the abstract element inherent in any concept and thus to obfuscate what one had wanted to clarify by theorising about it. Perhaps the main difficulty lies in the fact that psychoanalysis, in contradistinction to philosophy, does not operate purely on the level of ideas – which, it is recognised, contain their own coherence and consistence and therefore are worthy of considera- tion in their own right on account of their intellectual rigour. The psychoanalytic approach always refers to an experience which is seen initially from the point of view of positivity and the constraints involved. While a philosopher's thinking arises purely from its debates with itself and the world, the work which stems from it is the proof that the difficulties encountered have been surmounted – however partial and temporary this may be. There is no doubt that the solution was facilitated by bringing together under a single figurehead the identities of the one who questions and the one who answers.

14

Here, Plato is not just a model but a paradigm. On the contrary, psycho-analysis speaks of the opacity of another person's psyche which can *never be overcome* and is irreducible. Admittedly, psychoanalytic writing, as with the former example, is evidence that the process of questioning has ended up by providing the beginnings of a solution. At any rate, there will always be something which remains unanswered, unnegativised (*non negativé*) and which perhaps cannot be negativised (*non négativable*) because the lever necessary for triggering its negative reversal has not been found. Here, I am using the reference to the negative to denote that which, in psychoanalytic theory, commonly applies to the latent as opposed to the manifest meaning which I identify with positivity. The latter contains, in every sense of the term, negativity. This is not simply to set praxis against theory. Intersubjective con-frontation demands greater rigour in resorting to negativity because it implicates another subject, not only as an interlocutor or as the one who is addressed, but as a constituent part of the experience in which he must be included without being controlled. We are dealing with a *de facto* negativity, a reflexive subjectivity which must find an area of agreement, not only with itself but also with the theorising subjectivity which is implied by the existence of the other. Inter-subjectivity, if you like, but inter-subjectivity which must take account of the other as really being other and not simply being 'for-others'.[1] This form of negativity is therefore not pure reversal but reversal needing to find a certain form of intelligibility and recognition 'with regard to' that which is at work in the processes of the theorising subject. This is to say that it adopts a position 'against' (in the two senses of being close to and opposing) the other and that it allows for a vision which includes both subjectivities in a complementary way. This makes it possible to conceive of their union as a single and unique object (symbolic) while preserving the difference which enables us to distin-guish between them and to attach to each pole what is due. However, we know that being in contradiction with the other corresponds to our own self-con-tradiction. In other words, an inescapable subject, facing two others, with-in and with-out, who are 'against' him and having to say why he exists.

It is therefore more difficult to make it clear what the negative is when one is not speaking on a purely speculative level. Yet, more than any other field, psychoanalysis has the particularity of being the kind of work which makes the negative visible. Moreover, the deployment of such a concept strengthens the coherence of psychoanalytic theory by basing it on practice and increasing its explanatory power, giving psychoanalytic thought the possibility of deriving a source of lively speculation from experience and of giving its conceptuali-sations more substance on account of its incarnation in living exchanges. It is probable that the difficulty of being understood resides in a certain confusion as to the conceptual meaning of the term, but also in the polysemy which its empirical use refers to. But this polysemy is not a simple juxtaposition of meaning, as can sometimes be the case. All the diverse meanings which have become accepted through use are implied – a sort of implicit logic – as if those whose necessity has become apparent are subject to a regulated interplay of relationships forming an articulated whole.

The Polysemy of the Negative

The first sense can be defined as oppositional; that is to say, as an active opposition to a positive, in an antagonistic relationship in which each of the inferred terms struggles, either to resist the other or to supplant it, or even to make it disappear. We could characterise it as *polemic* meaning if we extend considerably the reach of this term. What is signified here is the dimension of refusal in the negative. To my mind, such a refusal always implies, in the shorter or longer term, not just resistance to another entity but its destruction; para-doxically, this can take the form of self-destruction. For we know that when we are unable to impose our power on another person, we can always elude the other's power by destroying ourselves. In this way, we control the situation. In this case, positive and negative are both positives of opposite value, each striving for eventual pre-eminence.

The second sense can be defined from the point of view of *symmetry*, ideally devoid of any element of struggle. It is simply the contrary of a positive of equivalent value but inverted. Positive and negative are both interchangeable because the point from which we define them does not select one or the other but arbitrates between them. They can, by agreement, be inverted. This implies a neutral point of reference around which the positive and negative dimensions are defined, occasionally switching place.

The third sense – more difficult to conceive of – refers to the state of a thing which, contrary to appearances, continues to exist even when the senses can no longer perceive it, not only in the external world but also in the internal world (of consciousness). It harks back to the notion of absence, of latency. Here, positive and negative entertain different relations of existence, the value of which depends on the circumstances.

The reference to the real (*le réel*)[2] or the imaginary, depending on the context, favours one or the other. This synchronic view is allied with another which is diachronic. The mind, not being able to absorb everything which happens within itself in the normal flux of events, only retains that part which occupies it in the present. Thenceforward, that which is no longer in the mind, existing in a state of virtuality (and yet which can be made present at the slightest suggestion), and which is absent, can be called negative (by reference to the presence). But as the mind is not a simple succession of figures, this transition to latency, to the state of resembling what it is not, is comparable with the *movement* which explores different scenarios while reversing the facts, the per-spective, the hypotheses and the aims. It has even been shown that the succession of figures, the movement itself of consciousness, proceeds in such a way that one can consider the period of time which follows the making of an utterance – in as far as it is not subject to redundancy – as a negation of the latter, then the affirmation, as a negation of the negation, according to whether the focus is on consciousness or on its objects (Hegel). So it is not by an intentional decision of reversal but by the simple process of the progression of consciousness that the figures of its own reversal are spontaneously formed; the structure of consciousness being caught between itself and its objects. Is not consciousness, moreover, 'what it is not' (Sartre), from the moment that its activity is not pure recognition but rather imagines or simply evokes what is not there or even takes pains to describe itself?

This last aspect which, theoretically, can be seen as an extension of the second meaning, from a neutral point of view (absence as the symmetrical complement of presence), in fact often combines aspects of the first and second meaning. For, since Freud, latency also refers to the state of what must not be made present and to what has even been forgotten; that is, deprived of its power of representation and even effaced as if it had never existed. It is this third meaning which psychoanalysis is concerned with since it is interested in unconscious representations (those which are no longer in consciousness, as well as those which are not permitted to cross the barrier of consciousness and are even thought not to exist).

The fourth and last sense is that of '*nothing*'. Here, something is not opposed to an adverse force with inverted or dissimulated symmetry, but to nothingness. This negative is, however, not just negative since it refers to 'having been so and being so no longer',[3] unless it is supposed that it is a reference to 'having never come into existence'.

It is the difference between what is dead and what has not been born; i.e., the aporia of that which, by expressing itself as 'nothing', makes this 'nothing' exist, which otherwise would be inconceivable.

Basically, one could show the meaning of negativity in psychoanalysis by speaking of the postulate of a psychic activity other than that of consciousness but acting in tandem with it, if it was not for the fact that, unlike the neutral ideality of symmetry, psychoanalysis presupposes a 'polemic' between the two states, one being conscious, the other not, and sees them as struggling for power. This brings us back to the first meaning, i.e., that the unconscious is periodically reactivated and seeks to break into consciousness which counter-invests it, thereby creating a greater or lesser degree of disturbance at its centre, provoking a conflict, a civil war below the surface. This is all the more the case in that the balance of power is disproportionate; the imbalance favouring the unconscious. On the other hand, it is not easy to appreciate this disparity due to the unconsciousness of the unconscious which leads us back again to the third meaning of the negative which refers to the status of absence and latency.

We are quite close now to the fourth meaning: the denial and resistance which hope to convince the subject that nothing has ever emerged from emptiness, as if to fend off the powers of the negative which are barely allowed to establish themselves. It is understandable then that if, between these different meanings, introspective analysis finds contradictions which it can only partially resolve and which are dealt with on a philosophical level, the application of the negative to the foundations of psychoanalytic theory relativises these contradictions, making them seem secondary, and even rendering them obsolete by putting forward a concept which goes beyond them. Would it be going too far to assert that the concept of the unconscious is perhaps the root from which the different meanings applicable to consciousness are to be differentiated? If this were true, one could imagine that the origin of these changes in meaning would only be discovered retrospectively.

These remarks on polysemy have emerged from reflections based on experience. But there is perhaps another, more legitimate procedure, i.e., that which inspired Freud's article on 'Negation' which is at the basis of any psychoanalytic elaboration on the subject. I am referring to the linguistic approach proper.

A Brief Linguistic Survey

Lacan's proposal to translate *Verwerfung* by 'foreclosure' was inspired by Damourette and Pichon. After the notion was introduced, Freud wrote his article on *Die Verneinung* (Negation) which had also been the object of a study by Damourette and Pichon. The latter, studying negation in French, pointed out the special richness of its forms. In general, it is expressed by two terms: *'ne'*, on the one hand, and the adverbs *'pas'*, *'rien'*, and *'jamais'*, on the other. *'Ne'* can be employed in two ways: accompanied by *'que'* to denote either an exception (*cela ne concerne que moi = personne sauf moi*) [that only concerns me = nobody but me] or a discordance (*il est moins pauvre qu'il ne le paraît*) [he is not as poor as he seems]. According to grammarians, this discordance corresponds to an authentic mental function. As for the adverbs characteristic of negation: *rien, pas, jamais,* they denote a wish to consider the facts to which they apply as no longer being part of reality. It is a question, therefore, of a form of nihilation (*néantisation*) which Damourette and Pichon called *'forclusion'* (foreclosure), borrowing this term from legal vocabulary. Foreclosure is the loss of a right on some practice after the period during which it has been authorised. In fact, this term denotes exclusion. When Lacan suggested this translation, he omitted to acknowledge his debt to Damourette and Pichon. In the case of the 'Wolf Man', Freud wanted to point out a form of denial, of negation – which cannot contemplate the hypothesis of what comes into the mind or what is suggested by an interlocutor (castration, for example). The psyche is unable to retain the representation which is alluded to (and so, unlike repression, cannot be attracted by what is already repressed, or link up with other representations, etc., in short, become part of a system of symbolisation) and so it is literally expelled from the psyche, including the unconscious.

The philosophical inclination of French psychoanalysis is particularly noticeable in the work of Lacan who, as we know, was the disciple of Kojève; that is to say, he was used to the conceptual handling of the negative. But the genius of the French language very much lent itself to this, the expressions for negation being richer than in other languages. And, doubtless, it is not entirely a coincidence if Freud, in his article on fetishism, discusses the theory of scotomisation which comes from another Frenchman, Laforgue.[4]

This was just an episode. In fact, French philosophical thought seems to be impregnated with the negative, far beyond its avowed or veiled Hegelianism. The negative appears to be a precondition of access to the concept of the subject. Indeed, ideas about the negative, although present, are not always explicit in other authors. It is difficult to see how any attempt to conceptualise representation could bypass this theoretical task.

Let us return to language, for after all it is by starting from negation that Freud explicitly tackles the category of the negative. Linguistic literature on negation is too abundant and specialised for psychoanalysis to be able to take cognisance of its content and assimilate it. I shall mention just one author, Antoine Culioli.[5] Without mastering all the data and implications of his thought, I shall, nonetheless, refer to a few of his ideas which seem to have a bearing on psychoanalysis, at least at certain tangential points between the two disciplines.

The interest of Culioli's position lies in his attempt to reconstruct the constituent operations of ideas which are at work in the significant activities of subjects. Culioli makes the point that there is no such thing as natural language where a pure negative operator can be observed; there is therefore no unique marker of an operation of negation. Culioli's analysis leads to two conclusions: there exists a primitive operation of negation. Significant behaviour, whether verbalised or not, can be found in two registers: that which is bad, inadequate, unfavourable, to be rejected, and that which consists of a void, a hiatus, an absence. It is striking to discover here that one again comes across the categories referred to by Freud in his article on 'Negation': judgement of attribution (which opposes the good and the bad) – and judgement of existence (which differentiates between what is and what is not), attribution and existence can be found in the cardinal distinction proposed by Freud between the two major principles of pleasure–unpleasure and reality. Culioli calls the two registers he has defined 'subjective valuation' and 'spatio-temporal localisation' (representation of the existent and the discontinued). This terminology makes Culioli's referents clear: the opposition good–bad is linked with a subjective value system (what I love and what I hate), whereas that of temporo-spatial localisation refers to an objective system of determination, what 'is', involving a definition by the coordinates: 'Where is it? When is it?' In other words, how can I locate it in order to find it or find it again and with what instruments of thought? Culioli infers that this primitive negation develops and gives birth to constructed negations. This is the second conclusion. It can only be constituted thanks to operations (scanning, disconnection, differentiation, inversion of the gradient, going beyond what can be validated). This is where Culioli's exposition becomes difficult to understand for the non-specialist, although it is possible to follow his reasoning intuitively. His way of thinking is constantly underpinned by references to representation, whether it be categorial or notional. The delicate question of positivising (*la positivation*) the negative (as a precondition for dealing with it) is clearly defined: it is 'the privileged nature of a lexis which is neither positive nor negative but compatible with the positive or the negative'.[6] Identification and alterity are the two basic positions. Here, identification is alterity taken into account and then eliminated; differentiation is alterity maintained. Thus alterity is the foundation.[7]

There is no negation without a preliminary construction of the notional domain, any more than it can be conceived apart from a set of relationships. I cannot make a detailed study of the mechanisms inferred by Culioli (Organising or Attractive centre, etc.); however, I should like to emphasise the importance for this author of a hierarchical and dynamic concept (a stable state, a state in relation to a different state). Let us recall his own remarks:

> In other words, there is no isolated marker, there is no marker without the memorised residue of its genesis, there is no marker (or organisation of markers) that does not come from the adjustment of two complementary ideas belonging to the same domain of a notional category; every (meta) linguistic object masks a constitutive alterity. It is this enunciative work of locating (subjective and intersubjective; spatio-temporal; quantitative and qualitative) which, by selecting the complex adjustment of representations and utterers, suppresses, highlights or conceals this alterity.[8]

Here we can appreciate the progress made since the contributions of Damourette and Pichon as well as the proximity of Culioli's thought with the psychoanalytic approach, i.e., a contextual associative approach, a 'historical' tracing of the verbal process, the necessity of a procedure founded on the complementary pair (the contrasted pair), a relationship of identity or difference between the terms, and a reference to alterity.

Negation, concludes Culioli, permits the idea of possibilities. Is this not a fundamental element in the definition of psychic activity? The fact that the author grounds it in abstraction and form, far from arousing our misgivings, enables us to pursue the dialogue further. For, how can we not be in agreement with a linguist when he comes to this conclusion? 'And what would language be without the detours and games which negation alone permits through the intertwining of markers and operations?'[9] 'Now you'll think that I mean to say something insulting, but really I've no such intention', Freud quoted one of his patients as saying at the beginning of his article on Negation.

A Psychoanalytic Overview: Varieties of the Negative

The linguistics of enunciation accords a privileged role to alterity in language although many theoretical studies in the past minimised its importance. And no doubt there is good reason to be surprised at the position Culioli holds which reveals a considerable familiarity with psychoanalysis. His desire to leave his mark on the formalistic approach to linguistics does not prevent us from being in agreement with him when he stresses that the aim of the 'texts' produced is that their forms can be identified by a co-enunciator or that their recognition implies that they can be interpreted. Acceptability therefore regulates the forms which are exchanged: recognition, acceptability, interpretability, all of which refer to an activity of representation and regulation. All of these intercessors make dialogue possible even if it involves a great deal of translation between linguists and psychoanalysts. For, the series of mechanisms which Freud discovered – repression, foreclosure (or rejection), negation (or disavowal) – which from a conceptual viewpoint are included under the general heading 'the work of the negative', is based on different modes – linguistic or non-linguistic – of acceptability, although the latter does not refer to defined forms but to categories of representation (and a need for regulation). The birth of psychoanalysis can be dated from the moment Freud recognised the importance of repression, that is, after the 'Project for a Scientific Psychology' where he had underestimated its role. One should also point out that later he felt the need to describe variations of it in an order which was not a matter of indifference: first, psychotic structures disclosed extreme forms of it; then came the analysand's discourse in a session (the pendulum swinging from the most pathological to the most normal); and finally, there was a particular case of fetishist perversion where affirmation and negation co-exist. These different forms require us to take into account phenomena which are situated at some distance from language: in the areas of unconscious representation, the drives, perception, etc. Hence the idea of including negation at the heart of a larger whole, i.e., the work of the negative, which I am endeavouring to define more clearly.

'What becomes of the words in our books when we no longer read them?', one analysand wondered. This poetic formulation was less personal than he thought, for one of his siblings in analysis asked me a very similar question, asking himself or me what became of his words when a session was over. It is a question about life and death and not just about presence and absence.

Freud was faced with the same question when he wanted to know what had become of thoughts which a moment before had still been in consciousness but were no longer there a moment later. The answer: 'in the unconscious', satisfied his curiosity and ours for a long time. What no longer was did not, strictly speaking, cease to exist; it simply changed its form, since it lived on in an unconscious state. That is, until psychoanalytic practice enlarged its understanding to include these forms of non-existence which allowed the unconscious to return to consciousness – at least partially and in a modified form – through the intermediary of the pre-conscious. Freud's archaeological metaphor never lost its value right up to the end of his life. Nonetheless, after Freud – in fact, this began while he was still alive, with Melanie Klein – analysts began to have experience of forms of thought which exposed them to structures which were more radically negative or nihilating than, say, unconscious representation. This was the discovery alongside *Verdrängung* (repression) of *Verwerfung* (rejection) – uncovered by Freud with respect to psychosis – which remained without an equivalent in French until Lacan proposed that it be translated by *forclusion* (foreclosure). Many years later, Laplanche was inclined to favour the term 'rejection' which gave rise to less confusion. In Freud's work, foreclosure applied to two extremely different cases. On the one hand, it could be postulated in the mechanism of psychotic projection, the case of Schreber, but, on the other, it was found in the case of the 'Wolf Man' (it was even in reference to him that it was used) whose psychic structure was not even suspected by Freud, although it was clearly apparent to numerous analysts after him. We were then in the presence of a phenomenon with a very open clinical spectrum, for it ranged from psychotic structures which were more or less latent (borderline cases) to the most serious manifest forms of psychosis (paranoia and paranoid psychoses). In comparison with the repression found in transference neuroses, foreclosure bore witness to a defensive functioning which was more mutilating. In fact, along the path from repression to foreclosure, we come across again the first intuition Freud had formulated in 1896, concerning the psychoneuroses of defence, where paranoia was grouped together with hysteria and obsessional neurosis. The only difference was that this frame of reference had now fallen apart, the entities which it comprised being divided up into transference neuroses (hysteria and obsessional neurosis) and narcissistic neuroses (paranoia) which Freud divided in turn into narcissistic neuroses proper (melancholy) and psychoses (paranoia and schizophrenia). Other surprises awaited Freud when he was led to recognise what he called splitting. In this case, it no longer just concerned a field which could be defined roughly in terms of intensity, depth, extension, etc., in comparison with repression. With foreclosure a correspondence could be established between this singular form of defence and the extent to which psychosis is far removed from the normal psyche. But in this case he noticed something stranger; the form of negation identified in splitting appeared at the core of a psyche which, apart from the symptom, was considered to be totally normal, notably from the viewpoint of reason. However, with such patients, analysis could reveal the co-existence of an acknowledgement of reality perceptions and the information which issued from them, and the disavowal of these so that yes and no lived side by side, so to speak, without disturbing each other: 'Yes, I know that women don't have a penis. No, I can't believe what I have seen (and which threatens me), I am therefore choosing a contingent substitute which I will take hold of as an equivalent for what my perception has taught me was missing.' Thus the panoply was enriched and psychic functioning became more complicated. But in any case it was implicitly acknowledged that a link existed between all these nosographical entities, viz. the different forms of defence which made it possible to differentiate them. Psychoanalysts since Freud have necessarily continued with this line of thinking although they have not always been aware of the continuity.

Conclusion

At the end of his article on 'Negation', Freud, who does not ask himself too many questions about this transition – and heaven only knows how many it raises – ties judgement (of attribution) to the operations corresponding to the opposition of two groups of drives. This relationship assigns symbolic negation with the role necessary for establishing judgement in as much as the latter endows thought with a first measure of emancipation from the consequences of repression and thereby from the compulsion of the pleasure principle. This passage no doubt deserves a more thorough commentary for it contains the essential issues at the heart of the work of the negative.

Freud invites us to distinguish:

– negation considered as an operation of language;

– repression considered as a psychic mechanism on which negation is founded;

– unpleasure caused by the bringing into play of repression. On this point, Freud appears to invoke the existence of a negation which is neither of the order of language nor of repression, for it is precisely in order to free itself from the consequences of the latter that this negation comes into play. In other words, it is the symbolic nature of negation which is highlighted which, for Freud, does not seem to be confused with its verbal expression. However, its nature remains unspecified.

– one of the two groups of drives contrary to Eros (forces of destruction). We cannot avoid noticing here the preserving more than the destructive effect of a factor whose intervention puts an end to the consequences of repression and to the *compulsion* of the pleasure principle.

The preceding remarks oblige us to review our definition of the work of the negative. Clinically, taking into account the differentiations pertaining to defences, which experience has shown to be necessary, has been enough to justify the hypothesis of a work of the negative by the simple regrouping of these defensive varieties, thoroughly justified by the kinship of their mechanisms. Theoretically, the question is more complicated. It obliges us to consider the work of the negative from different angles: the first is one whose study is based on forms which make it possible to analyse it. Although this is difficult and open to controversy, it has the advantage of being clear. It is the fact that negation belongs to language. This can be linked with philosophical analysis which is a continuation of it, i.e., from language to conscious thought. The second constitutes a circle which includes the first, for verbal negation becomes an integral part of the psychic defences with which it maintains the relations already mentioned but which places the verbal form alongside others belonging to a psyche which is not linked with language. Here I am switching from a verbal and discursive frame of reference to a new paradigm referring to the psyche, the unconscious psyche in particular. This is the work of the negative as reflection stemming from repression and its offshoots (implying the participation of psychic representatives, unconscious representations, affects, perception, etc.). In this case the aporia is the inexistence of 'no' in the unconscious which poses the question both of the non-verbal substratum of this negation and the relations which can exist between verbal and non-verbal aspects. If, as Freud thought, negation does not exist in the unconscious, the question raised here is that of the relations between language and the substitute (not subjected to the negative) for negation which corresponds to it in the unconscious. However, the category of the negative is not constituted and the hypothesis of the inexistence of 'no' in the unconscious is not thereby reduced to a pure and simple absence of negativity. We know, moreover, that Freud did not stop there and that the epistemological problem would raise its head again with the final theory of the drives and the second topographic model of the psychical apparatus.

As can be seen, this second circle is not the end of the analysis; it is included in another, larger one which includes negation as a symbol, enabling it to free itself from the compulsion of the pleasure principle. I think that here Freud is alluding to a mechanism which he neglected to describe – and which he continued to neglect – that is, negativisation (inhibiting?): with respect to pleasure, intimately tied up with drive life (which the reference to repetition compulsion shows) and perhaps situated outside the defensive variations already mentioned. Finally, the last circle concerns the relationship between the two groups of drives: Eros–destructive drives. In this last case, negativisation is linked with the functioning intrinsic to drive life in the antagonism specific to the opposition of two kinds of drives. Are we to think, as Freud gives us to understand, that a mysterious factor might have an inhibiting effect – thus negativising – affecting each of the two groups? It is difficult to see what this internal inhibition should be attached to. Be that as it may, we can see that Freud is far from thinking of the drive as a purely positive force which, in the absence of any limitations placed on it, could express its potential fully.

It is clear that we are not dealing with the same work in all cases. However, it cannot be overlooked that in the course of our exposition, we have brought into play increasingly speculative forms of the work of the negative.

To conclude, I shall distinguish three aspects:

– negation in languages and its philosophical derivatives;
– negation in the psyche, derived from clinical practice;
– negation in thought, deduced from the axiomatic elaboration of theory and whose speculative value in psychoanalysis lies in the obligation it places upon itself of considering the psyche as being anchored in the body as well as in the long dependence of physical and psychical structure on its objects. In this respect, we cannot study negation without taking into consideration its internal functioning and the way in which the latter is in opposition with philosophical thought. This conflict between psychoanalysis and other disciplines should not detract in any way from the originality of a conception of the work of the negative which focuses on the intrinsic potentiality of drives considered as a 'mythology' of psychoanalysts.

2
Hegel and Freud: Elements for an Improbable Comparison

In modern times, however, the individual finds the abstract form ready-made ... Hence the task nowadays consists not so much in purging the individual of an immediate, sensuous mode of apprehension, making him into a substance that is an object of thought and that thinks, but rather in just the opposite, in freeing determinate thoughts from their fixity so as to give actuality to the universal, and impart to it spiritual life. But it is far harder to bring fixed thoughts into a fluid state than to do so with sensuous existence.

G.W.F. Hegel, *Phenomenology of Spirit*[1]

In the *Phenomenology of Spirit* Hegel does not set out to examine the concepts of subjectivity or objectivity, the World or Truth, or any of the other concepts which have traditionally served as a point of departure for philosophical reflection; philosophy sets itself the task of studying the very act itself of philosophising. This dissociation concerning the philosophy of this philosophising makes it possible to establish certain points of reference which, ceasing to be more or less arbitrary, become necessary in as far as they are already present in philosophy, e.g., common knowledge and reflective knowledge, knowledge and science, philosophy as a science, the experience of consciousness, and so on. Experience, which is thereby located at the point of departure, is at the root of the act of philosophising. Now, such an act presupposes that all previous philosophical reflection has been taken into account. This can be conceived of, sometimes as a search for Truth, evaluated regardless of the position it explicitly occupies in the succession of philosophical systems, and sometimes as a historical development, i.e., a succession of more or less convincing attempts within the same quest. And in this theoretical construction, which takes as its starting-point the way its own products appear to consciousness, Truth manifests itself as rectifying past errors and as progress relative to its former gropings. The movement towards Truth is nonetheless limited by the period in which it unfolds; no one can jump ahead of his own shadow.

Notwithstanding these innovations, it is necessary to make allowances for the inaccessible. The postulation of concepts considered to be immutable, at the pinnacle of the philosophical quest – Absolute Knowledge – raises the need for a critique of the purpose of such a construction. Hegel could not escape the Christian orbit of his thought. By thinking of his own time as the fulfilment of history, he indirectly revealed the prophetic dimension of his system. Yet Hegel wanted to break with the transcendental idealism of Kant and Fichte. His project was to write a philosophy of Nature and a philosophy of Spirit. While the latter continues to claim our attention, the former is still sorely lacking. More than ever there is an urgent need to bring the two together. Was not Freud's thought inspired by an identical project? It is always more difficult to find answers to questions which are conditioned by the epistemological horizon of one's own era. It was because Freud had a taste for reflection, without being imprisoned by the yoke of philosophical concepts, that he was able to take the risk of laying the foundations of a much madder way of thinking, the intuition of which came with the invention of the unconscious.

With Freud, consciousness does not become aware of itself through a purely historical inspiration. In other words, it is not by adopting an exclusively retrospective point of view that the truth will be revealed. In psychoanalysis the rule is not: 'go back in time as far as you can, and recall to consciousness the earliest memory you have', but 'say everything that crosses your mind without omitting anything'. In my opinion, this position corresponds somewhat to Hegel's method, provided one is ready to free oneself from the historical claim of conscious temporality. Approached in this way, the quest for spontaneity of spirit reveals more clearly, through the apparent anarchy of its productions, what the products of its activity are and what constitutes it; in fact, that against which spirit has been established and which endeavours to preserve it as such. The meeting with history is not so much concealed as postponed; that is, until meaningful order has been restored to what had appeared as disorder from a rational point of view.

Visions of History and of Development

According to Hegel, the path consciousness follows is history detached from its making.[2] But which history? Not the history of the world but rather the history of the accession of the individual ego to culture, by means of which it can move towards Absolute Knowledge. There is nothing to stop us making a connection here with the Freudian approach which views sublimation – that is, social and cultural interests – as the outcome of a drive vicissitude which is both very common and necessary. But Freud certainly does not consider sublimation as something to be taken for granted, for he denies that there is any spontaneous tendency towards perfection. While the history of the world is not the subject of Hegel's work, his discourse is grounded on certain key moments in history (the Ancient City, the Roman Empire, the French Revolution) and one is reminded of the way Freud speaks of the cultural process by referring to earlier symbolic events which are more fundamental than others in his view. Freud relies more on myth than history because he thinks that it is the relic of a repressed history; hence, Christianity repeats the murder of the primitive father (in the person of the son) and the Oresteia celebrates the transition of matriarchal to patriarchal rights, not to mention the Oedipus myth, the symbolic effects of which we are familiar with. It might be considered that Freud's thought is inspired by what Althusser called a 'spontaneous philosophy' of nature and mind. For it has to be said that its coherence depends on onto- and phylogenetic historical premises which in Freud's mind were undoubtedly linked with the natural sciences. The introduction into psychoanalytic theory of phylogenetic schemes, otherwise referred to by Freud as primal fantasies, is a kind of introductory statement to the process of civilisation referring back to a pre-history of the species.

It is therefore fair to speak of an implicit negativity or even of a bio-anthropological form of a work of the negative with regard to these speculations. This is not simply because, in such a system of thought, theorising is faced with the necessity of producing theoretical postulates which make the work more coherent, but also because Freud considers that the events pertaining to the pre-history of the species have been assimilated by the psyche through internalisation and have become an integral part of the common psychic structure through hereditary transmission. Furthermore, unlike Jung, who considers they have a direct influence, Freud believes that they express themselves through the mediation of a reactivation of individual experience which has the power of triggering the organising attributes of these phylogenetic schemes ('aptitude for reacquisition'). In other words, one passes from a silent potentiality to an active potentiality which has become effective through externalising an internal structure. The latter is itself set in motion by remarkable events and is found to have a capacity as a symbolic trigger which is liable to actualise or activate what had hitherto remained latent, caught in the web of interiority. Moreover, for Freud, drives (internal today) were formerly actions, just as affects were 'attacks' (this is the case in hysteria), and language was an omnipotent form of thought, etc. The present state of these different aspects of psychic life can thus be considered as the outcome (by means of internalisation) of a negativisation and their activation, as negating the negation. Such a point of view is both historical and structural. Rather than wondering whether it is appropriate to link these ideas to Lamarck or Darwin – which is all the more debatable in that they appear to owe much more to Freud's spirit than to a biologist's – it would be more profitable to see in them the germ of an original conception of negativity in the history of development. This would account for the movement by which consciousness claimed on the one hand to establish its supremacy over the unconscious by means of repression, but, on the other, to show how this repertoire handed down by generations is preserved in the unconscious, destined to emerge from its latency into fully effective activity. Such a process of internalisation would guarantee the preservation of a patrimony from generation to generation in the form, not of these acquisitions, but of that which organises the capacity for acquisition and in accordance with the sense of acquisitive development. This is a speculation, as we all know, but it is not without substance.

It is clear that awareness only exists because consciousness is clouded by everything which has accumulated in it, preventing it from returning along its trajectory and retracing its evolution. Its significance cannot be ascertained unless a significant psychic work of dealienation takes place which meets with resistance before coming to an understanding of what this consciousness is, i.e., the means, the stakes and the *punctum caecum* of the analytic process.

If a parallel can be drawn between Hegel's and Freud's projects, it resides in their opposition. Hegel wrote the *Phenomenology* as an introduction to his *Logic* and *Metaphysics* – an introduction which has won its independence and will be regarded as much more than a mere introduction to the subject. Its goal is knowledge *in itself* and *for itself*. (Sartre remembered this, and, let it be said in passing, expressed the desire to see the birth of a new psychoanalysis which he hoped would be existential and without an unconscious.) As for Freud, he concludes his work on the rock of an imaginary biology. Primal fantasies serve as a hypothesis for the foundations of the psyche, inscribed in heredity.

Both base their theoretical constructions on principles of functioning seen from a developmental point of view. To avoid any misunderstanding, let me add here that modern developmental interpretations of post-Freudian psychoanalysis are totally contrary to Freud's thinking. This is also one of the reasons for exploring, in a spirit of research, other poles of comparison, even if they may seem remote from psychoanalytic productions. Hegel's work is of interest to the psychoanalyst for the way in which it lays down the premises on which knowledge is based. Freud's work can also interest the Hegelian philosopher because of the way 'spirituality' is envisaged from the angle of cultural development. And if we adopt the Freudian view that the murder of the primal father is the founding act of culture, the work of the negative acquires a basis which goes far beyond its individual effects. For Hegel and Freud are both fascinated by the mystery of the origins of the works of the human community as an expression of psychic life. But here, too, they have contrary views. Whereas Hegel considers Absolute Knowledge to be his greatest achievement, Freud believes salvation lies in the critique of religion, not just as an institution but as a mode of thought. A certain positivism gives Freud an unshakeable faith in the advent and future of science. Both Hegel and Freud are concerned to extend our knowledge of man, the psychological study of whom constitutes the loftiest of the sciences. But with Hegel, this first emerges from anthropology (whose subject of study is the soul), raises itself to the level of a phenomenology (the theoretical support of which is consciousness), and flourishes as a science of spirit. With Freud, on the other hand, the psyche emerges from biology (or from a natural science), develops into a psychology (whose subject is also consciousness) and finds its accomplishment in psychoanalysis (as *meta*psychology). We might say that for Freud, the mind's manifestations belong solely to the domain of metapsychology, because they are anchored in the drives to which a psychology of consciousness has no access.

Any psychoanalyst who immerses himself in Hegel is inevitably struck by the major break in the work between the phenomenology of consciousness and the phenomenology of spirit. The further he reads, the closer he comes to the philosopher's real purpose which his own way of thinking, however, is ill-disposed to accept, and he therefore has increasing difficulty in adhering to Hegel's conclusions. On the other hand, the exposition of the phenomenology of consciousness will interest him, with its three canonical stages (thereafter developed in greater depth): consciousness – self-consciousness – reason. In particular, he will find the study of consciousness–self-consciousness more valuable than any other work of philosophy. This, I think, was where Lacan started out from. What the psychoanalyst finds is a philosophical model evocative of the genetic myths constructed by psychoanalysts which are apparently compatible (to a certain extent) with the empirical findings of psychologists.

An example of this is the mirror stage where Lacan, imbued with both Hegel and Freud, takes up the psychological observations, first of Preyer, then of Wallon. Here we have the premises of a 'genesis and structure' of the psychoanalytic ego which is different from Freud's. We should bear in mind, however, that the Freudian model was developed on two occasions: the first occasion was in 'Instincts and their Vicissitudes' in 1915 and the second and last occasion was in 1925 in the article on 'Negation'.

Consciousness – Self-consciousness – Unconscious

For Hegel, this moment in the process corresponds to self-certainty. Self-certainty arises when the soul separates from its content which, for the world, is the Other. It is therefore through *separation* that subjectivity is discovered, as an unshakeable ground of being, as if this was what remained after the separation from the world and the Other – a separation assigned with the role of taking responsibility for the subject. Subjectivity thus arises from distress, like a wall erected against the risk of nihilation (*néantisation*) in a world from which one is separated. As such, it has become hostile since it does not coincide with the self.

In the very antithesis between consciousness and self-consciousness there is an interstice which leaves the conceptual position of the unconscious a chance to exist. For, if phenomenologically one admits of the distinction between the two states, an almost imperceptible period of time is sufficient for consciousness to change into self-consciousness, that is, a simple appeal or a slight withdrawal, involving major consequences. In order for there to be two genuinely distinct states, it is important that the transition from one to the other is not taken for granted, that there is a distance between them, and that the transition does not take place quasi-automatically, as is the case in ordinary intuitive experience. This is a moment of time in which it has become impossible for self-consciousness to return to consciousness. It is tempting to put forward the hypothesis of a state which would be like *the connotation, in unconscious terms, of plain consciousness which is not yet self-consciousness*. It is in the movement which attempts to unite them – because it is difficult to imagine a consciousness which is not self-consciousness – that we encounter the shadow of an unconscious.

Jean Hyppolite's commentary suggests as much: 'Undoubtedly conscious-ness is also self-consciousness; at the same time as it thinks it knows its object to be its truth, it knows its own knowledge, but it does not become aware of it as such, for it is only self-consciousness for us and not yet self-consciousness for itself.'[3]

With respect to this consciousness which is said not to be self-conscious-ness – unconscious self-consciousness, we might call it – can we, without letting ourselves be deterred by the paradoxical nature of the expression, extend the line of reasoning a step further by calling it unconscious-con-sciousness? That is to say, not an inferior form of consciousness, but a state of consciousness which would not involve referring either to a self (ego) or to a reflexivity and yet would be a form of investment. This is what I am proposing by inverting the basis of Hegelian thought. The starting-point would no longer be sense-certainty but the pair: need(internal)–sensibility(external). There would be a correspondence between sense-certainty, shaken from without, and the constraining force of feeling stemming from an internal need. May I be spared the sacrosanct distinction between need and desire – an invention of Lacan who, under the pretext of returning to Freud, said the opposite of what Freud wrote in his article 'Instincts and their Vicissitudes'. Here 'need' is understood in its widest sense. I should add, however, that the term relates exclusively to the drive and not to desire, and even less to wish. For perception, we should substitute the pair representation–perception as a dialectic of the interior and exterior. Finally, understanding should be linked to the construction of phantasy as the first form of causality. Hitherto, however, it has not been possible to speak either of ego or of self-consciousness. The belief that the ego is the light which manifests itself and the Other is a lofty Hegelian idea.[4]

Love, a Lack of the Work of the Negative

The appearance of a similar Other when self-consciousness emerges constitutes an enigma. The withdrawal of consciousness resulting in its separation from another person not only makes the self of consciousness appear as self-consciousness but transforms the Other, hitherto identified with a world, i.e., another ego, into an Other who presents himself as another Ego. This is when desire appears. It should be pointed out that desire manifests itself here as desire which is based not only on separation but on potential antagonism, a preliminary form of it. Moreover, what emerges here is not the repressed aspect of that which in consciousness would transform it into a desire in compensation for sense-certainty, as a first stage in the triad sense-certainty – perception – understanding. This consciousness from which self-consciousness is absent, is the desire of the Other, i.e., what is at stake in a struggle involving self-consciousness. The separation of the subject and the object and the position of consciousness seen as an object could be understood as a displacement of desire, linked to the separated and lost object, onto the ego – itself taken as an object, through reflection, in the search for a response to distress. This is where common ground may be found to exist between Hegel and Freud, failing which it is to be feared that the theory of desire may give way to ideological temptations. Without getting into possible areas of debate concerning Freudian axiology – I am thinking here of the hypothesis that the auto-erotic relation to the breast must be given up before the mother can be apprehended as a whole person, as well as of the whole question as to whether the object should be conceived of initially as a part-object – the intermittent sense one has of discovering surprising areas of correspondence between the philosopher's thoughts and the psychoanalyst's is immediately demolished by the unavoidable and complementary conviction that there remains a considerable gulf between their points of view which cannot be minimised. Hegel strives with all his being towards the goal to which his thought aspired, i.e., Absolute Knowledge; whereas Freud constantly insists on the need to analyse the basic elements out of which the psyche is constructed. Conversely, each of them is attracted by the pole which they chose not to make the goal of their project. Hegel returns to the most obscure and modest forms of consciousness, which has little relation to a phenomenology of nature, and Freud cannot avoid speculating on the vicissitudes of the cultural process. With Freud, the object is viewed with hate; that is, when the subject becomes aware of its separate existence. The psyche is confronted with the failure of its omnipotent belief in its capacity to satisfy its desires instantly. The concept of drive, rather than consciousness, gives a better account of this inaugural relationship which does not expect the object to come from the outside and to leave its imprint on the subject's sensibility. The certitude is based on the need which 'consciousness' – not yet self-consciousness – has for the object and for the necessary and inescapable nature of the link. This necessity finds its justification in anaclisis, for it is when there is a dependence on the object of the drives of self-preservation, which assure the organism's survival, that pleasure is discovered (linked to oral drives). Freud's meaning in defending this idea is clear: just as our species would die out if the power of the sexual drive did not compel us to seek out a partner (almost at any price), by the same token, if anaclisis did not complement the necessities of self-preservation, the individual would perish for lack of a sufficiently powerful motive compelling him to find again the object with whom the taste for pleasure had been found. This is how he will establish a solid basis for forming an attachment and for renewing the links which make his relationship to the object one of 'second nature'. This relationship will give pleasure its stamp of origin and endow it with its essential quality derived from the soldering together of the sexual drives and those of self-preservation. We still have to describe the entire process which paves the way for the reciprocal formation of the ego and the object, starting with the original referents of drive dualism. This situation enables us to understand the development, prior to self-consciousness, of an opportunity to summon the object, without the use of sensibility and perception, by the sole means of 'knowledge' of this consciousness as 'knowledge' of the object, i.e., the hallucinatory wish-fulfilment arising from the object's absence. For consciousness, which has separated itself from the world, the latter is only there to satisfy its desires, before it exists in itself, independently. Prior to consciousness (as with the unconscious), the very idea of desire is inconceivable; after, under the reign of reason, the latter wants to surpass the former by synthesising consciousness and self-consciousness.

For Hegel the emergence of desire in the process which occurs between consciousness and reason, fundamentally determining the relation with the Other, merely leads to the struggle of the two forms of consciousness for recognition. Let us bear in mind that this is a struggle to the death. Desire, Lacan reminds us, is the desire of the Other. An idea of conflict, implicit in the work, now comes to the fore. Whereas in Hegel, it sets master and slave in opposition, in Freud it takes place intrapsychically between the demands of the drive and the ego organisation, before acquiring an intersubjective form which results in the formation of the super-ego. This is because in this study of the phenomenology of consciousness, Hegel is already thinking about the *Phenomenology of Spirit* and about his works, whereas Freud dwells on the primal ties of hate and love because they continue to endure during the entire subsequent development. Now, it is precisely in connection with love that Hegel speaks – by omission, as if negatively – of a work of the negative. Indeed, the only mention he makes of the work of the negative concerns love. The latter is said to lack the 'suffering, the patience, and the labour of the negative' which influences the tragic character of separation.[5] Yet where, if not in love, is separation more tragic; and how many sublime works have not arisen from it?

If Hegel is right, and we would be justified in doubting it, love is to be understood here only in its most limited sense. In reality, love and separation are indissociable; for the accomplishment of love is the fusion which is so rarely achieved, being institutionalised in the relationship with God. Hegel may be said to have failed to recognise the nature of the fundamental link between consciousness and its objects, which alone explains the fundamental position of desire. For can the desire for recognition be separated entirely from the desire to be loved?

Moments of Consciousness and Topographical Models of the Psyche

Hegelian reason is what makes the unity of consciousness and self-consciousness possible, in which the object is both ego and object. Although the term 'reason' is not credited with the same unifying power in psychoanalysis, the allusion to the achievement of unity between the id and the ego makes unquestionable sense when we transpose it to narcissistic and object-investments. It is in this sense that we can speak of 'narcissistic objects' or of the ego taken as an object. Both the possibility of reversing the perspective and also of situating this concept in the light of a certain vertex (the ego as object, or the object as that to which the ego is tied) represent progress. The concept of relation may offer a way forward with respect to the terms linked by it, each of them being viewed separately. Sexuality should then be seen as its synonym. The three stages: consciousness – self-consciousness – reason can be thought of as three moments, which in turn denote the indivisible totality – the 'individuating separation' – the relation.

Initially, there is consciousness of an object without this consciousness being separated as such; the object is the other in general. Subsequently, the object is the ego itself, i.e., the ego 'takes itself' as the object, it is both ego and object. Here, we again come across some of the paradoxical aspects of the psychoanalytic theory of object-relations which concerns both the relations between the ego and the object and the idea of the ego itself seen as object. To return to the ego, we can therefore say that initially it is unaware of itself as ego; it then discovers itself as object, and finally realises the relativity of its status in which object is both ego and object. Becoming conscious of the self as ego marks a lull in the process, the moment in the analysis when 'its object is its own being-for-self; then, it is self-consciousness'.[6]

The transition from the phenomenology of consciousness to the phenomenology of spirit is unexpectedly echoed in Freud's work. In my view, this is one of the reasons why the first topographical model was replaced by the second. For self-consciousness is not the final stage in the phenomenology of consciousness which must also surpass individualism. This movement is inaugurated by reason, not so much in its reflective aspect as in its active, inquiring dimension; that is, in its return to the world. Let us consider the development of the figures of the other; first as an object, inseparable from consciousness, then as the Other who is the obverse of self-consciousness, and, finally, the Other of the spiritual community[7] and universal consciousness. The Truth of reason, that is, effective reason, finds its accomplishment in a world which is supposed to be the authentic expression of it, i.e., Spirit. Lastly, Spirit is surpassed as a substance in order to become a Subject. An equivalent idea cannot be found in psychoanalysis. However, can we not discern a similar inspiration in Freud when he introduces the super-ego as an agency into the theory? It has often been stressed that the death drive was the main reason for the creation of the second topographical model. It seems to me that another reason, not unconnected with the first, was the need to remedy a conceptual shortcoming which compelled Freud to create the super-ego. For it is only at the level of the super-ego that the agonistic and antagonistic relations between the drives of self-preservation (or love) and the destructive (or death) drives can be developed. It is in this way that a theory of culture is integrated into Freud's work as a complement to a theory of the individual where the effects of nature and culture intersect. The fact that it is based on the dead Father is not inconsequential for, on the one hand, it commemorates this murder, and, on the other, it celebrates the absence: the two aspects of the negative.

We may wonder why? In my opinion, the answer is that beyond the dialectics of master and slave, the values of the two systems became increasingly far removed. While Hegel pursued the historical and cultural path towards the crowning achievement of Absolute Knowledge, Freud arrived at the most accomplished and complete structure of conflictuality and drive antagonisms by introducing us to the Oedipus complex and its resolution through the intervention of the super-ego. There is now too great a distance between the two conceptions. It would no doubt be interesting to pick up the thread of the argument we have just left at the point where Freud returns to his project of setting out a psychoanalytic model of culture. But that would take us beyond the aims of this study. I would like to add, however, that Lacan, with his concept of the Other (with a capital) – although it is different from its Hegelian counterpart – helped to reduce the gap between Hegel and Freud, for a while at least. Unless, that is, one believes that the theoretical function of this concept, with the late additions to Lacanian theory, went even further than Hegel in the direction of Absolute Knowledge. In spite of appearances, I am inclined to believe this is so.

Arguments for the Negative in Psychoanalysis

It would not surprise me if the reader still has some difficulty in grasping the influence and the place of the negative in psychoanalysis. This is because what we are dealing with cannot be apprehended directly by consciousness or translated into its language, and because the latter, faced with the demands made upon it, is a prisoner of a *de facto* positivity. This is what makes it difficult to come to grips intellectually with negativity in relation to psychoanalysis, if for no other reason than that it is only by means of direct intuition that consciousness can conceive of what this term refers to, that is, the opposite of what is, which is just another mode of being, i.e., a positive once again. Thus, if the negative proves to be refractory to immediate intuition, it will have to be discovered, not just as an enigma of what is, but as another mode of being. This other mode cannot be conceived positively since all the criteria which would define the positive are lacking, and, furthermore, because the positive is itself contradicted by it in its very positivity. The negative displays the same consistency and the same resistance to being known as positivity, except that, where the former is concerned, apprehending what stands in the way does not help consciousness understand what is happening, for it is not even possible to resort to the artifices of elusiveness. What I mean is that we cannot content ourselves with characterising the negative by a sort of evanescent quality, rather like a fantasy one drives away by staring ahead wide-eyed, or a ghost one dispels by being wide awake.

On the contrary, owing to its ties with the drive process (*le pulsionnel*) the negative is apprehended with the implacable harshness conferred upon it by the compulsion to repeat – as the basis which defies its rationality. It must therefore be understood that the status of the negative has the particularity of being both the reverse of the positive, connoting a contrary type of valency to that which was affirmed initially, but it also brings to light what is radically different in nature from the positive, so that approaching the latter by the means which are appropriate to it will never be sufficient to disclose its nature. It is not a question of essence, i.e., of that which assures the positive of its continuity, its indissolubility, its 'property', beyond its manifestations such as structure and content, or as background which remains beyond the multiplicity and temporal succession of forms – a permanence which goes beyond the discontinuities of presence. On the contrary, the negative expresses the reversal of the perspective that essence is immutable and invariable. Behind the discovery of a figure of consciousness appearing in the course of its movement, if it is not created by the latter, one can sense both the shift in the movement of the quest towards the point which would represent the end of its course, coinciding with its essence, and the fixation on a form which is marked temporally and revealed by the movement itself. The latter continues to have a relation to consciousness and the object but brings into view – just like when one suddenly discovers a new way of seeing things – an unsuspected reality which uncovers retroactively what was concealed, without our suspecting it, in the quiescence prior to the movement which is echoed by the form born of the temporary cessation of the progression. This reality is not entirely new, for it finds its meaning in relation to the positive which is pre-existent, but does not itself give access to this revealed meaning of which it is by definition unaware. Furthermore, the negative has the power, retroactively, to confer the positive which pre-existed it with a meaning which could never have been achieved by a consideration of the properties evoked by its positivity alone. The experience of the lack of existence of that which is described as positive is necessary for the deployment of what cannot come into existence: simply being there. A final paradox is that this observation tends to suggest that the withdrawn position of the negative gives forewarning of the effect it can have (in space and time). This property would confer it with a more fundamental status than the positive, for the negative so conceived cannot be apprehended in experience by the senses without relying on such concepts as ideas, essence, transcendence etc. The danger is thus avoided of yielding to the lure of common sense, to the trap of sense-certainty. By concerning ourselves immediately with what is not apparent for consciousness, we are seeking the core of the negative in its multiple versions which range from the implacable manifestation of the compulsion to repeat, as a basic mode of drive functioning, to the most discreet signs by which the negative makes itself felt in the fleetingness of the moment. It is as if the essential nature of the negative were divided between the elusiveness of the ephemeral and the continuity of an inaccessible core resistant to any kind of reduction by the knowable, excluding the possibility of any knowledge by means of positivity alone. If this is the situation, for the negative to appear it is necessary to bring about a shift in the organisation of consciousness and to offer communication an artifice through language. The creation of this artifice is imposed by the hypothesis of the relations which govern the positive and the negative in speech. For it is clear that in ordinary communication the negative is subjected, at least apparently, to the positive. This subjection must therefore be attenuated. Free association, that is, the mimetic figure of the dream, is still the most prototypical expression of the negative. What does free association mean if not loosening the noose of the positive which constrains consciousness. While the fundamental rule has the effect of producing a discourse which can only lead us back to the dream, it is important not to fall into the trap of the latter's positivity (its manifest content) any more than to give way to the charm of its illogicality, the seductive nature of which was treasured by the surrealists. The negative has the logic of the shadow which claims its due, just at the point where the positive presents itself in the light and seeks to monopolise for itself the visibility of the subject's psyche, whether the latter is awake or asleep.

Ruptures and Openings

The periodical but repeated attempt to draw a sharp parallel between the ideas of Hegel and Freud, suggesting a possible comparison, quickly peters out because the difference between their conceptions is so flagrant. The gulf soon takes on the proportions of a chasm, so much so that one cannot help concluding that anything but the most general of comparisons is impertinent. We should nonetheless offer some explanation for this preposterous attempt to establish connections between them. And it is perhaps in so doing that we shall discover that it is less the content of their work which lends itself to a dialogue than the sense that both of them broke with what had gone before.

For it could be said that Hegel's philosophy represents the ultimate stage in the evolution of a philosophy of consciousness, containing in its recesses the prescience of what might be the unconscious. This is a point of view which was criticised and challenged by his successors, entailing a return to the past in order to start afresh from a new basis (Husserl), soon followed by a definitive rupture with any approach which made reference to 'consciousness', replacing it with a reminder that Being had been forgotten.

With Being, a line of reasoning was abandoned which Hegel had pushed to the limits, in spite of its evident limitations which suggested that openness towards other horizons was necessary. For example, logical positivism based on the logic of language alone.

Kierkegaard undoubtedly sensed in Hegel's system a threat for philosophy (and religion, in spite of everything). He was not satisfied that Hegel wanted Absolute Knowledge to have subject status. He no doubt felt that the subject in question was much too crudely exposed to the light and did violence to his desire for intimacy, to his need to protect the dark spaces of his subjectivity, ravaged by anxiety, whose mystery had to be preserved, and which had to be defended at all costs against the impingement of Existence. Nietzsche's radical critique was not so much concerned to look down from a superior vantage-point upon the road which history had taken up to the battle of Iena as it was anxious to see the future struggles for the advent of a new man unfold. In other words, there was indeed a programme to be accomplished – but it was not the one hinted at by Absolute Knowledge. The progressive (or progredient) movement had to return to the past in order to create its transvaluation of values announcing the coming of superman. But Nietzsche also had to face this hard necessity which resisted the great upheaval he hoped for. And it was finally with Heidegger that the new paradigm was born: a paradigm which both re-evaluates the past and establishes its authority, overcoming the impasses of all previous philosophies of consciousness. Since time immemorial, the past had 'forgotten' Being and the time had now come to remember it. Was it 'an oversight'? Or was it repression? However that may be, the reunion with Being had many advantages: firstly, by getting rid of the millstone of consciousness, since a certain Freud (sublimely ignored) had shown how little faith could be placed in it. Secondly, by posing an absolute which could only be approached through its 'fall' into manifestion (*l'étant*).[8] Finally, by abandoning a historian's vision, Hegelianism having demonstrated how it could be variously dressed up to serve different purposes. However, when we look at the thought of the pre-Socratic philosophers, this oversight had considerable advantages, for it facilitated the birth of a way of thinking which laid greater emphasis on spiritualism. And when Heidegger urges us to recall this, far from turning his back on the development which followed the pre-Socratics, it is on the basis of this spiritualism that he proposes the reunion. In this respect, we may wonder whether Freud's thought is not nearer to these pre-Socratic sources than to its renewal under Heidegger's leadership.

It has been said that twentieth-century thought is heir to the philosophers of suspicion, Nietzsche, Marx and Freud. But the origins of the rupture can be traced back further. It may be said to originate in Hegel and to realise itself diversely through different uses of the negative. Psychoanalysts do not have the same concerns as either Nietzsche or Marx. Psychoanalysis therefore does not aim to evaluate itself in relation to Hegel's ideas.

It can be seen from these remarks that Hegel's contribution to psychoanalysis cannot be limited to its conception of desire (the latter is already present in Spinoza, not to mention Aristotle or Kant), the desire of the Other, the desire for the Other's desire, but that it covers a much larger field. With Hegel, to the extent that the phenomenology of consciousness distinguishes the figures which represent the different stages of a journey, each of them implies the negation of the stage preceding it, even if it cannot be apprehended as negation and results in a creation. In the same way, one should realise that what comes at the end of the process is already present from the outset in an invisible or unconscious form. This state can therefore be qualified as negative (the absolute exists 'in a negative form' = a shadow in common phenomenal consciousness). To say that the state is negative is also to postulate that at this stage it is not possible as yet to 'positivise' it. It is a deduction made retrospectively at the end of the process, i.e., from the soul to the mind by the intermediary of consciousness. But what counts in making such an assertion is its commitment to experience and the negative character which results from this commitment in terms of doubt or disappointment; hence the *Aufhebung*, 'conserving while surpassing'. Negativity is the stage necessary for the emergence of consciousness, of the process and of the relations by which it is woven into the positivity of its connections. It is a determinate negation. It can no doubt be maintained that negation is not posed–opposed in the mind to a content from the outside, as something which denies the possibility or the existence of it, but is an integral part of this content, its stand-in. Negation is a constituent component of the process; it alone sheds light on the development which it entails. '*Si le grain ne meurt ...*' .[9] In the last analysis, the *Aufhebung* is transcendence and the movement of transcendence is the movement itself of knowledge – which must become knowledge of the knowledge of oneself, that is, consciousness of this knowledge. However, in this movement, consciousness experiences the object's insufficiency and it uses this as a motor for the movement of consciousness. And that of course is the characteristic of what does not take its origin in the causality which is specific to the natural order.

In the history of ideas this negation corresponds to their obsoleteness and even to their death which provokes cultural crises of consciousness. Here, one could look for a parallel on the one hand in the idea of a quest to be reunited with the primary object (while taking into account its retrospective idealisa-tion), and, on the other, with the disappointment at discovering that parents are not omniscient. The relation to the Other which such a position implies can be conceived of as a generalisation of the category, since the Other can just as well be nature, an object or the world. As far as we are concerned, this is the difficulty with the uniformity of a category obtained to the detriment of the properties of heterogeneity. Heterogeneity would indeed enable us to rediscover what the concept has sacrificed in terms of its diversity, by acquiring homogeneity thanks to the artifice of language, the use of which itself depends on a homogenisation operated by the signifier.

Freud did not believe there was any divorce between science and *his* science, psychoanalysis, even when the latter defended points of view which science considered erroneous. Hegel, too, thought of his work as a science and saw no separation at all between philosophy and science even when, at times, he was not sparing in his criticism of the science of his day, for science is 'true knowledge', i.e., science of the experience of consciousness.

The Unconscious without Content: Relations with Consciousness

One difficulty facing us in our reflections lies in the opposition between the philosophical perspective (of Hegel), which locates the negative in the movement of consciousness itself, and the psychoanalytic perspective which traces the negative back to a subsumable un-conscious by means of a freer deployment of conscious activity. The unconscious, let us remember, does not occupy a position of pure symmetry with respect to consciousness; it is not like a figure of the development of reflective consciousness which engenders the adverse position by its own movement alone; it cannot be identified either as being solely opposed to the positions taken by consciousness. The psycho-analytic unconscious goes beyond these different aspects, more or less explicitly, by ceasing to be identifiable as such by consciousness. For, as Freud reminds us, the unconscious cannot be seen, it can only be deduced. Moreover, it is a concept which is both descriptive, dynamic and systemic.

There is one observation, however, which will help us understand the degree of complexity involved here. When, after 1920, Freud modifies his theory by limiting the unconscious to being only a 'psychic quality', he justifies this modification by his conviction that there are a multiplicity of states which deserve to be included in the category of what is not conscious. Nonetheless, by affirming that the repressed and the unconscious are no longer synonymous, he does not call into question the description of the repressed as unconscious, but extends the domain of the unconscious beyond that, to certain forms of resistance and mechanisms of defence, for example. But although they are unconscious, this does not imply, as is the case for the repressed, a reference to latent content; the defences are entirely under the watchful eye of consciousness. The status of the 'mechanisms of unconscious defence' is therefore paradoxical for, henceforth, the description unconscious can refer to mental processes without content, or rather, without content other than that of consciousness. They are thus closely related to consciousness and can be compared with Hegel's analysis of consciousness. What is there to prevent us then from considering them as equivalent? It is the reference to anxiety which Kierkegaard did not miss. The functioning of the negative in psychoanalysis thus differs from that proposed by Hegel's philosophy in that it always implies a strategy whose aim is not to seek an answer in Absolute Knowledge but to establish a link with anxiety, a generic term covering a wide range of states from unpleasure to pain and which can go as far as effacing all trace of its strategic nature. The negative carries out its own nihilation of that which enabled its basic nature to be identified.

It has been maintained that Hegel's work marked the end of the era of philosophy. It seems to me, however, that something is continuing which started with Hegel: the idea of consciousness as a process which is self-revelatory through its discourse, the path from latency to actuality. Apparently the march of knowledge which confines itself to winning over territory from the domain of ignorance leaves a profound mark on the progression of the discourse which discovers, as it unfolds, how alienated it is from its own productions, thus paving the way, at its core, for the beginnings of alterity. For it is indeed with Hegel that alterity inhabited consciousness, not as the result of an exteriority which, coming from the outside, leaves its imprint on the subject, but as a different development of the figures of consciousness which henceforth see their unity constantly challenged by its own discursiveness. And it is here, providing we safeguard the possibility, that there is a potential point of contact with the unconscious.

There are two reasons, however, which have prevented this meeting from occurring. The first is the discredit which has been cast on the hierarchical conception which may serve as an alibi for hegemonic theses, for such a vision is crowned by the culmination of history. Moreover, like any theory which systematically conceals the realm of the real (*le champ du réel*), it provokes the opposition of all those who, in spite of themselves, feel engaged in the march for progress which this philosophy speaks of, and, at the same time, feel crushed by its steamrolling dogmatism. So the opposition to Hegel's ideas would inevitably come from the irreducible singularity (sometimes in the name of God) of Kierkegaard or from nihilistic protest. Curiously, it is in the negation of the Hegelian negation promoted by Nietzschean thought that we discover the potential source of what will later blossom with Freud. His theory, however, would not be able to bypass the demands of an ontogenetic viewpoint (which can always be exploited for normative ideological ends, as has often been stressed), which we could not do completely without. This is one of the weaknesses of Lacan's thought whose questioning of accepted ideas on development was nonetheless not unfounded.

The solution to the problems which are raised by this point of view should reveal the insufficiency of the developmental perspective – once a critique of its simplistic criteria has been made – with the aim of setting an extremely complex conception of temporality in opposition to it.

The second reason why this meeting did not materialise is that the discovery of the alterity which inhabits consciousness was not enough to persuade the philosopher to submit himself to the test of experiencing a situation of radical alterity, that of transference. The philosophical subject, in effect, can in no case give up the privilege of its transcendental solipsism. Which is why it was necessary to wait for psychoanalysis to establish favourable conditions for the flowering of this alterity and for the revelation of its conflictual nature. For the o(O)ther (*l'a(A)utre*), as Lacan observed, is itself caught in a double alterity. The first is situated, through its discourse, in its relation to the anti-language represented by the drive; the second relates to the person who is required to respond to the situation created by the drive exigency and who listens to the discourse by virtue of the role he or she occupies in the psychoanalytic situation.

Alterity Within Alterity, Intrapsychic and Intersubjective

Lacan's error, and the weak point of his theory, was to resist *alterity within alterity*, the heterogeneousness between drive and object; that is, between bodily demands and the singular status of the 'other-who-is-able-to-provide-satisfaction'. And Lacan opted for the easy solution by saying the unconscious is 'structured like a language'. In other words, in spite of everything, the other (object *and* speaking subject) could respond to the demand, 'potentially speaking', of the drive, on condition that language could still be found again in the area of the unconscious. Just as there is a great difference between desire and its satisfaction, equally there is a great difference between drive and the unconscious. On the contrary, we need to maintain the distance which prevents this homogenisation in order that alterity is assured of its status in discontinuity with consciousness. Alterity cannot be reduced to denoting simply another 'human being' (like me), called a *parlêtre* (a speaking being), for any conception which is based fundamentally on language implies a community of co-locutors, even if one shifts the essence of language in the direction of misunderstanding which puts serious limitations on the idea that communication is established through verbalising. No, the difference implied by alterity is more basic, more intransigent. It necessitates recourse to a more radical incompatibility because the basis of the exchange is to discover the compatibility and not to have it at the outset. That is why it is necessary to emphasise what can account for the clash within this alterity by which I am doubly inhabited, both within myself, and with respect to what is not me.

There is therefore – and this is the difficulty – on the one hand a potentialising of the elements in conflict which sets in opposition the aspects described by language and philosophical reflection, and, on the other, the absence of any possibility of using the resources of consciousness, which we have denoted as language and reflection, other than by a series of graded diffractions to know what is happening in the part of the psyche which escapes the jurisdiction of consciousness. This is even more true where the knowledge of my relations to others as *similar others* is concerned. What in conscious thought corresponds to a negativity of refusal refers in the conception of the unconscious to a silent claim, i.e., repression in the first topographical model and the ego's unconsciousness of its defences in the second. In other words, in both models the *negative is negativised* because resistance manifests itself as a *'no' which is not expressed and which denies its own negation by its very silence*. Repression, says Freud, exists between flight and condemnation. This means that condemnation, even when pronounced, effaces itself by turning away without ceasing to be active. The unconscious is thus not only the opposite of consciousness but that which is separated from it by repression. And as such, its status is one of absence. The situation gets worse when Freud has to deal with the *méconnaissance* of the patient who remains deaf and blind to the analyst's interpretation of his defences. In this case it is not resistance which is an obstacle but resistance to becoming aware of resistance.

Alterity becomes meaningful then in relation to a causality which originally was natural – consubstantial with the organisation of the ego – which constitutes one side of the psyche, the other side being formed by the relation which the latter maintains with another person who is separated from it and has the same constitutive heterogeneousness. This other is put in the position where he is supposed to have an answer (in the sense both of satisfying his demand and his desire, as well as providing clarification by his interpretation of what is happening to the one who is faced with the 'question' and expects to receive an answer. Reflexively, the power of being the one who has an answer will be re-appropriated by the one who desires an answer. Both sides closely combine their effects because the question, however enigmatic it may be, is the daughter of suffering and the elucidation does not only apply to what is happening to the subject – which would put the other into a position of exteriority with respect to the latter – but to *what links* the subject to the other. Thus there is a dual estrangement: estrangement from oneself by the revelation of a causality which is not conscious – non-discursive according to the canons of secondary processes – and estrangement from the other in terms of discursiveness ruled by a relationship of desire with an object who cannot be confined to the realm of discourse, even if discourse is the accepted convention of exchange.

It is the relationship of these two polarities, intrapsychic and intersubjective, which constitutes the essence of the work of the negative. Being a psychoanalyst does not mean that one has easy access to the idea of consciousness as a creative movement of figures carried along by negation and the negating of negation, but that one finds oneself right away in a universe marked by everything which is opposed to accomplished totality and plenitude. Symptoms, by their constraining presence, are like a screen formation. Their remarkable nature might make us forget the negative which they are a product of and induce us to topple over into a positivity which would then occupy the whole stage; all the more so in that the disturbance they cause shows that they take up more space than one would like.

When one is a philosopher, however open one may be to the idea of the opaqueness of consciousness to itself, it is difficult to let go of the luminous promontory of consciousness or of Being in favour of an unconscious which is uncontrollable. Furthermore, accepting the idea that the motor of development finds its source in the failure which suffering represents and that the deployment of thought, far from succeeding in averting its return, can only ensure – perhaps without realising it – that it is kept at a distance. This can even induce the philosopher to simulate – by controlled reflection – the detours of the unconscious by giving him the illusion he is undertaking a conceptual self-analysis. Not surprisingly, this will always land on its feet, lucidity being neither the surpassing nor the accomplishment of the psyche but simply the consolation afforded by the work of the negative faced with the impossibility of *jouissance*.[10]

What has been added to the domain of knowledge since the discovery of the unconscious is nothing other than the process of negativity which has extended its field from the existence of an unconscious psychic organisation in each individual to the conditions which determine the most disturbing forms of madness. It was already known that the negative works on the psyche; but the psyche in turn works to negate itself – which is precisely what we had not foreseen in acknowledging the work of the negative.

In the way the negative is thought about there is a tacit underlying affirmation that the negative is necessary, not only to oppose the positive, but for the very act which makes an understanding of the meaning of positivity possible. Positivity can thus be thought of as a form of negativity which has been warded off. Ultimately, one can also envisage that every positive affirmation must necessarily have its negative counterpart. But if ideally, one can, so to speak, immobilise the system to the point of paralysing it, one cannot reverse the process beyond a certain point. For we must imagine the case in which negation is invested in turn, not only with other values – also positive, albeit with an inverted meaning – which are opposed to the initial positivity in face of which negation establishes itself in a purely and exclusively negative way.

At first sight, this situation seems unlikely. If this is so, it is because it is often very difficult to transcend the polemic sense of negation which turns it into an inverted affirmation. This is what the ambiguities in modern linguistic analyses of the negative show.

To paint an extreme picture, lets imagine the case in which a positive existence has given way to nihilation but has reached a final state which, as such, could be taken as a paradigm: death. Man is so resistant to this final nothingness that religions grant an important place to the idea of life after death – the characteristics of which vary from one religion to another. Thus, while the idea of death, seen as putting an end to life seems acceptable, actual death – which definitively wipes out the life which preceded it – is viewed as something absolute going far beyond its relation to the existence which it takes over from, and it is when it is seen as death with no return that it becomes intolerable and has to be denied.

The form of negation which, ceasing to take a stand, withdraws and turns away from existence even to the point of non-existence, nonetheless remains within the framework of a relationship where the other's desire for affirmation is recognised. In order to increase the resistance which is offered, one robs it of its prey by doing away with oneself. But there are perhaps still more radical forms which are barely tenable for consciousness, where the other's desire for victory is nihilated by a unilateral change in the rules of the game. It is what we have detected in the 'he-who-loses-wins', better described as the 'he-who-wins-loses', of certain psychic organisations. Here, the indifference to loss, the withdrawal from unpleasure, the integration of suffering to the rank of an ordinary psychic condition, replace the search for pleasure, for well-being – everything which can give one the feeling that one exists. Indeed, the will to win inevitably runs the risk of incurring a loss which would cancel out the gain, and can become a possible cause of defeat. Whereas the cancelling out of any gain, which is always possible, puts the subject in an omnipotent position. He consents, if need be, to the other person's will to destroy him, even welcoming this will with jubilation, but on condition that he deprives the other person of the victor's pleasure in inflicting suffering on the vanquished.

Affirmation – Negating Negation – the Negative Denying Itself

It is now time to consider affirmation. Hegel thinks of it as negating negation. This may well be the only possibility for a notion of this kind. The consciousness-process implies that it is the very nature of its constitution which represents its own obstacle and yet, at the same time, assures its continued movement. This Hegelian view of consciousness in terms of movement and the surpassing of consciousness *in the name of movement* does not satisfy Freud and induces him to reject the equation psychic = conscious. He seeks movement not in consciousness where he soon senses a closure but rather, beyond this, in unconsciousness. It can never be stressed enough, however, that this is not the last word of Freudian thought, nor the ground on which the psyche is based. It is in the knot – the chiasmus, Meleau-Ponty would have said – defined by the bodily sphere which, more than any other, needs the object, i.e., the *drives*, that Freud locates the concept of movement. For the movement of the drives relates both to what is necessary for my continued existence and to my relation with my counterpart who, even before becoming an object of desire, was essential for my survival.

Let us look one last time at the reasons why the two systems are irreconcilable. With Hegel, affirmation is conceived of as negating negation because it can be posited that consciousness only apprehends itself in the movement of negation from the moment it ceases to be caught in the facticity of sense-certainty. Starting with sense-certainty introduces negation through the need to think of consciousness as having a capacity for differentiation and, therefore, for separation, compared with sense-certainty which is localised, identified and determinate, as Hegel would say. But if the starting point of sense-certainty is replaced by drive excitation, this changes everything. Firstly, because drive excitation does not offer the same determinate qualities as sense-certainty. The certainty is not that of the present in which it finds itself; it is overshadowed by the uncertainty of a future in which drive satisfaction alone – always hazardous and temporary – will bring the required relief. We should note in passing what this shift of certitude from the present to a future, oriented and focused uniquely on this uncertain perspective, will involve in the way of disappointments. These are not only possible but inevitable, challenging the aim of self-certainty in order to locate it with the other who holds the keys to it. On the other hand, compared with sensation, the 'certitude' which comes with satisfaction is further affirmed by the imperious nature of the claim arising from a bodily drive excitation. It is all the more 'certain' in that it cannot, like external sensory excitation, be avoided by flight. Furthermore, as long as it has not found relief it will increase in intensity. Nevertheless, this form of certitude, tied to the drive and its object, brings with it both the danger of exacerbating its dissatisfaction and of suppressing satisfaction, depending on the unpredictable nature of the object. It is thus both more certain (more complete) than sensibility and more uncertain with respect to the moment of its appearance, the assurance of its return and the precariousness of its renewal. The inaugural negative movement is in this case no longer consciousness seen as distance, contemplation, separation, that is, the first step towards what will and should be self-consciousness but, on the contrary, an expectation of the symmetrical movement of the other suppressing the desire arising from an undesirable drive excitation, or the bringing into play, as a negating symmetrical effect, of what occurs when satisfaction cannot take place, i.e., unpleasure and its corollary, repression. The process is repeated here differently. Through consciousness, sense-certainty is divided, for consciousness cannot stop itself from seeking certitude while at the same time distancing itself from it. It is the emergence of what will be an 'I' which begins to exist for itself through its enunciation, but whose enunciation can be distinguished from its utterance or, better still, appear in the utterance, to affect the relation between what it is saying and what it is speaking about, which does not belong to the world of discourse. The vicissitudes of drive excitation proceed quite differently, for its first purpose is to suppress the consciousness that one may have of it, not by dissociation or by constituting another way of being (consciousness vs. sense-certainty), but as a form of being which would only be accessible beyond the barrier which makes it become non-being (repression). Dissociation comes into play again here. That is, in place of consciousness the repression of drive excitation (or of its representatives) will form the core of the unconscious. Moreover – and it is at this juncture that the dissociation symmetrical to the one which gives rise to consciousness is carried out – it will have to see to it that the repression itself becomes unconscious.

In this case, then, negating negation is not affirmation but the disappearance of the trace of drive excitation by an internal modification of what denies it, so that this latest negation will not provide any clue to the meaning of its operation. In order to bear witness to the presence of the drives, Freudian thought would for a long time to come content itself with referring to the failure of repression and the return of the repressed which makes the unconscious appear to be the organiser of the drives via the concept of representation. This was true until the moment when the work of the negative was no longer limited to repression and its failures but was centred on its quite unexpected success: the ego's unconsciousness of its own defences. This accomplishment which was the original aim of the process, its total success, appears subsequently to be its most resounding failure, for it prevents any evolution in the relations between the unconscious and the conscious. Negating negation in the Hegelian sense does not however disappear, since it may be considered that the search for drive satisfaction and its success can be seen from this angle. But as the significance of what has been developed above can be expressed in the same way, it finds itself torn between opposite meanings.

The negating of negation is equally applicable to the overcoming of repression and the accomplishment of acts leading to a drive satisfaction freed from prohibition as to the operation which simultaneously denies both the drive and the prohibition. The same is true for the desire for transgression and for transgression itself. There is still room for a third way; that is, the belief that it is possible to do away with prohibitions altogether in order to return to the golden age of lost innocence, presuming that no drive exigency is itself dangerous but that the danger comes from the institution of prohibition and its frustrating effects. One difference separating Hegel and Freud is the philosopher's postulation of an appropriation towards transcendence. This only has an uncertain, extremely fragile and partial place in what Freud refers to as a renunciation of the drives in the quest for spirituality (*Moses and Monotheism*, 1939 [1934–8]). Further, one of the possible points of contention between Freud and his successors concerns the place and the role which Freud gives to sublimation as a solution to conflicts caused by drive vicissitudes. It is worth recalling that for a long time sublimation was given a role which it proved incapable of sustaining until it was supplanted by the creation of the super-ego.

Once again, it can be seen how Freud's and Hegel's projects differ. With Hegel, it is a question of arriving, thanks to an appropriate method, at a concept which the most acute commentators have difficulty in defining, that is, the accomplishment of the Spirit, the crowning of its activity and of the historical process of which it is the culmination. For Freud, the development of his work, the experience of his analytic practice, as well as his life experience, led him to take seriously the possibility of a nihilation which annihilates what has been accomplished through negativity. Not as a fatal outcome of the Destiny of Man or of History, but as one of the paths which we had not realised was taken by a work of the negative which has more than one solution. So, not one Destiny but one destiny among others. This direction of life which seems foreign to common mortals, who clearly seem to orient their activity in the opposite direction, possesses an unrivalled power of fascination, for some at least.

It is troubling to note that the idea of the negative can give rise to such different works as those of Hegel and Freud. Finally, if we are justified in speaking of the working-through of desire and defence as the works of the mind, how should we describe psychic organisations whose negativity takes on such a curiously deadly meaning, whereas the subjects who provide asylum for these negative vicissitudes just see them as a way of life which they say they would willingly exchange for any other which would deliver them from their suffering? Psychoanalytic work, however, which perceives the desperate undertakings of negativity, will often, in its attempts to avert its tentacular progression, come up against the most passionate attachment to this yoke which constitutes their subjectivity.

3
Traces of the Negative in Freud's Work

On examination, a return to Freud reveals a presence of the negative which undoubtedly accounts for Lacan's endeavours in this direction. The fact that he later abandoned his attempt allows us to come back to it now with a fresh vision.

Without in any way claiming to be exhaustive, a thoughtful consideration of certain major Freudian concepts indicates that they call for a theory of the negative: thus, dreams, mourning, the relation between drives and representations all lend themselves to such an inquiry. But it is with identification – a concept containing contradictions – that the work of the negative finds one of its most remarkable applications. This re-examination above all shows that the work of the negative is not so much a new category – a theoretical addition to an existing corpus – as a new interpretation which runs right through the theory. I will enlarge on this further later in this volume where an individual chapter is devoted to the study of the relation of the negative to the hallucinatory process.

Un-conscious

From the moment Freud breaks with the equation psychic = conscious and defends the idea of an un-conscious, the negative, a well-established notion in philosophy, takes root in a domain where it was hitherto unknown. Unconscious is that which is psychic without being conscious, what is 'beneath' consciousness and affects the latter without it knowing it. We know how this descriptive definition would subsequently give rise to a structural definition, i.e., the unconscious is not only an inferior or degraded type of psychic activity, a kind of storehouse; it is a system which possesses its own organisation governed by processes which are different from those of consciousness, and endowed with its own particular system of functioning, etc. Freud was not satisfied with pleading for the recognition of the unconscious. Indeed, he made himself the champion of a view of the psyche in which the conscious part, highly overestimated, was altogether dependent on and even subjected to the unconscious. This is all the more true in that we only have a vague idea of the unconscious. What we can perceive of it – the tip of the iceberg – only gives us a very limited appreciation of the extent of its influence and power. As soon as it was shown that psychic activity results from the tension between three agencies (or rather three, grouped together as two: conscious–preconscious and unconscious), whose relations are modified during dreaming, fantasy, symptoms, and transference, it became apparent that the functioning of the system-conscious may be dominated by the activity of the unconscious and the productions to which it gives birth. This conclusion indirectly implied the existence of a work of the negative, an inference which repression ought to have called for. There was already an inkling of this before the days of psychoanalysis with post-hypnotic suggestion, which was undoubtedly the starting-point for many earlier elaborations which contributed to its birth. We may ask ourselves what went on in the hypnotised patient's mind between the moment when the hypnotist instructed him, upon waking, to open his umbrella before leaving the room, and the moment when, having done this – without, however, linking this act to the instruction received under hypnosis – he explained this incongruity by a motive invented extemporaneously, whose unforeseeable eruption was no less puzzling than the execution of the instruction given. How can we conceive of what may have existed at the core of the psyche during the time when the idea suggested by another person was still latent? When one tried to penetrate the mystery of psychic functioning during this lapse of time, one could merely assume the existence of a persistent impression, outside the subject's consciousness, either asleep or awake (as the order is not executed immediately after the awakening), in which the command was deposited on a bare, empty background, so to speak. The performance demonstrated, in fact, less the unconscious of the 'impressionable or suggestible' subject, than the hypnotist's suggestive power. It suggested a work of the negative was possible but did not demonstrate it in the slightest, for one cannot denote the simple retention of an impression received by someone from outside himself as psychic work. However, one could infer the existence of such a work during the second stage of the procedure, i.e., an explanation by rationalising the act performed. This is what we would expect in the case of a lie but not of suggestion. To the question, 'Why are you opening your umbrella?', there would have been no difficulty in replying: 'I don't know' or 'It's a reflex'; but replying: 'To see if it works', means there is a wish, by affirming his own subjectivity, to efface the hypnotist's, breaking the link which unites them in the experience, letting the subject's will take centre stage.

In fact, the first example of a genuine work of the negative was the discovery of dream work; all the more so in that the unconscious expressed itself in the unconsciousness of sleep. It was just a beginning and the future looked promising. Later came the example of the work of mourning to denote another mode of the work of the negative. In the former case, one was dealing with a way of functioning which operated outside the sphere of the conscious mind; with mourning, it was the work which takes place following the loss of the object which enhanced the work of the negative in wakefulness.

This was yet another step forward. Sleep is necessary for dreams to occur and during sleep consciousness is suspended. But sleep is a positive state whereas it is the absence of consciousness which functions as the negative. Insomnia often reveals that it is the persistence of consciousness which is felt to be a disability. In other words, dreams which are the manifestation of the psychic work going on in this state of negativity, are not a direct consequence of the defect which unconsciousness represents. Rather, the latter reveals the impossibility of fulfilling wishes in a waking state. Nevertheless, apart from certain special cases which constitute failures of the dream function, their manifest content does not clearly reveal the lack for which the attempt to fulfil a wish is supposed to compensate. It is only after analysis that one will discover the unconscious fantasy on which the dream is based. There is therefore a work of the negative in dreams because negativity itself, the implicit lack to which the unconscious fantasy refers, is hidden.

Clearly, these remarks only concern the hypothesis of the discovery of the unconscious, without returning in detail in the analysis of dreams to the relations which the activity of censorship call for in the dream process and to the endless commentaries which the mechanisms of dream work might suggest in their relation to the work of the negative. It is not that the considerable literature which already exists on these topics makes further commentary unnecessary but that I prefer to devote this study to issues which are less often dealt with. So, for the moment, I simply want to draw attention to the negative source of certain basic concepts. This is why, equally, I will refrain from returning to Freud's first discoveries which particularly lend themselves to this kind of reflection such as *The Psychopathology of Everyday Life* (1901) with its list of acts of forgetting, parapraxes, slips and the study of *Jokes*. Undoubtedly they would enable us to approach the negative consciously, in the full light of day rather than under the cover of unconsciousness but there again that would largely mean retracing well-trodden paths where an intuitive apprehension of the work of the negative is sufficient in itself and would quickly become tiresome, if it was enlarged upon, since it would be confined to making a different description of phenomena which are already familiar. I have therefore preferred to focus on other psychic phenomena either because they seem to maximise, with regard to issues related to loss, the effect of the negative which is often discernible at first sight or, on the contrary, because the latter is disguised to such an extent that to begin with we hardly think of it at all. An example of the first case is mourning and an example of the second is identification, which covers a much more extensive field.

Mourning, Object-Loss, Melancholia

With mourning, the situation changes. Loss is patent, its effects are massive and recognisable at the outset. In this case, in contradistinction to dreams, the lack is identifiable straight away. It was at this point that Freud noticed the strange characteristics of this condition which had never been the object of a serious inquiry as they had seemed so straightforward. Sadness, painful dejection, certainly, but also idealisation of the lost object and a corresponding abasement of the other person who survives. At first sight, it is difficult to see what use these observations could have. Except that, due to a series of significant transitions (pathological mourning), Freud linked mourning to melancholia. Loss is evident, here, too – but the subject does not know what he has lost – and he does not know either how he has faced this loss. We are familiar with the answer: the ego identifies itself with the missing object and amputates a part of itself which then takes the place of the lost object, becoming divided within itself. In this case, the sense of loss, through being unaware of what is lost and of what will be replaced by the ego itself, gives the work of the negative an unparalleled scope of influence. The negative is no longer purely that which acts silently under cover of the censor or of sleep remaining almost completely unrecognisable – as will still be the case to a certain extent in neurosis. On the contrary, the negative, due to the fact that it afflicts the ego itself, will achieve a greater degree of complexity. For, on the one hand, the ego's affliction then renders this negativity more visible – the depressed subject is clearly in the grips of negativity in the image he has and presents of himself (and here the negative has a connotation which clearly links it with destruction) – on the other hand, this increased visibility of the negative is accompanied by a greater opaqueness vis-à-vis itself. In other words, although the negative is more visible from the outside, its work on the inside remains unrecognised. This is the major paradox which will cloud the vision of psychoanalysts: positivising the negative, making its existence obvious, results in negating the negative by this very positivisation. One is no longer in a world of absence inferred from the lack resulting from the unconscious desire which compensates for this defect. We are in an all-too-present world of suffering resulting from loss, but the one who is suffering cannot know either what he is suffering from or what has caused his suffering. The more the suffering presents itself as an excess of internal presence caused by the absence of the lost object, manifesting itself by a psychic pain, the less the ego knows the nature of this suffering (the hate which is underlying it) and that of the object which causes it. In the same way, it seems to know nothing about the way it has negativised itself in order to replace the lost object, losing its capacity for recognition and awareness, sacrificing the love it has for itself and the pleasure which it can draw from its own image.

Now we can understand how one of Freud's basic conceptual claims has two aspects which are apparently very different and to a certain extent antithetical. The subject necessarily remains unaware of some aspect of himself. When this *méconnaissance* applies to his desire (this is the case in neurosis which cannot be sharply distinguished from normality), the concealment leaves the ego intact. This is not noticeable for the ego, for the latter cannot take cognisance of it without admitting that, in this case, it would like to fly in the face of what is forbidden – which is inconceivable. The second possibility is that this *méconnaissance* applies not to what the ego cannot see of its desire, because it is separated from it by a screen, but to the structure which is inherent to it and which links its activity as a purveyor of satisfaction to the activity of upholding the function which guarantees the knowledge it has of itself. As a desiring subject, no doubt, but more with respect to the stance it takes towards the desire which inhabits it. A distinction of this kind became indispensable in the analysis of the defences described by Freud after 1925 – splitting in fetishism being the most probing example. This second case is one Freud discovered while he was studying melancholia and later he extended its general validity when he maintained that the ego is unconscious of its own defences. It is thus not only blind to a reality it cannot see but blind to itself, to its sacrificial mode of repairing and restoring the object to the detriment of its own unity and sense of existence. This *méconnaissance* furthermore effects the ego's blindness in the face of reality. In the dark, neither blind people nor sighted people can see anything. But as soon as day breaks a sighted person sees the world and the blind person is still in the dark. It is the existence of this structural blindness which obliged Freud to change his view of the ego and to construct the second topographical model.

We can forget this positivisation linked to the pathological context of melancholic depression and just retain the structural negativity which is present generally and independently of any particular circumstances: this is what justifies Freud's abandonment of the un-conscious as an agency and its relegation to the rank of psychic quality. The unconscious only exists for an ego which is capable of taking cognisance of it, or for a consciousness which is an ego attribute. If the ego is largely unconscious, the theory of the repressed un-conscious will be seen to be inadequate. For the unconsciousness of the ego betrays its clinging to anachronistic defences giving free rein to the drives over which it cannot extend its control. Thus the quality of what is not conscious in the form of representations (unconscious) in the first topographical model is not sufficient to define what can be opposed to the ego, for we are not so much concerned with fending off, by means of these functional reorganisations, the dysfunction they represent, as with taking account of the economic disturbance of object investments whose loss 'affects' the ego's very texture. This disorder shows we need to take into account something other than that which is denoted by the organisation of representations. This 'something other' which is affective by nature suggests that it involves the drives in a more immediate way than representations and brings about a dangerous short-circuit: drive (affect)–ego–object. All the more so in that the removal of the object and the ties which unite the latter with the drives and the ego point to the destructive vectorisation of drive investments which are brutally deprived of their principal source of supply. Hence, we can appreciate the impact of an unconscious which is marked by its 'oldest', oral, cannibalistic id impulses. Especially since the ego is taken over by another sort of unconsciousness which concerns its resistance to analytic work implying a change in its relations to the object. It is thus a question of finding an entity which is the polar opposite of the ego and which, under no circumstances, can pretend it resembles that which says 'I' *quite consciously* and which, in its structure, contains nothing at all which can be considered rational. The unconscious, by virtue of its organisation could pride itself in being a different kind of reason. The new agency will be deprived of any kind of rationality. It will only be demonic. This is the underlying reason for the theory of the id. And this is why its radically non-ego character (id) – negative of the ego (seen from its own point of view) – is in fact the effect of a radical positivisation: the drive. This is another way of saying that the negative (from the point of view of the drive) is the basic condition for psychic elaboration. In the chapter of the *New Introductory Lectures on Psychoanalysis* (1933 [1932]) which deals with the decomposition of the psychic personality, Freud notes the inescapable negativity which is present in the theory: 'what little we know of it [the id] we have learnt from our study of the dream-work and of the construction of neurotic symptoms, and most of that is of a negative character and can be described only as a contrast to the ego'.[1]

Freud had already come across the conjunction of the unconsciousness of the ego and a serious regression in the case of President Schreber. But if he did not give much attention to the work of the negative, it was perhaps because delusion had appeared to him to be a restorative mode of the ego, the void resulting from the repression of reality or the backward flow of investments towards the ego, making it more difficult to infer the underlying negativity of which it is the manifestation, than the positivity of the cover-up the delusion expresses. It was not until 1924 with his article on 'The Loss of Reality in Neurosis and Psychosis' that it was explicitly recognised that delusion is like a piece of cloth used to patch up a hole, hiding the tear in the ego. This is where the difference with melancholia lies, for in this case it is not enough that the ego sacrifices itself to replace the lost object. Delusion is like a dagger which must not be withdrawn from the victim's body unless one intends to treat the wound, otherwise he will die. Moreover, the relations of mourning to melancholia suggest a coherence which is much stronger than those of fantasy and delusion. The repression of reality is interpolated between fantasy and delusion creating a hiatus, without the link between them always being clearly noticeable. Whereas mourning and melancholia are united by a relation which can be sensed intuitively from the start because mourning is an ordinary experience of life, the relation of fantasy to delusion is looser and less common. Fantasy is a spontaneous activity of psychic work which possesses an appropriate and immediate means of giving shape to the realisation of its desires. It acts as consolation in face of the disappointment inflicted by reality and guarantees the continuity of psychic work, warding off what might interrupt it. Imaginal functioning is permanent whereas mourning, even if the experience is part of life's vicissitudes, is a crisis: a crisis which will be surpassed and surmounted, but which is nevertheless a temporary tear in the tissue of experience. This is why mourning can serve – due to its critical and reversible aspect – as a prototype for attacks of melancholia considered to be the expression of an acute and recurring psychosis which Freud prefers to call narcissistic neurosis.

If Freud had lived long enough to recognise the originality of borderline cases, he might have had the chance of discovering the prototypes of delusion in what I have called 'private madness',[2] i.e., between ordinary fantasy and the manifestations of chronic psychosis. An example of this kind would probably have been taken from the vicissitudes of social life, from political and xenophobic persecution, in the widest sense of the term, from which he himself would suffer. The problem arises here of the differences between ordinary and psychotic projection which we will return to later.

The train of thought which led to giving up any reference to the un-conscious as a concept – in fact, it is not so much that as radicalising the phenomenon in question by freeing oneself of the ideological and terminological presuppositions underlying it – obliges us to go back and look for its deepest roots.

Drives and Representations

By emphasising the effects of lack, psychoanalytic theory was linked with the negative from the outset. If one thinks of the basic model of the mind, i.e., hallucinatory wish-fulfilment, one possesses the most decisive argument for the existence of a work based on an unsatisfied wish. The sequence: experience of satisfaction – trace of this experience – lull – resurgence of the need – reinvestment of the traces of the experience of satisfaction (wish) – hallucinatory wish-fulfilment – failure of the hallucinatory fulfilment – signals of distress – return of the object having brought satisfaction and a new experience of satisfaction – in spite of its schematic character, allows us to understand the meaning of the work of the negative straight away. It is not just a matter of warding off the lack, but to show that the traces inscribed in the psychical apparatus are neither fixed nor inert. Not only are they capable of becoming active again but they can modify, enrich, or deform themselves through excess, defect or alteration, organise themselves, and so on.

This whole system would not have the slightest reality if it was not stimulated from within by drives constantly seeking satisfaction, thus always capable of arousing movements of desire. And as it is not possible for the latter to obtain immediate satisfaction which, moreover, can never be complete, it is precisely during this time and space that the work of the negative can take place. As we can see, the desire re-investing the traces of an experience of satisfaction is a movement. 'It is this movement which we call desire',[3] says Freud. A dynamic perspective of this kind which seeks out the object from its trace (that is, from the memory of experience) mimes the movement of the subject's mouth seeking the nipple. Desire replies intrapsychically to the memory of the attraction of the mouth prompted by the impulse towards the object, inscribed intersubjectively and reactivated intrapsychically. It should therefore now be clear that unconscious representations as an expression of the work of the negative (compared to the lack of the object guaranteeing satisfaction), are already the product of a negativisation of the drive since the latter at first only meets with a void before being transformed into a movement of desire. Later the imperious need for drive satisfaction will suffer various fates: it can be postponed and sometimes it will even have to be silent; the drive has therefore to be negativised. The initial polymorphous perversion will give way, not without difficulty or protest, to civilised childhood preparing the ground for the onset of neurosis. Neuroses are the negative of perversions.[4] This was the result of the measures taken against the fixations of drives by counter-investment. The negative cannot be reduced to a photographic comparison. It already implies, to my mind, the two-sided structure of symptoms: desire and *defence* and it is as such that neurosis is 'negative' whereas perversion is desire and *satisfaction* – according to Freud at least.

The idea of the negative, without following a definite course, progresses according to the circumstances, and needs to be interpreted differently in each case, in relationship to the context. Applied to hallucination it means the limits of perception are exceeded so that there is a kind of failure of reality-testing which I will come back to in due course. Later, employed to characterise certain kinds of transference, it implies that transference is not exclusively positive and it uncovers the role of hate towards the analyst (and above all the analysis) as an obstacle to the progression of treatment. There is no doubt that the discovery of the negative therapeutic reaction was one of the main reasons for introducing into the theory first, the death drive, and then, the second topographical model.

It is when the drive gives full expression to its positivity that it attaches itself paradoxically to those forms of the negative which are not derived from the repressed or from the unconscious but evoke rather the succession of the figures of consciousness deploying themselves by means of a reversal of perspective or by modifying the topography of the subject, the latter changing places with the object, the other. It is a clinical picture of this sort that emerges from the descriptions of voyeurism and exhibitionism as well as those of sadism and masochism in 'Instincts and their Vicissitudes' (1915). It is also in this study that Freud describes two mechanisms of defence: the reversal of a drive into its opposite and the turning round of a drive upon the subject's own self, of which he will later say that they pre-exist repression. Put another way, before the negative creates its own territory and space for working, it manifests itself first of all in the full light of day by producing configurations which are linked by symmetrical and complementary relations either by inverting the process of the subject's investment of the object, returning to the subjective source, or by changing the sign of the said investment, that is, by turning what is positive into a negative, by replacing love with hate. We will come across this tendency again later. Freud describes a similar process in 'A Child is Being Beaten' (1919). This contribution to our knowledge of the origin of sexual perversions does not concern the drives but their representatives organised as fantasies. In this article the successive stages of fantasy – each needing to be elaborated individually – appear to be controlled by the process of the free activity of conscious fantasy. Each position dislodges the one before giving rise to a new phase which also forms a 'different' picture, the scenario being modified as it proceeds. To the extent that each phase in fact is a denial of the one before, this creation of fantasy under the impetus of its own deployment is also one of the figures of the work of the negative. What is interesting is that it only alludes to repression and the unconscious indirectly, and unfolds, during most of the stages, in the light of consciousness. I should point out that the strong masochistic features foreshadow the central importance of masochism and future ideas of the death drive.

One would perhaps expect to see these developments lead to the inclusion of regression in the group of concepts directly concerned by the work of the negative. This is not the case. For while regression is readily seen as an inversion of development, this regressive orientation due to fixation is, in my opinion, a very bad example of the negative on account of its schematic character. I will return on another occasion to the undeniable reality of this dysfunctioning; now, I simply want to explain the reasons why regression has been excluded. Far from manifesting itself as a form of the negative, regression remains in fact the sign that the work of the negative has failed. The change in direction of the progression is a direct manifestation which does not deserve to be characterised as negative to the extent that it reveals an incapacity to detach itself

from positivity, accompanied by a desperate attempt to cling to another manifestation of it, due to its incapacity to tolerate the sacrifices necessary for the
accomplishment of the work of the negative (suspension of presence, intervention of counter-investment and other mechanisms of defence, etc.). Is this
to say that there are no 'regressive' forms of the work of the negative? Not at
all. But we are reserving these aspects for those constellations where the work
of the negative carries out a radical concentration of its offshoots, by short-
circuiting the forms of elaboration which play an intermediary role with the
drives and the ego. The regressive influence can be evaluated then by the
'uncompromising' character of the psychic productions involving a remarkable
shutting-down of the range of possibilities which allow mental life to breathe,
thereby safeguarding its mobility and dynamism. There is a coalescence of the
various psychic registers (psychic representatives of drives, object representations, affects, acts, etc.), capable of mobilising explosive tensions with a great
potential for disorganisation. This is another way of saying that there is a drive
investment extending to the mind and not simply a mechanical return to past
fixations. And yet, by acknowledging the regressive nature of these constrictive phenomena of mental life which seem to stem from the failure of the
psychical apparatus to create mediating formations, we are obliged to recognise
that in contesting that regression belongs to the work of the negative, our point
of view was biased and insufficient, for we were only thinking of dynamic
regression and of the way in which it can give rise to the denaturing of the
concept of negativity. This was not taking into account the other aspect of
regression (topographical) which has been the object of interesting developments in French psychoanalysis and whose theoretical use has served
fortunately to correct a schematic use of the concept. It is as if, once again, by
having recourse to the advantages of a certain use of dynamic regression
(including evoking its Jacksonian and Spencerian resonances) its exponents
revealed the same insufficiency as we found in the patients alluded to earlier:
a short-circuiting of thought processes cutting a swathe through our theories,
with some devastating spadework, resulting in an over-simplification bringing
inordinately close together the psychological and biological meanings of this
concept. The word alone suggests the idea of going backwards. Describing
regression as dynamic is almost a pleonasm. On the other hand, the idea of a
formal or topographical regression allows us to discover the rich range of
psychic productivity and the complex elaboration of a contradictory tendency
which is capable both of regressing and of staying put, in order to 'make
progress' in mental working-through along this indirect, 'oblique' path, in the
sense which the Ancients gave to this term. Topographical regression is perhaps
the essential aspect of what we are describing but we are justified in questioning
the description of this phenomenon as regression.

When the demands of clinical work, as well as the necessity for theory to make itself more coherent and responsive to those requirements, called for a new topographical model, the second model made an elaboration of the work of the negative even more vital, all the more so because the latest theory of drives had brought to light new findings – repetition as recollecting, for example. By replacing the unconscious with the id, by removing from the definition of the latter any allusion to representation and content, by dispossessing a large part of the ego of the property of consciousness and by applying the same treatment to the super-ego, the field of the work of the negative was extended; its forms or modes became more complex, its expression more varied. For the negative in this case is not simply the un-conscious; it goes beyond the criterion conscious–non-conscious, neither more, nor less. Here then is a change of paradigm which regards not the unconscious but the drives as the source of the mind, which themselves are now divided into figures of life and death. Compared with the idea of the unconscious which is unaware of negation, here is a revision favouring the replacement of the unconscious by the id inhabited by two kinds of drives.

The Death Drive and the Second Topographical Model

I have already drawn attention elsewhere to the importance of the change which differentiates the two models. In the first, the drive which you will recall is neither conscious nor unconscious, is by this very fact located outside the psychical apparatus. This is no longer so in the second where abandoning the criterion of 'consciousness' allows the drives to be included – through the mediation of the id – in the psychical apparatus. The following conclusion forces itself upon us: the main field of the work of the negative is no longer the unconscious. Although the latter still belongs to the field of psychic elaboration, it is no longer the raw material of transformation. The function formerly allotted to desire is now taken over by the drives, by drive motions.

Furthermore, the aspects of these drive motions which have undergone the most significant transformations are found under the auspices of the super-ego, which is capable of subverting the task and re-sexualising morality. The decisive change is certainly the one which preceded the adoption of the second topographical model, i.e., the attention given to the death drive. For it is this that is found at both ends of the new psychical apparatus: at its base with the destructive drives and at its summit with moral masochism. The whole field of primary masochism thus unfolds before our eyes.

The development is significant. At first, the work of the negative designates an unsuspected structuring of the non-conscious mind, a latent organisation, where until then one could only see randomness, uncertainty, the absence of structuring which is in principle neutral. At the end of its course, although the overall purpose of the organisation described remains, it is thwarted by a disorganising, destructuring force with multiple aspects, the most superficial of which look like an 'organised disorganisation' (the sense of unconscious guilt, for example), but the deepest of which is to be linked with a 'disorganising force of disorganisation', without structure and even opposed to being structured (to any form of intelligibility therefore) – *a pure culture of destructiveness.*

The negative is pulled between two extremes: the negative of repression at one end, and the negative of the masochism of the negative therapeutic reaction at the other. It must be pointed out that the negative of neurosis aims to preserve the relation to the object with the secret hope that desire will be fulfilled – without however giving way to perverse temptations – whereas the negative of the negative therapeutic reaction makes the subject cling to the object more than it preserves the link. In this case the hope of one day seeing its desire fulfilled is forever disappointed; nothing remains but the rigidity of a *'relation of non-relating'* destined always to remain the same, desire vanishing in the sand so that it is no longer discernible.

So in both cases, negativity remains a link, either in the hope of achieving its purposes in the future, or, on the contrary, of celebrating indefinitely its failure, soothing itself with incantations dedicated to what is irreparable. Wherein lies the difference? In the first case, awareness of the repressed wish (forbidden) allows for the resolution of transference and the search, following the work done in analysis, of objects in the external world which can offer, albeit partially, satisfaction (not just hallucinatory satisfaction) of the wish. We have played too much on the illusory, fallacious and inaccessible character of this satisfaction – under the pretext of realism and sometimes by leaning towards the cult of prophecy which has never been short of followers, however hopeless it was – to make ourselves the voice of a psychoanalytic nihilism. Without achieving the ideal which is expected of it, the satisfaction remains in the realm of the possible: it cannot, for all that, be equated with the promise of a happy end. Let us say that this comes about anyway, whatever happens. 'Everything works out in the end ... but badly', Alphonse Allais used to say; although the real problem is to know if other modes of satisfaction can be found which are less draining. There is no guarantee of this and even the worst is not always sure to happen. We should avoid falling here for the ruse of a generalised pessimism which is not without its advantages. Under the pretext of having foreseen this from the outset, the analyst no longer has to question the analytic act. He only has to have a feeling of horror for it (Lacan) to excuse himself for the outcome. I am referring here less to the comparison of the results of analysis or of the statistical analysis of successes, failures, stabilisations and decompensations, than to the comparison of practices and the different ways of understanding what is analysable, including the discussion of unanalysability (an unpronounceable word). This relative optimism is designed to emphasise the difference with the negative therapeutic reaction proper which is characterised – in contrast to the former – by the impossibility of renouncing the actualisation of desires with the transference object, despising everything else, putting it in a despicably inaccessible position, without, however, letting oneself be affected emotionally by it, and refusing any kind of satisfaction outside the analysis. Therefore it is indeed the fixation to the subject as an emanation of a primary imago which is being expressed here, taking the form of an unquenchable hate which is grounded in the feeling of an incessant refusal coming from it. This parasitic fixation would manifest itself again if the object had given way to the entreaties of the subject and *because he had given way*. This is not unconnected with the idea of Jean Guillaumin that self-destruction is 'the very perversion of the desire to live'.[5]

Identifications

Each of the different concepts that we have just considered shows how it can be interpreted in its own field according to the work of the negative. With identification, reference to the work of the negative is essential in order to throw light on and articulate the contradictions which are discernible at the centre of its multi-faceted problems. Hence the necessity for a wider and deeper examination of the subject.

If the drive can be seen as that which literally propels an emerging subjectivity towards its object and, if representation is, in a way, the first inevitable vicissitude in a situation where it cannot get an immediate response in conformity with its expectations – which is the fate it necessarily meets with, as Freud says, on account of life's exigencies – one can understand it as the delegation of an imperious bodily demand to restore internal peace and, at the same time, as a summoning of the resources which have to be found at the heart of the psychic structure in order to cope with the absence of satisfaction. There is a double negativity in fact: the first source of negativity can be understood as the effect of the drive waiting for a response in the absence of satisfaction (going hand in hand, very often, with the absence of the object which is supposed to be able to satisfy it) and the second is the shadow substitutive satisfaction which representation can become. But we are dealing with a reactive negativity, so to speak, which has to do first things first without, however, knowing in advance what the future holds.

One can always count on the eternal renewal of desire to assure the progressive movement of psychical organisation. Nevertheless, although the risk of inertia is averted, the set-up described does not help us at all to understand how the many ways of making the experience of lack of satisfaction less problematic are worked through. This occurs not only by making good the displeasure of dissatisfaction but by finding derivative forms of satisfaction, either as a consolation or as a displacement, both of which allow unprecedented solutions to be found. From this moment on, the resumption of drive movement becomes more complicated:

– by anticipating the non-immediateness of satisfaction and/or of its absence, i.e., desire;

– by gathering together temporary solutions thanks to a setting which makes it possible to remobilise, preventatively, the parameters of the means of satisfying desires: these are memory traces.

Other measures brought into play by this set-up regulate this basic pair:

– Repression by means of which unpleasure can be avoided or at least limited and which establishes a kind of second external world giving birth to the repressed material organising the unconscious. It now becomes possible to speak for the first time not only of a process of negativity but of a constituted negativity which will soon acquire the form of an instituted negativity. We can grasp, here, the first conjunction of two important senses of the negative: the negative as unpleasure or as the opposite of pleasure and the negative as the shadow of the positive experience sought after, i.e., the hallucinatory fulfilment of wishes and fantasies.

– All this is subjected to the dynamics of growing libidinal development, the strength of which cannot be overlooked – however obscure it is – inscribed, as it is, in the movement of life, constantly feeding the demands of the drives.

Everything I have just described reveals characteristics of greater complexity, accumulation, integration and, lastly, self-organisation of the mind. One fundamental factor, however, is missing here which relates exclusively to the unpredictable and uncontrollable dimension of the object. Up until now, we have only had to take into account non-satisfaction (immediate or partial) and we have considered the different means by which a solution can be found. The situation I have described can be summed up as the necessity and wish to prevent the emergence of anxiety (or of distress) which is in most cases a disorganisation which has the value of a message. When it gets worse, it is due to pain often linked to loss. We need to distinguish between a crisis which represents a response to the total unpredictability of the object, resulting in a disorganisation of the psychic structure which is pulled to bits, and the pain caused by the object disappearing, without there being a real disorganisation, or representing this itself as if it contained it within its limits or was its limit, triggering its harmful effects by means of what accompanies deprivation, i.e., the loss of substance, psychical amputation; all threatening situations which mobilise the psyche and are perhaps designed to avoid its collapse and disintegration through fragmentation. L. Guttières-Green[6] has described a syndrome of painful amnesia which shows the limiting function of pain, watching over a past whose traumatic significance has to be concealed. One understands how castration signifies the symbolisation of the catastrophe, mainly through the activity of two disorganising agents: the observation of the missing sexual organ, threatening the subject's integrity, and the representation undermining the formation of the object – which has thus become literally inconceivable – deprived of its organ of *jouissance*. Anxiety affects just as much what is, which seems unthinkable, as what might be, with the result that a fear of any form of change hangs over the future.

So from among the different approaches we have taken to the problem, we are bound to stress the role of the object, that is, to look at what is the most uncontrollable factor in the situation because it is external to the psyche and yet present within it (with a double status as a component of the drive organisation and representations originating from memory traces). The psychic structure must therefore find a solution which is precisely adjusted to its relation to the object, which is all the more restricting in that the tie of dependence which links them cannot be avoided if its survival is to be assured. The object is an attractive or repulsive agent generating unpredictability, master of gratification and frustrations, and finally a source of uncertainty in as far as the internal configuration of its inscription in the psyche can lead to confusion with external perception which is supposed to provide proof of its existence and of the reality of the satisfaction it gives. Not to mention the fact that its constancy is far from assured and that it does not cease to oscillate between the mad love it is capable of arousing and the most inexpiable hate which it can provoke. The worst thing is probably the royal indifference it can show in the face of expectations – a devastating indifference because it generates a loss of meaning.

The representation of the object assures a certain regulating or disorganising intrapsychic presence. Being part of the drive organisation, the object becomes an indispensable guide for purposive ideas. By linking itself to memory traces, it follows the paths which have been opened up, in part at least, by earlier experience and invites psychic organisation to construct itself around a memory, by means of which, what is to be avoided or sought after, can be identified less according to adaptive criteria than criteria which are torn between what are often incompatible polarities such as pleasure and unpleasure or the relative priority to be given to the ego and the object. Finally, by constituting itself as a representation, the said organisation gives the psyche itself an object of a new kind which will serve as a platform for future psychical development. Nevertheless, there is always the danger of being captive to the illusions which make one confuse reality with a fanciful alternative, namely representation for perception, and this is the most vulnerable link in psychic binding. Let us remember that the work of representation is carried out in the object's absence where there is a lack of the sensory qualities which ensure that a real relation is established with it.

It should also be borne in mind that relations with significant objects exist which do not originate in an immediate physical contact. Even when this happens, it does not involve the same investment as with the primary object – the close proximity with the mother's body and the attachment to the pleasure it affords being incomparable in all respects. But we should not conclude that all the other objects, whatever they may be, are only shadows or substitutes for the primary maternal object, thinking that its distinctive features efface all the others. On the contrary, we must assume that other types of investment exist which inscribe themselves in a way which complements the vicissitudes of the contact with the mother's body, opening the way to relations which are defined in different ways. This would be the case, for example, of the very early investments of the father whose eventual physical and bodily characteristics cannot compete with the maternal investments and whose specificity must be looked for elsewhere.

The solution which is supposed to correspond to these dangerously variable object relations, concerning the factor which the subject has the least control over, is identification. With identification, the structural organisation of the psychical apparatus shifts its gradient towards the object, i.e., in the pair intrapsychic–intersubjective, vectorisation no longer proceeds from the first to the second but goes in the opposite direction. For if in the kind of vectorisation which proceeds from the intrapsychic, the essential preoccupation – which, moreover, will never disappear – is the organisation by means of which a relative order can be established in the internal world, the second kind of vectorisation, from the intersubjective to the intrapsychic, shows that the earlier set-up takes insufficient account of the source which is external to the intrapsychic and that it is imperative to internalise it to preserve it with constancy. This is not purely and simply in order to carry out a sort of assimilation, as it is often said, but rather to reinforce the articulation inside–outside and to show that it is capable of warding off the hazards of that which escapes the control of the internal organisation and which cannot be regulated by repression. This is achieved, among other ways, by assuring the inside with a representation of the outside vis-à-vis which the inside will have to take a stand to cope with the problems posed, not only by the outside, but by that which on the inside is inevitably tied to the outside. In other words, it might be said that what is involved is the coming into contact of two modes of binding (intrapsychic and intersubjective), to fend off the dual danger of an excessive internal unbinding or of external unbinding. This set-up, guaranteeing the articulation of the two modes of binding, is supposedly better prepared to apprehend separately each front of disorganisation. Including the problematics of the object in the intrapsychic could be understood as a sort of mark of defiance regarding the fragility of the psyche. Knowing the irresistible partiality of the ego (invested by the drives) for the object and the object's aptitude for jeopardising psychical organisation, the latter protects itself by creating what is variously called an *ersatz*, a model, a mark, a simulacrum. On the other hand this result will paradoxically have to circumvent the temptation of being taken in by the lure it has itself created with the representation which fascinates the internal ego. It can increase still further the object's seductive nature, calling for urgent measures to be taken to cope with the undercurrents which risk sacrificing everything acquired by being under the sway of the object's magnetising effect. Conversely, it is necessary to ensure that losing the object does not leave the ego in a state of complete ruin without any other choice but to sink into hopelessness. Identification is thus the response of negativity to alterity which is necessary for the activation of negativity, driven by the illusion of its non-separation from the object and the promise of happiness expected from possessing it. Conversely, but arriving at the same conclusions, it is necessary to ward off the unhappiness, always dreaded, which is caused by the disappointment arising from the object's unavailability and, worse still, by the withdrawal of its love or interest, without having to suffer the sight of its favours being bestowed on another person. The work of alterity, aiming to free itself from the charms of fantasy and its representative mirage-effects, consists in abusing these distractions in turn, once they begin to lose their seductive power, by 'becoming' the object itself without giving up the wish to possess it. The representation doubtless loses some of its attraction in the process but the feeling of protecting itself against the disillusionment connected with the experience of its evanescence or of its versatility, makes an absorption necessary which, in order no longer to exhaust itself through its efforts to keep the object – 'the real one' – becomes the latter through a delegation obtained once and for all, but at the expense of what may amount to relinquishing its own subjectivity. Not to mention that we can also consider the fascinating case – from the point of view of psychic organisation – of an identification with an unconscious representation considered as a substitute for the object. While, in my opinion, this almost certainly occurs, analytic work sometimes has difficulty in providing examples of it, apart from the well-known forms of hysterical identification.

It is not necessary here to retrace the theoretical development of identification in Freud. Let us note, however, that it is first seen as a mechanism, a component part of a structure comprising other traits to which the significance of identification is subjected according to the context: identification with desire in hysteria, primary identification linked to cannibalistic oral incorporation in melancholia, narcissistic identification, etc.

It is only secondarily that identification is recognised as a basic process whose importance goes far beyond the contexts in which it manifests itself. It is not a matter of chance that it was in connection with *Group Psychology and the Analysis of the Ego* (1921) that Freud was led to speak of it in its own right. For it is not a question of yet another context, that of collective psychology. What up until then was still pending, i.e., the discovery of a fundamental unit which would give account retrospectively of its contextual diffractions, has now been achieved. With *Group Psychology*, the fundamental role which the relation to the other plays in the psyche was discovered as the second polarity which psychoanalysis had not given enough attention to up until then, having been exclusively concerned with the vicissitudes of the drives seen from an intrapsychic point of view. Admittedly, the importance accorded to the drives always implied that the object was considered as the object (partial) of a drive, but now the object has a second condition as similar other which does not originate in the maturational development of drive life but is apprehended as such. In other words, one could point out that the theory neglected the relations between the internal object in the drive organisation and the external object invested by the drives.

There is no doubt that the ground was already prepared for this by concluding *Papers on Metapsychology* (1915) with the article on 'Mourning and Melancholia'. The entire set of papers could be said to retrace the path which proceeds from the partial-object to the consideration of the lost object in melancholia: whole, perhaps, but that is not so much the problem as its effects on psychical topography. Although melancholia confronts us with one of the most extreme regressions, since it is of an oral-cannibalistic type, we should not expect only to find in it the activity of component drives, as was the case for the perverse positions described at the beginning of the volume in 'Instincts and their Vicissitudes'. Quite to the contrary, in this case, drive regression – because it is accompanied by the loss of the object – brings out the massive nature of the ego's desperate reactions. Seeing its investments withdraw for lack of an addressee, it alienates itself to fill the hole left by this loss. We should then be able to understand that the variable positions of the part-object, internal to the drive organisation, rest on the pedestal of a tutelary presence of the whole object even if it has not yet been apprehended or is still indiscernible. The ego's reaction of alienation to the loss of the object shows indirectly how much the latter shared the ego's structure even though at the time concerned – oral regression – it would not have had a distinct individual identity. It is in its absence that we can appreciate the importance retroactively:

– of the cover function of the object, before it is identifiable as such, that is, globally. Without regulating it, it allows for the play of partial-objects with erogenous zones where there is a predominance of drive activity which controls the ego's movements;

– of the mechanism which is linked to its spatial situation: incorporation;

– of the hidden and silent role it plays in the differentiation of the ego, since its action seems to be confused with elaborating the texture of the agency which feeds on it but works in favour of individual differentiation;

– of the destructiveness which its absence causes.

Identification appears to be a sort of obverse side of incorporation but cannot be entirely distinguished from it. In this respect, it does not treat the object in such a way as to create a kind of availability of recourse, as is the case for representation, it fixes it by making it disappear without there existing either consciousness of separation or consciousness of having it inside. For incorporation is supposed to have made the object disappear. For some (Winnicott), this assumption suffices to explain what underlies the death drive which now becomes superfluous.

The negativity which characterises the movement of incorporating the object speaks for itself. But here this would be to content oneself with only taking into account the simplest aspect of the phenomenon. Since the study of N. Abraham and M. Torok,[7] which reminds us of Ferenczi's ideas, it has been necessary to complete the mechanism of incorporating the object with the introjection of the drives in the ego. It is in fact precisely here that the work of the negative really takes place. All the more so because it is apparently an action which reduplicates incorporation, repeating it differently. But this is not the case: by speaking of introjecting the drives, we are no longer alluding to an operation which has any connection with the real act occurring in the body but to a reorganisation with topographical effects within the psychical apparatus.

When Freud decided to promote identification as a concept, he used its ontogenetic roots as a support. The conceptual nature of identification can be deduced by inference: if regression (oral) reveals its presence, that means we are dealing with a resurgence distorted by a paradigmatic primitive process. The number of contexts in which we come across it leads us to make the probable assumption that identification belongs to the basic data which are involved in the origin and structure of the mind. Until then, identification was fragmented into various types of situations which suggested the existence of an important but little-known function without however imposing itself as a basic model. The grouping together of these notions made it clear that their diversity, and even the contradictory nature of some of their figures, made it difficult for some time to appreciate the extent of the field in which the properties of this concept could make their influence felt.

We should note that the basic description of *Group Psychology and the Analysis of the Ego* is the child of the future Oedipus complex and not, for example, that of the oral phase already dealt with in 'Mourning and Melancholia' and still earlier in the *Three Essays on the Theory of Sexuality* (1905). Once again, while Freud cannot be thought of as a structuralist, without forcing the facts, he is certainly not a geneticist. Thus, at the beginning of the chapter on identification, he makes a vital distinction concerning investment. The child – the little boy here – shows two kinds of attachment which are psychologically different: 'a straightforward sexual object-investment towards his mother and an identification with the father which takes him as his model'. Freud places the two forms of attachment on the same level; they are at least of equal importance and dignity. As Freud is careful to introduce us to a notion which supposedly speaks of primitive times, how are we to reconcile this new version with the earlier description of the oral phase described in the *Three Essays*? Can the problem be disposed of by maintaining that the description given in *Group Psychology* is later than that of the *Three Essays*? We are obliged to recognise that Freud did not state clearly how he got from one to the other. For my part, I would say that the value of the situation described in *Group Psychology* does not reside in its dating; it shows that Freud can no longer manage without articulating *two* types of investments. It is in this respect that it represents progress over the *Three Essays* which is not only appreciated for the stage of development chosen for the theoretical construction but as a genuine change of paradigm. The following question arises: while the attachment to the mother as a sexual object is entirely in keeping with the drive investments which are the basis of any relationship, what does the identificatory mode of attachment towards the father correspond to? In fact, Freud supplied the answer to this question a few lines earlier: the child turns the father into his ideal and would like 'to grow like him and be like him, and take his place everywhere'.[8] It can be seen that here it is not a question of a dilemma between to be and to have – which will arise later when 'wanting to be like' the one who possesses the object will seem like a palliative for not having the object itself. Being means both being like the object and replacing it: 'taking its place everywhere'. But neither is it a question of a being which is just a form of having. As Freud suggests in one of his posthumous notes of 1938, it is a definite form like being but with a dynamic dimension in which, if one had to add an additional connotation to 'being', one would find the idea of becoming and substitution which no philosophical concept can account for. In this formulation we find the idea of being which sees no contradiction between its identity and the change in its evolving dynamism on the one hand, any more than it sees a contradiction between its property and its reference outside itself on the other – a polarity rendered necessary by its dynamic and temporal dimensions since they describe it less as being than as having to be in relation to other beings who have power over it. We should not forget that it also has power over them, for it is not only it which expects something from them; its being will also be formed by what they themselves expect of it. This relation always needs to be understood from the viewpoint of a propelling or extinguishing disequilibrium.

What kind of investment are we dealing with then? With idealisation, as Freud suggests? In this case what would be its relation with an object-investment considered to be 'purely sexual'? Would we be dealing with a non-drive investment? But what basic investment would be capable of escaping drive investment? Are we dealing with drives which are not aim-inhibited? By posing the question of the status of this idealisation we are raising the idea of the existence of a form of original primary investment which does not have the nature of a drive. Now, while such a solution is imaginable for Hartmann, Kohut or any other para- or post-Freudian theoretician centred on the ego or the self, it was unimaginable for Freud. The only possible compromise would be to make him say that this idealisation can be linked to the ego by a transformation of the id, the two types of attachment being separated by all the modifications of drive functioning (of the id) which were necessary for the emergence of the ego. The spirit of Freud's theorising is not to oppose two forms of attachment, the one primitive, the other secondary, but to consider two types which share the situation equally without giving up the *unique* reference point of drive life. Which is to say that the idealisation postulated here has to remain in close relation with the 'purely sexual' attachment as its shadow or its inverted figure and this is why I propose to consider it as a product within the drive metabolism. However, such a result seems to be more concerned with the object, whereas in the case of the 'purely sexual' attachment, the investment is anchored above all in drive sources. With this bipartition, the Freudian logic of drive–object relations is reinforced. It binds together drive satisfaction and object, while still being able to imagine the particular development of each of its polarities or the pre-eminence of one over the other according to the circumstances. What Freud describes under the heading of aim-inhibited drives (tenderness, friendship, etc.) is not in keeping with the 'entire' nature of a child's reactions: to grow like the father – in every respect – even to the point of replacing him. It is therefore necessary to imagine a transformation which is not so much a simple inhibition of aim (that is, a drive which does not achieve all the satisfaction expected) as a fulfilment of the aim along different, indirect paths. For, when all is said and done, what is involved is putting oneself in the father's place, making him disappear. The solution of idealisation does not explain precisely enough its relation to drive investment. To me, in any case, it seems to say that the defences (the unpleasure which results) against drive satisfaction are not the only response available in face of the pressure exerted by the drives. To the defences erected against the pressure of the drives, an operation must be added which will change the object they are addressing, distancing it by idealisation, just as the lack of satisfaction will in turn be idealised as if all the fronts had to form a league against a possible tidal wave of the drives. Freud adds to the identifications already listed (hysterical and primary), identification with the ego ideal which raises the difficulty of a kind of theoretical redundancy, i.e., idealisation frees itself from its objects (idealised) and becomes an agency capable of getting the better of the ego.

We are no doubt right to wonder about the narcissistic nature of an attachment of this kind, since the reference to idealisation refers back to it. But there is a need to clear up the ambiguity concerning which view of narcissism we are referring to. Are we going to link narcissism to the self, in order to separate it from the drives; or hypostasise the references to an egocosmic ego, i.e., to being, in order to claim it is different in nature from the drives? I will follow Freud by noting that narcissism, strictly speaking, is opposed only to the object, even though it may mean conceiving that the dialectics of their relation – as the phenomenon of identification suggests – can lead to the creation of narcissistic objects or a narcissism which is projected onto the object calling for its reintrojection through identification.

Indeed, when we are surprised at the weak position occupied by narcissism in the years which witnessed the birth of the final theory of the drives and the second topographical model, we need to look at identification to understand where things went adrift. Are we not justified in coming to this conclusion when we consider the relations of the ego or of the id, when the former wants to be loved by the latter by invoking its resemblance with the object?

Our assumption is that *idealisation ought to be considered as a negativised drive investment*. The ideal is the very type of the work of the negative which sets itself up as a mode of satisfaction when the drive is not satisfied, completely or incompletely (intentionally sometimes), which involves the following paradoxical effect: instead of the usual reactions following upon the absence of satisfaction (unpleasure, frustration, anger, rage, impotence, etc.) what we see is the denial of it and the unexpected appearance of a sort of contentment, as if the drive had been entirely, fully satisfied in the manner of an ideal perfection, more satisfying than if it was real because of its deliverance from its dependence on the object. The risk is thus avoided of the imperfection (of the object's response) giving rise either to an aggressive state of anxiety or an intensification of the demand, or the disappointed hope of a new satisfaction which is even more wounding because it increases the damage instead of effacing it. It is important to note that the pair of investments postulated by Freud create meaning and contrast: meaning, because they are two modalities which become significant through a common reference to attachment to the object; contrast, because this contrasted pair opposes – without emphasising it – two different modes of the said attachment: the first which is based on the mother's bodily pleasure (direct contact), the second on the distant relation of the person of the father (indirect contact). The figure of contact is basic to our thinking about the negative, both when it does not occur (due to the nature of the object), or when it cannot occur (because it is prohibited or impossible). Further, what is negativised – in the sense of a state of latency which will be lifted in the future – is the assumption, unimaginable at this point in time, of the contact which unites the two objects and which excludes the child from any closeness, from taking possession of its object of desire, by whatever the means may be.

The contrast manifests itself then by the demonstration of the fact that identification is understood as a counterpoint to desire. A little later, *The Ego and the Id* (1923) (employing the same opposition)[9] shows that identification can ensure a sort of reeling in. It is said to be appropriation, but I think above all it is a complementary mode of drive investment which achieves the aim of remaining attached to the object, outside the most ordinary possibilities of attachment marked out by the pathways of infantile sexuality. At the height of the latter's evolution, the Oedipus complex is resolved by means of a double identification which connotes the dual positive and negative expression of the desire for the parental imagos.

Never has the work of the negative been illustrated more fully,

1. at the beginning (in the oral relation), attachment and identification are not distinct;
2. identification is conceived of as the only condition for accepting the abandonment of the object;
3. sexual investment and identification are shared without conflict between the two parental objects, seen as two equal, symmetrical and opposed modalities, i.e., complementary;
4. at the time of the Oedipus complex, identification is transformed by the modification of its relation with the barred desires: the object of the preceding identification forms an obstacle to the realisation of desire;
5. the resolution of the Oedipus complex is accomplished by identification with the rival recognised as such: to be like him, for lack of having what he has, but to be like him while accepting certain limitations (not being able to do everything he does). It is important to note that the procedure for resolving the conflict implies making 'territorial' concessions towards the desired object which concern the fulfilment of the most basic wishes, i.e., those relating to incest. The meaning of identification is changed in that it makes use of the rival object to strengthen the prohibition of the desire (forbidden) or to complete its repression. Two measures of consolation are proposed: a deferred fulfilment ('when you are older') not with the same object, but with a similar substitute (an object of the same sex which could recall the object of the oedipal conflict);
6. the identification which leads to the resolution of the Oedipus complex occurs with both parental objects (balancing the desires) giving rise to a *double identification*;
7. there is a possibility of giving prevalence to the identification with the parent of the opposite sex (who should be a desired object) either on grounds of excessive castration anxiety or through the impossibility of giving up the desired object by keeping it as an identification, or again with hate which disparages the rival by refusing to identify with him (inverted Oedipus);

8. a special type of identification through libidinal detachment leads to identification with the ego ideal, perhaps as narcissistic revenge for the double identification of the Oedipal complex which remains under the superego's thumb.

This is the profoundest example of the way in which the same notion can take on different, and even antithetical meanings, in the course of development. The differentiation which the notion undergoes compels the earlier meaning to change and even to take on an opposite meaning to the one it had up until then, while nonetheless retaining something of what has had to be abandoned in the evolving process. That is how a concept comes about. The value of a concept, or to be more precise, the way in which it has evolved, is bound up with the nature of psychoanalytic thought.

Originally, therefore, drive satisfaction consumes the object and it is moreover this consumption that makes the said object disappear. It is by means of it that the transformation into common being (as one) (*l'être commun (comme un)*), or rather into being-one (*l'être-un*) of what has consumed with what has been consumed is achieved. Thus, this incorporation, by means of which the object extends its empire over the ego – for the ego and the object are one – inaugurates a union in which each party, giving up its individuality, merges into a community. In spite of the object's power of impregnation, the form, so to speak, of this mitigation no longer knows what belongs to either of the parties which have merged.

Once the separation from the object has occurred, identification changes status: it becomes the condition thanks to which an object can transform itself into a part of the ego, as if by an attraction aimed at re-establishing the broken unity, in a new context however, and with results which differ from the initial fusion. But in this case the two parties are distinct. It may not be so much a question, then, of two parties which are absolutely separated as an alternation of the presence and absence of an object which is the only one still concerned.

Finally, the crucial moment arrives when the two objects, being clearly distinct, mutually share the effects of drive satisfaction and idealisation, as the basis of identification.

We cannot help noticing the insistence of the reduplication. If what was unique, and seeking a common identity through the intimacy of the unifying action, ends up by consenting – not without unpleasure – to the object's separate existence, that is, to the birth of an ego–object pair, this form of coupling will repeat itself, but this time outside the ego, between the object and its other which is not the ego, which necessarily means taking into consideration more than one object, that is, at least two. But with the inauguration of this series by *the other of the object*, thanks to the displacements occasioned by the presence of this third party – the first other – the infinite perspectives of *'thirdness'* are opened up. The process of separation is, as it were, consummated, for a reunion with the primitive object can in no way re-establish the 'unifying' union (from which the feeling of being unique is born), since a second object is there calling in turn for his own investments. With the exception of orgasmic or mystical fusions, the chains of causality succeed each other endlessly. But in order for the dialectical movement to progress, it is necessary to envisage *another type of link* between the two objects and to conduct a re-evaluation retrospectively of the primitive link which brought ego and object into contact. This approach will enable the ego to establish a new relation to itself by replacing the old link uniting it with the object by a new relation where it will find *within itself* a relation to its objects. This will continue in the splitting between ego and super-ego now oriented towards the future. Thus, the original ideal has become autonomous, an integral part of the diverse ways by which psychical activity manages the problems submitted to it. A new category of psychic objects is created, thanks to the establishment of the function of the ideal in which Freud saw one of the major institutions of the ego. The detachment of the parental imagos makes the functions which have the greatest capacity for symbolisation anonymous; that is to say, it becomes capable of creating new forms of relations which are independent of the existence of concrete objects which were the reason they were brought into play. This process of disengagement has succeeded in transforming idealisation, incarnated as a motor of primary identification, into identification with the ego ideal.

This latest mode of identification has lost its links with objects which, through their power to grant or withhold love, initially controlled the situation. Now the ego ideal is no longer subject to the unpredictable nature of their desires. It is all the more demanding for having become the only master to be conferred with the task of evaluating the ego. This mutation, which could not have been foreseen at the time of the original idealisation, calls for clarification. In connection with primary narcissism I have put forward[10] hypotheses which could account for idealisation at much earlier stages than the Oedipus complex, but it is not indispensable to discuss them here because the situation speaks for itself. Consciousness of the object's separate existence necessarily precedes the stage of being able to distinguish between the two objects. This new stage has the effect, on the one hand, of putting an end to omnipotence, of exacerbating the demands of the drives and, on the other, of having to take into account that separation with the object brings into view as a consequence not only the mother, but in fact both parents: the mother from whom one has just separated and the father. It is clear, however, that the link between the two is not yet conspicuous. The non-conflictual, idealised investment of the father who offers a different form of investment, rather than being antagonistic towards drive satisfaction (where the object appears henceforth as an obstacle to the investment which is supposed to bring sexual gratification), experiences an interval of enticement (*leurre*). The father is then taken as a support for an imaginary identification where it is impossible to know if the admiration he receives results from hidden knowledge of his condition as the beneficiary of the satisfactions provided by the mother – in which case, it is clear that there is a desire to replace him – or the projection of an ideal ego. This projection implies that such an object has never had to suffer any frustration or hardship because its desires are automatically satisfied – this is the characteristic of the notion of an ideal ego – or again because an object of this kind is thought to have no needs. Something of the earlier mother–child dialectic and of the relation where they are united by a tie of mutual identification is broken now. In this type of relationship, it is not only the child who wants to be like the mother, but also the mother who becomes like the child, establishing the closed circularity of their relationship. The new relation to paternal distance no longer allows for this reciprocity; it is the child who wants to become like the father without a reciprocal relationship being established which would repeat the earlier circularity of the former relationship. Idealness arises from this forward impetus, curious to discover the unknown, which requires the assurance of being freed from necessity, expressed by overcoming the dependence on satisfaction from the primary object. The second reversal occurs when the child, having become aware of the parental tie – and in this respect the fantasy of the primal scene maximises oedipal intuitions and forces a radical stand to be taken – encounters the father's function as an obstacle. After the repeated failures of oedipal rivalry and of the wish to separate the parents in order to interrupt their mutual *jouissance* from which the child is excluded, identification now becomes the solution for getting out of the ties of oedipal attachment. The decisive reversal concerning the 'prehistoric' identification with the father can no longer be justified by the wish to 'replace him everywhere' but, on the contrary, by the obligation to accord him a place which the child cannot occupy. It is the energy which stirred him to become like the father which is once again employed to negativise the wish for sexual satis-faction, a necessary sacrifice in the interests of the whole. First identification was a mode of attachment, indistinguishable from drive satisfaction, then a consolation following the severing of the attachment, and finally a transfor-mation into a different kind of attachment, achieving at last the status of a mode of detachment. Further, the contradictory duality it formed with desire by means of the complementary negativisation of the positive oedipal complex (inverted oedipal complex), will create an interplay of crossed identifications and desires. The full oedipal complex will be resolved through a double iden-tification, as a precipitate of the imagos where the encounter of drives and objects in bisexuality seeks to find expression. There is, therefore, at the end of the process, and after the restructuring which has been accomplished at the significant moments of differentiation, a final synthesis in which the same concept applies to two objects, being the reverse side of opposing desires, the outcome of what, initially, only knew one form with one single object, generating antagonistic effects.

Freud did not go further than this. However, the accession to the second object, the distinction of the two objects, the repartition of contrary affects between them, creates a duality of desires: positive and negative, the negativising reversal of which we have seen in the formation of the inverted Oedipus complex. The work of the negative is what inhabits the relation between the two sides, positive and negative, of the Oedipus complex. Identification cannot answer all the questions which this situation raises. It is not until 1937 that Freud recognises the connection between bisexuality and the final theory of the drives. For, when all is said and done, the resolution of the Oedipus complex and the post-oedipal super-ego rely on the identification with the ego ideal or the super-ego. And it is a fact that these can also be subject to a new negativisation (the resexualising of morality at the heart of the super-ego). It is at this point that oedipal renunciation can take on the grim expression of primary masochism. Might we go so far as to postulate the existence of this negativisation from the beginnings of libidinal coexcitation, in order to understand that such a resexualisation not only integrates pain with pleasure, but can negativise itself further by installing an idealising indifference towards the solution, almost benign in comparison, of ordinary masochism capable of rediscovering the libidinal sources (disguised) of sexual excitement? This is the moment when idealisation appears not only as a negativisation of drive satisfaction, but as an attempt at repositivisation, that is, the omnipotent restoration of a withdrawal of investment, as a desperate means of struggling against the destructive effects of the lack of satisfaction. The latter is not satisfied with reversing the desire by preserving the object but, by getting rid of the object, thinks it can achieve the aim of liberating itself of a desire, the satisfaction of which depends too much on the object's goodwill alone. The result of such a withdrawal of investment is that denial of the object gives way to the illusion of a return to self-sufficiency. When this fails, the search for masochistic satisfaction transforms what is subjected and eroticised by being rendered passive into 'the order of things' in which the subject plays no part.

The procedures of negativity are seen to be even more complex when examined in detail, for they bring into play defensive activity combined with drive vicissitudes. Thus the effects of incorporation giving rise to the mimetic mechanism of introjection correspond, as we know, to excorporation and projection whose negative function is unmistakable. To repeat: internalisation makes the object disappear by consuming it. Later, the repressions of the oedipal stage obviously also have this negativising function of which identification is the consequence, although it is not conscious of its link with the repression which promoted it. But between these two extremes, the role of the double reversal has not been sufficiently recognised. The turning round against the self and the turning into its opposite are the very prototypes of a negativity which is produced *under the effect of the pressure alone of the unconscious and prior to repression,* as basic defences of the emerging psychical apparatus. If we think carefully, we should ask ourselves if something of the deep nature of these mechanisms of double reversal does not reappear as splitting or disavowal. They, too, seem to take place outside the orbit of repression and no doubt by means of the movement of an organisation more complex than foreclosure which rejects totally any control over the satisfaction of drive claims.

The case of disavowal enriches the possibilities of the psychical apparatus to respond in situations where it feels threatened. Until then, to defend the claims of reality faced with the seductions of fantasy, Freud relied on perception to compel recognition. But in fact the latter can fail, as the analysis of fetishism shows, which proves that this is not sufficient to do away completely with reality-testing since the fetishist has indeed noticed that women do not have a penis; but its anti-investment opens up a range of solutions which leave the way open for a contrary opinion. Disavowal now takes its place – which confers on it its originality – alongside the other procedures of psychic life, and doubtless this ambiguous relation to perception is also the occasion for examining its relation to representation. I will come back to that. It can be maintained that, between foreclosure – the rejection without further discussion of a threatening eventuality – and representation, disavowal holds the middle ground. For the second is always the result of a solution which implies that in the circumstances there is something to retain – in the sense both of preserving and remembering. Disavowal wants neither to reject nor to retain; it refuses to accept representation and seeks an alternative perception, i.e., the fetish. The relations – problematic, I agree – which I propose to consider between disavowal and double reversal rest on a dual setting aside (*mise à l'écart*) which I resume with the formula: neither repression, nor representation. Seen from this angle, disavowal could be understood as the inverse solution to that of identification which is also a response to the same double refusal: neither repression, nor representation. Disavowal keeps itself away from the (perception of) object for fear of being transformed by becoming like the latter. Identification proceeds to an assimilation–appropriation of the object by introducing it into the ego in a wide range of possibilities which go from total fusion to complete separation but still maintaining an internal tie with the risk of alienation. Disavowal comes into effect in order to ward off the danger of the loss of identity (sexual); identification strives to meet the threat of losing the object, the danger here being the alienation of the subject. It is this relation that I would like to define in order to explain the most mysterious phenomenon of the work of the negative in identification: namely, how, from a form of attachment involved in the relation to the object, this situation can alter to the point of becoming the only means by which an object relationship can be given up. A transition which we could describe by the formula of the change from the 'and' to the 'or', or again, having and being, having or being, being for lack of having. This first stage implies a dissociation between the two.

If we dwell for a moment on the primitive situation, we can explain it as a manifestation of insatiable greed. The attachment to the object manifests itself under the dual angle of need and pleasure, the conjunction of which creates completeness. Having (the mother's breast) and being (the breast or the mother) are operations which are both merged (and as such unthinkable), potentially capable of being distinguished during the encounters and interruptions of the relation with the object. Dissociation or differentiation, between having and being, can only arise in the context of the loss of having. It is then that the 'being-like' appears as the remains of the unity having-being which has survived the loss of having and which enables us to infer the signifying modality of 'hoping to rediscover having' without really doing so. By making a comparison, which will raise a lot of expectations, I will draw a parallel between this desire to rediscover and join up with having in the object's absence, with the disavowal instituting the search for an object displaced and chosen as a substitute, to be found in the vicinity of the mutilated sex, as the choice of the fetish shows. We can see how the loss of having incites the search for another 'common' having. Disavowal cancels out the feeling of the loss of having, whereas identification, itself seeking to make up for this loss of having, pushes for 'common' being with the object, now identified *as a souvenir of the time when having and being were one.* The aim of common being seeks to approximate, as far as possible, to the state where having and being were indissociable. The form taken by the work of the negative measures the transformation of the state in which having is changed into being, whereas, in the case of disavowal, the work of the negative can only rest on the illusion of having lost nothing, having enthroned another having within reach of what is lost ('at hand')[11] by shutting out the awareness which would oblige it to recognise that it is in fact only an imitation having. This is very different from a reversal of having with recognition of loss. Would it be going too far to suggest that this discovery of a 'counterpart with a lost sex' might be a replica of the discovery of the object as 'similar other'. In this case the model of the similar other could be used again in the discovery of symbolisation as a psychic process with unlimited possibilities. The effect of 'similitude', in symbolisation, is fundamental to the field of polysemy whose quasi-unlimited extension due to new developments operating through the multiplicity of meanings centred around the same formulation we are familiar with. Disavowal, here, plays a contrary role, i.e., of stopping the pursuit of a frantic and 'pointless' search, setting a limit once and for all to the process of intellectual curiosity by tying itself to it. In this case, the accepted loss offers the solution of a closure which allows nothing more to escape, but in which the subject has become his own prisoner.

The comparison with the double reversal has the advantage of getting us away from the simplification of identification as a simple variant of an imitation–replication. For it is obviously too easy to conceive of it as an imprint. In fact, as we keep on insisting, identification and representation are opposed. The representation is of an object, of an 'ob-ject', of that which presents itself before the psyche, to be taken into consideration, in its double aspect of transformation and new presentation, whereas identification, through its roots in incorporation, has nothing else to place in front of itself but itself, having made the object which has become 'in-ject' (introject) disappear, before being able to position itself as sub-ject (*sous-jet*), subject (*sujet*). It is thereby clear that its links with narcissism are self-evident, but a narcissism which is still unaware of what a self-image might be, and is therefore closer to its primary version, caught between the zero and the one (having absorbed the object), just being one with it and ceasing consequently to have a representation of it, 'feeling', on the contrary, that it is like it, or even it. At bottom, there are two forms of division, the first openly accepted and open to its contradictions, the second seemingly unaware of it but never being completely able to extinguish the idea of a more or less totally possessive bewitchment.

In the past, we have insisted on the effect of closure (comparable to that of a Möbius strip), of the *combination of the reversal into its opposite and of turning round upon the self.* We assume that an effect of this kind is at work in identification, hidden by the relation to the same, and rather evocative of a situation of confrontation face to face. While the turning round against the self is natural in such circumstances, we may wonder what underlies the turning into its opposite. The answer is that having and being, by separating, become antagonistic values; the transition from having to being is thus the sign of this turning.

This can justify the later explanation where identification opposes desire (a modality related to the search for having), finding support in the negativising force of renunciation and resolving itself in situations which place it in contradiction with itself, as is the case in double identification.

What's more, it would be a mistake to think that the process of identification remains inalterably fixed to this global form of appropriation; on the contrary, since identification with the desire of another (hysteric) may only concern this limited aspect. And just as disavowal only attaches itself to the signifying object, in this case the penis, identification – the work of mourning reveals this fragmentation – has, in its most differentiated aspects, repercussions on only very limited features. This does not prevent it, elsewhere, from taking the forms of identification for an abstraction, such as the ego ideal, bearing witness to a more complex psychical working-through, freeing itself from the trappings of form, in order to invest the perfection of the form as such.

The production of negation at the heart of language pushes this self-organising complexity to a degree of culmination never achieved before and refers, through retroactive reflection, to forms which preceded it, all of which had the purpose of treating negatively an excess raw material which needed neutralising.

All things considered, with identification Freud poses the question of the psychical structure *from the object's point of view and not from that of drive gratification* at a level of generalisation which takes up, from the angle of psychoanalysis, the classical question of subject–object in terms which have no resemblance with its earlier treatment. We can conclude that it is by this thread that he holds, as far as the cure is concerned, the postulate of transference complemented by counter-transference as well as the foundations of interpretation. In a larger sense, it also touches upon the inter-human link at the base of the cultural process to the extent that this process is founded largely on drive renunciation. The question which arises, then, is to know whether culture can reflect a state of organisation which would have some relation to what results from the analysis of the transference in treatment. This is what Freud began to hint at in *Group Psychology and the Analysis of the Ego*. And it is the question he returns to in *Moses and Monotheism*. It is also a question which was addressed implicitly to the psychoanalytic community once Freud had died. Is identification with Freud the solution? Probably not. It remains to be seen whether the cults which succeeded him represent the return of the golden calf or celebrate the virtues of the heirs of his most legitimate filiation. The real solution, but we know how difficult, hazardous, precarious and highly falsifiable it is, would be an identification with the search for truth which motivated Freud. But who does not lay claim to this and what right do we have to exclude the eventuality of this procedure leading us away from Freudian paths and perhaps even to opposite points of view? This is the risk involved in any de-idealisation.

4

The Death Drive, Negative Narcissism and the Disobjectalising Function

Any discussion of the concept of the death drive today must be centred on two kinds of thinking:

1. *Retrospective interpretation* of what Freud wanted to denote and signify by this concept which was introduced at a late stage into his theory. This interpretation requires that we distinguish three aspects whose inter-connections need to be emphasised:

(a) the ongoing lessons of clinical experience which have led to a revaluation of the basic mechanisms considered to be at the foundations of psychopathology;

(b) reflection on past and present cultural phenomena and on certain factors influencing their determinism, at a distance from the observable facts, on the one hand, and metascientific speculation about natural phenomena which are the concern of biology on the other;

(c) the articulation of the hypotheses arising from the two foregoing aspects, leading to the insertion of the concept of the death drive at the heart of a theoretical model called the psychical apparatus of the second topography, whose creation follows closely upon the final theory of the drives. It is on this last level that the question arises of the place, function and economy of the death drive at the heart of the psychical apparatus, that is, of its heuristic value in the attempt to make a theoretical representation of psychic functioning.

2. *Current interpretation* of what Freud denotes and signifies by the death drive posing the problem of its maintenance or its replacement and this depends on a large number of data:

(a) The modification, as a result of psychoanalytic experience, of the configuration of the clinical field which served as a basis for Freud's theoretical
elaborations. The general picture which emerges from current practice
obliges us to take into account the weight of factors linked to narcissism
and destructiveness together with what stems from the fixations of object
libido.

(b) The breaking-up of the unity of the post-Freudian theoretical field through
various theoretical reformulations, many of which are not simply complements to Freud's work or developments of such and such an aspect of
his thought, but real theoretical alternatives. As far as the death drive is
concerned, let us note that none of the post-Freudian theoretical systems
follows Freudian theory to the letter. This is even true for the Kleinian
system which openly adopts its existence. We know, moreover, that while
the role of aggressivity is accorded a fundamental place in many of the
systems, the theoretical framework in which it is conceptualised differs
from Freud's.

(c) The view of the general theoretical model of psychic activity, that is,
Freud's psychical apparatus. There is no longer general agreement about
it. To stick to the main point, let us say that the current understanding
of what such a model should be, tends to make the object, in its internal
and external status, play a formative role in this functioning. Furthermore,
ego theory has also seen complementary concepts emerge such as the self,
the subject, the I, etc.

(d) The elimination from the discussion of one of the sources of Freudian
thought. Reflection on cultural phenomena and metabiological speculation no longer plays a part in the debate for complex reasons. One of these
could stem from the contradiction between what tends to accord with
Freud's assumption on a cultural level where the development of the
means of destruction is more and more worrying (man's attitude towards
nature and his own relationships) and what to date, in the biological
sciences, has weakened this hypothesis by not providing it with any
material backing.[1]

II

Whatever differences exist concerning the interpretation of clinical facts and
the theories put forward to explain them, all psychoanalysts recognise the basic
postulate of psychic conflict. Disagreements only appear when it is a question
of specifying the nature of the elements in conflict, its forms, and the consequences which proceed from it. We have arrived at a situation where one can
no longer say that there is a consensus on the hypothesis of a primal conflict
setting two major groups of drives in conflict with each other – seen as the

expression of matrix and primitive psychic powers. One of the arguments advanced most frequently by the adversaries of the death drive is to maintain that it is difficult to see how one can apply the characteristics described for the sexual drive to the death drive (source, pressure, aim, object). More radically still, current psychoanalytic literature contains numerous examples of positions taken, either against the idea that drives represent the most basic element in the psyche or, more extremely, defending the opinion that the concept of drive is inadequate and useless. What the majority of these critics forget is that the thesis of fundamental drive conflict corresponds in Freud to an exigency, that is to say, of explaining the fact that the conflict can be repeated, displaced, transposed and that its permanence resists all the transformations of the psychical apparatus (intersystemic or intrasystemic conflicts, or between narcissistic and objectal libido or between agencies and external reality, etc.). It is this observation which compels Freud to postulate theoretically an original, fundamental and initial conflict bringing into play the most primitive forms of psychical activity, which explains his inflexibility concerning the dualism of the drives.

The theoretical daring of the Freudian assumption of the death drive has led to intense debate amongst analysts and has diverted their attention from the fact that Freud no longer sets it in opposition to the sexual drives but to the life drives which he later calls Eros or love drives (*An Outline of Psycho-Analysis* (1940 [1938])). This slight semantic shift leads Freud no longer to speak of sexual drive but of sexual function as the means of knowing Eros, with which it cannot be confused. On the other hand, Freud admits that we do not possess an indication analogous to that which libido represents for the sexual function enabling us to know the death drive in such a direct way.

III

As the drives are only knowable by means of their psychical representatives, which are no longer to be confused with ideational representatives, we are led to assume that the sexual function and its manifestation the libido is the representative of Eros, the life drives or love drives, provided it is understood that this representative function does not possess all the characteristics of Eros – which, incidentally, raises a considerable number of clinical and metapsychological problems concerning the relations between Eros and sexuality.

The real question is to try and find an answer to the puzzle left in the air by Freud, i.e., what function could play the corresponding role of representative of the death drive, remembering, that for him, it is self-destruction which is its basic expression, hetero-destruction being simply an attempt to relieve the internal tension – a point of view which many post-Freudian theories call into question. As far as I am concerned, I fully adhere to the assumption that the self-destructive function plays a corresponding role for the death drive to that played by the sexual function for Eros. However, in contradistinction to Freud, I do not believe that we should defend the idea that the self-destructive function expresses itself primitively, spontaneously and automatically.

The difficulty, as far as the death drive is concerned, arises from the fact that it cannot be attributed so precisely with a function corresponding to that of sexuality in relation to the life drives (or love). What we are more sure of is that it may alloy with the sexual drive in sado-masochism. But we also have the acute feeling that there are forms of destruction which do not exhibit this fusion of the two drives. This is evidently the case for serious forms of depression leading to suicide and in psychoses revealing ego disintegration. Without going as far as these extreme forms of pathology, contemporary psychoanalytic clinical experience has no difficulty in identifying non-fused forms of destructivity, more or less apparent in serious neuroses and character neuroses, narcissistic structures, borderline cases, etc. It must be noted that in all these clinical configurations, the dominant mechanism often mentioned is insurmountable mourning and the defensive reactions it gives rise to. Finally, in addition to the series of painful affects observed in the psychopathological field under consideration, alongside well-known forms of anxiety, we come across catastrophic or unthinkable anxieties, fears of annihilation or breakdown, feelings of futility, of devitalisation or of psychic death, sensations of a gap, of bottomless holes, of an abyss. We are justified in wondering whether these manifestations as a whole cannot be connected, in part or in totality, to what Freud described as primary masochism which for him was located at an endopsychic level, prior to any form of expression. Nonetheless, it is true that there is no clinical argument which provides proof of the death drive, for any clinical picture is open to various interpretations and cannot be a direct expression of drive functioning. Although the problem is based on clinical experience it is still a theoretical one. On this point, I agree with J. Laplanche.

IV

The hypothesis I wish to advance comprises two presuppositions:

1. It is impossible to say anything at all about the death drive without referring to the life drive which together form an indissociable conceptual pair. The corollary of this is that in order to gain a more precise idea of the death drive, we are obliged to go deeper into the theory of the life or love drives which Freud gave us.

2. Although we have not lost sight of the fact that drive theory belongs to the order of concepts and is therefore never completely verifiable by experience, these concepts are designed to elucidate experience and cannot be dissociated from it. This leads us to say that even if drives are considered as basic, first

entities, that is to say, primary, we nevertheless must assume that *the object reveals the drives*. It does not create them – and no doubt it can be said that it is at least partly created by them – but it is the condition for their coming into existence. It is, moreover, through this existence that it is created although it is already there. This is the explanation found in Winnicott's idea of 'found created'.

In the light of these two remarks, we must bear in mind Freud's idea that the major mechanisms which he described as being characteristic of the life and death drives are binding and unbinding. This idea is sound but insufficient. The life drive can accommodate the existence of both these mechanisms of binding and unbinding, just as it can absorb a portion of the death drive which it transforms by so doing. The manifestations which result from this can no longer be interpreted in the register which is characteristic of the death drive. On the other hand, the death drive only involves unbinding. But the unbinding of what?

Our assumption is that the essential purpose of the life drive is to ensure an *objectalising function*. This does not simply mean that its role is to form a relation with the object (internal and external), but that it is capable of transforming structures into an object, even when the object is no longer directly involved. To put it another way, the objectalising function is not limited to transformations of the object but can promote to the rank of object that which has none of the qualities, characteristics and attributes of the object, provided that just one characteristic is maintained in the psychical work achieved, i.e., *meaningful investment*. From this follow the apparent paradoxes of classical theory where the ego can itself become an object (of the id) as well as the reference to self objects in certain contemporary theories. This process of objectalisation is not restricted to transformations of structures which are as organised as the ego but can involve modes of psychical activity in such a way that, ultimately, *it is the investment itself which is objectalised*. This requires that we distinguish the object of the objectalising function where, of course, binding, coupled or not with unbinding, comes into play. This justifies the attention which has been given to object relations theory whose error however is not to have clearly noticed the objectalising function, being too attached to the object *stricto sensu*. This explains that the sexual function and its 'exponent' (Freud) the libido, are the means by which Eros is known, for this is inconceivable without the object being included and accounts for the classical theory of narcissism which nonetheless needs completing.

On the contrary, the purpose of the death drive is to fulfil as far as is possible a *disobjectalising function* by means of unbinding. This qualification enables us to understand that it is not only the object relation which finds itself under attack, but also all its substitutes – the ego, for example and *the fact itself of investment in so far as it has undergone the process of objectalisation*. Most of the time, we only observe the concurrent functioning of the activities related to the two groups of drives. But the manifestation characteristic of the destructivity of the death drive is *withdrawal of investment.*

In this respect, the destructive manifestations of psychosis are linked much less to projective identification than to what accompanies or succeeds it – the impoverishment of the ego abandoned to a withdrawal of investment. In spite of the considerable contribution of Melanie Klein's ideas for our understanding of psychosis, she betrayed herself somewhat by overlooking that the schizo-paranoid stage was 'schizo', not in the sense in which the term alluded to splitting (the schize) into good and bad but in the sense of opposing paranoid investment to schizoid withdrawal of investment. In this connection we can mention one of the most troubling paradoxes in psychoanalytic experience; namely, that the disobjectalising function, far from being confused with mourning, is the most extreme way of preventing the work of mourning which is at the centre of the transformation processes characteristic of the objectalising function.[2] This, I think, is the logical explanation in Freudian theory for the transition from the theoretical step opposing object libido–narcissistic libido to the final theory of drives, i.e., Eros and the destructive drives. This has led me to support the hypothesis of *negative narcissism* as an aspiration towards the level zero, the expression of a disobjectalising function which is not content with focusing on objects or their substitutes but focuses on the objectalising process itself.

The central issue with regard to the objectalising function is that the theory of it must take into account a contradiction which is inherent to it; namely, that the role of the primary object is decisive and that *there is always more than one object.* We are not for all that justified in thinking that the second object (the father in the oedipal complex) can be attributed with a secondary role in any sense of the term. Nor should we consider it as a reflected projection of the primary object. These remarks are not beyond the limits of the subject under discussion to the extent that we are trying to determine the *primary* manifestations of the death drive and their link with the object (primary). We should be aware, in this respect, that the good enough mother (Winnicott) implicitly contains the bad enough mother to get out of the impasse of idealisation–persecution and to promote the mourning which preserves the disobjectalising function. The technical implications of these observations are important.

The disobjectalising function is seen to play a dominant role in other clinical situations than melancholia such as infantile autism or non-paranoid forms of chronic psychosis, mental anorexia and various expressions of the somatic pathology of the infant. The studies of the Paris Psychosomatic School (P. Marty: operative thinking, essential depression, regressive desublimation, progressive disorganisation, pathology of the preconscious) constitute an extremely valuable contribution to the reflections on the subject which concerns us. They appear to corroborate the assumption of a withdrawal of investment and the disobjectalising purposes of the death drive.

V

The mechanisms of defence against anxiety and other disorganising, painful affects can equally be reinterpreted in the light of our reflections on the conflict between the life and death drives. It is necessary, with this view in mind, to make a prior distinction between the ego's primary and secondary defences. The primary defences form a category of which repression is the prototype (*Verdrängung*). This was later enriched by the discovery of other analogous mechanisms such as disavowal correlated with splitting (*Verleugnung*), foreclosure (*Verwerfung*), negation (*Verneinung*), whereas the other defences should be considered as having a secondary role of reinforcing or completing the task of the primordial mechanisms.

However, the closer one is to repression proper, the more the polarity binding–unbinding is accompanied by a rebinding in the unconscious, thanks to other mechanisms (displacement, condensation, double reversal, etc.). The further one is from repression, the more one notices in the activity of the other types of primary defences (splitting, foreclosure) that unbinding tends to win through, limiting or preventing rebinding. Thus, just to mention one case which often arises in psychoanalytic literature, that of projective identification, its function seems to be to reinforce the disavowal of splitting which encourages disobjectalisation, in spite of the apparent objectalisation which projection and identification attempt with the projected parts. However destructive its action is, it is above all in its attack on linking (Bion, Lacan) that its fundamentally disobjectalising function is seen. The success of a disobjectalising withdrawal of investment is manifested by the extinction of projective activity which is translated particularly by the feeling of psychic death (negative hallucination of the ego) which sometimes barely precedes the threat of a loss of external and *internal* reality. An interesting parallel has been drawn between foreclosure (radical repudiation) – assumed to be at the basis of psychotic structures – and a corresponding mechanism thought to be at the source of serious somatic disorganisation (P. Marty), translated by disturbances in mental functioning characterised by a poverty of psychical activity or a deficiency in its investment. Of course, I am speaking here of asymptotic functioning which evinces less the fulfilment of the project than its orientation towards the pursuit of its ultimate goal: the disobjectalising withdrawal of investment.

Negation, which is expressed through language, no doubt has a special place in this category in that it seems to cover the entire field occupied by each of these terms. Thus it turns out that it participates just as much in the pair binding-unbinding as in unbinding alone, as Freud had already pointed out.

These remarks call for our attention. They show how the characteristics which mark the modes of action of the drives (binding–unbinding) can be found in the ego, either because it carries their certificate of origin or because it mimes the drive functioning revealed by the object. Might we go as far as to speak of an identification of the ego with drive functioning or with its objects?

VI

Freud's view of the psychical apparatus resists the revaluation which we have just undertaken. But it gains from being elucidated by the conflict objectalisation–disobjectalisation.

The joint use of both topographical models shows itself to be necessary, provided we understand the essential difference between the id of the second topography and the unconscious of the first. The unconscious then appears as the organisation which best preserves the objectalising function.

The hypothesis of the objectalising function clearly deserves to be developed further than I have done here. If I had done so, it would have diverted the focus of this discussion on the death drive to a debate about the life drive, which we tend to do too often in our exchanges on this difficult theme. So I will confine myself to making just one further but fundamental point: the objectalising aim of the life or erotic (libidinal) drives has the major consequence of achieving, through the mediation of the sexual function, *symbolisation* (Bion, Winnicott, Lacan). Such an achievement guarantees the intrication of two major drive groups whose axiomatics remain, for me, indispensable for the theory of psychic functioning.

5
Masochism(s) and Narcissism in Analytic Failures and the Negative Therapeutic Reaction

High in the midst exalted as a God
Th'Apostate in Sun-bright Chariot sat
Idol of Majesty Divine, enclos'd
With Flaming Cherubim, and golden Shields ;
Then 'lighted from his gorgeous Throne, for now
'Twixt Host and Host but narrow space was left,
A dreadful interval, and Front to Front
Presented stood in terrible array
of hideous length: before the cloudy Van,
On the rough edge of battle ere it join'd,
Satan with vast and haughty strides advanc't
Came tow'ring, armed in Adamant and Gold ;
Abdiel that sight endur'd not, where he stood
Among the mightiest, bent on highest deeds,
And thus his own undaunted heart explores.
'O Heav'n ! that such resemblance of the
Highest
Should yet remain, where faith and reality
Remain not;

> J. Milton, *Paradise Lost & Paradise Regained*,
> Book VI, v. 99–116

And nothing is,
But what is not
Macbeth Act 1, scene 3, 141–2

Masochisms and the Negative Therapeutic Reaction

If it is difficult for us to conceive in psychoanalysis of a pure negativity which is not opposed to an implicit positivity with a contrary meaning, it is in reference to psychopathology. Up until now we have based our analysis on general concepts which transcend the differences between normality and pathology and which therefore cannot be confined to therapeutic applications. This indeed is the spirit of the Freudian approach. By starting out with neurosis which led him into an exploration of the dream process, Freud managed to free himself from the presence of psychopathology so that he could build his model of the mind on a phenomenon common to all humans. Similarly, the transition from the analysis of the symptoms of transference neuro-psychosis to the manifestations of transference neurosis, whilst being immersed in thera-peutic experience, subjected the latter to a grid of decoding which relativises pathology, for it is said that transference is by no means the prerogative of psychoanalysis and is met with beyond the confines of psychoanalytic treatment. The latter is simply concerned to provide the optimal conditions for analysability. It has always been understood, moreover, that neurosis occupies the very favourable position of being perceived both as pathological and of showing, upon examination, that all the intermediary stages between it and normality exist without there being a clear line of demarcation between the two. Neurosis has become the most auspicious case for enabling pathology to come out of its ghetto, its structure allowing it to become part of the general human condition once again. Conversely, it makes it possible to demonstrate at the very heart of normality the presence of discreet pathological traits which it is by no means free of but which, no doubt for ideological reasons, one preferred to overlook. It would be a mistake to infer that the notions of normal and pathological have lost their meaning for it was known that other clinical entities existed which stood out more visibly from the ordinary and which were more clearly stamped with the mark of abnormality. Freud only approached them from afar, with the memory of the psychiatrist he was or with his talent for textual analysis. He said he found psychosis too destructive for his taste, even doubting whether it was accessible to analysis.

Analytic experience has demonstrated that we cannot so easily get rid of this fallow field by concentrating too much on neurosis. However, apart from a few exceptions where there was a direct confrontation with psychosis, this field was not tackled. With time, psychoanalysts have been surprised to discover it – sometimes without even being aware of the nature of their discovery – hidden under the cloak of neurosis. The analysis of the 'Wolf Man' has turned out, retrospectively, to be a new paradigm.

While Freud demonstrated that neurosis and normality, at bottom, belonged to the same category, it may equally be said that perversion simply enlarged the Freudian field a little but was legitimately included within it. Neurosis as the negative of perversion – the felicitous expression found in the *Three Essays* (1905) – reveals a notion full of implications. Freud did much to de-alienate perversion by referring to the normal state of polymorphous perversion in childhood, a source of potential fixations. There was no justification for seg-regating the perverted from the rest of humanity for, when all is said and done, Freud saw them simply as backward children whereas his contemporaries thought of them as sinners, troublemakers, disturbers of the moral and social order. Freud was perhaps right to demystify the dangers of perversion in face of the values of honest people, but he came to realise that the perversion which was apparently the least perilous for the social order was the most formidable, for it would soon show itself to be a threat to psychic and vital order.

At the start, masochism was just one of numerous sexual perversions; at the end of the Freudian opus it becomes (isolated from the pair it forms with sadism) the model, the source and the outcome of all kinds of perversion as well as of the other pathological entities. Now is not the moment to take up the discussion on the relations between death drives, unconscious guilt feelings and masochism. It remains true, however, that at the end of his work, Freud finally possesses in masochism an intelligible structure which is rooted in sexuality, with a leaning towards its non-phallic aspects, which means that sexuality inverts its key value and pervades its relation both to *jouissance* and the law.

Generally speaking, Freud felt the theoretical need to have a structure at his disposal which was more intermediary than primary in nature in order to construct his table of orientation. Thus he focused his interest on dreams, in the oneiric world, neglecting other forms of the dreamer's psychic life (nightmares, for example), just as in the world of pathology, he chose neurosis as the starting-point of his reflection, leaving aside other categories involving deeper regressions to earlier stages. The discovery of masochism involved the same procedure: uncovering the intermediary process responsible for the failure of treatment and the maintenance of unhappiness. The essential thing for Freud was to bring to light the significant structure whose extensions and unfurling would make it possible to take in the whole psychoanalytical field at a glance. Masochism, in this last sense, caused a problem. The human sensibility of analysts made it difficult to accept the idea that extreme suffering could be a source of hidden *jouissance*. Moreover, the width of the masochistic spectrum in its triptych form was not immediately appreciated. Primary masochism put in question the pre-eminence of the pleasure–unpleasure principle. Admittedly, from 1921, Freud had proposed a 'beyond the pleasure principle'. In fact this 'beyond' was a negation of the latter in favour of an original binding, maintained as a compulsion to repeat which is suggestive of a deadly automatism. With primal masochism, Freud discovers a solution which can account for the turning away from the pleasure principle. At the beginning of life, binding ties sexuality to pain in the name of libidinal coexcitation, which gives rise to a certain form of pleasure, i.e., masochism. We can thus speak of the beyond the pleasure–unpleasure principle as a matrix form where pleasure and unpleasure are not separated; it is in the eyes of the other that they appear as 'negativised' pleasure (in every sense of the term), whereas for the subject they form a mixture which is neither pleasure – under any circumstances – nor unpleasure: a coexcitation which can perhaps be defined as a tensional intensity. We could even speak of a beyond unpleasure, i.e., distress, unhappiness, etc., in this case, warded-off by a sort of requisition of fused sensations. Furthermore, this *dolorism* finds ways of feeding itself in social life in the form of moral masochism. The latter, far from rebelling against authority, reinforces it – in spite of appearances – but finds considerable compensation in denouncing it. The powers that be are accused of being unjust, iniquitous, despotic and, what is more, indestructible and all-powerful, which is supposed to show that one takes them to be the enemy, whereas in fact it is we who are their accomplices.

The link between these two forms of masochism, primary and moral, seemed defensible, but what then does feminine masochism represent? It has rightly been pointed out that Freud makes reference to cases of masculine masochism as if his prejudices concerning femininity meant it could only appear in the regressive form that it takes in men. I believe that there are deeper motives underlying this point of view and it is only by standing back a little that we can uncover them.

If we recall that for Freud libido is masculine in nature, it is necessary before protesting on behalf of our wives, sisters and mothers, to understand the quasi-biological perspective of his position. Moreover, biology tallied with his viewpoint by discovering that sexual desire – in both sexes – is found in humans to be dependent on androgenic secretions! But let us return to psycho-sexuality. Freud identifies sexual desire with activity, physical energy, hence its 'masculine' nature. Does this imply that women have no sexuality because they are considered to be passive? I believe that here Freud shows that he had a great sense of the negative. Firstly, he separates sexuality and maternity. Maternity is a biological function, secondarily invested by female sexuality. For Freud, female (psycho) sexuality is masculine in nature, as is all sexuality but it is inverted according to feminine characteristics: namely, that sexual activity (phallic) finds itself inverted (with a passive, receptive aim) – aiming to achieve a centripetal *jouissance* – in order to welcome and integrate what is received from the man (penis, child). In this way, it acquires phallic functions which will later be manifested explicitly in raising children. It was concluded rather too quickly (Lacan) that women do not care so much about phallic *jouissance* which is characteristic of men; for them it is the whole body which offers itself to be invested with *jouissance*. This statement needs qualifying. It is not that women are not concerned with this local phallic *jouissance* but they need to negativise it by delocalising it onto the whole of their bodily erogeneity and to relocalise it (vaginally) in the meeting with the male organ.

In connecting masochism with femininity Freud was relying on certain situations in feminine sexuality ('being castrated, being subjected to coitus, and giving birth in pain') which he interpreted in a way which has been considered questionable. For him, passivity becomes synonymous with castration by rape (subjection to coitus) and painful extraction of the child (giving birth in pain), because passivity in this case is experienced less as a form of *jouissance* than as being reduced to impotence, i.e., phallic and penile castration. What is at stake in the examples Freud cites is the foreclosure of the phallic dimension in *all* forms of sexuality and its identification in women with a basic masochism which is not the product of a reversal but the consequence of an imaginary traumatic event. The latter, through libidinal coexcitation, may become a source of *jouissance*. Freud confuses, it has been maintained, the regressive situation of men with the general structure of female sexuality. In fact, for normal (phallic) female sexuality the feminine attributes would be: having a vagina, enjoying coitus, giving birth with pride. Under these conditions, Freud's feminine masochism refers to what is expressed by the displacement of the phallic function reduced to an overvaluation of the penile function and the return to the infantile genital organisation based on the distinction phallic-castrated. In other words, feminine masochism results from an unconscious working-through of a general castration complex, which in this case, however, does not manifest itself by castration anxiety. It is rather the price which must be paid for phallic recuperation which must then follow the paths borrowed from the male sexual organ. What remains indisputable for Freud (and intolerable for women) is the discovery of penis envy. For if men, dominated by castration anxiety, have difficulty in conceiving of envy for the penis, women, for their part, have just as much difficulty understanding the impact of castration anxiety which is unthinkable for them. They have trouble in recognising their envious attitude towards a sexual organ which they consider to be uncastratable and therefore non-transferable. On the other hand, masochism – in the form of fantasies – is an important source of pleasure whose function is to increase libidinal coexcitation and to heighten the orgastic *jouissance* obtained from an overvaluation of the penis. In short, it is a masochism for pretence, or even better, for fun, but which can, occasionally, as with men, make them come 'for real'. The masochistic triptych thus signifies: its origins in sexuality (in its relation to pain but with the possibility of inversion which ensures the pre-eminence of the latter as a condition of *jouissance*), a reversal of the sexual phallic value and a 'subversion of the moral order'. It is the accomplishment of the negative as a reverse value of life, derisive of inter-human relations: the more it hurts, the better it is and the more it makes you think that having it is a way of becoming invulnerable. Not having it leaves open the possibility of making it exist in the form of power attributed to it.

This is not to deny the advantages of the female genitals. Penis envy is not at all the same as the desire to change sex. Far from it; it is, as we say, a 'bonus'. Can the same reasoning be applied to men? This would mean calling into question the referential position of the phallus. And so what? The fact remains that men seem to have more talent for simulating femininity than women masculinity. Feminine masochism arises from this simulation. Male castration anxiety is often masked by a denial of their dependence on women.

We are perhaps now in a better position to understand how the general model of negativity, which took its roots in drive life as a vicissitude of natural causality, underwent a transformation in man by subordinating its claims to intersubjective relations (with reference to the similar other). In order to found the human order the work of the negative was necessary. It is as if it were to show us, tacitly, that psychic vulnerability is the price to be paid for the establishment of such an order, the burden to be carried by the human condition at large, variations from one culture to another often masking the permanent features which unite them where sexual issues are concerned. We still need to account for the reasons why the male organ, the erection of which is a symbol of life, potency and accomplishment, provides the model for a function which is called phallic. There is no doubt that there are cultural answers to the question but it is not certain that these are adequate. In any case, it cannot remove the sense of injustice felt by women at not being able to be the source of a transcendental symbol. The answers are not easy to establish, explain and justify. Even though it may arouse some scepticism, I attribute the phallic privilege to its link with external space (the conquest of the world) and to the risks which are involved in exposing it (castration anxiety). This is in no way contradictory with the fact that a symbolic choice of this kind rests on the warding-off of the dangers imputed projectively to feminine powers – *dangers which are shared by women themselves* – and because of which they prefer to adhere to the phallic supremacy of men by building up fantasies of appropriating the latter. Such a conquest could not be achieved without suffering: the greater the price paid for this transfer of power, the more important is the imaginary value placed on it. The more 'the pain' is overcome, the more valorous is the woman and the stronger her constitution. It is by means of this fantasy of pain and endurance that women establish their equality with masculine power. And it is this pain, with its ambiguities, which is found in the reality of giving birth.

The Negative Deviation of Repression

The discovery of a new type of human relation, thanks to the special conditions of exchange defined by the analytic setting, implies having recourse to the negative. Its use has given rise to another structural form which we might conceive of as a manifestation of the mobilisation of the negative linked to masochistic matrices, i.e., the negative therapeutic reaction. It might be that we are dealing with an iatrogenic pathology, a neo-neurosis (or neo-psychosis? or neo-perversion?) created by analysis itself and absent from 'spontaneous' pathology or from ordinary social life. This new type has therefore arisen from the vicissitudes of the negative brought to light by psychoanalytic treatment. By what deviation, by what process of turning away does the work of the negative turn here into a 'negativistic' work? For it is certainly an intuition of this sort that led Freud to conclude his article on 'Negation' by making an allusion to the negativism of schizophrenics.

We shall have to turn to one of the vicissitudes of negativity which is found within the drive model. The pressure of the drives and their imperious demand for satisfaction are succeeded by the need for preservation, the development of the capacity to defer, and the alternative between elaboration and rejection. Elaboration, contrary to generally accepted ideas, is not the prerogative of the ego; it is present at the heart of drive functioning and is part of its very essence: arising from soma, the excitation which 'reaches' the psyche is a measure of the amount of work imposed on the psyche by its link with the body. This means the formation of messages formulated in terms decipherable by the psyche to which they are addressed, the expectation of a response and, if need be, an attempt at a more adequate formulation, a search for other means of satisfaction apart from the object or by means of other objects, and finally the discovery of more efficient means which are capable of providing a solution. It is clear that all the means of psychical figuration will come into play (hallucinatory wish-fulfilment, representation) and will be adopted as solutions, temporarily at least, even if they do not provide conclusive results immediately. They can nevertheless serve other secondary aims which gives them a usefulness thanks to which they will not disappear. Here, once again, we must distinguish the self-informative and hetero-informative value of what is produced at the heart of psychic activity. The first is considerable, the second weak. A means of combining the two aspects remains to be found. But during this basically self-informative period we are dealing with the negative in the sense that we are still in a state of virtuality. For the negative is not only the image in relation to the thing, it is the image in its capacity to pass itself off as the object.

However, whether it be due to the delay of the response or to its unsatisfactory nature, rejection sometimes occurs. We have brought in a new parameter which is not based on natural causality but originates in the production of the negative. Hallucinatory wish-fulfilment reiterates the satisfaction obtained by means of hallucinating an object, onto which are projected all the concomitant characteristics of well-being and pleasure. During the test of satisfaction which follows, the child will rediscover, *through the reality of experience* all the characteristics projected onto the object as it appeared at the time of the hallucinatory wish-fulfilment. However, the latter is less likely to correspond to the memory of the experience than to its retrospective idealisation. If the real object satisfies the need without presenting all the positive characteristics of the projection of the hallucinatory wish-fulfilment, the negative will change from the state of positive virtuality into the condition of the negative 'coming into being' as the contrary of the positive, owing to the unexpected disappointment. The tension between the memory of the hallucinated experience and the actual present experience which satisfies the need but disappoints the desire, has a frustrating effect necessitating the expulsion of violent affects, condensed with the object to which they are addressed. This object, as Freud pointed out, is seen to be responsible for the lack of well-being, for the badness, identified with the extraneous and the outside. This leads to the early separation of the good and the bad object and the rejection of the latter. We have moved from the dimension of virtuality to that of an evil spell which means that a part of oneself finds itself identified with an intrusive part, not-me, which has penetrated and colonised the ego. The other is born from this expulsion so that its own existence – distinct from the ego which experiences it – coincides with the negative affects banished by expulsion.

To avoid recourse to such an extreme solution the subject, in those cases where it suffices to ward off the situation, resorts to repression. The displeasure caused by a lack of satisfaction, the delay of the expected response, or its inadequacy, create the space necessary for desire to preserve the object after all, provided that the experience is not entirely negative. This involves making a renunciation. *Repression becomes the consequence of a renunciation of destruction so as not to endanger either the desiring organisation of the subject or its relation to the object of desire.* Repression thus becomes a sort of geometrical locus of the subject–object relation, representing simultaneously the subject's renunciation and the object's demand ('if you love me ...'). The wish to preserve the bestowal of the object's love as well as the love felt for it, leads the subject to accept the need to make sacrifices because, through experience, he has gained a sense of the value of its existence – through being loved, certainly, but also through being recognised as a being of desire. Under these conditions, the Other can exist separately and even demand certain renunciations in exchange for the love bestowed. The necessary condition for *jouissance* is to authorise the union of what is remote and separated in the imaginary. But this relation is never perfect and cannot avoid certain hiccups, i.e., the necessity to give up denouncing the inadequacies, lack of adaptation and imperfections of the response is never quite achieved; the ego's control over the drives is never complete allowing numerous offshoots which cannot be integrated to escape;

the safety valves for unsatisfied desires tend to fail, etc. – hence the continuity between the notions of normality and neurosis.

However, in certain cases, when the distance between drive 'alterity' and subjective alterity cannot avoid rejection, the knot formed by the two forms of alterity becomes inextricable. This means that drive life is identified as such with the object which can never satisfy it. It becomes somewhat demonic. In this case there is a subjective dispossession of the drive and, as I have already pointed out on several occasions, a displacement from the source of the drive to the object. There thus develops a kind of rampant paranoia which attributes all the manifestations of drive life, experienced as an intrusion destined to repeat an eternal frustration, to the movements, not to mention the manipulation, of the other. Persecution is not directly experienced as such. It filters through because from the point of view of the drives, the subject only exists when he is activated from the outside, i.e., is directed, manipulated by the other who, it might be said, has no other goal than to 'see what effect this has'. Which means he enjoys exercising his power. Conversely, any form of relation to the other is invested by the drive with the aim of provoking dissatisfaction. The negative is as common as in a country where there is no experience of satisfaction. This leads to an increase in masochistic resources but above all provokes a shift in the life struggle which now takes the form of a struggle for territorial integrity alone. The search for a relation to the other no longer simply nourishes a claim for autonomy, that is to say that the objective is to achieve a state of separation and individuality necessary for self-esteem founded on independence, the recognition of alterity fading conjecturally and necessarily at the same time. This is to say that the aim of a struggle of this nature is not the sharing of pleasure but the possibility of finding refuge in narcissistic withdrawal and self-sufficiency. In extreme cases, this solution is achieved in isolation through auto-eroticism. Then we are dealing with a form of narcissism whose extreme limit is what I have called negative narcissism, an attempt to reduce tensions to the level zero.

The principal characteristic of this deviation of the negative is related to the vicissitudes of the other, at the heart of intersubjectivity. The transformation which it undergoes depends on a number of characteristics which are potentialised:

– The distance between hallucinatory wish-fulfilment and real experience of satisfaction makes it look as if the other does not desire the subject's desire. This is a prime motive of grievance.

– On closer inspection, the experience of satisfaction is seen to satisfy the object more than the subject who is at the source and origin of the desire. The subject then feels dispossessed of his satisfaction in favour of the one who should be providing it.

– The paradox of the situation arises from the fact that the object, who is supposed not to desire the subject's desire and is accused of having attempted to divert for his own benefit the subject's satisfaction, has not separated from the latter with whom he is one. The Other can therefore never constitute himself through separation.

– It follows that the Other is represented as a persecutory agency of satisfaction within the subject who only has one representation of it, without relief or volume (just like his own).

– The subject's whole strategy consists in escaping, by laying claim to a separate domain, the power of the persecutor it has set up within itself. Such a domain only procures momentary joys, destined in the last instance to be persecuted by the ascendancy of the Other, hence the adoption of a strategy of desire for no-desire, in a perpetual flight.

– Being unable to escape the Other, the subject's reaction is to adopt a strategy of mutual asphyxiation. By suffocating oneself, that is, by inhibiting one's own capacities for development, one hopes to suffocate the Other. In fact, in contradistinction to what is observed in neurosis, murder is indissociable from suicidal designs.

– In any event, the Other remains the agency of a deadly authority which wants neither life, nor development, nor creative capacities but the preservation of a parasitic, cold and rigid relation. Here the negative has once again acquired its attributes of potentiality, of virtuality, but simply to fix them for ever in a state of psychical immobility with the negation of time which passes.

These are some of the effects of the imprint of the masochistic model discovered by psychoanalysis, in the form of the negative therapeutic reaction, constituting a deviation of creative negativity. At this juncture I shall conclude by trying to understand what it is that forms a bridge between the two.

Freud states that masochism resexualises morality. This implies that morality takes part in this process. It was concealed behind the anonymity of repression and it took Freud a certain time before he ascribed an agency to it: the super-ego. But the negative therapeutic reaction makes a mockery of the latter. It makes it appear as an egoist, concerned only with its own pleasure; cruel, insensitive and even sarcastic. A sort of 'sub-ego' which, once stripped of its flashiness, looks very much like the id, which is another way of saying that when one speaks of the Good Lord, the Devil is never far away. But we must also understand that they form two sides of the same question: that which concerns the relation between the parental authorities of whom the subject is the product. One can only be delivered from them by having a sense of the contingency of one's own condition. For a long time psychoanalysis focused on the manifestations of the subject's sexuality, interpreting them as vicissitudes of its infantile roots. Today, there seems to be an unjust tendency to neglect problems concerning the acceptance of parental sexuality. We had thought as much since the case of the 'Wolf Man'. The future will show that it is in the interaction of these two negativities that the vicissitudes of desire are played out.

The Negative Trap

Jean Guillaumin has pointed out that the negative is in a way fundamental to the experience which makes psychoanalysis possible. The setting requires the analyst's withdrawal, not only because he is out of the patient's sight and is assigned a role limited to listening to the latter – which certainly 'negativises' this presence all the more in that it evokes a potential absence, favoured by his being out of sight – but also because the analyst intervenes less in person than through his interpretations. It is not his opinions or ideas which he communicates but those which he lends to his analysand. Undoubtedly, the loan is not entirely neutral and it is certainly the analyst who makes up his mind as to what he thinks the patient's unconscious message is, but it is quite clear that it is not as an individual that he expresses himself but as an imago 'created' by the situation.

These remarks lead us from the analyst to the function of the setting, of which the analyst is certainly the most significant element, but nonetheless he is only the representative of it.

Furthermore, the analyst's lack of response to the patient's demands, the silence which he opposes to the desires addressed to him as well as, in spite of everything, the exciting nature of the analytic set-up, mean that the setting may function, to use Guillaumin's expression, like a *negative trap* – modelled on bodily erogeneity: mouth or anus.

With regard to theoretical ideas concerning the setting, it has been objected that the modifications of it by using the face-to-face situation were no less interesting, psychoanalytically speaking, than the classical treatment of neurotics. No doubt. But would that not be overlooking, rather too hastily, the fact that many of the indications for this 'variation' have as their motive that the patient could neither tolerate not seeing the analyst nor not hearing him (by his silence in so-called classical analysis)? Invoking the case of these variations is to allude implicitly to the intolerance of the negativity of patients who are unanalysable according to the classical procedure. However that may be, the modifications of the setting mentioned here retain their basic negative position; namely, the fate reserved for the patient's demand, i.e., abstaining from responding to it – which implies refusing to consider the question as 'real' within the analytic space and limiting the analyst's interventions to interpreting the discourse of the patient who is there 'to speak'.

However, I am not certain that I go along with Jean Guillaumin's decision to focus his thinking on the transfer–counter-transferential interaction – however pertinent and fruitful this position may be. The foundation of negativity in psychoanalysis rests on the effects of the object's non-presence and the attribute which the human psyche has of responding to this absence by means of representation (hallucinatory, fantasmatic, cognitive, etc.). In short, the 'trap' is not designed to poach some game but to create a mimesis of the conditions which obtain in nature. And it would not be demeaning to admit that there is indeed a strategy in the setting created by the analyst, that is, the invention of a relation which has unsuspected effects. But this invention, however original it may be, compared with the usual modes of human inter-action, does not escape comparison with other prototypes. It has often been pointed out, with daring or vulgarity, that the psychoanalytic relation is somewhat evocative of certain forms of religious experience. I will not dwell on the comparison – a very poor one – with confession, but you may recall that Lacan compared the analyst–analysand relation with that which unites the Zen master and his disciple. I also recollect the indignant protests aroused by the paper of a respected colleague who dared, during a meeting gathering together an international group of psychoanalysts exercising tasks of great responsibility, to claim that the effect of an analysis could be compared with the result of a conversion. I have on numerous occasions drawn attention to the ambiguity of the concept of the capital Other (*grand Autre*) behind which the analyst is tempted to shelter in order to eliminate any propensity to take advantage of the situation in which he finds himself. At the very minimum, he will feebly resist the easy gains to be had from his position without needing much persuasion; at worst, he will let himself be captivated by the fascination of the *jouissance* experienced from being in a position of strength, while invoking, beyond the setting, the structure of the 'subject'.

A continuity can be inferred between the experience of regressive alienation which occurs in certain forms of treatment – negative therapeutic reaction and moral masochism – and certain aspects of cultural life. Far from being destined to remain outside the human community due to the strange economy of desire which inhabits them, these psychical organisations, whose pathologi-cal character is little doubted, are close to certain forms of sublimation. It is not because they are differentiated from the latter by different characteristics that one feels inclined to state that they must be set aside from the general organisation of human desire.

If these forms of alienation are different from those known to psychiatry, the reason is to be found in the maintenance of a relation to the other as someone who is similar. For here the work of the negative does not cease to militate against the dissolution of relational moorings, sometimes under the cover of a masochistic organisation capable of resisting anything. The constancy of a passionate attachment to a primary object, viewed as thoroughly bad but yet impossible to relinquish, can ensure these patients' survival. Their suffering is offered as the only gift of love which is permissible, even if it is bound up with the most tenacious hate, forever entangled.

Reflections on the Failures of Psychoanalytic Treatment

Since Freud's quasi-testimentary text 'Analysis Terminable and Interminable' (1937), negative therapeutic reaction has been the subject of incessant reflection. Its re-interpretation invited psychoanalysts to go further back to acquire a better understanding of the infantile mind, based on the assumption that the cases which demonstrated this development in the cure presented fixations which were much older than those which we are used to dealing with in neuroses. It is already striking to note that this was not the point of view held by Freud who did not think that these kinds of early fixations were the sole obstacles to recovery. Nevertheless, many of the factors mentioned by Freud (the constitutional strength of the drives or ego distortions of similar aetiology, the sexual nature of traumas) have seen their role questioned and minimised in favour of others whose aetiopathological role might well not have received Freud's backing.

Moreover, as J.B. Pontalis rightly points out, we must not confuse failure in psychoanalytic treatment with negative therapeutic reaction. I now propose to look at some of the factors which I consider are often responsible for unsuccessful treatments.

The analyst's feelings when confronted with failure can be divided broadly into two categories: paranoiac projection ('it's the patient's fault; he was unanalysable and is therefore responsible for the negative outcome of the analysis') and depressive self-accusation ('it's the fault of the bad analyst who was badly analysed'). In that the latter is more disposed to recognising the analyst's role in the failure of treatment, it cannot be misleading. For one could interpret the criticism directed at oneself as a protective ploy against the much severer reprobation of others. In both cases the feeling of guilt is easy to detect. Also surprising – besides the fact that the limits of analysis are not being taken into account here – is the pure and simple omission of any reference to our persisting ignorance of the possibilities of psychic change, as if there were no need to admit that there are many aspects of this which remain unknown to us. In defending such a line of argument (paranoiac or depressive) we can scarcely notice, behind the contrasted nature of the defensive strategies adopted, the mirror situation which in both cases unites the two partners of the analytic couple. This is not a matter of chance and this is what I wish to demonstrate. While the role played by guilt feelings and masochism in psycho-analytic failures has long been recognised, the role of narcissism, although suspected, has been taken into consideration to a lesser extent. One would like to have an explanation at hand which would account both for the *non-lieu* of analysis (the case where the latter, decided by common agreement, does not in fact take place) and for the negative therapeutic reaction (where the treatment begins well but continues badly) as well as for cases where the obstacles put in the way of the analyst's efforts lead inexorably to failure. It is also necessary to throw light on the paradoxical nature of a relationship which is as attached to its continuation as it is to its sterile effects, in such a way that the analysand's failure as well as the analyst's become indissociable, each of them in the end being confronted with themselves; both, however, remaining united in a relationship which is in fact a tenacious non-relationship capable of withstanding any ordeal.

Unconscious Sense of Guilt and Narcissism

It is in 'A Child is Being Beaten' (1919), where he studies the origin of sexual perversions, that Freud comes across what he calls 'a sense of guilt'. He does not insist on its unconscious character, no doubt because his attention is focused on the unconscious forms of pleasure linked to the activity of the drives, to their regressive substitutes, to the representations and imagos which they stage, and the aims which they pursue. Initially, therefore, there is only one discovery related to certain masochistic scenarios in the reference to the ordinariness of the fantasy of 'A Child is Being Beaten'. Such a situation is ultimately as unremarkable as one in a family romance where the child invents different parents for himself in order to protect himself against the disappointments and hurts which his own cause him. In other words, what is only glimpsed in passing here is the significance of the connotation of 'consciousness' which guilt acquires. The 'consciousness' of guilt should have led Freud away from perversion to its opposite, as an effect of a division in the ego, already described at the time when narcissism was introduced into the theory, and which was liable to acquire characteristics of splitting. Freud had already come across this division in the ego as a pathological mode of organisation, i.e., in the delusion of observance, the most general basis of which makes it possible to recognise narcissism as a part of the ego detaching itself from the rest in order to evaluate its worth and aspiring to perfection in what is then called, without there being a clear difference between them, ideal ego or ego ideal. Curiously, although one of the arguments which underlay Freud's project for introducing narcissism was based, on the one hand, on the existence of a *perversion* described by *Näcke* and, on the other, on the myth of Narcissus which ends with the suicide of the legendary figure, he had great difficulty in bringing these two aspects together. He accorded less and less interest to the perverse side of narcissism (seldom observed in fact) and more and more to that of depression (melancholic) which later alone would have the privilege of being qualified as narcissistic neurosis. Freud seemed to want to turn away from perversion of a narcissistic type to another, more enlightening to his eyes, that is, masochistic perversion. Henceforth, the whole discussion, although it was not stated clearly, skated over the different varieties of masochism on the one hand and depression on the other. Although depression was not explicitly linked to the different forms of masochism, it was to become the focal point of the relations between the death drive and narcissism, as in melancholy. These links stood out even more clearly than those which Freud established when he was elaborating his theoretical ideas on psychosis, as if the regression of the ego towards the auto-erotic state of fragmentation situated the latter short of a narcissistic fixation proper. The opportunity was missed, however, of opening up an original path, alloying masochism and narcissism as a model of invulnerability to the object's undertakings.

It is not difficult to find reasons why Freud did not think of a solution of this kind. It was just at the time when he was beginning to get an idea of the mode of activity and the really fundamental importance of the destructive drives that he became aware of how important it was to take the sense of guilt into account. This consideration swept away the earlier theoretical framework whose heuristic value was based on the opposition object libido–narcissistic libido. In other words, negativity was divided between destruction and withdrawal into the self. As destruction was a more extreme measure, leaving hardly any possibility open for the libido to turn towards the ego, it made, so to speak, the thesis of withdrawal superfluous. The error obviously was not to see that the consequence of withdrawal was to avoid the temptation for destruction to direct itself towards the object or to become intricately bound up with the object's erotic libido.

And besides, although clinical experience was the favoured basis for theoretical work, how was the sustained transference relationship compatible with a prevalent narcissistic position obstructing the transference process? Freud struggled considerably when faced with the paradoxical existence of unconscious guilt – a paradox which he thought he could resolve by calling it instead a 'need for self-punishment' to avoid the almost contradictory character of a formulation denoting an 'unconscious sense'. His argument did not gain in strength for, to my mind, his line of reasoning was wrong. The real paradox did not lie in the 'unconscious' sense (of guilt) but rather in a 'narcissistic' sense of guilt and, more precisely, in an *unconscious sense of guilty narcissism*. Far from it being a matter here of just a simple reversal of pleasure or of unpleasure, it was necessary to understand that the consequences of such a reversal only made sense if one envisaged the object from the position of narcissism. Resistance was already at its peak in having to admit – sometimes as much for the analyst as for the patient – that the most extreme unpleasure masked a hidden *jouissance*. It was asking too much to have to supplement this reversal with another which would have consisted in admitting that the relation to the object served as a disguise for a narcissistic relation whose ultimate goal was to call into question, in its principle, the object relationship *as such*. The interest shown in the content of the latter made it difficult to see the wood from the trees, i.e., what the discussion was all about.

It is because this path was not followed that Freud's elaborations thereafter would reveal contradictions which we will do no more than mention in passing.

The Ego and the Drives

If we agreed to stand back somewhat from the issues involved, we would see that the deepest contradictions stem from the basic separation between the ego on the one hand and the drives on the other. Of course, it is the drives which are most hypothetical here since they can only be apprehended indirectly and their mode of functioning can only be inferred from the unconscious, thus according to a certain conception of the latter, that of the first topography, outside its sphere of influence (given that the drives are neither conscious nor unconscious). As far as the drives are concerned this raises two problems. The first concerns the need to delineate their direct or indirect mode of functioning according to the reactions they arouse from the ego; the second concerns the need to define the minimum order that their action may be supposed to have, as well as the internal principle of their functioning based on the mode of opposition which separates and unites them. Concerning the ego, the problem is absolutely complementary and remains so throughout Freud's work: what is the ego's specific mode of functioning and what is the mode of functioning which is exercised in relation to the drives or, more precisely, according to the internal organisation of the drives?

Freud comes to the following conclusion: if the internal organisation of the drives is understood in terms of union and separation, ego functioning can be considered on various levels:

1. A mode of functioning vis-à-vis the drives;
2. A functioning in relation to its internal organisation;
3. An activity oriented towards the exterior.

At the level of the ego's internal functioning:

(a) it will never entirely escape from the modes of activity specific to the drives from which it has marked itself off while at the same time retaining – by imprint? – certain characteristics in a toned down and disguised form – which means that the ego's functioning proper will be more or less 'coloured by'[1] the drive and not simply be invested by the drive. Although this may seem scarcely imaginable, it can perhaps be elucidated by the functioning of the secondary defences in obsessional neurosis.

(b) it will comprise organisational factors homologous to those of the drives, that is, it will be caught between union (cohesion) and division (splitting). These general terms show that they can apply, depending on the case, to the parts it is made up of (or which are constituted as effects of these mechanisms), to the relations of these parts to the drives or again to objects.

(c) it will have to bring this internal functioning into harmony – in accordance with the laws which govern it – with the drives and with the external world.

What distorts our judgement is the global rather than rigorous approach to chronology in the theory. Thus, by saying that the discovery of narcissism comes before the hypothesis of the death drives, the latter supplanting the former, we are in fact not recognising that with narcissism Freud anticipates his discovery of the opposition between the death drives and the life drives. He understands the importance of the factors of union (transition from auto-eroticism to narcissism) in antagonism with those which bespeak of separation (narcissism versus object relation). He already defends the idea of an internal destructivity in the form of a self-sufficiency which denies the object's existence. This destructive modality is quite different from aggressivity directed outwards or turned back against the ego.

The fruitfulness of this approach to narcissism will be confirmed, in fact, less in relation to the drives, than by the re-interpretation of the ego which it made possible. And this is what accounts for the ego being conceived of, first and foremost, as a bodily ego but which corresponds to the projection of a surface differentiated from the id and separate from it, with the aim of constituting itself by means of unification into a totalising entity. Against this tendency, however, are opposed the internal divisions which set one part of the ego against the other, the splitting-off of one part enabling it to set itself up as a judge of what the other part is, or does, and to exercise functions of internal surveillance. The encounter of the two series occurs at the level of sublimation, on the one hand, and of the super-ego on the other. The influences of drive vicissitudes on the one hand, the development of the ego detaching itself from objects, on the other, and, finally, the 'destruction' of the Oedipus complex, come into play here. Alongside sublimation and the super-ego, we should not forget the role played by the idealisation both of the object and the ego.

We can now understand the theoretical route Freud took prior to developing his theory of 'The Economic Problem of Masochism' in 1924, a study which is usually seen as the turning-point in Freudian thought although it is made up of threads woven since 1914, even if they were not all interlaced at that time. With regard to the question we are studying – 'On Narcissism: An Introduction' being 'put aside in a state of latency' – it is from the angle of the sexual perversions, which were the surest and most demonstrative for Freud, that the question is inaugurated ('A Child is Being Beaten'). It is followed up in the more conjectural but original domain of repetition compulsion introduced in *Beyond the Pleasure Principle* (1920) and blossoms for the first time in *The Ego and the Id* (1923) under the thereafter accepted term of negative therapeutic reaction. But the major novelty consists in the statement, following this last work, that a major part of our moral conscience is unconscious. By upholding that man is not only far more immoral than he believes, but also far more moral than he knows, Freud is reaching out both towards the drives (immorality) and towards the ego (morality, that is, an inference of the superego, as a division of the ego).

The Situation of Narcissism Guilt and Masochism

We have traced the line of thought which leads to masochism. It is nevertheless a fact that numerous collaterals become detached from the main trunk and follow their own path or flow like many tributaries into the main current, widening its course. We will confine ourselves to just mentioning them at this point because the problems which are connected with them will surface again later on. One of these, for certain, has appeared as a paradigm of the reversals which we referred to earlier. It is the inversion of the Oedipus complex in the 'Wolf Man' which, it will be remembered, Kraepelin, who was consulted before Freud, considered to be a case of manic-depressive psychosis. As far as we are concerned, it should be emphasised that for the first time castration anxiety finds itself intensified by *an aspiration for castration* – without, for all that, being accompanied, as in the case of President Schreber, by an obvious state of alienation. Moreover, there is a correspondence between this oedipal inversion and a fixation to anal eroticism which differs from that of the 'Rat Man' in that it opens up new perspectives on what elsewhere I have called *primary anality* whose relations with masochism are very pronounced. What's more, it is striking that the 'Wolf Man' – considered by most authors today as a psychotic structure and the first case of failure in psychoanalysis – did not go through a more pronounced decompensation than the one he presented during his analysis with Ruth Mack Brunswick. His equilibrium seems to have been organised around a stabilised narcissistic position. Against the 'Wolf Man's' masochism – also in a state of equilibrium – we would set his melancholic decompensation. If the latter existed, it was not he who was affected by it but his wife who committed suicide. Freud confined the relations between narcissism and masochism, as a 'pure culture of death drives', too much to melancholia while neglecting the possibilities presented by the intervention of a projective mechanism and a 'delegation' of the conflicts to another relative. Contemporary psychoanalysis has identified this mechanism in the re-evaluations it has made of the functions of counter-transference which, in certain cases, may become the only means of gaining access to aspects of the transference which are not identifiable in the patient. Freud's inquiries are located at the cross-roads connecting an unconscious sense of guilt, masochisms (in the plural) and destructive drives. In melancholia it is the latter which predominate. It would not be very convincing to explain the essence of melancholia by an unconscious sense of guilt alone, perhaps because of the grotesque, depersonalised, and even mechanical nature of guilt in this affection. Furthermore, the fact that we are dealing with a clinical entity beyond the reach of psychoanalytic treatment somewhat diminishes the interest of the conclusions which can be drawn from it. Consequently, it was better to look for the causes of failure in the different forms of masochism. These would offer the opportunity of testing the latest theories of the drives and the most recent conception of the psychical apparatus, instituting the ego and postulating the division between ego–super-ego.

As for the sense of guilt, it deserves a separate study in itself as its effects manifest themselves well beyond the domain of neurosis and are a source of reflection on the human condition as a whole and, more specifically, on the effects of the process of civilisation.

Henceforward, it is around the various forms of masochism that the question of analytic failures will revolve. To what extent the unconscious sense of guilt is connected with it is not easy to determine: it is as if it were easier to find the sense of guilt in masochism than always to invoke masochism in the sense of guilt, even though Freud writes that the unconscious sense of guilt induces the patient to 'fall in love with being miserable' (*An Outline of Psychoanalysis*, 1938). It is not enough to base the comparison on the intensity of the attachment. What Freud designates is an impermeability which in either case makes the subject inaccessible to the opinion of others. Thus it is not only the exclusive character of this love which needs to be taken into account but the fact that such exclusivity comes down in the end to a narcissistic retreat. We can simply make a link between this observation and the one Freud makes about patients being 'unable to tolerate recovery through our treatment' in the negative therapeutic reaction. Now, given that the treatment is based on transference, how can we not conclude that alongside the apparent object transference there is an inaccessible, narcissistic 'transference' which is only perceptible through the impermeability and negativity of the transferential experience? That is, not negative transference but transference–non-transference, 'negativised' transference. It is always, of course, possible to point out the defensive character of such a narcissistic cover. So the old debate rears its head again: is masochism a defence against narcissism or, conversely, is narcissism a defence against masochism? Or again, there is the hypothesis, which radicalises either one or the other of them, or both, that it is a defence against psychotic disintegration. But there is nothing to prevent us from explaining this as a defence since, for someone like Winnicott, even psychotic disintegration is a defence against primitive agonies. Would it not be more honest to say, like Freud: 'But we must confess that this is a case which we have not yet succeeded in explaining completely' (*An Outline of Psychoanalysis*). The best way forward would seem to be to make a detailed break-down of the factors which are involved in these configurations:

(a) *The transtructural character of masochism*: moral masochism which is the phenomenon to which failures in treatment are related, is not limited to a particular sector of the psychoanalytic field. It is found just as often in the severe neuroses i.e., symptomatic or character neuroses, as in personalities with a dominant pathological or narcissistic trait, or in depressive patients, etc. It seems therefore to involve a crystallisation which we are liable to come across extensively.

(b) The difference established by Freud between *moral masochism and feminine masochism* as an 'expression of the feminine nature' is based on examples taken from masochism observed in men (F. Begoin). While it is not rare, phenomenologically, to note the existence of masochistic fantasies in women, the demonstration of their structural worth calls for more commentary than Freud offers. Nonetheless, this could suggest the existence in masochism of a distinction between an identification with women and a position of identification in relation to the mother. We should therefore distinguish between:

– masochism which is tied up with a feminine identification vis-à-vis the paternal imago;

– masochism which is tied up with an identification with the mother's maternal masochism with respect to the child (the mother's spirit of sacrifice towards her children).

(c) *The objectal 'disqualification'* which accompanies feminine masochism–moral masochism gives prevalence to the goal of suffering rather than to the attempt to find the object needed to achieve this goal. In this connection, Freud recalls that in moral masochism the sufferings no longer derive from the loved person but from anyone at all. This observation seems to lean in the direction of a *narcissisation of suffering*, more concerned with the condition sought after than attachment to an object.

(d) Moreover, the metapsychological interpretation of the clinical phenomena will lead Freud to distinguish – while at the same time pointing out their similarities which at times can lead to confusion – between *the sadism of the super-ego and the masochism of the ego*. Indeed, what Freud designates as *primary sadism* is in fact identical with masochism. B. Rosenberg admits that this auto-sadism resulting from the internal structure of the first expressions of the death drive poses a lot of problems.[2]

(e) As a last point, it would seem that with *libidinal coexcitation* Freud put his finger on an essential factor, the importance of which he did not entirely appreciate, when he noted that its effect died out soon after the beginnings of life. I should emphasise that it can have two registers of expression. The first, which is the usual sense, is where the different kinds of drive potentialise their effects, with the implication that the result of this potentialisation always occurs along erotic lines. The second is where one could imagine the same mechanism of coexcitation, between the subject's drive and the object's – which could, depending on the case, give rise to either another version of the former case, or to a different way of seeing the relation of a drive to something other than itself. So the partner it pairs up with will, according to the circumstances, be an object, the ego or another drive. This would make it possible, even in the case where masochistic functioning was operative, to conceive of a thoroughly narcissistic version of this masochism.

Destructiveness and Aggressiveness

The common factor between masochism and the sense of guilt is aggressiveness. The further one advances in Freud's work, the more mysterious it becomes. One becomes aware of the obstacles which work against an understanding of its functioning in *Civilization and its Discontents* where Freud has a go at elucidating the sense of guilt. In it he states that aggression is rendered harmless because it is 'introjected, internalised; it is, in point of fact, sent back to where it came from – that is, directed towards his own ego'.[3] Secondarily, it is taken over again by the super-ego. Here, there is a paradox which is not immediately obvious. For, as Freud refuses to assign a centrifugal origin to destructiveness, unlike those who think it is primitively directed outwards, it is an *internal* aggressiveness which undergoes this vicissitude towards *interiorisation*. It is as if a recurrence of this sort resulted from the fact that, *tempted to exteriorise itself, it turned back and took stock of itself,* constituting thereby *a retroactive loop without any action as an outcome.* It may be that it is from such a loop that the first link of aggressiveness to narcissism arises, the specular basis of which was rightly observed by Lacan.

How are we to account for this pathway inverting its trajectory? In the same text, Freud postulates the hypothesis of this reversion with renunciation: 'A considerable amount of aggressiveness must be developed in the child against the authority which prevents him from having his first, but nonetheless his most important, satisfactions, whatever the kind of instinctual deprivation that is demanded of him may be; but he is obliged to renounce the satisfaction of this revengeful aggressiveness.'[4]

Freud's formulations are remarkable on more than one account. The 'external authority' leaves a certain mystery hanging over the indefiniteness of the father or mother. While it is the father to whom he generally gives this role, the fact that it is the 'first but nonetheless the most important satisfactions' leaves the specific nature of the prohibited satisfactions in the dark: oral (in relation to the breast), anal, phallic, genital? The question is not asked and is even considered as 'of little consequence'. This is unlike Freud and indicates he was in a real quandary. Clearly, this left the door open for Kleinian interpretations. But there are still other questions which can be raised in this connection, for it is not enough to refer to erogenous zones in this allusion to the 'first but ... most important satisfactions'. Does it not also involve questions which relate to erotic and/or aggressive satisfactions, primal sadism, masochism, and lastly libidinal coexcitation? From a more modern standpoint, the question of the object's safekeeping or survival is raised implicitly. The problems of drive theory (fusion and defusion) and its relations with those of object relations theory can be read between the lines. To these I would wish to add the inescapable question of narcissism and to raise again the hypothesis of negative narcissism. The latter, instead of drawing ego investments towards unity, points them towards a search for the level zero in a bid to find a solution to the problems of destructiveness by dissociating them from aggressiveness which can be linked up with expressions of positive narcissism.

A Detour via the Narcissistic Organisation

In his *Papers on Metapsychology* (1915), Freud attributes different origins to love and hate. We know that as far as the object is concerned, Freud makes its appearance depend on its awareness of being separate, thereby postulating that hate is older than love. It is when the non-realisation of desires which require the object's participation occurs that primal hate appears, preceding love. Non-separation maintains the belief that the object is a part of the ego and therefore has no autonomous existence. This belief serves the claims of omnipotence. This goes to say that Freud is pleading here for a narcissistic organisation in which the ego and the object are not distinct. It is not possible, within the framework of the drive functioning thus described (which supposes maternal care), to speak of a love of the object from the start in spite of numerous attempts to promote this view. On the other hand, the exchanges only have meaning when they are situated within a narcissistic organisation generally called fusional. This designation does not exclude 'moments' of object love or dialogue between the mother and the child, but these soon get lost in the overall structure of the situation.

Nevertheless, Freud suspects that it is not so much the libido as the ego which is at the origin of hate. 'Indeed, it may be asserted that the true prototypes of the relation of hate are derived not from sexual life, but from the ego's struggle to preserve and maintain itself.'[5]

Moreover, Freud stresses the fact that primitive love closely resembles hate, which Winnicott calls 'ruthless love'. The confusion of the two suggests a mirror relationship: when the subject–object separation has occurred, there can still be moments of alternation between a return to the narcissistic organisation when they are once again momentarily merged and others when the hate for the object's independence, marking its separation, is still permeated with nostalgia for the time when it was syntonic with the subject's omnipotence. Here again the differences are less striking than the rapprochements allowing for substitutions arising from the mirror relationship. In any case, the tendency to restore a closed system of narcissistic autarchy encloses this alternation within a unity, largely shut in on itself and subjected to the potentialisation of libidinal coexcitation. It is indeed within the context of attempts to resurrect infantile omnipotence, in spite of its numerous failures, that the drive for mastery and will to power emerge, as offshoots of hate, but also as a way of neutralising love. Freud makes this Nietzschean expression his own in 'The Economic Problem of Masochism' (1924).

The subject–object distinction does not distribute the places and functions of the two partners in an intangible way within the framework of a relation which has clearly defined limits. Freud's study of 'Instincts and their Vicissitudes' reveals the sense which he attributes to the narcissistic organisation. It is not limited to subject–object confusion and does not end with their distinction. On the contrary, it is never more attested than when, separation having occurred, there is an exchange of places. Thus the transformation of sadism into masochism signifies a return to the narcissistic object, 'and in both these cases [i.e., in passive scopophilia and masochism] the narcissistic *subject* is, through identification, replaced by another, extraneous ego'.[6] We see then that when Freud began to develop his theory, he could only think of the relations between sadism and masochism in the context of narcissism. While the progress that he made later in his theoretical position does not explicitly renege on positions he defended formerly in the *Papers on Metapsychology*, it does not continue with them either. It is not so much that they have become obsolete as that it would have been necessary to reconsider the relations between an unconscious sense of guilt and masochism from the perspective of primary narcissism and even of absolute primary narcissism.

Admittedly, the resonance echoed by the link between masochism and pain is not easily reconcilable with a narcissistic universe, evocative of insensibility. But is it not paradoxical to observe, in the extreme situation represented by masochism, the subject's own complaint that he is prey to 'a painful anaesthesia'. To the puzzle of having *jouissance* in pain, we should add that of being insensible in unhappiness.

In another passage in the text on 'Instincts and their Vicissitudes', Freud states that in sadism, as in masochism, it is less the pain itself (inflicted or received) which is enjoyed than the 'accompanying sexual excitation'. A strange sentence gives us an unexpected lead. 'The enjoyment of pain would thus be an aim which was originally masochistic, but which can only become an instinctual aim in someone who was originally sadistic.'[7] Is this not to say that primary masochism is not in itself an aim of the drive? Is it not so that in the uncertainties of Freud's writing we come across an allusion to something which is 'anti-drive', often confused nowadays with narcissism? This is another way of asserting that a genuine aim of the drive always implies the existence of a distinct object needing to be invested by the drives. This does not mean this possibility is completely excluded when the distinction is not established but it should be reinscribed at the heart of the narcissistic organisation.

It is clear then that the expression 'narcissistic organisation' can be understood in different ways:

– as a modality of exchange (due, in particular, to identifications) between objects, between subjects – 'through identification with an extraneous ego' – even between object and subject, when *partial drives* are in play. We are dealing with the vicissitudes of secondary narcissism in sado-masochistic transactions, which are not so much synonymous with stagnation as with circularity and do not exclude certain spiral progressions.

– as closed systems in which the subject–object distinction is not clearly established. This non-differentiation creates, between the dominant drives of love and hate, confusions which equally affect the sources and make the id intervene for love or the ego for hate – but with the reservations that primitive love resembles hate and that the latter must be distinguished from destructiveness. At this point we are at the level of positive narcissism which is what is at stake in the love–hate relation entailing a reference to an object in the process of separation–totalisation.

– as a closure in which the narcissistic organisation works for the non-accomplishment of totalisation and pulls the process less towards the maintenance of an unchanging unity (or stagnant as in the former case) than towards the zero of negative narcissism, masochism and the failure of the treatment being the guardians of a disobjectalising function,[8] when the transference is subjected to a work of Penelopy between sessions.

The various positions can only be characterised descriptively. They can alternate at different moments in an analysis and be of greater or lesser importance. But the analyst ends up having the feeling that what really counts in the treatment is preserving the narcissistic organisation, as a resistance to transformation through analysis, faced with the danger of compromising a system of values and *negative* investments whose disappearance would mean the end of the *raison d'être* for their investment. The analyst's interpretations bring about a defensive impasse and suggest implicitly the possibility of parting company with this implacable fate, far from always succeeding – not by a long chalk – in achieving this change.

Freud said privately that one could never convince a pervert that he could find more pleasure in practising a heterosexual genital sexuality. In cases of analytic failure, it is important to know whether the treatment gives a glimpse of a more reliable system for the narcissistic organisation than the culture of masochistic retreat.

Post-Freudian Reflections

When, while examining the effects of the destructive drives in 'Analysis Terminable and Interminable' (1937), Freud distinguished between a bound destructiveness, represented by the super-ego, and a floating destructiveness, existing freely and distributed throughout the psychical apparatus as a whole, in which he saw the deepest cause of analytic failures, he wanted to draw attention, by means of this image, to the non-transferable part of this destructiveness – that is, the part which was not capable of becoming attached to the transferential object and which can be qualified as narcissistic. It is understood that it refers not to unitary narcissism but to negative narcissism whose ideal is zero. Extremely difficult questions arise here concerning the relations of chaos (as dispersed energy) and nothingness (attached particularly to the negative as inexistence).

Other authors since Freud have tried to emphasise the link between masochism and narcissism. Thus Fenichel, in 1928[9] (well before 'Analysis Terminable and Interminable', but after 'The Economic Problem of Masochism'), reported a case in which the denial of castration led the patient to believe in the existence of a hollow penis in the place of the vagina. In this case, too, masochism sustains the fantasy of a deliverance from sexuality. The paternal function shows here that it is marked by the same denial favouring the omniscience of the mother's parents and auto-eroticism fulfils a function of self-sufficiency by swallowing the sperm resulting from masturbation.

Similarly, Bergler,[10] by granting masochism pride of place in the genesis of neuroses, saw it as deriving from the narcissistic wound marking the end of infantile omnipotence. It indeed seems as if masochism here is like a paradoxical vengeance trying to recover omnipotence which has been lost. Among the Kleinians, Joan Riviere[11] has distinguished the attacks of the super-ego from those which stem from narcissism which, in fact, denigrates and rejects the ego.[12] Following her, Rosenfeld recognised the existence of a destructive narcissism to which he strangely enough accorded the status of an object relation.

But it is thanks to Michel de M'Uzan,[13] with the description of a case of perverse masochism, that we are in a position to realise the extent of the lure which attributes the object of the masochist with an all-powerfulness stemming in fact from projected narcissism. An all-powerfulness which is reflected on the subject who makes the object suffer the vicissitudes of mockery, denigration, attempts to break his will, and who simply makes use of erotic symbolisation to deny symbolism any value, solely to the advantage of a megalomania thought to be indestructible.

In an earlier study[14] I proposed to differentiate from a psychoanalytic point of view two kinds of power: *power* and *potency*. In my opinion *power*, in contradistinction to *potency*, can be shared. *Potency* oscillates between two opposite poles: impotence or omnipotence. The archaic distributes its effects between situations which are equally marked by extreme states. From the object's standpoint, the super-ego only knows of alternations between the ego's obedience and revolt; from the angle of narcissism, it is the ego ideal which leads to the exacerbated reactions of humiliation and pride. Such are the forms, in the context of what I have called primary anality – a structure oriented more towards grasping or clinging than towards retention – by means of which the culture of masochistic failure can be constructed. Its narcissistic purpose is the invulnerability conferred on the unavowed reversal of the rules of the game: he who wins loses (he who loses wins, would signify already a will to win which is sabotaged here). For while any gain involves a risk of loss, transforming everything gained into a loss – always a possibility – is the only way to guarantee the outcome every time, by systematically annulling any dependence on the object, while maintaining control, since the Other – adverse by definition – is thus preventively deprived of an eventual victory.

How do we get from the ordinary situation where a subject, lacking satisfaction, desires and seeks out the object supposed to be able to provide him with it, with the possibility of shared pleasure, to one in which masochism dominates in the systematic culture of solitary unpleasure? I will put forward a hypothesis based on the preceding remarks. The subject I have just described effaces himself to give way to *an object of the object*. In other words, he is no longer the subject as an agent of desire which institutes him as the initiator, but he accords this place to the object. Up to this point there is simply a banal reversal of roles. As a matter of fact, the situation is more complicated for the subject has not only become the object but through dissociation the object of the object. In the unconscious, he keeps his place as subject being the instigator of a scenario in which his eclipse is pure pretence since he is pulling all the strings. What is more, the object (for whom he has in turn become the object), is put in an omnipotent position. The object then has complete power over the object of the object but in fact it only uses this power to signify to the object of the object that it, the omnipotent object, is self-sufficient. In asserting that in his narcissistic tower where he remains inaccessible, he does not, when all is said and done, have any need, and still less desire, for anyone, all that is left for this subject, now the object of the object, is to love himself passively, in the sacrificial pain of a vain offering. This situation disguises a narcissistic *jouissance* which is symmetrical with that of the omnipotent object.

By denying the lack, and by means of a hidden reflexivity, an apparent unity is accomplished which masks what it disguises: the confinement of an object sequestered in the psyche, dispensing pain as if to celebrate the moment of its capture. It is out of this confusion that an active libido, which mobilises a subject seeking an object, comes to love itself in a passively masochistic way. This triumph is the consequence of having captured[15] the object. Hate here changes course, ceasing to be addressed to the object due to its separation from the latter and turns into hate for its own dependence on the object, self-hate because the self has tied its fate to an object. Perhaps the subject can only find a solution by dispersing this self, whose nihilation is vainly and repeatedly sought after, giving rise to a symbolisation which has negativised its meaning. It is no longer to be sought for in the reunion of separate fragments, but in the repetition of separations which – in order for the union to be repeated – will only need to destroy it untiringly and indefinitely.

It is understandable that masochism and narcissism go hand in hand, each striving to achieve their effects. To put it succinctly: for the psyche which pursues this unending venture of destruction, it is necessary to divide through narcissism and to unite through masochism.

6
Splitting: from Disavowal to Disengagement in Borderline Cases

Hold pleasure and pain, profit and loss,
victory and defeat to be the same; ...
La Bhagavad Gîtâ
Chant II – 38–9

'I would prefer not to.'
H. Melville, *Bartleby*

Perplexity

The year 1920 is often seen as a turning-point in psychoanalysis. It is less frequently observed that, having undertaken the theoretical modifications which he deemed necessary, Freud in fact found he was at a standstill.[1] The different stages in the development of his ideas did not follow the order one would expect. The fact is, Freud's intuition of what he thought was the truth came long before a more detailed understanding. His way of thinking reflected the curious idea he had that the truth can only be reached by means of its distortions. To put it another way, it was easier for him to put his finger on the distortions underlying the errors he wanted to do away with than it was to know clearly what they could be replaced with.

At the beginning of his work, he identifies the obstacles to true knowledge which lay in the ideas which reigned at the time concerning the normal or pathological mind, but later – and in this respect he shows that he is a conquistador of a different mettle from those who are simply content to exploit their territorial conquests – it is in his own conception that he discovers new obstacles compromising the construction of a model of psychic functioning which would be more promising heuristically. When he becomes aware of something hindering progression towards the truth, he relentlessly – as if he feared being outstripped by one of his detractors – points out the error and proposes that the theory be reviewed. This provides him, moreover, with an excellent opportunity for reaffirming his convictions with regard to the inalienable basis of his thought, for introducing new concepts which demonstrate, retrospectively, the inadequacy of the previous theory from which they were absent, and for reconsidering the internal relations of the different component parts of the intellectual construction in the new equilibrium arising from the recent changes. As far as the details are concerned, the material evidence will follow. It is just that sometimes the material evidence reveals perspectives whose importance had not been sufficiently appreciated during the global reinterpretation, and which turn out retrospectively to be a propitious opportunity for discovering new and unsuspected horizons.

So it was well after 1920[2] – seven years after! – that the concept of disavowal (*Verleugnung*) was introduced. With it appeared the remarkable effects of splitting. Yet Freud already knew that repression was not the only mechanism of its kind, but this observation had not been followed up. The idea of *Verwerfung* had slipped from his pen when he was writing up the case of the 'Wolf Man', although he did not think of making a concept of it. Negation (*Verneinung*) had given him more cause for thought, but perhaps only as an 'intellectual substitute' for the primary defence: repression. In fact, it is at the heart of the article 'Negation' (1925) that the contradiction arises. Having clearly linked the fate of the latter to repression, just as he is about to conclude, he puts forward the thesis of a negativity at work at the centre of drive life, linking affirmation and negation with the two main groups of drives: Eros and destruction, through the acts of swallowing and spitting. The link is symptomatic. As soon as Freud is attracted linguistically by a development, whose necessity is acknowledged retrospectively, and which closely associates theory and practice, he appears to want to remind the reader, before concluding, that it would be a great mistake to underestimate the importance of this new shift of emphasis by minimising the fact that the basis of his thought, i.e., both its original basis and central axiomatics, are only to be found in the oldest drive impulses linked to elementary bodily functions whose biological bedrock is allusively referred to.

What a strange notion disavowal is! It is the sign of an *Ichspaltung* which had difficulty in cutting a path for itself between the existing *Spaltung* of Bleuler, in use since 1911 (translated in French by dissociation), which only has marginal connections, if any at all, with what Freud describes, and the introduction shortly afterwards by Melanie Klein – who nonetheless claimed to be an heir to his thought – of an altogether different sense of the same *Spaltung*. The question is complicated further if we recall that when he was bringing his work to a close, Freud widened the scope of his own *Spaltung* which, starting from the limited splitting found in fetishism, was extended to the extreme forms found in psychosis, as is the case with fragmentation. It is as if, late in the day, Freud seemed keen to make a link with the concept introduced by Bleuler. Was it not in an attempt to win over psychiatric thinking – which had to a large extent joined ranks with the master of Zurich – that the nuclear, one might even say, primal form of this process, was recognised in sexual life, as the example of fetishism goes to show? But as we read of Freud's extension to psychosis of a mechanism described originally in relation to perversion, it seems that many transitional stages have been left out.

The novelty of the situation resides in the fact that Freud discovers that infantile sexuality is not only a source of fixations in which the singular sexuality of adults is outlined, but that the elaboration of its early forms in its relation to the ego produces modes of thought, certain of them prototypical (repression–negation), others more disconcerting (disavowal–splitting), even bordering on the incomprehensible (foreclosure, rejection), which could prompt one to look for the links between these logical matrices – where unexpected relations between sexuality and the ego are formed – and the later impressive constructions produced by psychotics, of which delusions are the most striking examples, but not the only ones. Furthermore, Kleinian thought, developing along its own path, would express itself (in English, its new language by force of circumstances) in terms of 'split off' parts (of the ego, the self or of the baby, depending on the context) which henceforth have nothing to do with the initial sense of Freud, except that they show that there can be no question of explaining what repression involves, an approach which was implicitly at the origin of the introduction of splitting into the theory concerning fetishism. Nonetheless, if our speculations about the surreptitious reappearance of the Bleulerian reference in Freud's thought are accepted, they could also account for the singular fate of Melanie Klein's legacy, remodelled by Bion. His work is only intelligible if we understand how its coherence obliged him to build a 'bypass' permitting him to join up again with the Freudian road, as can be inferred from the way he uses projective identification, reinserting it within the framework of the functioning of thought processes.

There is good reason to suppose that Freud felt that in disavowal he had found a theme which was liable to lead to a considerable modification of his most solid theoretical gains. We need only think of the beginning of his unfinished article on 'Splitting of the Ego in the Process of Defence' (1940), published posthumously, in which he cannot decide if what he is about to say belongs to the domain of what is already known or whether it should be considered as something entirely new and strange.[3] This was more than ten years after the article on fetishism, whose content is nonetheless very similar. What are the reasons for this perplexity?

Between Perversion and Psychosis

In order to find out, we shall have to retrace the meanderings of Freud's thought: to differentiate between the use – which initially does not seem to have any precise intention – of a verb, *leugnen*, translated by 'disavow' or 'deny', and its later designation for a specific use. This term does not apply to the attempt to oppose the manifestation of a content carried by a movement which has surged up from within, but to the wish to ignore information arising from a perception – related to sexual difference and thus centred on the castration complex. This had already been established by the article on fetishism.[4] It is not this line of thought – because it is the safest, the least likely to be challenged – which explains Freud's hesitation, but another, less constant, more obscure, and in every respect uncertain, which explores the theory in more depth and with an increasing sense of urgency, raising many new questions.[5]

Two short references will be sufficient to identify it. They contradict each other at times but this does not exempt us from giving them our closest attention. Let us begin with the second of them – the last on this theme – set out in the final part of *An Outline of Psychoanalysis* in the chapter devoted to the relations between the psychical apparatus and the external world. There, Freud speaks of psychical splitting with reference to a case of paranoia. (It is interesting to note in passing that he makes this hypothesis after giving an account of what he has observed in a patient afflicted by delusional jealous thoughts: each attack was followed by a dream which enabled the analyst to get a clear idea of the non-delusional cause which set off the attack.[6]) On this occasion Freud uncovers, for the first time, mechanisms which link the sphere of perversion to that of psychosis. He also notes that disavowals are always incomplete. They are supplemented by an acknowledgement – without which one could not speak of real splitting – a consideration which is absent from the later Kleinian usage.

Even though the rapprochement perversion–psychosis is undeniably something new in the Freudian elaboration, the chapter is cut short and finishes with the observation that splitting is equally present in neurosis.[7] This remark suggests there is a regret, rather like when a painter corrects a primitive idea which he has had. So the feeling that Freud gives the impression of wanting to generalise the validity of the mechanism which he describes, by including the neuroses within its sphere of influence as well, does not dissipate our impression that he does not allow himself to recognise the importance of the discovery of a close and singular link, capable of uniting certain psychic mechanisms of psychosis and perversion. It seems that Freud was afraid of isolating the neuroses in this new redistribution of the cards, for what he says about disavowal in connection with them is not enough to convince us that the rapprochement in the two other cases is justified. Here again we see him swaying between the sense of having discovered a specific mechanism and that of making a simple reformulation of something very general. What is new is the identification of a specific mechanism of denial, the clinical importance of which goes far beyond its semantic importance, making it possible to imagine its relations with the more developed forms met with in psychosis, at the heart of deeper and more extensive forms of disorganisation.

A Revision Which Was Not to Be: Splitting and Disavowal in Penumbra

Since *The Ego and the Id* (1923) which succeeded in integrating the concept of the death drive into the theoretical revision of the psychical apparatus, Freud seemed open to the idea of splitting and shows a new sensibility vis-à-vis the negative in different forms. He wrote a series of articles on masochism, negation, and, later, on disavowal in fetishist splitting: sexuality, language and reality, his thinking wandering between these three poles. In fact, what needs to be emphasised in Freud's work is, first and foremost, the ego's unsuccessful defensive efforts in various contexts. The perplexity of the article of 1938 can be explained, therefore, by his doubts about the legitimacy of generalising this mode of defence; that is, I think, about the necessity, after introducing the death drive and the second topography, of making a *general revision of the notion of defence*, comparable to the one he had undertaken for anxiety, the need for which he seemed to have foreseen.[8] As usual, when what is new concerns sexuality, he is unassailed by doubt and his vision is clear. When the ego is involved, however, his interpretations are more conjectural and his progress more hesitant.

What needs to be seen clearly is that whereas, until the second topography was formulated – following the initial evaluation of the issues – Freud dealt with the neuroses, psychoses and perversions separately; as soon as he had completed *The Ego and the Id* these relatively autonomous theoretical formulations were more and more difficult to maintain due to the intricate nature of the problems they created. His thinking then bifurcated in two directions: the first was the comparison between neurosis and perversion which continued a thread which had been present from the outset, but which now somewhat relativised the enlightening equation he had made at the start, i.e., neurosis = the negative of perversion; and the second, which moved forward on much more uncertain ground because it was not the fruit of direct experience, was the comparison between neurosis and psychosis. Now this distinction, inferred retrospectively, was translated in the process of writing by a permanent entanglement of these two procedures, his thinking returning back and forth from one to the other. For if one accepts that Freud's psychoanalytic experience, where psychosis is concerned, had little chance of being deepened after 1920 since, by his own admission, he felt little inclination for treating psychotics and it became increasingly possible for him to select those he accepted for analysis, it is fair to assume that the newest line of thought arose from his apperception of the similarities between the mechanisms pertaining to psychosis and others, akin to these, which were more or less identifiable in clinical phenomena considered, nonetheless, to be neurotic. Are we to believe that this sliding of perspectives was favoured by the increasing proportion of training analyses in his practice?

I shall, however, add a rider to account for these trials and errors. Freud's extremely tentative advance into the territory of the ego, the most mysterious of all, can be explained by a link which he gave us a glimpse of although he did not pursue it further.[9] Namely, that if the idea of normality has some substance to it – and I would say that it can not be otherwise, for although norms vary, the reference to the norm is constant – it can only be linked to the ego and to not to anything else.[10] Now any consideration of the ego from an angle which aims to analyse its foundations as well as the its modes of functioning reveals the necessary character of its relation – so to speak intrinsic – to psychosis. Its relation to psychosis cannot be translated by: 'founded on a primary psychosis', nor by the allusion to a constant factor designated as 'the psychotic part of the personality', but rather as a recognition of the defensive vulnerability of the ego in view of its dependent relations vis-à-vis other instances and the constraints imposed by its contact with reality, the most important of which is the function of recognition which disavowal can put in check. It might as well be said that if we were to discover the appropriate theoretical tools, they would be more than put to the test along this risky path. *On Private Madness* was the fruit of this thinking.

The two-fold orientation of research in which neurosis is compared now to perversion, now to psychosis, constitutes the precarious, discontinuous and problematic thread of the development between perversion and psychosis, centred upon the notion of disavowal. This is what reading the articles of 1924 on 'Neurosis and Psychosis' and 'The Loss of Reality in Neurosis and Psychosis' reveals. It is reading which is both stimulating and left in suspense, containing a promise of future developments curtailed by returns to the past and a hope of overcoming contradictions which nonetheless remain unresolved.[11] In 'Neurosis and Psychosis' – the first, chronologically, of the two references to which we alluded above – Freud does not so much offer new insights as order and articulate the entities of the psychopathological field, but it is precisely at the bend in the path that something new appears. This is directly related to our subject because cases are considered where it is possible for the ego to avoid a rupture by deforming itself, by sacrificing its unity, and even by effecting a cleavage or division of itself. The idea of splitting (and of disavowal) is very present here, and yet not explicitly spelled out. And Freud adds, using a comparison which he does not take any further, that we could see the inconsistencies, eccentricities and follies of men in a similar light to their sexual perversions – thanks to which, when they are accepted, they avoid acts of repression.

There is no doubt here that his intuition goes further than its explicit form suggests. Its most powerful moment is the creation of a hypothetical field which is to the ego what perversion is to sexuality.[12] Today the evolution of psychoanalytic thought leads us to wonder if Freud's remarks do not open up a new horizon rich with possibilities. And it goes without saying that we feel less bound to the letter of these eccentricities and bizarre phenomena than to the search for what underlies, for us today, the allusion to these 'follies' which go far beyond what one might attribute to plain originality.

The Hateful Ego[13]

The ego's specific vocation still awaits clarification. Freud left it to us to define it, although he was not sure that the examples he gave were the best for grasping its most striking manifestations. From the end of the 1950s in France, all reflection on the ego was exposed to attacks designed to denigrate discussion of a subject considered as mystifying, the vehicle of a normative ideology suspected of political collusion with those in power.

There was a desire to give substance to the idea of a psychoanalysis reconciled with a psychology or psychosociology in the service of a repressive morality, the 'watch dog' of a conformism which was thought to be collaborating in maintaining the social peace necessary for the development of capitalistic turpitudes. There was some truth in the diatribes of the period and a lot of untruth, too. The little truth there was concerned the debatable value of the elaborations of American psychoanalysis led by Hartmann,[14] in which the large majority of analysts from the other side of the Atlantic recognised themselves. Was there really a danger of French psychoanalysis succumbing to this deviation which, furthermore, saw itself as orthodox? There are very few indications to this effect. Evidence of this can be found in the fact that English psychoanalysis, which was exposed to the same influence, even more so due to the common language, remained largely unconvinced, without needing for all that to cry wolf. We are therefore bound to think that the polemic very much exploited imaginary dangers to favour the diffusion of another theory and to dissimulate behind this Lacanian smokescreen other interests, i.e., the desire to dress up with chimerical virtues a rebellion whose success was supposed to be ensured by the salvation it offered to the imperilled souls of deluded psychoanalysts.[15] The denunciation of an ideology, which was above all guilty of theoretical weakness, succeeded in playing the game of the defence proclaiming a real veto on all thinking about the problematics of the ego, except under Lacan's directives. Even on this condition, there was no longer to be any question of it. The intimidation was successful. In truth, if the undertaking was discouraged, it was because it threatened the entire Lacanian theoretical construction, as the works of ex-Lacanians would later show.[16]

So we need to return to the abandoned path which leads to the ego, to its relations with the subject, to its heterogeneous constitution, and to its inevitable doubling. And to return as well to the sexualisation of the ego, acknowledged as early as 'On Narcissism: An Introduction' (1914), but thereafter minimised. I also believe that we must reflect further on its relations with the death drive, by reconsidering and re-interpreting what experience has taught us.[17]

I began to tackle the work of the negative as early as 1960, concerning myself with aspects which principally involved the ego, although at that stage I did not have sufficient experience of conducting analyses with patients who display the work of the negative in terms of a lack of well-being making them oscillate between the necessity to survive and the impossibility of facing their life aspirations. However, suicide or attempted suicide is far from being the fullest expression of the desire to die. Faced with such a challenge, the analyst's narcissism, which is subjected to very great jolts, is the most vulnerable point and, if undermined, can jeopardise confidence in the analytic process. It would be equally dangerous to count on the soothing virtues of kindness (in reality the surest means of getting rid of the most recalcitrant patients). Seduction and/or reliance on the authority which is conferred by the power the analyst is supposed to possess keeps the analysand's fundamental alienation alive for ever. But the essential thing is not that, it is simply a question of surviving.

Thwarting the Agency of the Ego

However urgent it is to get out of the impasse of a debilitating theory of the ego, it is not my purpose here to undertake this reformulation. I will simply confine myself to establishing certain points of reference. These will always be subject to later revisions but we should be on our guard against falling into past errors. We should therefore resist the complacent but reassuring tendency – especially as it is legitimised by a significant section of contemporary analysis which is inclined to disregard the difficulties which the concept of the ego raises – to make a surreptitious return to an ante-psychoanalytic academicism. This is not always immediately noticeable for it now circulates under the guise of a technical rehash in an operational style which poorly disguises its behaviourist origins (although supposed officially to be defunct). In addition to this, there is another misrepresentation of the ego which is inspired by a way of thinking claiming to be at variance with the precedent conception and to offer an alternative solution. This focuses in an almost exclusive manner on the effects of imaginary identifications but can scarcely escape the criticism that it is guilty of a complacency which, while it is in other respects reassuring, is symmetrical to the previous one, making it an accomplice of the very conception it claims to replace. Both are united in their refusal to take seriously what underlies the ego's status as an agency. This cannot be resolved easily by simply pointing out the ego's disputable and disputed authority, hoping thereby to convince everyone that the interest devoted to it is unjustified.

Furthermore, it is not by implying that the manifestation of what we call the ego is simply a fiction governing a space inhabited by mirages, that we will provide an answer to the questions raised by modes of psychical functioning which are so strange and so peculiar that it is difficult to see what else they could refer to other than the agency concerned.

It is only negatively that this reference becomes fully apparent. This is perhaps precisely because the way the ego is shaped by the defences, themselves infiltrated by what they are supposed to protect against (the drives), thwarts its status as an agency. Astonishingly, a common feature of these two conceptions is that they present an ego purged of its drives and conflict-free. Let us therefore leave this revision of the theory of the ego until later and draw instead on what we have learnt from the interpretation of transference experiences which are quite different from those we are familiar with.

It is in the very nature of the work of the negative to favour indirectly an ambiguous, sometimes contradictory, and often even paradoxical apprehension of psychical activity of a high intellectual level. But when it is oriented in a direction which primarily has the goal of opposing the elaboration of the drives, there follows, as an indirect consequence, a powerful thrust and irruption of the latter in forms which make their influence in the domain of consciousness barely recognisable. It is as if secondary thought processes were unable to establish a boundary allowing them to exist at a sufficient distance from primary processes (contact barriers, Bion), especially as the latter have been transformed by the transfiguration of the logic of hope into the logic of despair.[18] The secondary processes which are not sufficiently isolated will not be left intact by this reversal. This is to say that the task of the processes which govern the unconscious and which come to our awareness is less to represent desire than to oppose the disclosure, even indirect, of the transformation which they have undergone. I will comment on this transformation at a later point. Any hint that the 'reasons' for this transformation might be uncovered leads to a counter-offensive which endeavours to barricade all the avenues leading there in the name of a mute violence which is just as much attached to the analytic relation as it is vigilant not to subscribe to the pact of liberty which its deployment requires. This situation should not be confused with a straightforward resistance, even if highly active. For in the latter case what is blocked is simply an unconscious desire, because it is forbidden and, as such, only mobilises what opposes awareness of it. In the cases we are discussing, the blocking of psychical work combines the ordinary work of resistance with effects which relate to the transformation of desire: that is to say, the work of the negative does not simply reject its manifestation but affects the core of the manifestation itself and is no longer simply against it.

In addition to a desire, conceived of ordinarily as 'perverse', there is the panic of seeing it take on the shape of a wave which sweeps away everything standing between itself and its unlimited satisfaction – thus transferring the perversion, as if to displace and turn it against itself, onto that which decrees its prohibition. Strangely enough, this transfer onto frustration is not only opposed to satisfaction; it shifts it onto the object which we can sense behind the prohibition. Losing its anonymity, the prohibition makes the object re-emerge, not in a form which can be thought of or imagined, but with the aid of the 'embodied' sense of a constraint to grant itself as little freedom as possible. There is the intuition that what is taking place has less to do with adhering to values than to the obligation to subject oneself to an object which manifests itself more through its arbitrariness than in order to 'defend' – that is, to preserve – a precious possession, a value.

Idealness, which contrapuntally evaluates the ego, stands for unhindered, complete and total satisfaction. But while the ideal ego is conceived of as a 'purified' pleasure ego, nothing has been said about how it sometimes feels dispossessed of its objectives. The implicit all-powerfulness of such an ideally satisfied ego is transformed into an all-powerfulness capable of destroying both the cause of its frustration and the frustration itself, by means of a radical suppression, as if both were radically set aside – occasionally being challenged by the return of anxiety. To come back to authority – this is how Freud refers to the precursor of the super-ego in *Civilization and its Discontents* – it is not so much tyrannical as devoid of meaning. We can even say that any emergence of meaning would endanger it, that is, would alter the nature of its power by integrating it within a greater whole, where the will to submission, which is a reason unto itself, would be surpassed. Yet, the subject is barred from acquiring an understanding of an 'order in things' which would make sense of the prohibition, because he has not yet acquired the combined sense of his individuality and its relation to the hierarchical and differentiated distribution of object-investments, nor a sense of desires which can be interpreted according to generational and sexual differences. Whatever the circumstances, the object's absolute domination regarding its capacity to create disorganising effects, as well as the chaos caused by its moods, choices and decrees, stands out. It is the fixation to this authority which seems to be purely self-concerned, shut in on its own activity, avoiding, without appearing even to be aware of it, all consideration of the consequences and implications of its injunctions which are evoked by its 'implicit' perversion. The satisfaction which is at the root of the desire of the object's authority neither provides the meaning it requires, nor indicates a way forward towards a new transformation. It can be seen that the perversion we are speaking of is not directly sexual but is consonant with the comparison Freud made concerning the 'follies of men'.

There is no need to go into lengthy explanations to understand that the ego which originates in the collusive activity between this desire and what is supposed to restrain it in order to give it a human face, can, in turn, only inherit a 'perversion' which manifests itself by the way it deals with obstacles standing in the way of its enterprises. This is to say that the ego models itself on the identification with the agent of authority to which we have just alluded – an identification which is not limited to its prohibiting function, but is based on the absence of perspectives which goes with it. Such an omission to replace what the prohibition has banned by an offer of symbolic substitution leads the ego to carry out a similar operation on itself.

That is to say, it feels stronger for having avoided the conflict in which it is divided between a satisfaction which is always in danger of veering towards destruction (through its own movement or its reactions to the object's movements) and its cessation by means of a brake which opposes its manifestation, provoking a feeling of intolerable capitulation. It achieves this by throwing itself away, thanks to a combination of the paralysis which has gripped it with the scotoma making it blind to itself, and with which it identifies, thereby losing all lucidity with respect to its defensive strategy. It can then elude consciousness which would reveal the massively negativising character of its operations (often imperceptible, as such, due to their integration in the form of habitus), an undeniable indication of the mutation it has undergone, the revelation of which shows that its aim is to ascribe a monstrous status to man's most commonly shared aspirations in order to protect its self-idealisation which, in this case, becomes the idealisation of its capacities for denial. In point of fact the monstrous character is not the direct expression of the drive pole of the psyche but the image that this acquires when, for one reason or another, it is thwarted. What is most paradoxical here is that the very freedom that it is given to express itself may sometimes become the most exacerbated form of its annoyance due to the simple fact of having to take the object's existence into account. An opportunity of this kind splits the drive process (*pulsionnalité*) off from the ego, obliging one to declare that it is radically alien to it, whereas one would have thought the ego capable of acting as its spokesman, so much are the circumstances and objectives pursued common to both. We can see clearly to what extent this drive process is unintegrated and deprived of resources in the course of the displacement, thus burdening alternatively the ego and the object with its hate whenever they appear to expect something unpredictable from it or require it to modify its demands or to defer them. The worst thing is having to respond to the manifestations – which are symmetrically imperious but in a completely different way – produced by the object's drives and their integration with reality, together forming a bloc of painful adversity.

All this is by no means easy to understand. I am alluding to the way in which the prohibition carries out the negativisation of desire which aims less to protect the latter than to deny its existence as desire, only being able to conceive of it as the clastic effect which its satisfaction would involve well beyond (or short of?) itself, like an explosion causing a collapse to which the ego would succumb. Such a transformation is accompanied by the object's substitution as an object of desire, or even as an investment centreing attraction on it with the aim of approaching the source of an expected happiness, or as a complementarity carrying the hope of contact with it through the object of the drive. The latter is different from the precedent object in that it can scarcely be represented; it exercises an imperious solicitation without giving rise to an idea of well-being which can be rediscovered in any other way than by eliminating tension. The consequence of the threatening confusion between the object and the drive is that the satisfaction of the drive gives rise, not so much to an introjection, as to a violent excorporation which attacks the ego, engulfed by the drive, as well as the object which is swallowed and spat out simultaneously.

What is involved here is not a kind of psychical primitivism, but rather should be thought of as the consequence of an intense compression of drive violence, unchannelled by the paths of desire, generating itself at a time marked by the equipollence between the exhaustion of the satisfaction and the catastrophe of the object's loss. The latter is now felt to be irremediably inaccessible and impossible to find again because it is left to its own desire which has no choice but to reject the subject in order to be free of it. Because there are no structures of desire available which, thanks to the deployment of fantasies, make it possible to offer the psyche the hope of future encounters, everything appears to be totally consumed at each imagined encounter. It is now that the experience of satisfaction is transformed, turning, as Freud said, into an experience of pain. Classically, this comes about by means of the hostile mnemonic image, linked with the impossibility of satisfaction. In this case, on the contrary, it is related to a satisfaction which has indeed occurred. The registered trace of that experience above all contains the danger of a kind of psychic earthquake occurring, involving a satisfaction in the shape of the self-absorption of tension accompanying a disorganisation which leaves no possibility for the earlier state to be recovered, an emptying of the ego during the easing of tension following the consumption of the vanishing object, and the putting out of reach of the structures of desire preventing the psyche from benefiting them. Normally, they form a reserve for the primary processes to draw on when it becomes necessary to mobilise the hope of reviving what has been, and what is capable of being reanimated. Everything outside consciousness which aspires, hopes and constructs both its lack and what is supposed to fulfil it at the same time, i.e., what we call unconscious fantasy, is now in scattered bits and is scarcely fit to serve the pleasure principle later on. This is not the functioning we expected to find behind the fear raised by the vicissitudes of satisfaction we were speaking about earlier. The danger lies rather with the drive base which disengages itself and acts on its own account, suspending all connection with the subject's historicity and his difference from the object. In other words, thanks to the fantasy's potential or real representability (*figurabilité*), it is deprived of its capacity to seduce the psyche and to solicit its appetite for representative anticipation in order to awaken in it the charm of the nourishing diversion of illusion. It is precisely because of the real threat of this vicissitude, at a time when any possibility of imaginary substitution may be lacking, thereby leaving the psyche completely exposed to the drives, that measures are taken to ward off the appearance of desire, behind which the emissaries of the drive cyclone emerge. This will require the activation of anti-investments with a view to a remission of pleasure in which the subject 'runs for his life' – in every sense of the expression – in the name of this transvaluation whose effects will extend to turning the child's so-called primal perversion into a *diversion of the functions of the ego*. The latter will have paid the price of abandoning drive aims involving another person's participation, through the 'colouring' of its defences by the drives[19] secretly hidden from the services they are supposed to provide.

The Colouring of the Defences by the Drives

What is meant when we speak of the ego defences being coloured by the drives? Three characteristics may be noted. First, the *transfer of force* which underlies the fulfilment of a drive aim. That is, the ego benefits from a diversion stemming from an affluence of destructive drives deflected from their aim, conferring it with an energy for refusal just when one expected to see it actively mobilising its capacities, with the aim of achieving pleasure by allying itself with the drives. Secondly, the *reversal of aim* which henceforth links the ego's enrichment, not with what it experiences through the satisfactions offered to it, or which it sets out to take advantage of, but with the way in which it manages to withdraw, not by an act of its will or as a result of a deliberate decision, but through a spontaneous circumvention. The avoidance which is so characteristic of phobia inevitably comes to mind here. Such a comparison is deceptive, for if one had to make use of an analogy, the existing mechanisms could only correspond to a mode of action combining phobic avoidance with the obsessional's internal counter-investment, with the difference that, in this case, all trace of the displacement onto either an object or a phobogenic situation, or onto an 'obsessive' thought or content, would have disappeared, leaving simply the necessity to remain unaware of what must not be identified, even in a displaced form, by means of a constant vigilance which is insensible to its own wakefulness and unaware that it is involved in a struggle. What is going on within the psyche must not be recognisable either by the displaced content of a thought, or as a mode of activity of an ego which is becoming aware – the centre of the psychic event lies within it – that it is involved in what is happening. An automatic precautionary measure of distancing or brushing aside (*écartement*) is observed. This differs considerably from the displacement which proposes another link, enriching the chain of representations with new associations which are added to those which existed prior to its intervention, overlaying rather than replacing them; whereas here the gap effaces the trace of the link which governs the constitution of meaning while at the same time pursuing its course. The analyst lets himself be guided by the dynamism which reflects the progression of the discursive process in which he is tempted to see an analogical figure of the quest, admittedly more hazardous, and thus subject to errancy, of desire in search of its object. Here, the distancing appears to imitate this errancy, with the sole difference that it is driven by the tendency to avert the encounter with what is being pursued. This is a procedure which is more involuted than evolved, silently sustained on the outside as on the inside, managing at the same time to avoid revealing itself through its action, hiding that in the ego which ensures its salvation by denying itself in this way. It is clear that it is the same action which prevents the onset of the process which could lead to satisfaction (involving its object) and which signifies, by this very hindrance, the negative intention motivating it. In other words, the super-ego no longer exists except in the form of tensions exerted on the ego, tensions which cannot easily be differentiated from those generated by the id. Finally, we come to the last aspect of this drive investment, *the replacement of the orientations of psychical activity in the contradiction between the two principles (pleasure–unpleasure and reality)*, by means which are already at its disposal or must be acquired. This principal contradictory pair is replaced here by a *system of beliefs* intended to provide an infrastructure for the ego's rationalisations with the sole aim of averting possible catastrophes.

It may not be easy to see how this situation differs from ordinary cases. Let us try and clarify things. When Freud tries to illustrate what underlies the concept of repression, he defines its action in terms of a combination of flight and condemnation. And he undoubtedly implies that this reflex of setting aside is necessary for the organisation of the ego's structure. Later, when he discovered that the ego was itself drive-invested, he understood that it was necessary to refine the existing idea of its functioning, but the idea of repression averting something remains valid. When he describes – in a veiled way – foreclosure (or rejection), he implies the existence of mechanisms translating an internal *abolition* which goes hand in hand with the return of what is foreclosed by the path of the real (*le réel*). But there would be no return if it were not for a lack of internal symbolisation, as Lacan maintains, and also a displacement outwards of this mobilising power which returns to its place of origin, without being in the slightest bit aware that it belongs to the psyche (in contradistinction to what happens in phobia or obsession and even in conversion, where psychical exclusion nevertheless remains contained within the perimeter of the individual).

The case of splitting cannot be linked with either of the two precedent eventualities; nor can it be understood either in terms of internal distancing or in terms of external exclusion. Its originality lies in the maintenance of a contradictory co-existence, both acknowledged and denied, whose mode of negation, in contradistinction to the other two, is only sustained by an intimate and secret belief which obliges it to turn away from drive satisfaction. In the latter, object, alterity and coming-out-of-oneself converge towards the same aim, experiencing a pleasure which, owing to the loosening of the ego's links with its usual functions, sees the phantom of an unpredictable collapse rise up before it. Belief, in this case, is the effect of the ego being invested by the drive for negativising purposes which are intended to destroy the aspiration of psychical activity to pursue its adventure of testing itself against whatever refuses to be confined within its boundaries. It achieves the perfect crime; that is, of remaining within the jurisdiction where the real (*le réel*), the other and the ego are acknowledged to be separate, while deep down inside preserving the possibility of covering up this recognition with a creation (the fetish, in the initial example) which is not so much designed to serve as a consolation or even to present itself as being of greater benefit to the ego as to guarantee the triumph of the alternative which negation offers. This is because negation conceals its existence from itself, taking cover behind the promotion, the election and the very elevation of a portion of reality which is removed from the picture of which it is a part, and is detached from the links which bind it with elements of the whole to which it belonged, setting itself up in an affirmation of its unquestionable singularity. In this case the positive is, strictly speaking, neither the contrary of the negative nor even the inverted image of it, nor again the being which thwarts nothingness. Through the subjective projection by which it comes into existence, the positive is, by the way it appears, and by the peculiar and absurd value it acquires, what gives the illusion of accomplishing the deed which makes the negative inexistent (castration in the initial example). A feat of this order only becomes intelligible in relation to the hallucinatory wish-fulfilment which enables us to infer that the latter has no need either to realise itself or to hallucinate itself (internal exigencies of the model on which it is based), or to be dominated by perception in order to be recognised as the basis of psychical reality which is stronger than any ego and never under the subject's control. The ultimate aim in establishing this belief is to maintain the ego's *méconnaissance* of itself, as an investing activity, moved by the drive process devoted to desire and to its transformations.

On the Need for Recourse to the Subject

Let us begin with Freud's observation which establishes an elliptical parallel between the ego's distortions and perversion. Do our descriptions allow us to speak of a category which has not been described, i.e., ego perversion? The latter already exists and was the basis of the first ideas on narcissism. Later descriptions of 'narcissistic perversion' do not seem to match up with these. So here is a category of phenomena we do not know how to characterise other than by comparing it with the role played by perversion in sexuality, whose metapsychology is very difficult to conceive of except in terms of a certain perversion of the tasks which the ego is supposed to carry out. What can be set against sexuality or in opposition to it? It is characterised by its relation to the body, to pleasure, to its transformations and to the alterity necessary for its accomplishment. The field of the ego which is equivalent to it cannot, however, be determined so precisely. To give reality a position equivalent to that occupied by sexuality would be to wrongly restrict its status as an agency. The ego might be envisaged in terms of the constraints which Freud recognised in its dependent relations with its masters (id, super-ego, reality), but that would not give us a clear enough idea of its intrinsic nature. I will therefore assume that the ego should be thought of as being dominated by the search for an equilibrium which is more optimal than maximal, that is, open to disequilibrium. This is the fundamental mode of its activity as a source of internal and external transformations coming within the jurisdiction of the judgement which relates them respectively to the modalities governing the internal and external worlds by means of interpretation. So its situation relative to the object enables it to gather around itself the components distinguished by the reference to other agencies and to reality. Finally, we cannot overlook the contradiction which characterises it, noted by Jean Laplanche, of being alternately considered as part of the psychical apparatus and yet also as the representative of its empirical totality.

In my opinion, this is what makes recourse to the concept of the subject inevitable, which I intend to include here under the concept of the psychical apparatus. If the ego can play these two roles as a part and a representative of the totality, it is necessary to redefine its relations to the subject as well as those which bind it to the conceptual whole to which the empirical totality refers. Whereas the ego as an empirical totality carries out a temporary global unification, the subject – in the psychoanalytic sense – can only reflect its divisions, its heterogeneousness, its contradictory designs, and particularly the diverse forms of the links which connect its constituent parts. And this should not be confused with what Freud designated as the ego's dependent relations. For it is one thing to point out the ego's dependence on the id and quite another to indicate in what way the id contains the seeds of subjectivity. In the ego's logic, dependence leads to compromises; in the subject's logic it leads to contradictions which can, moreover, give rise to 'real' transformations in the ego, as observable findings at the level of defence mechanisms show.

It can be seen that giving such a subject properties of this kind is enough to indicate the originality of its position in psychoanalysis. We have already looked at the complex relations between masochism and narcissism in cases of analytic failure. If we come back now to the modalities of this alliance or alloyment, it could be said that the variations of dominance between one or the other of these two terms can be interpreted as a stable fluctuation (in its very instability). Or again, that the stability is due to the refusal to let oneself be completely gripped by either one of the two eventualities – masochism or narcissism – the one dominated by the prevalence of the object, the other by the prevalence of the ego. In fact, this distinction is not entirely satisfying for it will be seen that the *objectal* perspective plays a fundamental role in our assessment of narcissism. It might therefore be preferable to reformulate things and to speak, where masochism is concerned, of the object and of identification with the object as a pole for appeasing the drives. In the case of narcissism, however, one is much nearer the pole which seeks the reasons for its variations within the ego itself, regarding the constraints imposed by its *objectal* ties and the withdrawal they provoke. The very meaning of the appeasement and of the way in which the ego can be affected is called into question by the work of the negative. Returning then to the idea of the trauma-object, of the object as a 'trouble-maker' causing excitation, I would want to add the idea that the object represents hazardous alterity owing to its nature as a desiring object and, as such, it exposes the subject to its variations.

No conception of the ego is worth its salt which overlooks the fact that not everything which occurs in it can be understood by psychoanalytic thinking – unless it underlines the paradox that we have to deal with a double stumbling-block: on the one hand, it is in the nature of such an ego to be coloured by the drives and on the other, this colouring goes hand in hand with its being unconscious of its defences.

Inhibitions, Symptoms and Anxiety

We should make it clear that the 'colouring' in question concerns the ego's own love for itself, whereas the colouring of the defences by the drives, which we were just referring to, is connected with the destructive drives. By their act of refusal, the defences, which are supposed to foresee the effects of these drives, themselves acquire a potential for nihilation which is akin to that which they are erected against.

There are various ways in which the ego is coloured by the drives. The least important of them concerns its relation to the drives of self-preservation, the imprecise theoretical status of which must nevertheless include both their constitutive role and the possible deviation of their aims in certain extreme situations (in psychosomatic syndromes, for example). Contrary to notions which are increasingly widespread, let us remember that narcissism, the ego's principal characteristic, is not opposed to the drives but, being subject to their activity, represents one of their destinies. Finally, in addition to these two contingents, self-preservation and narcissism, there exists a third sector of the colouring of the ego by the drives which Freud called 'erotisation'. This type of sexualisation must not be confused with the sexualisation of the drives of self-preservation at work in narcissism. Narcissism does not have the monopoly on the sexual processes affecting the ego. It is perhaps when narcissism is engaged principally in conflictualising its positive and negative sides that sexuality meets with the conditions which are favourable for infiltrating the ego. The converse of this, i.e., the primitive invasion of the ego by sexuality provoking a secondary reaction of narcissism revealing its difficulty in determining between its positive and negative aspects, can also arise, but this time it is more likely to be through the object's mediation (sexual trauma which exceeds the capacities of the constitutive seduction to absorb – on this specific point I am in agreement with the ideas put forward by Jean Laplanche).

Be that as it may, Freud's proposition is to consider that an erotisation of this kind gives rise to three possibilities: anxiety, symptoms and inhibitions, the latter being understood as a *restriction of an ego-function* brought into operation to avoid a conflict. It would be interesting to clarify the nature of such avoidance. Are we dealing with an identical procedure to that which is met with in phobia? I would not bet on it because if the answer involves the ego itself, obliging it to restrict itself, it means there is a possibility that the ego's conflict with the other agencies cannot be resolved by repression alone. There is some reason to think that the result of inhibition, far from being confined to a mere restriction, can in certain cases be invasive, even to the point of compromising the vital functions of self-preservation (as is the case with anorexia, for example). It may be that the erotisation of the ego, which is expressed here in an extraordinarily rigid and stereotyped way, occurs at the level of a drive functioning operating in the least differentiated mode.

After 1926 the triptych: inhibition, symptoms, and anxiety leaves unexplored the road opened up by the idea of the ego's restriction. Although it raises some problems concerning its connections with certain symptoms (phobic, obsessional, depressive), it nonetheless possesses a specific tonality which extends beyond the sphere of influence of neurotic symptoms. It is interesting to consider the pair drive–inhibition for, as far as the first term is concerned, more often than not, we are in fact dealing with a gradient 'drive–erotisation' with a variable potential which we should also evaluate in terms of the register objectalisation–disobjectalisation. This gradient can slide from the most patent erotisation – enabling us to infer the displacement which has been carried out onto the functions which are less suspected of collusion with sexual desires, whose link with the censor is clearly visible – to a sort of uncoercible energy in which the erotic dimension has given way to a disqualified internal constraint leaving its contents with no other alternative but to empty themselves inter-mittently through secondary paths of discharge (crying, alcoholism, bulimia, smoking, addictive sexuality, compulsive and sterile work), seeking relief which, even when it occurs, is very ephemeral. We may suspect that behind this 'neutralising' degradation there is an effect of disobjectalisation. Its link with inhibition is masked by an outward activity which puts us off the track.

As for the other registers of symptoms and anxiety, I do not intend to dwell on them here because our main concern is the ego. With regard to symptoms I would, however, like to emphasise the forms of encystment and of hemming-in which are only sustained thanks to the maintenance of the general equilibrium: intrapsychic and intersubjective. The efficiency of these defence mechanisms is very relative, for if the equilibrium is challenged at all, it results in an onslaught of worsening symptoms, at an alarming speed, similar to a traumatic neurosis in which there is a subterranean war. What is being tested here is the necessity, which I have stressed elsewhere,[20] for the ego to be able to draw up frontiers which are both firm and flexible. This apparently phe-nomenological formulation simply aims to accentuate the ego's capacity for investment and the constant work of transformation to which it is subjected. However valuable the 'frontier' image may be, what is certain is that the subject, who tells of his tormented state faced with his incapacity to express himself, feels intense anxiety at being dispossessed. Anxiety of being dispos-sessed can come as a surprise, mostly passing unnoticed, for everything which is expressed leaves, as a result, the domain where the sense of belonging exists, and when what has been said is repeated by the analyst, its attribution is changed in the patient's eyes. When it is returned in the form of an interpre-tation it is, as it were, despoiled property. It is then no longer seen as originating from oneself and is experienced as something extraneous, coming from the outside. In other words, it is not so much that the communication is trans-mitted as that it appears retrospectively to have been foreclosed as soon as it was uttered. The interpretation is thus received as the analyst's unconscious projection, and as such is incomprehensible, whereas it originated in the hidden recesses of the patient's conscious mind. It is simply the fact that this has become part of the analyst's discourse which dispossesses the analysand of his own words and alienates them in the new forms in which they return, as he listens to the analyst's understanding of what they are thought to refer to. It may be that giving expression to the thoughts out loud is enough to anticipate, in a form which is more of a virtuality than an actual discourse, their potential dangerousness owing to the flooding of imagery which has to be warded off urgently with scorched earth tactics. It is at this point that the image of the void associated with dispossession is combined with the feeling that things are getting out of hand in the face of such extremely condensed imaginary content. What is occurring enables us initially to recognise the double impact of the anxieties of separation and intrusion and the concurrence of *objectal* and narcissistic ties. The patient's communication makes it possible to give meaning to the modalities of the introjective and projective processes which constitute the other major type of operations, complementing those of the work of the negative. The differentiation between interior and exterior paves the way for elaborations on the positive and the negative, freed from modes of expression which are bound up with bodily functions and call for a higher level of integration. Occasionally, the existence of psychic zones can be observed in which this differentiation has occurred unsatisfactorily, constituting delusional recesses whose content is half way between popular beliefs and themes belonging to pathology. This formation of isolates does not always enable us to appreciate how impossible to assimilate and potentially threatening they are. They are rather like some Erinyes who have little confidence in the promises that have been made in order to obtain their transformation into Eumenides and who, having lost their power to govern the world, retreat to isolated places, pretending they have disappeared only to reappear at the most unpredictable moments, when their claim is awakened by the echo of some wrong-doing by which they feel slighted. Such a state of affairs is incompatible with the deployment of the ego's capacities; worse still, this seismic activation sometimes claims to be in the service of the ego in order to defend it against the snubbing it suffers. In fact the ego is caught between two fronts: that of the drives – often ignored as such and disguised as defences, as is sometimes the case in narcissism – and that of the object, too often hesitant, if not dissimulated. Now, of these two elements, the second is considered to be the most dangerous, if only because its drives have to be reckoned with.

Castration, the Oedipus Complex and their Relations

As Freud rightly observed, none of all this succeeds in warding off anxiety ... nor depression, I would want to add today. For they both alternate constantly. Either the ego finds itself threatened by drive satisfactions which have not been mediatised by purposive representation, their realisation resulting in the capacity for representation being overwhelmed, for the main part; or it succumbs to the crushing sense of guilt which has less to do with its drive aims (which are said to be bad, harmful, or forbidden, depending on the circumstances) than with lightning flashes which overwhelm it intermittently when it suddenly realises the extent of the threat of the reciprocal collapse of the object and the ego during an encounter burdened by the contentious nature of their unresolved conflicts. This is probably the repetition of a catastrophe which Winnicott rightly believed had not occurred but was potentially always liable to occur. There was not even any hope of resolving it by getting rid of its potential for conflict.

Kernberg has stressed the confusion between genital and pregenital aims. That is right. I feel bound to add, though, that this frequent excess of pregenital drives cannot be explained by a simple fixation or a spontaneous regressive capacity. There are two causes which set it off: first, the narcissistic wound, which I think is non-specific, welling up in connection with anything and everything and which, I think, is very often the result of what I would call the conversion of an *objectal* conflict into a narcissistic wound, with the aim of denying it. Secondly, the genital threat which calls for a reconsideration of the entire economic, topographical and dynamic equilibrium due to the existence of an object who is different. It is the conjunction of sexuality–love which gives this situation its specific character. Becoming the object of the other's desire, which is the perfectly normal goal of ordinary relations, constitutes the major danger. Is it the potential loss of love which is anticipated? That is the answer given in cheap novels. 'No, it's impossible, I don't want to suffer.' The real reason is the fear of an irreversible, destructive catastrophe, mutually damaging for the object and the ego, due to their confusion in what I shall call the trauma of their encounter. It is not the collusion between their desires which is in question here but the confusion between the mobilisation of the drives in search of long-awaited satisfaction and the actual possibility of giving free rein to vengeance whose main offence is to have suffered the effects of the non-coincidence of the subject's and object's desire. It is not the threat of separation or of loss which is the agent of the negative attitude towards love but the sense that there is a danger of an annihilating negation of everything which has been acquired and that the best of what has been, as well as everything else, can be made to disappear for ever, with the aim of warding off the worst. Genitality is threatening because it involves the risk of negativising the active wish for the fusion of subject and object, which is the purpose and sign of the paroxysm of genital love. How are we to understand the central, underlying issue? Is there any room in Freudian theory for a reference other than that of castration? The answer is far from clear in spite of forty years of debate.

It is well-known that the ideational strength of the concept of castration resides in its polysemic value bringing together the threat to bodily integrity, the punishment related to the transgressive search for pleasure with the incestuous object, the saturation of a potentially infinite relation with alterity and the closure of a dimension of symbolic substitution for a lack. This set of ideas is completed by the metaphorical power of the concept which implicitly opens up ways of relating to death which are unknown to the unconscious. It is nonetheless true that while, theoretically, castration remains an irreplaceable operator, the various and poorly structured forms it sometimes acquires raise the question of its relations to the manifestations of the complex of the same name, where its presence can be fairly clearly identified. There is no doubt that we cannot be satisfied with a conception comprising different layers in which the concept of castration crowns the edifice of limitations threatening psychical organisation, the foundations of which are represented by fears of annihilation or collapse which are thought to be incomparable with the risks, regarded as relatively minor, which sexuality runs with castration anxiety. There is no time here to discuss in detail a problem which would involve the study of diachrony in psychoanalysis as well as the intergenerational overlapping of complex organisations. I shall therefore restrict myself to offering pointers, forged by human psychic experience, based on anthropological[21] arguments linked to the difference between the sexes and the generations. Thus the value of castration lies less in the revelation of the ups-and-downs which mark the emergence of the complex from its latency than in the demonstration, in non-neurotic structures, of masking thanks to which its revelation can be kept at a distance and delayed. This is so even when these structures which hold it captive reduce it to silence or render it unrecognisable. For while it is natural to see the early fixations or the more global regressions affecting the ego as responsible, none of these clinical descriptions – the authenticity and partic-ularities of which give them their own validity on a clinical level which no one questions – convince me that they would find in themselves their own *raisons d'être* which would be very different from those of the Oedipus complex. On the contrary, I believe that these clinical pictures which impress us by their rigidity and by the limitations which they impose on those who suffer from them, deserve to be viewed as a system of fortifications, permanently in place and periodically renewed, against the possibility – which must always be kept as far away as possible – of seeing a real oedipal organisation appear in the psyche which, in the last analysis, is considered to be the supreme danger. This danger must be interpreted and herein lies the misunderstanding. It is not the danger which accompanies the sanctioning of oedipal desires, i.e., castration, but the danger arising from the accession of the Oedipus complex, i.e., the rupture of the relation with the primary object and the subject's exclusion through recognition of the parental link. This does not occur through the primal scene alone but quite openly through the perception of discreet signs which show that they have their own separate life. The object had become something of a danger due to its separate existence exposing the subject to the sufferings caused by the non-coincidence of desires. Now there is something worse, i.e., the secret collusion of the desires of the two parental objects, even though their relations show the most obvious signs of radical discord. They agree to disagree. The question remains: is it the nucleus which has secreted the interferences or, should we consider, on the contrary, that the nucleus only reveals a sediment, when the rest has more or less been dissolved by a favourable evolution – which serves to remind us that we shall never achieve a state of transparency or innocence. We shall have to think in a more 'complex' way about how the various structuring processes which overlay the latent Oedipus are produced. This does not happen by chance, nor in accordance with the actual configurations of the period in which they are organised, that is, at a time clearly prior to any recognisable form of the Oedipus, but in a way which only becomes intelligible when it is related to its future accession where what matters is to prevent the stages which precede it from leading to its appearance. This is another aspect of the fecundity of the negative. What takes place only does so within a context of negativisation which is not only defined in relation to what is, but in relation to what, because it exists, can only be understood in the light of a future which has not yet occurred, and, which is never really recognisable in what is but only allusively in its potential for prefiguration. It is as if one were to build a labyrinth in which, at every turning, there would be a sign indicating the path to follow for the exit which had been systematically erased in order to indicate the opposite direction, which would lead one to other signposts also pointing the wrong way, leading one even further from the goal. The image of an anarchic psyche, resulting from such a development, apparently resembling the various fixations of the libido's evolution, should be envisaged behind the deceptive appearances from the angle of an oedipal vectorisation. The latter is never perceptible as such because it would only be brought into play in order to accomplish its negativisation, so that one is always evoking it without ever finding it; not because it does not exist, but because we can never see more than its outline. Of course, I can already anticipate the question: 'Who does that and why?' I would have preferred each person to find his own answer. But since it is necessary to justify what one advances, I shall put it like this: 'An unequal couple in which both parties are unaware of the reasons why this situation suits them. What is certain is that in the end both of them find the situation disturbing in the light of their original intentions.'

The Implications of Dependence

With regard to the work of the negative of the ego, an examination of its relations with the object allows us to verify Winnicott's ideas on the central role played by dependence and the struggle against dependence. But this is only an intermediary level which we will come back to later; dependence in this case being the deployment of the 'external' aspect of a certain type of conflictual situation between the drive and the ego. In the end, this question is no longer about independence and autonomy, which is more demanded than really sought after, whereas the three forms of segregation which adults experience: psychosis (confinement in a psychiatric hospital), somatic illness (electing to live in a general hospital), and delinquency (barricaded behind the prison gates),[22] may be regarded as general orientations rather than as actual realities. These capitulations are the most tragic, but they are far from being the only ones or the most common. They are above all useful for defining the different scenarios to show how far the work of the negative can extend. But it is as if the ego were betraying itself, perceiving itself too late, on the other side of a frontier which it is trying to cross in both directions, until one day unpredictably, it is obliged to recognise where it has to stay put, the way back being closed off for a greater or lesser length of time. It is not that the means do not exist to make it return across the border to where it came from, but rather that the compulsion to repeat seems to have a magnetic attraction which is stronger than the pleasure of living, the latter requiring that other people be taken into consideration. It may seem excessive to have to think about these extreme situations in order to understand what the negative involves. There is no getting round it even when the main subject of reflection concerns the ego's structures which do not fall within any of these three categories and can only be defined in relation to them.

We have been unable to refrain from interpreting these ego limitations as a consequence of the demands made on it by the so-called 'cruel' super-ego. The super-ego is not responsible alone for this devastation. It is undoubtedly necessary to take into account the ego ideal as well, but that does not exhaust the question either. This implicit reminder of the irremissible nature of narcissism perhaps gives us the sense that we are drawing near to our goal.

It is often difficult to understand clearly how the agencies protecting moral standards, as we see them at work in adulthood, function – just as it is difficult to understand the role they are assumed to have played in childhood, there being few remaining signs of the inhibiting effect which they may have had on the ego's development with the exception of the neuroses. It is as if the adult psychic structure – that is, what may be conjectured about it, including the unconscious – were cut off from its infantile sources. Nothing in personal recollections or in the recollections of parents has made it possible to foresee, in most cases, the grave consequences for later development. I suggest that it is the subject's choices of love objects which expose him brutally to affective fluctuations which often prove to be cataclysmic.

We enter the world which others call pathological by different means. Through depression – that goes without saying – but also through disappointment, when the ego is overwhelmed by situations which are highly libidinally charged and extremely symbolic, as well as through insurrection, more or less acted out, which is motivated by a desire to be free of an inner constraint which, even if one is in a position to identify its agents in a general way (family, childhood, current conflicting circumstances, personal achievements which leave behind them a sense of lack or of shortcomings etc.), remains oppressively opaque, driving one to look for its origins in anxiety which is sometimes explicit but more often unidentified. This anxiety, however, spares itself such painful awareness by wholeheartedly adopting ready-made systems of rationalisation. More often than not, this is expressed by a significant arrest, giving the impression that the future has closed down just when the acquisition of independence ought to allow a space to open up infinitely before one; a space which is often indistinct, but without immediate boundaries, even if the future looks far from rosy and is not clearly traced out.

In fact all of this combines to give the impression that *time is not passing as it should* ... The reason for this is not always identifiable or manifested consciously. When it declares itself, considerable damage has already been done which it will take a long time to repair. There is a feeling of uncertainty and precariousness concerning the nature of the attachments with people one is close to; attachments which cannot simply be described as conflictual and which are marked by the dereliction of the voice crying in the desert, or are broken off even before they have had time to develop because the mould in which the new experience is supposed to be cast remains imprisoned by past conflicts which repression has not succeeded in silencing. What is at stake in all cases is the investment of alterity, always irritating, always disappointing, always threatening, always, in the end, *a burden to love*, whereas the other person has been chosen in such a way that he cannot arouse love or be loved unless he ceases to love himself.

All the forms of the work of the negative marked by inhibition and dependence see an increase in the potential for insidious undermining processes, hints of mistrust, manoeuvres aimed at frustrating personal undertakings, *proportional to the subjective involvement* they require. An insurmountable wall seems to prevent any kind of project from being realised in spite of the benefits which it would bring. Self-depreciation, self-abasement, allegations of inferiority are used to explain the disappointment which is frequently experienced following any action which requires a personal investment, whatever the outcome of it is. Disappointment makes one regret the action, whereas before it occurred a desert of solitude exerted its sway over the psyche while the subject desperately hoped for something to happen – sometimes anything at all – which would put an end to it. And if at first one is tempted to ascribe these lamentations to masochism, one would do well to try and find out what is hidden behind this label. It would be better to think in terms of a seduction exercised over the internal object designed to show allegiance which is even prepared to accept self-effacement, provided the attachment remains and at the same time covers up, without leaving any evidence of it, every slightest fragment of identifiable drive activity. Such reasoning – which is based on the only grounds it considers valid – strives to stop up all the holes through which it might betray itself. It does this in various ways: by concealing its implicit accusation of an object which is assumed to demand this self-anulling recognition without even having to ask for it; by denouncing the purely narcissistic aim, only concerned for its own glory, which is ascribed to the object; by showing cunning in not challenging – except in purely conventional forms (a concession to selective reality testing) – the fallacy of the object's so-called all-powerfulness, preventing the idea that this idol might only be made of clay from being disclosed, a possibility which is feared even more than the personal sacrifices made on its behalf, thereby ensuring the preservation of the object's 'secret' which has been 'glimpsed', but concerning which it is always important to give the impression that one has neither seen it nor knows anything about it; and finally, by 'discharging', as Laplanche would say, an avidity for power which never manages to organise itself as sadism, except in cases where it can make use of an eventual phallic issue (which is then compensated for by castration anxiety). In a girl this might express itself by penis envy, which aims at an impossible rivalry with the father, in as far as he is not so much a phallophor, the representative of the law, as someone who supplies the mother with children. It is in this respect that his own presence is hurtful in as far as it is itself a sign of her incapacity to feel she has value in the mother's eyes (it is immaterial that she herself devalues the father on occasions), for in any case the child who is there, in person, is indeed the proof that something is going on between the parents which goes quite beyond his or her own control. While this last characteristic is acknowledged, the reason for it is hidden. Once we have uncovered all these aspects, we are in possession of the most intimate image which the ego gives of itself. It would be tempting to say that everything which has already been said on this subject and which is the outcome of the object relationship in 'mundane' conditions (in the philosophical sense), needs to be reconsidered. Not that it is enough to shift from relations to external objects to relations with internal objects. While our description is at times based on events, or ways of feeling, reacting and living with others, it is very much about the way we apprehend them, from the perspective of the inner world. (How could it be otherwise in analysis?) At moments which are often unforeseeable, certain figures appear furtively, giving the analyst the impression that they are the key to what lies beneath the patient's complaints that he is suffering. What we see is an ego (without) skin (Anzieu) always in danger of emptying itself, suffering from the impossibility of putting its stamp on the other, that is, of making him admit that he is not what he seems to be, and of impressing him (literally speaking) by leaving a trace of the way it sees itself as being the object's last line of defence and as having a vital hold over its object which cannot be challenged – that is, analysed in the name of the defence which serves as a cover for the unconscious. It is as if the unmasking of this other conscious ego had already involved so much effort that it could not let go of this figure by itself. Strangely enough, the fear is not of what one might discover about the unconscious, but of the possibility that the conscious 'public' ego, as the subject thinks it appears to others, might be authenticated. This ego with a false bottom is the very opposite of the idea one may have of the relations between the conscious and the unconscious. For this way of neg-ativising the self-image, which can only be defined in terms of insufficiency and lack, will go to any length to ignore the fact that by ratifying the so-called diktat of the super-ego, one subscribes to it simply to monopolise the object which is at its source and to assure it that one is simply speaking through its voice. Such a manoeuvre serves to block off the manifestations of the drive process which is always afraid to express itself without mediation and, as such, is liable to endanger the self-idealisation which appears behind the masochis-tic allegations. A system of elaborate rationalisations strives to isolate rather than repress drive life. To be more precise, the sexuality which escapes repression is subject to conditions designed to show that it is not so much rejected by the subject as by life which usually results in creating a state of privation giving rise periodically to reversals in the shape of violent drive motions, detached from significant objects. It is not so much a matter of component drives, as one might think, as of sexuality which is not lacking a genital dimension but seems only to be able to express itself towards indifferent, conjunctural, insignificant objects. Or, if they are significant, it can only express itself in a way which makes their expression insignificant by taking it out of any kind of context which could have meaning for their object and which gives the sat-isfaction sought after a note of urgent necessity and determination to push the experience towards a resolution which is as radical as possible. This means that in this case *jouissance* coincides with its own exhaustion. When the objectali-sation has not been sacrificed, we can observe that the affects accompanying it combine an activation of the drives with a total submission to the object, struggling obstinately to get it to admit that it has no other reasons for existing than to fit in with the subject's fantasy, thereby hoping to model it on what the latter imagines to be an ideal primary object, whereas the said object has been chosen precisely in order to repeat the environmental deficiencies of the infant. In any case, the libido can only appear on the psychic stage when its manifestations are related to their unconscious sources, in the form of a brute, savage, unbridled appetite, rendered ferocious by the absence of any outlet in the world of others, inadmissible as such in the chains of the various repre-sentative systems, only offering highly insufficient satisfactions in the activities onto which they have been displaced. It is only too easy to interpret these aspects as stemming directly from unelaborated fixations whose expression should be linked up with 'early' object relations. I believe we need to lay greater emphasis on the unflagging work of dissociation between the psychical representatives of the drives and the object representations which give them meaning. If such a disunity between the fundamental psychical matrices succeeds in accomplishing the goals of a work of the negative whose absence would reveal a subversion of the Oedipal structure, it makes narcissism respon-sible for this unfettered libido and impairs ego investments. The effect of any relaxation of censorship is that the preconscious manifestations, revealing this absence of mediation, will at first be experienced as deeply wounding for the ego ideal, without even being able to idealise the drive process in the name of regenerative spontaneity and without there being an integration of its manifestations with the ego through ongoing investment. They are left with no other possibility than to burn up at the exact spot where these manifestations would have succeeded in making themselves heard or to render themselves futile by affecting decorative sectors which are not so much intended to embellish life as to make one forget its roots. Worse still, driven into a corner by its modes of relating to the object and the obscure claims which characterise it, the ego is sometimes obliged to accept the image of its self-reflection, in dreams for example, and yields to the pressure of the drives by occasionally becoming its own object. Imaginary formations then emerge which surprise their host, revealing a fragmentation, a parcelling of the body in which certain parts of it are split off from the rest and, under the effect of the sanction which hits them, suffer the repercussions of their erogeneity which uses the displacement to concentrate in it all the available libido, escaping any form of control. Sometimes the imagination is unable to contain anxiety by offering it its potential for representation and the process of depersonalisation bears witness to the ego's detachment in face of the loss of the means of representation, making the subject experience the brutal effects of his inexorable libido, as Freud said. A vicious circle ensues when these drive manifestations finally break through the censorship. They are coloured by the enormous burden of frustration which results from being repeatedly denied expression and when they erupt it is always under the auspices of a vindictive rage. One then discovers that their partner in the order of things is a megalomaniac ego which completely splits the opinions it has of itself from those which the objects have of it (the same opinion which it expresses and which is taken over by the analyst is inadmissible in the interpreted version which is only an echo of it). The ego is certainly desperate and its only chance of rediscovering the 'narcissistic' conditions organised by maternal madness is to reconstitute the situation, but this time by attempting to make the other person desperate just as it had been desperate about having to relinquish itself. For it is only by means of the language of affective symmetry that it can make itself understood. We discover then that it has invested the all-powerfulness of the negative as an ultimate weapon against the threat of disorganisation.

The Object's Vocation and Limitations

In transference we are faced with a paradoxical situation. The transference of desire, as such, is, I will not say denied, but unidentifiable (more than resistance, it is a question of non-recognition) whereas transference as a need (without object, in the sense of without reason) dominates the relationship.[23] In other words, the awareness of the vital nature of the attachment to the analyst masks the fact that what is binding does not have the slightest connection with what is known – even by hearsay – as desire. For him, moreover, there is no understandable reason for it. It would be naive to link this condition with some kind of regression to the mother–baby relationship on the pretext that the baby who is taken away from its mother is visibly distressed and that the patient's behaviour is suggestive of this. In fact we are left with the distinct impression that for the analysand the main point is to affirm that he is unaware of having desires in as far as acknowledging them always results in the same problems occurring again. Firstly, his attachment to the object is always hazardous with regard to the way the latter sees fit to respond to the patient's unconscious fantasy; unconsciously the object is suspected of acting in a way which involves subjecting his partner both to his whims and to his self-interest (projected sadism). Secondly, the possibility of there being the slightest snag in the idea of a pure symmetry of desires, or that their state of perfect complementarity might cease, raises the threat of unleashing drive activity which is capable of sweeping away, like a tidal wave, all the acquisitions achieved through repression, stripping the psyche of its capacity to deal with the danger of disorganisation, with the ever-present risk that the object may disappear from the subject's mental universe.

In actual fact it is not the drives as such which are feared, but the sudden conversion of an ego which has been won over unexpectedly to their cause and which falls in with a thirsting aspiration for facticity whose catastrophic quality is viewed as arising either from the satisfactions blindly demanded, or from having scuppered everything which it seemed to want to protect, well away from these external perils and self-traumatic temptations. It is therefore impossible to ascribe the fear of a disastrous outcome to the object relation alone since there is the risk of seeing the ego itself dragged into the disorganisation.

I am perfectly aware of the important role which the object plays in these fragile structures. I would simply like to emphasise the following: while we accept that drive investment is the basis of one's relations with oneself, with others and with the world, not simply in the form of satisfactions of erogenous zones and component drives, but as a source of the pleasure of being alive, we should add that this can never be provided by the object relationship. This has other functions, e.g., seeing to it that vitality is not stifled, sharing the beauty and goodness of erotic encounters with objects (which requires the object to own up to its own eroticism), recognising and preserving the mystery itself of the new-found pleasure in loving, admitting one's own inevitable spitefulness as well as that of others and even recognising the healthy aspect which may sometimes be contained in destructivity, dealing with the inevitability of suffering, accepting the limited means we have of reducing the feelings of enmity which take hold of us when other people refuse to give us what we want, and even admitting the pleasure we take in causing suffering – with the complementary roles of victim and executioner – rebelling, showing compassion, accepting one's impotency, tolerating waiting etc. But none of this should be confused with the essential core of our involvement in life which can only depend on the meaning we give to this drive life which links us emotionally with the world and other people and which means that we are affected by them, none of which can be created in us by the object alone.

The idea of the object relationship arises from an overestimation of the part played by the analyst in the transference, considered as a collimator of all the patient's communications. It is as if the source of the communication could only refer to other objects and other relations, without it being clear how these objects acquire this particular form of existence and are modified, even to the point of being denied, and as if there was no idea of analysis being first and foremost a confrontation with oneself, albeit a self which barely has any idea of what this self might be, which it will have to invent in order to be able to conceive of the other as well as of itself.

It is clear that the key to this should not be sought exclusively with the object nor with compulsive drive activity of the kind one sees triggered in psychopathological structures which seem to stem more from a deficiency than from a subverted functioning, anxiety mobilising reactions in which the primary need is for discharge. What we are dealing with is dominated by the fear of internal disorganisation following the encounter between the drive-invested ego and the object. In fact it is more like a vicissitude of drive life which only seems so unbearable because the ego has not managed to appropriate it. And if it is incorrect to challenge the role of unconscious identifications here, it is also because the figures which underlie these 'captations',[24] as Lacan aptly called them, exude an indefinable mixture of passionate energy and seduction which, while not always lacking in generosity, is nonetheless the mark of incoherence, uncontrolled effusion, alternating with the most indiscriminate negligence concerning the other person's expectations. In the object's responses there is a total lack of distinction between the thinking of an adult and the psyche of a child, a dramatisation of what is not essential existing alongside an unawareness of what is essential, an almost animal vitality co-existing with a kind of day-to-day mechanical mode of functioning in which its whole existence is concerned with doing. Affects are not ignored but are used for warding off any other possible outlook. And this is how there is an excess of excitation making identification into a pole which saturates the capacity to imagine solutions (fantasmatic, of course) to expectations which have been created, questions which have no answer, the difficulty of defining the exact content of the most familiar experiences, the need to recognise that the other will always be opposed to the need we have to know that we represent for him the mystery of his own ignorance on this subject. In short, the saturation in question strives to thwart the certainty of the uncertainty in the facticity of the other. This refocuses the questioning around key signifiers, first in the sexual domain and in the unfurling of its ramifications which always lead back to the self. Above all, the subject's questions will be mobilised in order to detect the orientation of the organising axis of psychic life which, because it cannot be found in himself through recognising the libido and the need for its transformation, will be assumed to reside in the unthinkable chaos which characterises parental relations. It is not the presence of conflicts in itself which is a handicap for the organisation of thought, but the fact that when they involve figures of the same family group they assume an irreconcilable and incommensurable character. The principle of the excluded third party loses ground to the mutually exclusive relationship. This tonality is not itself the cause of internal division; it is more the unanswered questioning concerning the identification of what the relationship is based on which keeps the parental couple together.

We know that the primal scene is unthinkable. Ordinarily, its status is such that it does not admit of any representation, otherwise the latter would acquire so many attachments through magnetisation that it would compromise the preservation of the link as an infinite process and basis of the psychic system. In this case, however, the erotisation of external conflicts results in the link being frozen, so that it is even more difficult to shift – to transfer – from its repressed form. Because it is even less 'conceivable' for the repressed unconscious, the parental link cannot be expressed in a metaphorical form (to do so would be tantamount to accepting it); it is left no other choice but to repeat itself in external conflicts over and over in the most banal circumstances. The idea that the cause of their insistence should be sought elsewhere is eclipsed, apparently forbidding such an investigation by a kind of occupation of psychic space in such a way that the ego is obliged to yield more and more territory only to find shelter in a position where it simply becomes a spectator of what is happening. This failure to come to grips with the conflict is often the prelude to a renewed unleashing of drive activity. This is because the exuberant derivatives which psychic activation engenders have, so to speak, exceeded the capacities for transformation and linking. I have said that these are frozen by the erotisation of external conflicts with the result that what remains at the ego's disposition is insufficient for the task of linking these repeated eruptions together in a meaningful way.

We are once again confronted with masochism when we think of the endless tears shed which alone seem to ensure a continuity of existence for this distressed ego, the appalling solitude finally suggesting that in the absence of any other form of expression it is perhaps after all the erotisation that needs to be recognised as underlying such a useless expenditure of energy. In spite of appearances, I do not think that we can speak here of auto-eroticism. For it is not a question of substituting the object but of a negativised relation to an object judged *in absentia*. Nothing fruitful ever comes out of this despair. I would be willing to bet that in this case masochism has a function differentiating it from those organisations in which its central role is recognised. The invasion of the whole psychical field by sadness, which in this extreme isolation no doubt constitutes a *tête à tête* with the captive object within the enclosed space of psychic suffering, has the essential function of blocking thought processes. Thinking means becoming aware of separation from the object and discovering the advantages of this, rather than exhausting oneself by trying to recreate its presence, i.e., concentrating the energies used to obtain its reappearance in the background where its form is expected to emerge. A space is provided here, not simply as a consolation or as a hallucinatory habitat, but as an opportunity to create in it one's own object not only as an analogon of the one before but as a receptacle replacing the figuration which in one way or another links its representation with its perception by means of a system of relations freed from the obligation to produce what can be represented. It therefore subordinates the functioning which governs its production of what can be represented to exercising its freedom to exhibit, not something similar, but meaningful properties which are able, in turn, to engender forms. Their aim of figuration is reduced to preserving an attachment to the object by means of the grid of operations which have found their place within the space of thought. The advantage of the operation is not only that it loosens the attachment which is too demanding, responding to the need to make the object present and to stay riveted to the task of reconstituting its equal, but also that it creates in its place not so much a system of equivalence as a generating matrix of psychic formations which are able to evolve in multiple directions in its own space. The latter remains linked to the object which has facilitated its creation, less by reference to its presence, aided by its localisation within a definite space, or by identifying its forms, qualities and properties, than by a relation of investment. Now I have shown that the affective satisfaction invading the psyche has reduced the ego to the condition of a spectator. Under these circumstances, it can only project the image of emptiness clearing the way for the invasion of narcissistic affects over which it no longer, thereby, has any control. On the other hand, suffering, despair, impotence and rage all arise from the need to hang on to an elusive reality and to steer all the investments back to the ego, as if the latter were sacrificing itself as a replacement for what it is losing, eluding any approach. However, although autonomy is constantly demanded in social life – or in the transference – it is in fact secretly hated, because it is also a sign of the object's independence. Suffering thus maintains the object's presence in oneself. It prohibits any exercise of subjectivity. It destroys any perspective other than the present, as if each period of solitude might lead to the moment when mourning had exhausted itself.

When thought has cut out a path for itself, it is extremely difficult to bring it back within the analytic experience for the same reason. Thinking distances one from the analyst.

It is therefore necessary to wait for a reversal of perspective in which thinking is seen as a way of putting between the partners of the analysis a kind of third object which will have a life of its own.

Subjectal[25] Unbinding

This is the moment to demonstrate the trap involved in this so-called pursuit of the object, the 'collage' which would have us believe that the explanation lies in some sort of primitive fixation. The reality is quite different, its specificity affecting investment in the work of the negative. None of the terms we use to define it (*objectal*, narcissistic) seem adequate to describe the situation. In its extreme form we must postulate a dissociation between the ego and the subject – in which the investment accomplished in the name of the former frees itself from the second, that is, it withdraws investment from the adhesive function of the attachment which is a sign of involvement. The attachment is maintained, so we are not dealing with an attack on linking; neither is there a withdrawal of investment – on the contrary, it can be strongly invested – but it is the involvement with the object through the drive which comes undone. It is an involvement which does not simply imply, under normal conditions, acceptance of the satisfaction obtained or expected, thanks to this new level of unity formed by the subject–object pair, but recognises itself in this realisation of desire and goes on to recognise itself – without being consciously aware of it – as the source, origin, pursuit and hope expected from the realisation. This means that the subject has to put all his strength into the struggle to bring about the desired aim, to preserve this acquisition or to support the calls for the return of what is henceforth established in the field of desire, marked by the longing which the hope of rediscovering it arouses. Therefore the precondition of the object relationship can be admitted. The binding established by necessity is proof of this but, on the other hand, the persistence of danger – which in this case not only consists in its non-realisation but also includes, when on the contrary this occurs, the object's unpredictability, the investment of the ego by the drive etc. – involves, in the most extreme cases, *subjectal disengagement*. This occurs when the modalities of the ego's work of the negative have not been able to accept the vicissitudes of the lack at the heart of the network of systems of representation which are supposed to offer a range of orientations and diverse choices constantly diffracting their essential core, as if repression had been ineffective. Certainly, the remoteness from consciousness has achieved its objectives; on the other hand, the attraction which lies in what was formerly repressed appears to have been unsuccessful in distributing the urgent appeal of the original demand for satisfaction, thanks to the operations of primary processes, by linking them up with key signifiers, and then diffusing them onto the symbolisations which might give them the right to exist.

Freud's last article on the role of splitting in the process of defence referred to such defensive activity, showing how revolutionary his observation was, even though its modalities could not yet be guessed. I shall call it the *fantasy of the subjectal unbinding of the ego.*

Why fantasy, since such activity really takes place? Because it is based on resorting to supposedly controlled omnipotence whereas, when the ego resorts to these radical solutions, it is increasingly driven by a competitive struggle of which it paradoxically becomes the victim, i.e., between the drives which are less and less bound by the psychic structures which derive from them (fantasmatic representations, sublimatory activities, the transition to secondary psychic processes) and the objects whose own resistance is not always in the service of the compromises required or which demand as a condition a preliminary sacrifice which is felt to be exorbitant. This situation obliges the ego, while continuing to follow the normal 'course of things', to disconnect itself from the grounds of its subjectivity, an ordeal which will be on a par with desire. What gives the illusion that these subjects remain involved in the ups and downs of which life provides endless varieties, is that they appear to be playing the social game like everyone else. With one difference: they obscure (without realising the difference) the distinction between desiring and being desired and assume that they are both the same. It is in order to hide from themselves the *subjectal* disengagement which they have carried out towards their drives that they claim that the latter are simply awaiting satisfaction, provided there is a consenting object; the latter, however, never meets their needs.

Should this be seen as a contemporary form of hysteria? I would think it is more likely that we are dealing with the essence of what Winnicott called the false self, which is very often misunderstood, being confused with some kind of inauthenticity which is not in question here. The desire of unsatisfied desire is quite secondary to the need to maintain the damaged ideal developed as a counterpoint to the primary object, rather than being derived from it. And this is what deceives the analyst in these cases. Every analysis which stays close to the material and brings its impact to bear on the ego's relation to the drives, immediately brings to the surface their preoccupation with the object and the extent of its potential control.

There is also a masochistic paradox behind certain aspects of these configurations. The subject puts himself in situations which inevitably result in punishment, all the while pretending that he will be able to avoid it – whereas in fact he knows that sooner or later he will not be able to do so – on the pretext that he thinks he has already suffered enough in life. In fact, the explanation stems from an animistic regression which consists in attributing all the circumstances calling for renunciation with the finery of the primary objects which must be excited without relief so that they maintain their mastery over the subject. Mastery is by no means always an active phenomenon. Thus satisfaction is found for the passive need to be mastered by an object which is anonymous but decked with projections. These are all the easier to pin on it in these circumstances since those which belong to the original objects have acquired a rigidity – making them hard, impersonal, abstract, almost stripped of humanity – all characteristics which are attributed to the social products to which they are transferred (administrative agencies, the law, etc.) These frequently encountered examples indicate an obvious absurdity which is not entirely removed by interpreting the situation in terms of self-punishment. They shed light on other situations which are much more intensely invested on the amorous level we have described above by the untimely manifestations of drive life. All this emphasis on the pole of the object, its unpredictability, its incomprehensible variations, its deficiencies is deceptive. Even if one is persuaded that certain characteristics are real and not necessarily projected, they only play their role in the subject's psychic economy on the condition that they are subordinated to a postulate which consists in shifting the source of drive activity onto the object and in presenting itself as the object of the object's drives. Hence the tragic character of attempts to make the partner of a dialogue, which seems to reflect an alienating fixation, see reason. In fact what is obscured is the manoeuvre in which the projection of the source of the drive onto the object evinces the ego's withdrawal from its own drive excitation. This situation absorbs the ego by making it try desperately to respond to the incomprehensible character of the other person's drives which become distracting. There is a misunderstanding since the subject thinks he is trying to realise his desires whereas the main part of his activity is really aimed at escaping what he assumes to be the other person's drives by withdrawing further into himself and by deserting his own drive investments. The paradox of this situation is that it can take a passionate turn owing to reciprocal accusations and justifications whereas, at bottom, when the subject's discourse is listened to attentively, the complaints that he makes about the bad treatment he receives from the object mask his disengagement. This is to protect him from becoming aware of his own desire for the desperate subservience of a fantasised object on whom he wishes to impose unconditional surrender, in anticipation of the fate which it might want to make him suffer.

However disconcerting this behaviour may be – one can interpret it in terms of the combined parameters of a denial of reality, masochistic provocation and the need for self-punishment – it comes within the scope of the work of the negative. Thus in situations considerably less loaded with symbolic implications – for in the ones we spoke of earlier there is a link between the animism mentioned and parental power – caused by minor annoyances, last minute disruptions of planned activities, or disappointment caused by certain objects whose intentions, moods, and momentary preoccupations do not coincide with the fantasmatic scenario of the event as it has been imagined (in fact there is no scenario; it only appears after reality has quashed what the encounter *should have been*), there is a sudden reaction – apparently unrelated to the reason for the annoyance, the unpleasant surprise, the displeasure at noticing how little reality has collaborated in fulfilling the expectations one has of it – dissociated from any discernible structuring by a conscious causality and taking on a quasi-hallucinatory form even though it mainly manifests itself affectively. This reaction is virulent, minimally significant, peremptory and incomprehensible in view of the facts of the situation. It has two aspects to it: on the one hand, a radical, imperative and irrevocable 'no', and, on the other, a reaction of withdrawal, isolation and rupture with others and the world. One might think one was just dealing with an unstable or sullen reaction, if one was not struck by the fact that even from the subject's point of view the reaction seems uncalled for, inexplicable and incoherent; it is not even as if anything specific is even expected from it. It is not the 'no' of the undisciplined person but rather the no of the anorexic, perhaps at the greatest moment of risk lest the situation topple over into bulimia. Only reconstruction can enable us to find meaning in the event retrospectively and to understand – for clearly one has thought about identification with the aggressor, which does not explain the situation adequately – the consequences of the intervention of reality which has a prejudicial effect on the realisation of an implicit inner project. A simple series of actions succeeding one another, but in the wrong order, is interpreted as a sudden separation between the mother and child which requires that we enact a scene in which reality becomes a metaphorical representation uniting a mother who rejects (herself) and a child who is exiled from the world which she alone represents. Frequently there is an outburst of tears. Overall, the situation remains surprising and irrational, prompted by an obscure will whose aims are unclear. Actually the 'negativising' scenario is already in oneself, a mode of representation standing in the way of nihilation. And it is because these reactive features are part of a much more co-ordinated whole – at least from the analyst's point of view – that particular attention is paid to them for what they may reveal as they emerge. What is nonetheless troubling is the eruptive, spontaneous character of it, the meaning of which seems to escape one's grasp. The fact is that owing to a striking regression we can observe a capitulation of ordinary reason in order to explain an emotional reaction which one is trying to communicate. One may see here a desire to hold the reaction in – as if to protect the objects which it is aimed at (indirectly but in a very exposed way, revealing their proximity with childhood objects) or as if the idea of motive needed replacing by that of automatic reaction so as to deprive the psychic event of all significant influence. In this case, affect does not describe representation; it exhausts, through its explosion, the possibilities of transmission in the systems of representation. It could be said that everything comes down to the psychical representative of the drive.

If we correlate these outbursts – which are not so much outbursts of protest as of denial, when one thinks about it – and if the indictment of reality is just the screen which makes it possible to camouflage the outburst directed at objects which occasionally come to life again, the latter do not seem to me to be rejected for the reasons which are usually given in these banal situations ('He or she isn't nice.' 'He or she is selfish.' 'He or she doesn't care about me' etc.), based on a predicative logic which I think is less present here than a logic of mutual exclusion between the subject and the object. While fusion is not the active paradigm of the relation, the object's existence – as a subject with its own independent intentionality – desubjectivises the subject. From this follows the immediate reconstitution of the couple under a negative paradigm which nevertheless means that the link is not broken off and that the de-subjectivisation itself can contemplate itself, as it were, from the outside in the movements which herald the subject's exile. The intensity of the reaction is on a scale equivalent to the object's evanescence. In times of peace one lets it go to avoid *subjectal* engagement; in war one pins it down, as well as oneself, so as not to lose one's hold and to be able to immobilise it.

These strategies as a whole are not easy to understand: all the arguments we have developed, even when combined, scarcely allow us to guess the secret roots from which their branches grow, no doubt because the analyst is reluctant to think about what appears to be extremely audacious. The unavowed – unavowable – goal which one finally uncovers at the bottom of this transvaluation which has no trouble in declaring itself, while revealing nothing of its methods, is to stop time. Here we discover the problems which the analyst faces with regard to the constitution of such psychical formations. Are we dealing with regression? Circumstantially, yes – one even finds a repetitive series of traumatic situations which call for such an explanation. And it is quite clear that if the functioning which we have described had not been preceded by a development which had been stopped at a certain point along the way, we would not have had to deal with such complex psychopathology. Will the notions of immaturity, infantilism and ordinary inhibition suffice to provide us with an answer? What we have observed here does not suggest they will.

Withdrawal and Disengagement

This regression cannot, however, be characterised as a return to a fixation giving less conflictual pleasure. There is indeed regression but not a return to a mode of pleasure which has escaped repression because obtaining it has not met with obstacles in the past. It is more a question of a regressive wall; the fixation is above all designed to ward off a risk which lies less in the permitted or prohibited nature of what desire is seeking than in the danger of seeing its course disturbed, being obliged to make sure that nothing stands in the way of what can be obtained from the subject providing he is 'willing'. What is agreeable is not what is desirable – 'pleasurable' (to use the English word); it is what I agree to. Here we come across a variety of narcissism which has very little to do with the love which the ego has for itself – there is every reason to believe the contrary, which in no way impedes megalomania – and which seems primarily to be exercised towards the object whose indispensable participation in the pleasure is above all the vehicle of a traumatic potential turning it into a trauma-object, as I have called it elsewhere.

This narcissism can never be discerned directly by the features which usually characterise it (hypertrophy of the ego, infatuation, a self-admiring attitude, coldness or arrogance, etc.); it only becomes apparent through deduction and retroactively, as a result of transference. What is revealed is the singular way in which the object is treated. It is rare that the analysand allows us to examine his close, intimate relationships with objects to whom he is attached by shared erotic ties which would enable us to infer, by observing the fantasies or the way desire is mobilised, a libidinal organisation whose effects might shed light on their unconscious psychical activity. In general, the anxiety aroused by the drives, the fear of rejection and the loss involving interminable pains of mourning, rage, devaluation, apprehension of intolerance to frustration, drive the subject to refrain from responding to the object's advances, or even to frankly discourage them or to flee from all situations of closeness. It is not a fear of sexuality which is involved – when the situation lends itself, this can be experienced without conflict, temporarily at least – but the subject is then totally blind to what this experience represents for the partner. This is another way of saying that it is indeed the object who poses problems. Even though we must be careful not to oversimplify when writing, it is to some extent unavoidable if we are to underline the essential characteristic which we want to draw attention to concerning the splitting of the ego.

The narcissistic nature of libidinal expression leads to an 'encounter' with an object who happens to coincide, by the miraculous effect of a divine act or a law of nature, with what one has always thought he should be like, corresponding perfectly to the subject's shape. But in this case a subtle difference distinguishes him from the ordinary love object. Whereas the latter gives the pleasant impression of being the answer to a long-standing quest, giving a sense of having made a find and quickening desire for a loving relationship seen as an ultimate longing, here the unexpected experience of love short-circuits, as it were, desire because the fusion of love is more a state of fact than the realisation of a long-awaited hope. In other words, object love does not enable us to come out of ourselves and to approach the other because it is the other who has come to us – without even arousing anxiety as to whether the experience will live up to expectations. The subject thinks he is in love, whereas love in this case is merely the idea he has of himself being in love.

After all, is this not the essential point, is it not what each and every one of us tries to rediscover in paradise lost? Therein lies the illusion. For paradise is lost for ever: in fact it is only a retroactive fantasy arising from our difficulty in accepting the obstacles our love meets with. Nobody can escape from himself, Freud said, and it is a great illusion to think that being loved can replace the experience of loving to the extent that the latter may entail the risk of not seeing all one's hopes fulfilled. For it is where there is love that we see drive involvement, the encounter between the ego and the drives, the revelation of the subject of the drive, because a human being in this world is a hollow shell if he is not a 'being-to-others'(*être-à-autre*) and not only for others (*pour autrui*). No doubt because it is through the other that being can be perceived of as a possibility. This means that this potentiality of diverse circumstances amounts to nothing if it does not involve risking or putting a price on one's own head. The inversion which consists in seeing oneself as a receptacle for the other person's love has performed a turning away – rather than a detour – without having the slightest awareness that this way of experiencing love will have made him miss out on the essential aspect of the experience, i.e., the risk of loving, a gamble where there is no guarantee of the benefits to be gained. How mistaken he is about the virtues of being loved. In the quest for love he confuses the satisfaction of the drives (active) with a passive aim, and the fact that he is the passive object of the other person's drives. This is a narcissistic refuge which may go as far as remaining ignorant of itself and pass for something quite different in other people's eyes. It is not infrequent that the relationship thus established fails and is abandoned. For however satisfying the condition of being loved may be – however fully satisfying its accomplishment is – the fact remains that it will inevitably lead the subject to withdraw into the most hidden areas of his being, fearing exposure and wishing to escape his vulnerability. It is this dimension which will affect all object libidinal investments and will only be sensed at a late stage in the transference experience. The latter will always be marked – whether it be through fear of the drives or through fear of the loss of love – by this disengagement which is the scar left over from the relationship with the primary object but which means that later the appropriation will leave its mark on the ego through its absence. As the subject is unable to avoid the object's existence, he wards off the pain which the latter may inflict on him, believing he is thereby sheltering the ego in order to create the space which is absolutely essential to avoid the shock of psychic interpenetration, and in so doing causes, without realising it, a breach between the ego and the drives. This is the major difference between repression and splitting. This was already evident in the case of the 'Wolf Man' but we did not see it. The drive (*la pulsion*) becomes re-pulsion (*ré-pulsion*), but it cannot be explained by disgust because the allusion to taste has been erased, making way for pouting which gives the impression there is *always* something better to offer.

This position reveals the pivotal point of the whole libidinal organisation diffusing its modes of action. The admired object (even if he does not arouse feelings of love) will be a fascinating object because of his libidinal manifestations, outwardly displaying investments which look like fireworks: but the admiration is a pure fascination for the outward appearance and the subject rarely allows himself to be permeated by it, to grasp it, so that he can enter the exchange. And the object which will be a source of frustration – even if it is not for reasons of love – will provoke a withdrawal, if anger or the feeling of impingement begin to invade the mind, for the narcissistic organisation strives above all to preserve the possibility of disengagement.

In any case the analyst, who may occupy, at given moments, the different roles in these dramas, provokes so much splitting, in the shape of *subjectal* withdrawal, that it is always the same issue which arises – it becomes a sort of blazon of the analytic relationship – 'I don't know what I'm doing here and what I'm looking for.' Not without adding, 'You, I suppose you know ... ' True enough, except that what the analyst is 'supposed to know' is never agreed upon.

A multitude of misfortunes have been described, which the object can easily be held responsible for: faltering in its function as a container (a new *pons asinorum*), failing to 'disintoxicate' projections, being devouring, incapable of mourning, vampire-like, insufficiently interactive, etc. I do not, of course, have a definitive answer to offer for such a problem and it is difficult to see how one can be found in these terms. What is important is to identify as precisely as possible the nature of the manifestations which are at the basis of the experience as it appears to the analyst.

In this case, it seems to me that the work of the negative, whose influence, as we have seen, extends over a wide spectrum, revolves around a double polarity. On the one hand, there is a drive process which is unacceptable because its refractions throughout the systems of representation and their mediating role vis-à-vis reality have received little recognition because they have not been appropriated by the ego – it is up to it to defend itself, if need be – and, on the other, an ego which remains for ever marked by the wound caused by its awareness of the object's independent life, i.e., the object's attachments to other objects (the other of the object). This same ego finds itself doomed to solitude and distress, all the more so in that it has not found satisfaction in the acquisition of its own autonomy. Lastly, it has made itself into a bastion, living according to the principle of *the inhibition of relations of alterity* in a temporo-spatial suspense, in spite of an existence which lets itself be carried along by traversing familiar spaces and domestic rhythms. But one should not jump to the conclusion that it is simply a matter of a denial of difference, as one might suggest in the context of positive narcissism.

It is not always easy to grasp the nuance between egocentricity and this unthinkable alterity because the latter struggles, without knowing it, on two fronts: that of the other in oneself (unconscious) and that of the other as not-self, outside oneself, obliging the subject to make use of narcissism as a source of negativisation.

These modes of activity and reactivity will be subjected to the severe test of transference. The ego's precarious journey exposes it to the threat of disorganisation when the possibilities of maintaining the suspense are compromised. The hazardous nature of the object (causing states of imbalance, triggering anarchic and defensive modes of drive functioning) may then not only lead to a withdrawal of investment, a habitual and familiar procedure, but to *subjectal* disengagement which may at certain critical moments affect – much more radically than the desire to commit suicide, because it becomes a *modus vivendi* – his basic sense of existence to the point of loosening the ego's bodily moorings. This is manifested by a range of diverse states from the most typical bouts of depersonalisation to extreme states of anxiety about greater or lesser degrees of bodily fragmentation. The symbolisation of these symptoms, although not totally opaque, often only gives a rough indication, making it difficult to situate it within the overall context of psychical activity. The reference to castration is not absent, but the dominant narcissistic and aggressive aspects of the symptom affecting the body ego severs its relation with the oedipal context as a whole. The main impression we get is of a tear in the ego's psychical tissue which allows underlying foreclosed drive processes to escape.

Thus the disengagement which occurs when analysis fends off the reconstitution of blocks tending to 'mineralise' psychic life can have repercussions creating extreme anxiety. For it can even reach the ego which ends up feeling that it is dying. We have provided a foretaste of negative hallucination but, however formidable it may be, it only concerns the sphere of representability (*figurabilité*) of the presence to-itself (*présence à soi*) from the angle of self-perception and not as a basis of investment. When this is affected, the sudden threat of the ego's disappearance is felt to be a forewarning of death. This affect of non-existence, resulting from an anxiety of internal loss concerning its own form (more a silhouette or even an impression, according to Tustin), conceives of itself as an 'unrepresentable form' which appears to itself as its presence withdraws. It is not easy to speak precisely about one's own relation to the ego but there can be no doubt that the portion of the ego which sustained it has vanished too. The ego itself is wrenched away from the internal world by the all-powerfulness conferred on the object which drags the ego with it as it disappears. The negative has reached its limit.

Generally, it is in literature and art that the most successful images of this are conjured up. There can be a source of misunderstanding here between what literature and art lovers attribute to creative fantasy and the effort in these works to express, for the benefit of those who still have their feet on the ground, this tormented experience. In a more trivial manner and by safeguarding the priority of what can be represented, we slip insensibly each night towards the danger of this submersion from which we escape through dreaming, although there is no guarantee that we will be able to return from it. This is the price to be paid for dreaming.

On the Non-Triangular Oedipus Complex and the Dimension of Thirdness

While the 'murder of the thing' used to be a fashionable way of evoking the powers of absence and the heuristics of language accession, the infinite opening up of a negative which is constitutive of the human being, we are a long way from this idea here. For it is perhaps the matrix murder of the ego by the almightiness of thought turning against itself which achieves, unwittingly, that which is probably not unrelated to what Schreber called the murder of the soul.

As life continues, nonetheless, and time does not stop, all psychical work takes place on the edges of this rupture.

It is customary to account for the clinical structures presenting the type of mental functioning which I have examined in somewhat more detail than is generally the case, as evocative of the dyadic relationship of early life. Without reiterating my reserve about the notion of the dyadic relationship, I shall endeavour to express my astonishment at what I have observed in this respect. In our description of *blank psychosis* (Donnet and Green, 1973),[26] we put forward the idea of oedipal bi-triangulation. As far as the present description is concerned we have concluded that in contrast to the former structures there is a *non-triangular Oedipus complex*. That is, both the imagos are present, and, as far as we can tell, clearly differentiated. What causes a problem is, on the one hand, the subject's feeling that he is excluded from the said triangle, and, seen from another point of view, the extreme difficulty in determining the nature of the relations which exist between the different summits of the triangle. Only sibling–parent relations are clearly intelligible. However, neither the attachment *between* the parents, nor that which makes the subject's relation with the parental couple binding, beyond the one he has with them separately, makes any sense. Under these conditions, describing the relation in terms of love or hostility vis-à-vis such and such a person or characterising it in terms of a positive or inverted Oedipus has little meaning; it is largely overshadowed by the *fundamental basis* of the attachment. We have characterised it in various ways without claiming to be exhaustive. To the foregoing general remarks let me add the following: it seems that one of the manifestations of the work of the negative is the dissociation of the pleasure–unpleasure principle and its reformulation in terms of the principle of *not-unpleasure*. The formula itself indicates clearly that the 'not' has taken the place of desire, that is, the most primary mental processes are governed by the avoidance of unpleasure and this avoidance implies giving up the aim of seeking pleasure. Of course, this modification is a distortion. Pleasure can only come back to 'squat' the psyche. It is only experienced as such in the intrusive form of a rape. Hence a vicious circle is set up which increasingly tends to immobilise the psyche and establish a state of vigilance in face of the possible return of the destabilising situation. We may even wonder about the pertinence of the term conflict. It is not that there is any doubt about the permanent state of tension felt by these subjects but what needs questioning is the almost unrecognisable character of the facts which structure it. These subjects themselves have difficulty in knowing what they expect from a relation which seems indispensable to them. Perhaps the essential question, although they do not realise it, is to rediscover their condition as beings of desire. But in this case, is desiring anything other than the wish to bruise or be bruised? In fact, the conflict cannot be identified because it is too fundamental and involves the choice which has to be made between surviving and living. A choice between devitalising repetitive timelessness and the perishable time of desire which only has in its favour the uncertain promise of a renewal. Perhaps.

But the hypothesis that an attachment of this kind, by its mixture of fragility and intemperance, of variability and obstination, in short, which seems at times only to know the solution of 'all or nothing', is to be thought of as a fixation to pre-oedipal stages, is one which we would do well to challenge seriously. I think we are justified in preferring one which sees each new stage of evolution undergo a new drive investment and a defensive reorganisation with changes of object type, from the two-fold perspective of their erotic libidinal qualification and the narcissistic repercussions of the change with the aim of determining structural meanings. This seems more fruitful to me than relating these findings to developmental stages described by psychoanalytic theory, the reliability of which is likely to be challenged again soon. A wealth of arguments is already being put forward based on an 'interactive psychology', promoted by the pervading vogue of established research. And we shall be asked to believe in its claims to greater objectivity resulting from a methodology which relies on technological equipment onto which the properties of instruments which achieve wonders in advancing our knowledge of the physical world are fallaciously projected. This is another mode – ideological this time – of desubjectivisation, in the form of an ideal of knowledge![27]

A hundred years of history should have taught us that in the field of psychoanalysis, that is, in the domain of the analysis of the psyche, we cannot treat the question of the premises of knowledge lightly. Psychoanalytic theory has suffered greatly from being dispersed in different directions – whether one was aware of it and preferred to pass over it in silence or whether one ignored it – because, all too often, those who thought they had a worthwhile contribution to make to the body of existing knowledge were rarely prepared to take the necessary steps which would make it possible to pinpoint what deserved to be brought to light and analysed, and then, if need be – analysis of the previous analysis – to announce the new paradigm, i.e., all the basic hypotheses – which were either already known, or modified or completely new – thereby giving full meaning to their proposals. It is strange that it is precisely where the psyche is concerned that these precautions – which are more necessary in this domain than in any other – have been neglected. Negligence apart, it looks as if we are faced with a kind of sacrilegious intimidation. However, having decided one is going to deal with the adventures of the mind, one cannot avoid the necessity of meeting the requirements of what is demanded of someone who undertakes such a project. That is, one must state one's position – like a ship at sea. In a field where there are no two concordant positions one must be willing, before expressing one's point of view, to question one's own position, not as a subjective statement, but as an agent of an *'opus incertum'*.[28] It is not enough for perception to detect its eventual imperfection; it is also necessary that it is capable of showing judgement concerning the options which govern what it can, wants or chooses to elucidate.

To put it rather bluntly: if, finally, I restrict myself to the drive–object pair, and even if I can only think of it as a pair, as soon as this pairing is formed, I find myself faced with the contradiction of the object–object and of the object as a component of the drive. One might just as well say that if the object is you, the drive is as much me as you, or again *me in me and you in me together*.

When the latter is directed at the 'you in you' which is the object, how else could this relation be expressed than as an *'it'* before anyone has even intervened in this intimacy. For if the *'you in you'* of the object and the portion of the drive which is *'you in me'* connect up, what then can the *'me in me'* be, if it is not an *'it'* to which one will address the thing by making it a mediator for everything which is to come in the encounter?

Linking this model to pleasure is doing no more than meeting the need to give birth to the sign, whose accession becomes the target of the world, to be tracked, surrounded and perpetuated by being linked up with other signs. And what is this *'it'*, in any case, if it is not a sign because it may intervene independently of me and you and be the root of this second world which brings within its jurisdiction what seems to be capable of persisting by continuing to take shelter behind the proximity of a natural spontaneity? As soon as one recognises the indivisibility between what is psychic and the interpreter, the dimension of *thirdness*[29] (which is always present) becomes recognisable in the endless constitution of systems where in each case it finds its meaning through the simultaneous definition of its modes of linking and of its objects.

At the same time, this concept is liable to give rise to as many counter-models – which only our limited minds will consider absurd – claiming the right to be heard, urged on by the cry which these networks, holding the world and the subject tightly within the same system, have tried to force down the throat of what cannot be identified in any other way than by this appeal.

7

The Work of the Negative
and Hallucinatory Activity
(Negative Hallucination)

By intangible we mean what has the quality of the tangible to an extremely small extent, as is the case with air and also those tangibles which show excess such as those which are destructive.

Aristotle, *On the Soul*, II, XI.[1]

... perceptual investments are never investments of single neurones but always of complexes. So far we have neglected this feature; it is time to take account of it.

S. Freud, 'A Project for a Scientific Psychology'
SE, **1**: 327

Any proposal to introduce yet another notion into psychoanalytic vocabulary is usually met with reserve. It is feared that such an addition would simply further encumber a theoretical machinery which one would prefer to lighten if anything. This is especially true when the notion proposed can neither claim to be a novelty nor to meet a lack, but seems rather to emerge from the depths of what one thought had been definitively forgotten – a sanction for its unjustified claim of usefulness.

The notion of negative hallucination which I shall examine in this chapter can be traced back to the heyday of hypnotism, before the birth of psycho-analysis even. Nowadays, perhaps, psychoanalysts are less familiar with it than the public who have come across it in books or films, even though the term itself may not be familiar to them. Its posterity was ensured by Maupassant's *Le Horla* written in 1887, a work whose literary filiation goes back to Hoffmann, Gogol and Dostoevski. We also need to take into account the part played in its conception by the demonstrations of Charcot and Bernheim, great masters in hypnotism, which the author witnessed, as did Freud. Barely three years later, in 1890, Freud mentioned negative hallucination for the first time in an article entitled 'Psychic Treatment'. The hypnotist's order was sufficient to suppress the perception of an object which 'tried to impose itself' on the hypnotised patient's senses. This was just the first of quite a long series of examples taken from hysterics as well as normal people. Occasionally, Freud cites one of his own experiences, the phenomenon appearing independently of any context of suggestion and in a thoroughly spontaneous manner. What may be surprising is the link established unhesitatingly between hallucination and a phenomenon of negation – since what is involved is the denial of an object's existence. From the first, it was accepted that it was not enough to compare the observation with normal perception as being a simple lack, but that it should be compared with hallucination as its counterpart. In positive hallucination ('perception without an object') there is something in excess (*l'en-plus*) which corresponds to what is lacking (*l'en-moins*) in negative hallucination ('non-perception of an object'). One must also note in the initial descriptions the common reference to a force which weighs upon the hypnotic subject from without, having the power to make him see what is not there or coercing him into remaining insensible – in the etymological sense of the term – to what is there. Yet, as we have already seen, the phenomenon can appear without the intervention of this external force. This extraneous will may also be replaced by an *internal* force which the subject does not recognise as being part of himself. Nor does he realise that it acts against his own will or without his knowing it, but the motive is always the same: to act against what he seems to want consciously. Breuer, who was less scrupulous than Freud with regard to the terms he used, speaks in this connection of a 'negative attitude'.[2] When the force acts from inside the subject there are clues which enable one to infer its existence indirectly, e.g., hysterical conversion, which shows that it derives from outside the psyche; obsessive representation, whose content does not appear to account for its obsidian tenacity, leading us to look for the displacement which it was subject to; and, finally, hallucination which designates quite clearly the projection of its offshoots recognised in Freud's earliest writings. The discovery of this internal force soon makes it clear what it is that resists its manifestation, i.e., repression, which now becomes the focus of attention. These first investigations relied on an active investigative method, whether hypnotic or not.

One can easily imagine how the invention of psychoanalysis would greatly diminish interest in negative hallucination by laying emphasis on the organisation of the internal world. However, the paradigmatic value of the symptom remains. And even if it has not given rise to many new developments, we are reminded of it through direct and indirect signs at key moments during the re-examination of central concepts of analytic theory. We will have ample cause to come back to this later.

Thus negative hallucination is a psychic mechanism which relates to two categories: hallucinatory activity and the negative. The former will lead us to study its relations with perception and unconscious representation and the latter calls for a close analysis of its relation to other more familiar defences (repression, splitting, negation, etc.).

Hallucination: A Defence Neurosis or Psychosis?

However frequent the allusions to the strange phenomenon of negative hallucination in Freud's writings[3] were, particularly at the beginning, though less so thereafter, it is clear that the institution of the psychoanalytic setting and the selection of those for whom the method was suitable would favour other notions which needed to be given prior consideration, i.e., representation rather than perception, psychical reality rather than external reality, the reaction to absence rather than presence, the reference to memory rather than sensibility to the present, the understanding of fantasy rather than the relation to the observable world. Whereas in his early clinical contributions Freud never tired of comparing hysteria and obsessional neurosis to paranoia and to hallucinatory confusion (Meynert's amentia), little by little, these two latter conditions ceased to be a part of this comparative approach.[4] However, they both present hallucinations, either in the clinical picture of chronic delusion in paranoia, or during the oneirism caused by hallucinatory confusion. One would be wrong in thinking, however, that hallucination is a synonym for psychosis – acute or chronic. Quite the opposite. During the period when Freud was almost exclusively interested in hysteria, he included the hallucinations of hysterics among the symptoms he examined. The fact is that at this stage in his thinking all these conditions which I have just mentioned were seen as belonging to the 'psycho-neuroses of defence'. It was at this point that the mental process of 'defence' or of 'repression'[5] entered the picture, one year *after* the publication of the the the 'Project'.

A reading of 'Further Remarks on the Neuro-Psychoses of Defence' (1896) is of interest on two accounts. On the one hand, Freud analyses the various symptoms (hysteric, obsessional, paranoiac – hallucination playing, of course, a major role in the last of these) in relation to each other, comparing the psychical mechanisms specific to each category. But, on the other hand, however interesting these psychical constructions may be, he relativises their distinctive features by tracing them back to the common mechanism which accounts for them: repression and its corollary, the return of the repressed. Hallucinatory activity loses importance in two respects. First, the privilege – which it has sometimes enjoyed in semiology – of being a sign by means of which psychosis can be identified, is erased by being included within a neurotic framework. Secondly, the analysis of its mechanism subordinates it to being simply one of the vicissitudes of the return of the repressed. From then on the problem lies elsewhere. Rather than wearing oneself out searching for the meaning and function of hallucination by means of an active technique of investigation, the priority now is how to gain access to the repressed. Instead of searching for it actively, it turns out to be better to arrange things in such a way that it reveals itself spontaneously: this is the invention of analysis. But that implies sacrificing hallucination which does not lend itself so easily to the analytic game as the other two neuroses. Negative hallucination and positive hallucination make way for more manageable subjects of study. To put it another way, negativising the therapeutic situation by the adopting of criteria such as free association, floating attention, and benevolent neutrality, is less favourable to the observation of negative symptoms which appear under normal conditions of observation or during hypnosis.

As analytic treatment became increasingly codified, the clinical features of hallucination were no longer taken into account. Does this mean that hallucinatory activity ceased to have a place in Freud's thinking? As we shall soon see, nothing could be further from the truth. On the one hand, we cannot help thinking that he needed little persuasion to turn away from the psychoses, which were considered unsuitable for psychoanalysis; we know that he had no great inclination for tackling them. On the other hand, Freud had the ambition of being much more than a specialist in neuroses; his theories were intended to cover the whole field of psychopathology. And much more than that even, since their range of application extends beyond clinical practice. It might as well be said that he could not neglect the study of psychosis even though its fixations and regressions might have prevented its analysis. Under these circumstances the publication of Schreber's *Memoirs* was a godsend: the richness of the patient's introspection, the quality of the document which he puts at the disposition of his doctors and the precision and insight which he demonstrates, surpass by far the most in-depth psychiatric observations. The possibility we have of studying it carefully compensates largely, under these circumstances, for the lack of immediate data which only an analysis can gather. This is then an unhoped-for opportunity to renew our understanding of psychosis which will make it possible to test the conceptions developed by psychoanalysis over the last dozen years or so.

While we can only admire the way Freud elucidates and interprets the pathology of the *Senatspräsident*, there is also good reason to be surprised in certain respects. Dr Weber's diagnosis, which Freud reports without further discussion, is 'hallucinatory insanity'.[6] Now Freud's brilliant analysis says almost nothing of Schreber's hallucinations. What I mean is that Freud approaches the case from the angle of delusion and the mechanism of paranoia but shows only very limited interest in hallucination. Admittedly, from time

immemorial, the analysis of hallucinatory delusions has laid emphasis alternatively either on the aspect of delusion or on that of hallucination in order
to maintain that one was responsible for the genesis of the other. Did Freud
simply join ranks with those who opted to give pride of place to delusion? Can
the priority which was given to the study of repression, the libido, the ego and
their relations only be explained by the place accorded to delusion? Even if
this is so, it scarcely exempts us from examining more closely the hallucinatory phenomenon which remains the sign of a very distinctive mental
functioning. Moreover, Freud does not shirk this completely: he defines hallucination briefly with a formulation of great importance when he describes
the return, by an external path, that of perception, of what was *abolished* on
the inside – and not just suppressed or repressed. This is no doubt the essential
point, but stopping there means being content to note the fact in passing, giving
the impression that we do not want to dwell on the implications of what we
have put forward. Freud practically acknowledges this himself, deferring further
discussion until later.[7] Once again, Freud's approach has two aspects to it. On
the one hand, as we have seen, the elucidation of hallucinations in psychosis,
qualified nonetheless as hallucinatory, disappears with the analysis of repression
– as in neurosis. But on the other, with hindsight and not immediately, Freud
pinpoints a difference. He revises his position: what is involved is not suppression affecting the inside (that is an action connected with repression) but
of *abolition*. Is it repression which is involved? Freud does not say and asks us
to wait until he is ready to communicate his thoughts on projection, which,
however, he never does. We know we are indebted to Lacan for his contribution on foreclosure but I am not certain that his commentaries exhaust the
question either. What is important is to explain how hallucination is related
to an *abolition,* considered by Lacan to be a flaw in symbolisation. The Phallus
and the foreclosure of the Name of the Father are supposed to satisfy our
curiosity and fulfil our expectations. Really?

The enigma of Freud's declining interest in the symptom of 'hallucination'
can be explained by the connection established between this pathological
phenomenon and dreams whose normality cannot be contested. We are led
to look for their common denominator by constructing a model which accounts
for each of them and is worthy of consideration in its own right for its general
validity which goes far beyond any theoretical forms resulting from it.

An Outline for a Model – Drifting towards Dreams

While Freud's interest in the symptomatology of hallucination waned, he
wanted to get to the core of hallucinatory activity. Even before the discovery
of repression which did not play the slightest part in his first theoretical construction, he prepared the ground for his future model in the '*Project*' of 1895.
The advantage of this work – even if Freud disowned it – is that it gives us a

very precise idea of the notion he had of the basic elements of psychical life and the essential principles of their functioning. Accordingly, after the definition of neurones and quantities in motion, that is, minimal 'atomic' elements – in the etymological sense of the word – and the relations uniting them, comes the first description of the two major experiences of 'psychology': satisfaction and pain. The experience of satisfaction brings out the analogy between perception and hallucination.[8] The reactivation, under the pressure of states of tension and wishing, of *mnemonic memories of the wished-for object and of the reflex movement* produces a hallucination, he writes. There is no difficulty in recognising what was later to become hallucinatory wish-fulfilment although it is not named as such at this stage. On the contrary, the experience of pain aims at avoiding the return to the psyche of the memory of painful experiences. The coupling of the two 'experiences' will form the basis of the future pleasure–unpleasure principle. Already in this first attempt to organise his theories into a whole, Freud establishes a close connection between hallucination and primary process.[9] In spite of modern interpretations which have attempted to separate the temporal and structural meanings of the term primary, for Freud, the term undoubtedly covers both aspects. Thus primary denotes what is assumed to exist at the beginning of psychical life in the short-circuit 'reflex', desired object–presented object as (if it was) real, by constructing theoretically what constitutes its foundations to which the psyche may be obliged to return, flouting many earlier acquisitions when, for example, reality becomes too unbearable because of the deficiencies which have to be endured.

We can therefore understand the paradoxical position in which Freud found himself: as a clinician he appears to give less and less importance to hallucination; as a theoretician, on the contrary, he gives it a place which it had never been given before. Once the model was 'outlined' it gave rise to all sorts of developments and constructions which generation upon generation of psychoanalysts would try and amend in order to improve it.

Alongside these neurobiological fictions, however, Freud's essay contains two parts which are still of great interest today: the analysis of a hysterical symptom (the Proton Pseudos) and an initial exposition of his ideas on dreams in which this phenomenon is linked with hallucination ('we shut our eyes and hallucinate'), announcing what is to follow, that is, the book on dreams and the case of Dora, subtitled 'Dreams and Hysteria'. There was another reason which led Freud to turn his attention to dreams. He had been misled by clinical experience. He had believed in the trauma of seduction. There was a great danger of giving too much credit to what patients say. For, in spite of claims to the contrary, it was not a question of fantasy having replaced seduction. Finding the solution so easily would be too much to hope for. It was much more troublesome to have to admit that the criteria available were insufficient to determine when seduction had occurred and when it had not. By considering the problem in terms of the subject's psychic productions alone, the field of fantasy was circumscribed more adequately. With the phenomenon of dreaming this anticipated 'reality-testing' was no longer an issue. Furthermore, in response to the drawback of the subject's eventual fantasising (conscious? unconscious?), Freud does not make use of the illusory measure of a verification which would rely on the power of consciousness but, on the contrary, turns towards the analysis of a mechanism of fantasy freed from the suspicion of being intentional in origin. The truth of a dream would dispel any doubts as to the narrator's intentionality. Clinical considerations were to be dealt with later. It was an exemplary approach bearing witness to a deep familiarity with the powers of the negative.

This *'Project'* was to lead to the theoretical development set out in *The Interpretation of Dreams* (1900). It might be helpful here to recapitulate on a number of well-known findings with the purpose of shedding new light on them. Instead of proceeding in a progressive way, we shall adopt another approach. Let us consider that the conclusions Freud drew from *The Interpretation of Dreams* were not so much discoveries made in the course of an investigation, whose eventual outcome was unknown, as demonstrations of hypotheses drawn from his earlier trials and errors. They may be summarised as follows:

1. Nothing can be learnt directly from clinical experience. Comparative semiology itself can say nothing about the *raison d'être* and meaning of symptoms. Only recourse to psychic mechanisms seen from a dynamic and comparative standpoint can throw light on the diversity, the structure and the function of symptoms which are subject to more general key principles.

2. The distinction between normal and pathological is based on different modes of functioning originating in a group of common factors. In other words, normal and neurotic people are inhabited by the same desires and the same fears, but these have got nothing to do with what they admit to each other spontaneously in the course of ordinary exchanges. Pathology is only mysterious and often incomprehensible because it arises from an intensification (involuntary) of the procedures which habitually contribute to the concealment of these preoccupations, an intensification which is proportionate to the increasing fear (often justified) that their activation makes them visible in spite of precautions taken to prevent this. One cannot simply say that what is pathological is mysterious and enigmatic. It would be better to admit that what is mysterious and enigmatic in a normal person is liable to become the source of pathology in a neurotic. This mysterious, enigmatic characteristic – which Laplanche focused on – no doubt comes from the complexity of psychical structure, but before asserting this in too transcendental a manner, we need to find out what men 'openly' hide, if I may put it like this, and draw all the

necessary conclusions concerning the way this constrains them to function psychically in relation to what they conceal from themselves, without being aware of it. This is all the more true in that Freud was led by experience to make the following observation: although men have secrets, they are incapable of keeping them. Furthermore, it is not so much others whom they betray as themselves. The key to this, then, is to be found in the disclosure of what exists within the normal person, without his being aware of it, but which, unlike the neurotic, he has managed to render unintelligible. In other words, the pathology corresponds to the visible struggle between the return of the repressed and repression, whereas this same struggle is indiscernible in the normal person because of successful repression. But the fact that there is no apparent struggle should not deflect our attention from what is some distance from it and makes its return at a later time. So, if the common factor is repression, this must be related to what it seeks to repress.

3. The success of repression in the normal person is very relative. Not only are there signs of misfunctioning, but there is a space and a time in which the lessening of censorships, even if it does not lift repression, attenuates the act of repression enough for 'steam to be let off' and to relieve the internal tension created by it. Dreams are an attempt to prevent the untimely return of the repressed and, more often than not, they enable the normal person to avoid the outcome of the conflict. However, unlike in cases of misfunctioning, it is not possible with dreams to cancel immediately what they have betrayed, by correcting them. They succeed in forming *another* reality. So man has the power to create a second world within the confines of sleep in which he can fulfil desires, making himself believe in the reality of this other world where this fulfilment occurs. This is what hallucinatory wish-fulfilment achieves. The 'realisation' signifies just as much the achievement of satisfaction as the creation of a reality in which such a satisfaction becomes possible. Finally, hallucination is the mode of functioning which manages to create this other world in which desire, by not succumbing to repression, exists in a form, thanks to which, the wish, which is disguised so that it cannot be identified, can take its place in a universe of 'realisation', indiscernible from reality. Nevertheless, the lowering of censorship in dreams is far from being equivalent to a suppression of repression. It is only through dream work that wish-fulfilment is achieved. It is also important to emphasise that even at the heart of this other reality of dreams, the dreamer is not conscious that the wish has been fulfilled. This can only be inferred from dream analysis. In spite of these special conditions, what takes place – the manifest content – is unavoidably subject to compromise. The hallucinatory fulfilment is complemented by the dream work which widens the gap between the latent content – which remains unsuspected – and the manifest content which the dreamer beholds in its hallucinated form. But the price to be paid for dreams creating a second reality is the sense of inco-

herence and absurdity experienced by the dreamer. There are thus two effects of the negative which need to be explored successively in dream work and in secondary elaboration.

4. What is instructive then is not so much the dream itself but what can be inferred from the study of its functioning which results in hallucinatory wish-fulfilment. This is useful as a model. The observation we made earlier about the hallucinatory nature of the primary process can therefore be sustained. It does not follow from this that all wish-fulfilment is accomplished by means of hallucination, just as the primary process does not necessarily take on a hallucinatory form. It is sufficient to admit that the wish can take on these extreme forms in certain cases, convincing us thereby of the power it can occasionally deploy. The advantage of the full model is that it shows us how far we can go. We must still bear in mind, however, that there is a risk involved in functioning beyond the permitted limits of the biological activity of sleep by exceeding the latter's restricted spatio-temporal conditions. On the other hand, confining wish-fulfilment and the primary process to their hallucinatory mode is too restrictive. The example of unconscious fantasy shows that the primary process may fall short of its hallucinatory fulfilment and its conscious form in order to be 'dreamed', but it is not, however, a dream. This being so, wish-fulfilment and primary process will be able to monopolise the psychical characteristics of dream functioning, *without however going as far as hallucinatory functioning*, but knowing that it is a possibility. Unconscious representations will take over from hallucinations. Sometimes both can merge, as in dreams. Usually they can be distinguished, as in waking life, where one can designate by a process of deduction an unconscious representation for which, by definition, there is no evidence in consciousness. What conclusions can be drawn then about the relations between unconscious representation and hallucination? Quite simply: the unconscious representation can never be *perceived* either from the inside or from the outside. It can acquire a form which can be represented after it has first been elaborated by the subject himself or by another person who elaborates the subject's thought for him. But in this case it will only be a conscious representation which is supposed to have some similarity with the unconscious representation which cannot be known. The preconscious representation is perceived from the inside, and only in this way. Hallucination is a representation, essentially unconscious, which is transformed into perception by being transposed outwards, due to the impossibility of its acquiring an acceptable form for the subject even just within himself. It can only be perceived from the outside (unlike the preconscious representation) by passing itself off, if need be, as a perception, that is, as originating from the outside. When we speak of an internal perception, we are not referring to a representation or a psychical event which can be represented or thought about, in other words which can be apprehended as an object (*ob-jet*) of the psyche, but rather which

is sensed in the way sensations coming from the outside are, sometimes carrying very little significance. On the other hand, we are bound to conclude that wish-fulfilment and primary process tend towards hallucinatory activity, so much so that the problem arises *a contrario*: how is the spontaneous tendency towards hallucinatory activity to be restrained? Freud was to wrestle with this problem for more than twenty years.[10]

The Return of Negative Hallucination

In 'A Metapsychological Supplement to the Theory of Dreams' (1917), a major revision of his *Papers on Metapsychology* (1915), Freud comes back to the comparison between dreams and hallucination understood in the light of the first topography and with the help of the notion of investment. Three states are seen as being very similar: dreaming, acute hallucinatory confusion and the hallucinatory phase of schizophrenia (which replaces here what was formerly known as paranoia). The first two can be included under the general title of 'wishful hallucinatory psychosis',[11] the third can be accounted for by the return of investments towards objects. Freud then comments that it is not enough to bring unconscious wishes into consciousness for them to be taken as realities. Belief in reality seems to be bound up with perception through the senses or regression to hallucination. But how does hallucination come about? Regression would be an unsatisfactory answer since we can let very clear visual mnemic-images invade consciousness without taking them for real perceptions. In other words, twenty years later, the hallucinations of hysterics were no longer necessarily considered to be hallucinatory. Reliving (regressive) is not hallucination.

What is at stake in this discussion is the relationship to reality. This task falls to perception but as (wishful) hallucination is so similar to it that it is difficult to tell them apart, it may be assumed that the psyche has equipped itself with a supplementary contrivance: reality-testing. Under normal conditions, perception and wishful hallucination can be differentiated, i.e., the subject does not take his wishful hallucinations for realities any more than he takes the shadow of the object for the object, thanks to the contrivance in question. Nonetheless, amentia and dreams can succeed in putting it out of action.

The following solution may be given: the system Cs., otherwise called P (perception) can be invested from within and not, as is normally the case, from without alone. It is in this sense that regression can lead to hallucination. What is involved then is not only vividness or regressive reliving, i.e., the aesthesic intensity of the representation, but also the possibility it has of occupying the terrain of consciousness and seeing to it that there is no longer any distinction between internal and external reality. Or, to be more exact, that internal reality succeeds in passing for external reality. The reality principle, postulated for some time and recently theorised in the 'Formulations on the Two Principles of Mental Functioning' (1911) arms itself with a test before being subjected to a 'judgement' (of existence). It is now that Freud adds the note which was the starting-point for my elaboration: 'I may add by way of supplement that any attempt to explain hallucination would have to start out from *negative* rather than positive hallucination.'[12]

With this single notation, Freud gives us a glimpse of an entire psychical constellation at the origin of hallucinatory production. The latter is thought to result from a dual action originating from an interface between:

– its external face, an undesirable, insupportable or intolerable perception leads to a negative hallucination expressing the wish to reject it to the point of denying the existence of the perceived objects;

– its internal face, an unconscious representation of a wish (abolished) which seeks to enter consciousness but which finds itself prevented from doing so by the barrier of the system *Cs.* (*P*). The latter gives way to the pressure put on it and the space occupied by the denied perception is now vacant.

The conjunction of these two aspects gives us reason to suppose that a potentialising of effects may be involved, that is to say, the unbearable perception is 'irreconcilable' (to use an old expression of Freud's) with the unconscious representation and, rather than the latter disappearing, it is the perception which is invalidated. The space which has been liberated by the negative hallucination is occupied, through projection, by the unconscious representation in a form which cannot easily be defined. But we could imagine that it takes on the attributes of perception, not in a way which would lead to their being confused, but through the form which denial takes in this case which 'whitens' whatever presents itself to the mind, suggesting the intervention of a mechanism which Freud qualifies as 'pulling away' from what is perceived. Between external reality which presses against internal reality, and internal reality which refuses to give way, the psychical apparatus has decided in favour of the latter, to the point of giving it the credence accorded to perceptions, as if the latter had done away with censorships. Thus negative hallucination is the process by which the ego can break off or interrupt its relations to reality. It can therefore justifiably be considered as the major process which governs relations between reality and the ego and which can, in extreme cases, extend to the durable process of repressing reality which Freud describes in psychosis. This is carried out thanks to a withdrawal of investment, or in more extreme circumstances by a disinvestment.[13] With respect to this, the voluntary renunciation occurring in dreams can be distinguished from the extensive and obligatory 'repression'[14] found in amentia.

Perception and Denial – Splitting

Freud was to come back to this question at a later date. With the benefit of the hindsight needed for presenting an overview of his ideas and trying to focus on the essential points on the pretext – a fortunate one for us – that he was giving a talk (imaginary) to an audience which was keen to learn of the recent acquisitions of psychoanalysis, Freud wrote:

> This system (*Pcpt.-Cs.*) is turned towards the external world, it is the medium for the perceptions arising thence, and during its functioning the phenomenon of consciousness arises in it. It is the sense-organ of the entire apparatus; moreover it is receptive not only to excitations from outside but also to those arising from the interior of the mind. We need scarcely look for a justification of the view that the ego is that portion of the id which was modified by the proximity and influence of the external world, which is adapted for the reception of stimuli, comparable to the cortical layer by which a small piece of living substance is surrounded. [...] In accomplishing this function [representing the external world 'to the id'] the ego must observe the external world, must lay down an accurate picture of it in the memory-traces of its perceptions, and by its exercise of the function of 'reality-testing' must put aside whatever in this picture of the external world is an addition derived from internal sources of excitation.[15]

He added that thought activity is interposed between a need and an action. Two functions are emphasised here:

– the task of reproducing an accurate picture of the external world with particular insistence on the distinction between the internal or external source of excitations and information;

– the setting up of a limit which functions as an interface adapted both for the reception of stimuli and as a protective shield against them.

It is not difficult to see that these two functions are bound to contradict each other.

Freud's clarification of the relations between hallucination and perception should not lead us to believe that they are the only cases where the question of the relations of reality perception arises. There is a new allusion to it in the short article on 'The Loss of Reality in Neurosis and Psychosis' (1924).[16] The importance of hallucinatory activity corresponds to the need to create a new reality by procuring a constant influx of new perceptions. Alongside this hallucinatory excess, of which psychosis is an example, we should also consider the case where negative hallucination (of which positive hallucination is the corollary) does not occur, although there is indeed a misfunctioning of perception. This is the case with fetishism. Here too the perception is intolerable: the boy refused 'to take cognisance of the fact of his having perceived that a woman does not have a penis'.[17] What is happening exactly? Freud raises the question: is this scotomization? This would however suggest that the perception had been completely erased. He adds: 'In the situation we are considering, on the contrary, we see that the perception has persisted, and that a very energetic action has been undertaken to maintain the disavowal.'[18] He proposes instead the mechanism of *Verleugnung* or – following Jean Laplanche's translation – disavowal. In other words, in negative hallucination disavowal involves doing away with perception and in *Verleugnung* it involves denial: the subject cannot believe his eyes, but it is precisely because he can see and not because he is blind.

All these situations suggest that it is necessary, where perception is concerned, to separate its object from the judgement which it makes of what it perceives. From now on the idea of a 'neutral' perception is seriously challenged. And the difference between perception and wishful representation is not so clear as one might think. However, it is precisely the preservation of perception which interests us as well as the introduction of a split mode of judgement in which the correlate of perception is the creation of a double language which both recognises and denies castration simultaneously. Furthermore, what results is a clinging to the fetish as a substitute for the penis which perception showed to be lacking. The article on 'Fetishism' (1927) not only sheds light on perversions, it is also a remarkable analysis of certain thought processes which are no less instructive than those which can be inferred from the couple representation–hallucination.

Internal Perceptions – Body and Thought

We are naturally inclined to associate perception with the ego's relation to the external world. This restriction of the perceptive field is in fact a convenient oversimplification. In Chapter 2 of *The Ego and the Id*, which is also the title of the work as a whole, Freud sets himself the task of redefining the different ways in which something becomes conscious, for this is our only means of knowing. With this purpose in mind, he divides up perceptions according to their origin. He contrasts those which come from without through the senses with those which come from within: sensations and feelings. To them he adds thought-processes which will become perceptions through the interposition of word-representations.

Two kinds of internal perceptions can thus be contrasted: those arising from the body and those connected with thought. As far as the first are concerned, Freud reneges, in order to state the opposite, on the opinion he had expressed in the *Papers on Metapsychology* with respect to the non-existence of feelings, that is, of unconscious affects. Feelings therefore can indeed be repressed (and not just suppressed).

But that is not all. Classical psychiatry taught us long ago of the existence of Cotard's 'delusion of negations' which is observed much less frequently now because the evolution of the affection, during which it appeared, has been stopped, thereby preventing its manifestation. In the course of Cotard's syndrome, after a melancholic phase, the patient often presents a far-reaching negativist attitude. The whole world is dead, the subject no longer has any parents, etc. But the most curious thing is the negation of organs: the patient claims he has no organs any more inside his body. This generates as an indirect consequence a delusional megalomania: the absence of organs leads to the idea of immortality and at the same time the body, losing its limits, feels it is expanding so that it comes to occupy the whole universe.[19] Thus the sense of one's own body, on which the most immediate consciousness of one's existence is based, can be disavowed which destroys the perception of it.

Although nowadays these strange clinical pictures are less frequently observed, other much more discreet forms can be seen to stem from comparable problems. Thus alexithymia, as described by Sifneos, does not only designate an absence of words to name affects but also, in the sense in which I understand it, the inability to experience affective states, that is to say, to become conscious of them. J. McDougall has gone more deeply into the analysis of patients presenting manifestations of this kind, postulating that unconscious affect is cut off from the system of word-presentations.[20]

In other words, without an appropriate 'reading' which would make it possible to think about their meaning, affects can never be nominated. All these cases, which are similar to those studied by P. Marty's Psychosomatic School, lead us to compare psychosis and *psychosomatosis*. This approach raises such complicated and far-reaching problems that they cannot be discussed here. We have confined ourselves to mentioning briefly the possible negativising of sensations linked to the body itself and to affects. By linking them with negative hallucination, we are making the hypothesis that hypochondria or certain passionate manifestations, which are more or less delusional, occur against a background of negative hallucination in the sphere of the body or that of the emotions. As for the eventual relevance of such a hypothesis, applied to psychosomatic disturbances, we may suppose that the shutting-down of the preconscious barrier mentioned by P. Marty might stem from the same phenomenon whose extension would also be relevant to other topographical barriers.

In the comparative analysis of symptoms which Freud undertakes in the article 'Further Remarks on the Neuro-Psychoses of Defence' (1896) we can read:

A thing which is quite peculiar to paranoia and on which no further light can be shed by this comparison [with obsessional neurosis], is that repressed self-reproaches return in the form of thoughts spoken aloud. In the course of this process, they are obliged to submit to a two-fold distortion: they are subjected to a censorship, which leads to their being replaced by other, associated thoughts or to their being concealed by an indefinite mode of expression, and they are referred to recent experiences which are no more than analogous to the old ones.[21]

This hallucinatory activity is amply illustrated in Schreber's *Memoirs,* even if it is not given particular attention. However, in his later works, Freud proposes an original and new conception of language. He attributes it with the function, thanks to verbal mnemic residues, of making thought-processes perceptible. In short, language allows thought to be 'externalised'. Nevertheless, it is clear that language is only perceived from the outside by the person who is listening; the person who is speaking, who hears his thoughts externalised, knows he is their author and only experiences language as a projection of his thoughts in the way that conscious reverie can be. Neither of them lose their sense of what belongs to them as subjects, whereas in auditory hallucinations voices are attributed to another person who also has the power of knowing their thoughts even when they are not verbalised. The interpretation of these symptoms assumes that there is a splitting of thought-processes accompanied by a projection and a return of what is projected in a hallucinatory form.

The question which arises then is to know whether, in this case too, positive hallucinations are preceded by negative hallucinations, that is, by a denial of the perception of verbalised thoughts, belonging to internal language, without being expressed out loud. This is very probably the case.

Nonetheless, if negative hallucination can exist as an entity apart, without necessarily being followed by positive hallucinations, as is usually the case, we may wonder if we should not refer to it under certain circumstances in analytic treatment. I am alluding here to certain moments in the analysis of borderline cases where the analysand does not understand certain of the analyst's inter-pretations, or even does not seem to recognise his own words when the analyst reminds him of them. In the first instance, the analyst thinks it is an ordinary resistance or an act of repression. But I have come to think that what is involved here is a real psychical agnosia which stems not only from an attempt to avert consciousness but also from a non-recognition of words, phrases and propo-sitions, whether they are his own, or whether they are repeated by the analyst or again have recently been expressed by the latter but are too closely related to what has to be disavowed.

Our remarks so far have led us from negative hallucination in hypnosis, encountered above all in connection with visual perceptions, to the analysis of the model of hallucinatory wish-fulfilment which again concerns the sphere of vision and is prevalent in the phenomena of representability (*figurabilité*) in dreams, then to the comparisons between unconscious representations, hal-lucinations and perceptions, looking finally at the case of auditory hallucinations and their relations with language and thought. This last approach reconciles, to some degree, the investigation of the phenomenon of hallucination with the conditions of the analytic setting which imply a perceptive restriction, above all visual. Although it is rare for auditory hallucination to be compatible with the practice of so-called classical analysis, it at least has the advantage of refocusing the investigation on speech and language, the subject's internal splitting reduplicating the analysand–analyst relationship in the 'classical' cure. In fact the main interest of such a rapprochement is to shed light on cases involving non-neurotic structures which, when they are the object of analytic treatment within the modified setting required for them, can face the analyst with unexpected situations which he naturally tends to interpret within the parameters operating for neuroses, but which soon make it felt that they call for other types of interpretation evoking not so much the logic of repression as that of disavowal seen from the specific angle of perceptive non-recognition.

The Exemplary Case of the 'Wolf Man'

Most of the issues we have been considering are to be found in the case of the 'Wolf Man'. In an earlier study,[22] I made a detailed analysis of the hallucination of the severed finger which the patient talked about. Let us recall the circumstances: Serguei recollects a scene which took place when he was five years old: 'I was playing in the garden near my nurse, and was carving with my pocket-knife in the bark of one of the walnut trees that come into my dream as well. Suddenly, to my unspeakable horror, I noticed that I had cut through the little finger of my (right or left?) hand, so that it was only hanging on by its skin. I felt no pain, but great fear.'

At this point Freud inserts a note to report another version given by the patient on a later occasion in which he says he has confused this recollection with another, 'hallucinatorily falsified', in which he made a cut in the tree with his knife and had seen blood coming out of the tree. The recollection of this passage in the 'Wolf Man' calls for a number of observations. Little Serguei says that he cannot bear to cast a glance at his finger. The fear of seeing the fantasy materialised, which would be confirmed by the sight of the finger, results in his refusing to look. Moreover, he manages in his hallucination – that is, at a time when perception is replaced by its equivalent – not 'seeing' the blood which the cut causes. In other words, at the moment when the hallucination occurs, the fantasy of blood is negativised.

Equally, no pain is felt. Nonetheless his state of dejection is so intense (and the impression of reality apparently so convincing) that the child does not try to reassure himself immediately by telling himself his senses are tricking him. The observation, at the heart of this 'moment of hallucination' which rarely occurs in states of confusion or of clouded consciousness but, on the contrary, occurs in a context of play and in the presence of the nurse, of traces of neg-ativisation, makes it possible to construct a symbolic matrix: a woman–mother

... turning his eyes away from ... feeling blood running from a cut ... causing an intolerable pain (through the *jouissance* it brings) ... making me think about [the tree in] my dream. The rest of the associations show the numerous ramifications which such a memory can have. Of all these, let us simply mention the one Freud refers to in a note as a 'correction' of the patient: 'I don't believe I was cutting the tree. That was a confusion with another recollection which must also have been hallucinatorily falsified, of having made a cut in a tree with my knife and of *blood* having come out of the tree.'[23] Somewhat surprising here is the phenomenon of *déjà raconté* evoked by the account of the recollection and contested by the analyst.

In the case of the 'Wolf Man', the childhood object of denial returns by means of a temporary hallucination and also as an anxiety-provoking repetitive dream. But the work of the negative, so patent in the cure under the mask of rationalisation which Freud, admiring his patient's intellectual qualities, is taken in by, suggests that there is good reason to question the nature of this repression and to assume that foreclosure is at work. Moreover, a reading of Freud's reflections on anal eroticism suggest the possible link – which he himself, however, does not make – between the Russian and Schreber.[24] Instead of enabling us to clarify unconscious desires, the hallucinatory connotation of the associations results in a negativising potentiation of the psychical work which carries out their elaboration.

So, 'I was cutting the tree ...' is denied secondarily in order to make room for another recollection in which the bark was indeed cut 'on' the tree itself, after which there was no hallucination of the severed finger but instead blood was seen coming out of the trunk. Apparently, one hallucination is simply being replaced by another. The rectified version even seems preferable to the initial version because there is an essential semantic element in it which is clearly visible: the link between the cut and the blood. *For us*, the previous semanteme is still present, i.e., the allusion to the severed finger. And it is probably here that we miss the essential point: namely, that for the 'Wolf Man' the correction does not complete the previous memory by adding a meaning which was lacking. On the contrary, the fact of drawing nearer to consciousness, which is expressed by the explanation of the semanteme 'blood', giving us the illusion that there is a closer link between the wound and the sexual member, in fact has the function of trying to invalidate the unconscious link between the cut finger and the sexual member. In the same way, what the recollection allows us to infer from the trauma about the nature of hallucination which, surpassing the boundaries of fantasy, emerges in the surprising context of an unexpected and apparently very 'real' event, plunging the subject into a state of collapse and leaving him without reaction, has now been trivialised during the reporting of the story by the familiar innocuousness of the *déjà raconté*. To this may be added the hypothesis of a repressed thought ('and nothing terrible happened'), thereby neutralising a transferential reliving of the fantasy of a castrating Freud, in contradistinction to the Rat Man leaping off the couch at the mention of the rat torture.

Such a way of thinking leads to the hypothesis of a disconnection of causality similar to that evoked by obsessional neurosis. But in this case the manipulations of representation must be interpreted, not in terms of the semantic links of representations – or at any rate not in terms of them – but in terms of the relation between investments and representations. In other words, the links only refer to the relations of meaning in as far as these relate to *claims,* that is, to the quest of the drives in which relations to the other and to oneself are rooted. Let us look again at the successive versions of the hallucinated memories.

On the one hand, a severed finger without blood; on the other, blood without a severed finger. Now we know that if there is some liquid oozing from a tree, it is very likely that the *first* thing it will conjure up is seminal liquid. The blood is thus linked to the denied thought and to the negativised representation of sperm, and therefore to the penis. We should bear in mind, however, that what instigated this hallucination, according to the patient, was the story that a relative of his had been born with six toes, and that the extra one had been chopped off with an axe.[25] Recognition and denial: there is indeed a cut connected with a violent bodily amputation, but it leaves bodily integrity intact and even makes it more 'normal'. We are not far from the idea: 'yes, women are castrated because the *extra* penis they have is taken away from them, which however does not suggest in any way the idea that a consequence of castration might be that I have a member *lacking*, since in fact castration makes her the same as me and means we are constituted in the same way'.

This is a good example of what I have called the 'Wolf Man's dual-logic.[26] It is worth pointing out that the manifestations of this logic are not based solely on representation. Furthermore, due to the evasive possibilities which are created by the conjunction and disjunction of conscious and unconscious thing-representations, negativisation is at work and, what is more, is deeply rooted in drive activity. We are reminded here of the contradiction between the different 'trends' concerning castration which gives Freud the opportunity of describing the (attitude) 'I won't have it', since designated as foreclosure by Lacan and as rejection by Laplanche. This blunt refusal blossoms into affective and intellectual ambivalence, as those who worked with Serguei Pankejeff after Freud had every opportunity to experience.

The case of the 'Wolf Man' is exemplary in more than one respect, but how? In the first place because negative hallucination goes unnoticed, being covered over by the recollection of a positive hallucination in which it is hidden. Secondly, because the patient's serious thought disturbances did not lead to the development of the hallucinatory potentialities he possessed. On the other hand, in his case, when regression takes a form which is evocative of psychosis, it manifests itself as a quasi-delusional, if not delusional, hypochondria. Lastly, this hypochondria is focused on an organ – the nose – which is the object of a symbolic contraction, a real short-circuiting of representation. This leads to constant perceptive verifications with all the possible gains to be had from eroticising care to breakdown – which is a repetition of the hallucination of the severed finger – when the patient learns that his lesion is definitive. In a previous analysis of this fragment of 'The Wolf Man', I concluded as follows:

> *The hallucination of the severed finger is preceded by the negative hallucination of the extra finger overshadowed in the hallucinatory content; the latter simply positivises, on the basis of this negative hallucination, an amputation which has already been carried out on the level of thought.*[27]

We cannot overlook the relation between this radical investment of the part of his body which is perceptible as much as it is exhibited, and the total absence of perception of the changes in his wife's state of mind – their union was one of the issues at stake in his analysis with Freud who did not hesitate to give his imprimatur to this project of marriage after having met Theresa. These changes led her to commit suicide which, according to the Russian, came as a total surprise for him.

Freud probably underestimated with this patient the part played by psychical work in the subject's relations to perception for he was entirely preoccupied with the analysis of representations (dreams), the memories of infantile neurosis and finally the reconstitution of the primal scene. The latter mobilised the whole of Freud's energy in the search for proof (against Jung) of his perception of things which was more than likely true. It distracted him from addressing the relations between the internal and external world from any other angle than that of amnesia and memory to which he would have to return at a later date.

In a word, the exemplary nature of the 'Wolf Man's case resides in the fact that for a long time the patient, who had served as a first case for the demonstration of infantile 'neurosis', made us overlook the fact that his psychopathological structure in adulthood could no longer be envisaged satisfactorily from the angle of neurosis. This was a fact which the analysts involved had difficulty in integrating with their theory, believing that they were thereby respecting Freud's work – a negative hallucination, no doubt, which concerned both Freud's text and the perception of the case which gave rise to it, as well as the relationship which bound them to each other. In describing *Verwerfung*, Freud implicitly supported the hypothesis – which would be considered impossible today – that the transference could be spared this very 'rejection'. In fact this implicit assumption burdens Freud's entire theoretical construction. The discovery of the 'primal scene' was coloured by it as the 'Wolf Man's remarks, after his analysis, would show.

Hallucinatory Wish-Fulfilment Revised

The way in which Freud's work lends support to the idea of a work of the negative has left us in no doubt as to its interest. Furthermore, its study shows the original way in which this notion can be enriched by psychoanalysis. But that is not enough. One hopes a better model will be put forward to account for clinical experience and to give a more satisfying picture of the human psyche.

In what ways are the Freudian models no longer satisfying for the psycho-analyst today? As far as I am concerned, it is not Freud's most daring concepts which I would want to call into question. I accept the fact that they are often conjectural in character because – given our present state of knowledge – it seems to me to be inevitable. To my mind, it is not so much a question of rejecting Freudian concepts as of emphasising their shortcomings. To be more exact, we need to uncover the implicit assumptions on which they rest.

Let us take for example the model of hallucinatory wish-fulfilment. It supposes from the outset the prevalent and sufficiently assured inscription of residues of an experience of satisfaction which serves as a point of reference, 'in case of need', through recourse to the representation (hallucinatory fulfilment) of the said experience of satisfaction, as an aim to be achieved if a state of calm is to be regained. This means that the experience of satisfaction took place and was repeated sufficiently often to give rise to a referential inscription without contrary effects – that is, without unpleasure, anxiety or pain which contest its prevalence. Equally, the models of the psychical apparatus, and notably the one Freud puts forward in the article on 'Negation' (1925) rely on the efficiency of the psychical apparatus to get rid of what it feels is bad by expelling it outwards, a process I have proposed to call excor-poration. This is so that incorporation, and then introjection, lead to a purified pleasure-ego, the structural core of the psychism whose constitution is a pre-requisite for any development. Now, we may recall Freud's note concerning the pleasure–unpleasure system in the 'Two Principles' where he hints at the need to include maternal care if the system is to work. We can say as much here: in order for hallucinatory wish-fulfilment to occur, and for the purified pleasure-ego to establish itself, it is necessary that the system of functioning which they imply benefits from maternal coverage.

Hallucinatory wish-fulfilment is grounded, as it were, in drive activity always in search of satisfaction. The role of quasi-object which hallucinatory wish-fulfilment offers the psyche leads us to stress this dependence of the constitution of imaginary objects on the real primary object evoked by hallucinatory wish-fulfilment. Consequently, while it is necessary to implicate the subject's drive structure which pushes for the creation of these formations, it should not be forgotten that it is based on the traces of real experiences which imply the action of a *real* object. This quality of being real (*ce réel*) should not be taken into account so much for its nature which is opposed to the imaginary as for its influence on the productions of the latter and for its relations with the psyche's other modes of functioning.

The development of Freud's work culminates in the final drive theory. The model of hallucinatory wish-fulfilment is contemporary with a drive duality which opposes preservation and sexuality. It proves itself to be perfectly adequate in this theoretical context since hallucinatory wish-fulfilment is a response to hunger (thus to self-preservation) and to sexuality (the pleasure of sucking). Hallucinatory fulfilment will not be affected by the introduction into the theory of the destructive drives, which is rather surprising.

In certain of his late writings,[28] Freud often speaks of the importance of very early experiences and of those which are opposed to them. Manifestly, he is alluding here to the 'opposite' of experiences of satisfaction. Now, taking into account the equilibrium or the antagonism of the experiences of satisfaction with those of pain (or of unpleasure) brings in the function of the object. Whereas in the experience of satisfaction it plays above all a protective role confining itself to guaranteeing the conditions which make satisfaction possible, in the experience of pain, its deficiency, leaving the subject exposed, has the effect of provoking a forceful destructiveness which gradually spreads. It does not succeed in preventing a hallucinatory fulfilment of pain or of unpleasure and is responsible for the creation of a 'bad' breast which the subject can end up identifying with (I am the breast), or for the destruction of any representation which signifies the loss of all hope of a hallucinatory wish-fulfilment (satisfactory).

It is clear that such a rectification of the Freudian model, based on the need to take into account the effects of the destructive drives and the object's role in the production of experiences of satisfaction and pain, sheds light on the paradigmatic value of the model of the setting and of the cure, and, consequently, the function of the object in the work of the negative.

This reformulation has given us a better understanding of the two aspects of the work of the negative: the function of hallucinatory wish-fulfilment on which dream theories are based and neurosis, both of which can be linked up with Winnicott's function of illusion and the negativism in borderline cases where it takes on the forms of moral masochism, the negative therapeutic reaction, the 'negative side of relationships' (Winnicott) and the experience of beta function with Bion. In the first case, the life or love drives imply an attachment to an object based on hope which will allow other objects to be invested and prohibition to be recognised. In the second case, the reference to the destructive drives explains the negative attitude towards the object which paradoxically aims at a state of parasitical clinging which in most cases is mutually sterilising. A lot of patience, endurance, stoicism and tenacity are necessary to be able to stand this in transference. Here the work of the negative oscillates on the one hand between the analysis of negative transference and destructive projections towards the analyst and, on the other, states of non-representation, emptiness and blankness in which thought becomes anaemic against the background of the negative hallucination of its own psychical productions. This process of turning the cure into a desert is the work of the destructive drives. This situation enables us to understand the extent to which the function of representation is more an acquisition than something given.

The reference to consciousness, in a negative form (the unconscious), was not far away due to the spirit of intentionality which certainly did not disappear from the new context of the psychical apparatus of the second topography but broke with the idea that there is a causality which is fully intelligible. There remains the idea of a wilful accomplishment: this is not inspired by the model of a projected action but one which has not been carried out, finding a way to realise itself in the mind and through this internal fulfilment to acquire a status which makes it close to an idea. Even the reference to action would be improper here and I think there is a need to make a slight distinction between action and acting. And yet we would be betraying the spirit of the concept if we were to see its content as a blind force, predestined, unmotivated, and 'soulless', if I may put it like that. It is here that one realises that the drive is a borderline concept and one can understand Freud's choice in favour of the id. 'Id' can be neither me nor another; id cannot be a thing either, and still less the manifestation of a spiritual power. Id is an indeterminate determination. It is a determination because its effects are controlled by a number of factors which are inherent to the structure of the human being. It is indeterminate because no subject is able to give a clear and unambiguous idea of it. But on the other hand, id claims to be the source of all later intentionality whether one calls it ego, subject or other, these being bound up with an action which is called desire, wish, intention, project, etc. There can be no doubt whatsoever that for Freud the id has an equivocal position in relation to the natural organisation. It depends on it, but cannot be reduced to it, and has no independent identity from it. In fact, the id is neither part of the natural organisation nor outside it. It is by means of it that the sense that such an organisation exists is manifested and that it is necessary to make good its imperfections. When the psychical apparatus is functioning smoothly there is scarcely any reason to refer to it. But the integration which removes the sense of its individuality, dissolved through operations in which the various agencies collaborate, obscuring the fact that they exist separately, is quick, at a time when its unifying power is failing, to remind us of its determining weight and of the difficulty in seeing its influence wane in the presence of more differentiated psychical forms. Id is an inchoate pre-form, an early form which detaches itself from physiological functioning without yet being able to apprehend it, not to mention feel it, but it is perhaps able to feel there is a connection and to seek to establish a state in which this impression of constraint disappears, either by eliminating the confining tension or by freeing itself from it. One can see here the cross-roads, whose paths are sometimes indiscernible, between the avenues of drive exigency and those of the object capable of satisfying it, from which an ego can emerge in both cases.

What does this change mean? In the first topography, hallucinatory wish-fulfilment is based on a postulate, i.e., that there has been an experience of satisfaction, that this has been registered and that its inscription serves as a reference and model guiding later experiences. This is the reason for adopting the criterion of representation as a basic fact of experience and as an issue at stake in satisfaction. It is up to the latter to transform this exigency for satisfaction into wish-fulfilment, the condition for the emergence of the pleasure which is sought after. Pleasure arises from its roots in need. Desire is a pivotal concept for one cannot overlook the fact that it is the satisfaction of need which sets it in motion. This happens in such a way that it appears to be concerned about the vital protection of the satisfaction of need, whereas it is aiming in a more hidden way (because covered by need) at the reproduction of pleasure. We are now in a better position to understand the function of pleasure. By procuring pleasant sensations, which are the essence of its manifestation, and by establishing an object to dispense them, pleasure binds the ego to the object in such a way that the attachment is not confined to providing for need (owing to the immaturity of the organism), but continues, in another form, ceasing to be determined by the fulfilment of aims dependent on biological conditions. It is by this means that the operation of searching for a transferable aim is carried out. Not simply from one aim to another but also from one object to another within a generational, historical and temporal dimension. Furthermore, the object is necessary for pleasure; pleasure is the relation of the ego to itself and can, under certain restricted circumstances, find an object-substitute in the subject's own body. It is clear that the main importance of these ideas is that they enable us to imagine the interlacing of the various registers and the pattern of certain functional circuits.

We are now in a position to understand the function of the *double link* of pleasure. By attaching to itself an embryonic ego (which perhaps only emerges after the relation has occurred) it binds this something, which does not yet exist, to something else which is not itself and which can only be a double 'without'. At the same time, however, by finding within itself the means to procure a substitute pleasure, it divides this ego (through auto-eroticism) thereby constituting its internal double 'within'. The ego is thus born from this double division 'without' and 'within'. It is only pleasure which can accomplish this; that is, which can constitute the mediation needed to oblige the subject to place himself 'between' in order to avoid the confinement of the inside and the decentring solicited from the outside.

We can understand that 'it' relates to this pre-ego designation which is bound up with both that (without) and this (within). And 'it' becomes 'id' as the prelude to an ego.

The difference with the initial model of hallucinatory wish-fulfilment is that under these conditions, which vary in function of the parameter of satisfaction derived from the object, nothing is less guaranteed than its 'later fulfilment'. It is likely that the set-up provided by the species seeks to tip the balance towards the hope of fulfilment which the wishful hallucination satisfies, so that the purified pleasure-ego can constitute itself in a wide range of situations. But by envisaging the passage from need to pleasure, and thus to desire (which will construct its hallucinatory satisfaction), by linking pleasure on the one hand to the object (that) and, on the other, to the erogenous zone (this), it is assumed that, whereas need limits itself to the elimination of tension, pleasure seeks in turn a similar elimination of tension. It achieves this not simply by obtaining pleasure in the erogenous zone but, given the divided status that the ego has acquired, by means of the relationship between the pleasure of the erogenous zone *with the projected reflection of this pleasure on the object*. The fact that this elimination (of tension) is accompanied by the bonus of pleasure which is the plus-value of the operation explains why this modality is preferred, but it does not however eliminate the aim which it continues to pursue, i.e., getting rid of unpleasant tensions. In this way the ego has found a way to link itself with the erotogenic zone and to be sure of the object's attachment in the first stages of the apprehension of time, in anticipation of future experiences in which the object will be needed.

Now while the pleasure of the erotogenic zone comprises an element of automaticity due to the natural organisation, the part which is projected and reflected on the object must receive from the latter, for want of satisfaction, a response which does not contradict it at least. In other words, if the projection is not confirmed – that is to say, in the case where there is a clear contradiction between what is experienced and what is perceived – pleasure emerges which is torn between its strengthening in the ego and the aggravation of its hiatus with the object. In these situations hallucinatory wish-fulfilment is conflictualised; the outcome is either the aggressive version of pleasure (owing to the object's disappointed expectations) or the masochistic reflection of the object's pleasure on the erogenous zone, or finally the attempt to eliminate pleasure through the impossibility of warding off extreme unpleasure, i.e., a blank, aphanisis.

The foregoing remarks are an attempt to show that the second topography coincides with a modification of the status of representation. The latter is no longer uniform (a drive-invested thing or object representation) but divided into psychical representation of the drive *and* thing and object representation; it is no longer a given for the construction of the psyche but an accomplishment of it; it is marked by the body and at the same time it accentuates, in spite of appearances, the object's practicality as a necessary complement. Speaking of the drive means speaking of the division of the object (internal to its organisation and external to the drive). And this is what explains the paradoxical nature of the final stage of the theory, i.e., a psychical apparatus which, grounded in the id, seems more solipsistic than ever, whereas the matrix agency of the psyche, comprised of destructive drives and of life or love drives, makes the object indispensable in the latter case.

The work of the negative will no longer involve psychical activity as it can be imagined independently of the positive aspects of consciousness; it will concern itself with the relation to the object caught in the cross-fire of the destructive drives on the one hand, and the life or love drives on the other. The work of the negative thus comes down to one question: how, faced with the destruction which threatens everything, can a way be found for desire to live and love? And reciprocally, how should we interpret the results of the work of the negative which inhabits this fundamental conflict, i.e., the dilemma which we are caught in between the anvil of absolute satisfaction, to which omnipotence and masochism bear witness, and the hammer of renunciation for which sublimation is a possible outcome? Beyond this conflict looms detachment, a step towards the disinvestment which is supposed to free one from all dependence on anyone or anything, so as to be able to encounter oneself at the price of murdering the other person.

These remarks which study the effects of the conditions determining hallucinatory wish-fulfilment should not be considered as relativising its importance. It remains the natural aim of the psychical apparatus: nightly oneiric activity shows this. But we have also learnt that nocturnal hallucinatory activity is not limited to dreams. And if it was possible for Freud to save his theory by a brilliant interpretation of anxiety dreams – as hypocritical dreams – psychoanalysts today generally agree that nightmares should be considered separately. This confirms our belief that there is a tendency for unconscious psychical activity to create hallucinations, wish-fulfilment only applying to a part of its production. We might mention here the reasons which pushed Freud to replace the unconscious by the id. The substitution of psychical forms (representational) by drives (of life and death) may have led Freud to neglect to take into account certain forms of representativeness in which the capacity for representation finds itself, so to speak, overwhelmed by a dynamic coefficient with a more or less disorganising effect on representation or, more precisely, capable of breaking the link of representation with wish-fulfilment. Either the dynamic quality takes it upon itself to invest the representative potential by enacting a destruction of the relation to the object, or this destructivity turns against the representative power itself. These are many of the points which work against the vocation, which we have called 'natural', of representation to compensate for the obstacles which reality puts in the way of wish-fulfilment. Perhaps we can go as far as to affirm, on the contrary, that through representation reproducibility offers the increased possibility of shifting the motifs which underlie this preferred mode of functioning towards wish-fulfilment. It was reflections of the same order which led Freud in *Beyond the Pleasure Principle* (1920) to the conclusion that its institution must be preceded by an inaugural mode of concatenation, the establishment of which is a pre-requisite for the sovereignty of the pleasure principle. Binding is the first operation: pleasure, by maintaining its rich variety of effects, invests it, as it were, with a supremacy which will make it its herald. It would be worth looking again at the object's status, doubly divided between its participation in the drive set-up and its position outside it. We are now in a position to express this differently by distinguishing between a desiring-object and a caution-object. Our hypothesis is that the latter may only be apprehended within the 'framework' of maternal care and is neither perceptible nor capable of being represented – its function being to facilitate the production of hallucinatory wish-fulfilment. This contributes to the construction of the fantasy-object as well as to the object objectively perceived, in as far as it is the *guarantor* of the fantasmatic object. Coming full circle, but without it being possible, however, to make them meet up, the real object represents the form of the caution-object which can be conceptualised. Thus hallucinatory wish-fulfilment and object caution are closely linked without however becoming one, for hallucinatory fulfilment can only occur with the object's caution and even with the object's desire which the ego (of the infant) desires, and which desires it too. But this cannot be represented. The paradox then is that Freud goes to extreme lengths to defend the solipsistic hypothesis of a death drive whereas everything suggests that what he is describing is explainable in terms of the vicissitudes of dependence on the object. Conversely, it would be an error to attribute the latter with the accomplishments performed by the psychical structure considered in the light of its intrinsic properties. At this point it is necessary to distinguish between the position of hallucinatory fulfilment which gives prevalence to the intrapsychic (Freud), and that of the object relation (from Melanie Klein to authors describing early interactions) which favours a relational, or better, an intersubjective approach. The aim here is not to come up with some sort of fallacious synthesis, but to show the point of view offered by each of them, the analyst needing to alternate between them by examining the characteristics of the theoretical field to which they belong.

But if this is the case, i.e., if binding is to be given pre-eminence, the relation to hallucination then appears as an exigency for repeatability, reproductiveness, representability and reorganisation subject to the pleasure principle. In other words the ego, left to its own devices in sleep, is driven to verify the validity of the object's caution, the latter being an integrated part of its internal organisation. At the same time it tests the validity of the accomplishments of the introjections which made its constitution possible. Let us not lose sight of the fact that Freud takes traumatic dreams as an example to justify abandoning any reference to the pleasure principle as the first organising factor of psychical processes. Nightmares, which have a very similar structure, enable us to follow the evolution of the modifications which Freud deemed necessary. The child's nocturnal terrors fit into the same scheme of things. What is important in these oneiric structures which do not fall within the sovereignty of the pleasure principle is not, as is the case with dreams, the preservation of sleep, but waking which frees the dreamer from a situation in which he is threatened by dangers. We can draw a parallel here between the end of the nightmare which comes with waking and the intervention of negative hallucination to suppress a perception, insufficiently protected, of the boundaries which make it possible to keep the latter well away from unconscious representations – or separated from them by a certain number of filters. When one thinks of the nightmares in stage 4 of sleep which are accompanied by a re-somatisation of anxiety and by a lifting of the motor inhibitions which normally occur during sleep, causing a disorganised state of agitation, there are good reasons for supposing that, under the influence of pathogenic factors, it is the system of boundaries as a whole which is unable to ensure that the different registers of psychical life are kept apart: so it is also the somato-psychic boundary, the preconscious and the protective-shield which seem to be subject to threatening infiltrations. Claude Janin has described the collapses of the psychical topography which occur in a less obtrusive manner and which are valuable indicators of the movements taking place in classical psychoanalytic treatment.[29] It seems to us therefore that negative hallucination fits in with Freud's remarks on perceptive activity. It is not so much that these represent a theme which has been insufficiently explored, and which needs to be cleared up, as that they command attention because the problems raised by certain psychical phenomena have not been resolved. But we must nonetheless bear in mind that here, as elsewhere, it is the dependence of this activity on the pleasure principle and its acolytes, the binding of repetition and the reality principle, which will serve as a guide for reflection.

Rediscovering the World and Reflexive Constraint

No view of perception can afford to overlook the issues raised by studies ranging from neuro-physiology to experimental psychology. Faced with the precise nature of the data which the scientific approach offers, it is difficult for clinical practice to obtain the recognition it deserves. The wide spectrum which extends from *Méconnaissances et hallucinations corporelles*[30] to agnosias following cerebral attacks of various kinds is a source of perplexity. But it is also true that clinical work sometimes presents us with facts of incomparable richness, inviting us to speculate further on the basis of experience which may teach us much more than we can learn from years of experimenting.

At this point I wish to relate the story of a shoemaker who was blind from the age of ten months and came from the lower-middle class. He liked his job which he was able to do almost perfectly in spite of his amblyopia. He had never lost hope that scientific progress would one day enable him to recover his sight and he consulted doctors over a period of thirty years requesting an operation to this end (a graft of the cornea). In other respects he was a confident, open and cheerful person. After his requests had been turned down several times owing to the uncertainty of the prognosis, an operation was finally carried out when he was fifty-two years of age. This case, reported by R.L. Gregory and J.G. Wallace,[31] is of considerable interest on several accounts, but I shall just focus on the aspects which seem particularly relevant to my purpose. When he was examined forty-eight days after the operation, there was already astonishment that as soon as his long-awaited wish to see again had been satisfied he showed no surprise upon rediscovering the world. It is easier to understand that, in spite of recovering his sight, his world of blindness persisted in many ways. If he was asked to make a drawing of objects, he could only make a correct graphic representation of the parts which were accessible to his blind man's faculty of touch. To acquire a new capacity for seeing he had to be able to transfer experiences related to touching. He was unable to learn to read.

For six weeks he lived in a state of euphoria, but soon his mood changed. He became gloomy and no longer enjoyed looking at his wife, whose appearance displeased him, any more than he liked looking at his own face. He was forced to admit that he found the world disappointing; it was different from how he had imagined it. He would start at anything which smacked of imperfection or degradation and developed a phobia for dirt. When the sun was setting, he seemed preoccupied. Worse still, whereas when he was blind he had been well-adapted to his daily tasks, now that he had got his sight back again he was incapable of carrying out ordinary tasks and felt handicapped compared with people who could see. In the home where he lived, he would sit at night in front of a very large mirror with his back turned to his friends. He became progressively more depressed and died two and a half years after the operation. In retrospect, the surgeons believed that the operation which had given him his sight back had been a mistake.

There are many things to be learnt from this case and it is a crucial experience for perceptive knowledge because the lesion affected neither the retina nor the visual brain but the extreme periphery of the eye, at the most superficial point of the perceptive organ. Gregory and Wallace point out that the dangers encountered by individuals who have regained their sight concern the non-optical properties of objects. This draws our attention to the fact that, according to existing models of vision, the interpretation of the cerebral cortex makes information meaningful when it applies to the non-optical properties of objects. The fascination for mirrors remains a puzzle, since the image they reflect is disagreeable. The spectacle of the world is only bearable if one turns one's back to it and if one receives a reflected image of it. The mirror image, far from supplying more information, is an attempt to turn away from reality. When he was shaving and had to take care not to cut himself, he found closing his eyes more reliable than seeing. In his *Traité de la peinture*, Leonardo recommended that painters who were worried about the quality of a painting should look at it in a mirror, saying they would then be able to get a better idea of it, as if it had been painted by another master.

It is well-known now that perception goes hand in hand with a questioning of internal models which is just as active as the investigation of the external perceptive field. Such an 'internal view' is a component of all visual or cognitive movement. Diffuse exploratory activities – scanning – complete the information coming from the specialised focusing of touch or sight. In this way the latter are able to communicate more fully, nothing occurring without the aid of the detection of symbolised features, identifiable in the external world, during an activity which is not only quite active but in which searching is concomitant with creating information.

Perception and memory are perhaps mutually exclusive in the way they appear to consciousness, but external view and internal view mutually reflect each other in their task of ensuring immersion in the present, grounded invisibly in the quest which links what is currently relevant with what is not.

The Phenomenal Field of Negative Hallucination

If 'reflection' is the basis – imperceptible – of the most general theory of perception, hallucination is equally fundamental to any psychoanalytic conception. The analysis of the occurrences of negative hallucination shows that it can occur in the most ordinary situations as well as in the most extreme pathological states. Once one is no longer surprised by the psychic plasticity which hypnotic suggestion reveals, it is in the manifestations of everyday psychopathology, or during fleeting impressions which are out of the ordinary and contain something strange about them, but which are of very short duration (*déjà raconté, déjà vu, fausse reconnaissance*), that one can discern in people who experience these manifestations the very marked presence of mechanisms of denial. Periodically, then, everyone may resort to the mechanism of negative hallucination without there being any serious consequences for their psychical functioning. However, the fact that this is possible obliges us to reconsider the theory of the virginity of the receptors of the perceptual system. In fact, what most of the examples show, is that the negative hallucination which occurs in non-pathological states vouches for the proximity of unconscious thoughts and external perceptions, with an unconscious representation having the value of a figuration of a primal fantasy or better still, serving as a bridge of communication between several of them. Whereas psychical functioning offers unconscious representation the possibility of separating into its elements, of displacing or condensing certain aspects of this decomposition, or even to subject the investments of affects to the same treatment, the occurrence of negative hallucination reveals subsequently – that is, after restoring either eclipsed perceptions or, failing that, reconstituting the continuity of perceptive sequences – the more or less complete series of thought associations. In an almost identical but inverted mode, this amounts to quasi-material *proof* of the interpenetration between unconscious representation and external perception without any diversion being possible. What I mean is, in contrast to the hypothesis which, in order to render more intelligible a sequence of psychical phenomena considered complete from the point of view of consciousness, consists in proposing the insertion of an unconscious representation, which as a result is conjectural and dubitable, in the case we are considering it is the quite noticeable lack of something perceived which makes it necessary, in order to reconstitute the completeness of the sequence it is part of, to relate this lack to a representation whose unconscious character does not raise the same doubts concerning its existence, because the assumption that it participates in the advent of perceptive negativisation takes on a more compelling character when the interrupted continuity is re-established. The connection which thus exists between perception and its suppression makes it quite clear that it needs to be accounted for in terms of the unconscious representation whose previously hypothetical character now looks more convincing. Why is this the only solution possible? The answer may lie in the fact that the unconscious representation is invested by the drive motion but in such a way that the affective aspect remains entirely unconscious, only manifesting itself through the meaningful connotation marked by the unconscious representation. Such a connotation denotes a mere marking of the unconscious representation, without an affective quality capable of entering consciousness, but manifesting itself through the difficulty of displacing such a representation – replacing it by another which is not so immediately meaningful. From then on, the collision with the external perception gives the situation a traumatic dimension in the shape of 'an excessive perception' which is intolerable, dethroning the submission to external material reality, in order to lend credibility to psychical reality without modifying the former. Now Freud always distinguished internal excitations from external excitations by saying that while it was impossible to free oneself from the former by means of motricity, this could be achieved with the latter. It really seems as though a 'motor image' were mobilised in the opposite direction from that which is normally the case in the experience of satisfaction, contributing to a withdrawal of the investment of the perception. In these cases, rather than speaking of a real denial, it would be better to speak of an *inadmissible recognition* (rather than disavowed). Of course, the main interest of these phenomena is to show us the range of the possibilities for the intervention of the defences which show that even external reality cannot escape their influence.

Two other cases remain to be considered. The first is that of the psychoses in which there is a powerful hallucinatory investment. Without going into details, we shall simply mention the two major examples of amentia and paranoia. As far as the first of these is concerned, we shall elucidate the oneirism which occurs in it by the following observation from the 'XXIXth Lecture on the Revision of Dream-Theory' in which Freud writes:

> The state of sleep involves a turning-away from the real external world, and there we have the necessary condition for the development of a psychosis. The most careful study of the severe psychoses will not reveal to us a single feature that is more characteristic of those pathological conditions. In psychoses, however, the turning-away from reality is brought about in two kinds of way: either by the unconscious repressed becoming excessively strong so that it overwhelms the conscious, which is attached to reality, or because reality has become so intolerably distressing that the threatened ego throws itself into the arms of the unconscious instinctual forces in a desperate revolt. The harmless dream-psychosis is the result of a withdrawal from the external world which is consciously willed and only temporary, and it disappears when relations to the external world are resumed.[32]

The comparison of dreams with psychosis is an indication of the attention which Freud now pays to the latter, in spite of himself, no doubt. We therefore need to be alert to whatever leaves the psychical space vacant allowing the ego to throw itself 'into the arms of unconscious drive activity' and to understand that it is not so much unpleasure which is involved as whatever causes intolerable pain. This can only be accounted for by what he called the repression of reality. He was not specific about the mechanism he was referring to but it has now become partially more intelligible.

In this case, it is not only inadmissible recognition but disavowed reality which prevails. And if hallucination is proof of the psyche's almost unlimited capacity to carry out transformations even to the point of creating the neo-reality required for its accomplishments or of rendering the intolerable perception innocuous, the same result can be achieved by the mere thought which is satisfied with ignoring the world instead of constructing a new one. In short, if negative hallucination negativises itself by being covered over by positive hallucination, we may assume that in purely interpretative paranoia potential hallucinatory activity is negativised. Thus disavowal will not have to apply to the materiality of a perceived reality – the 'intolerably excessive perception' which we were speaking about – but this would, as it were, be 'let be', becoming the object of the ego's perceptions, whereas it is the relation of perceptions to representations which would be altered by the investment coming from drive motions acting on the links between representations. The relations between drive motions, unconscious representations and representations of reality would then be modified. In the case of paranoia, we can understand Bion's remark that hallucination is the obstacle encountered by that which cannot be. It is around the pivotal point of preconscious representations, whose major role in thought processes needs to be kept in mind, that the intervention of the negative comes into play in the relation between thing-representations and word-representations. This is how we can imagine psychotic functioning becoming perceptible. For word-representations have two essential functions. On the one hand, it is by means of their activity that our thought processes can become perceptible – they are so to speak their principal, if not exclusive, material support, their signifier – and, on the other hand, they are closely linked with thing-representations (themselves originating in perceptions). There is therefore a contrivance which unites thought, language and the perceptivo-representative sphere. Furthermore, as conscious thing-representations are themselves inter-connected with the unconscious representations energised by the drives which have not been integrated by the ego, we can observe the subversive production of thing-representations. This is how the infiltration of drive motions tends to spread to the whole of the chain we have described, having its strongest effect on the weakest link (unconscious representations), bringing drastic defences into play which are mobilised under the circumstances to the detriment of perceptions, where the external world is concerned, and of judgements and ideas representing reality in the ego, i.e., the activity of thinking, where the internal world is concerned. The 'abolition' which Freud speaks of, namely, the withdrawal of investment, throws the whole system out of balance for what is involved is a 'local' rather than a global mechanism – the latter corresponding more to amentia. This 'hole', or this vacancy of the unconscious psyche, does not bring about, as it does in repression, a cut or an amputation on the basis of which the system then reorganises itself to disguise this alteration. On the contrary, in this case, what is left 'suspended'[33] – at least provisionally – creates a space weakened by this evacuation which initially makes it necessary to exclude whatever is liable to awaken the memory of this action, undermining psychical integrity. This has two serious consequences. The first is that external excitations, meeting less resistance, tend to surge into the hole left by the abolition of key signifiers, disrupting what remains of the organisation of representations which cannot cope with handling the invested sensory information. On the other hand, however, the disorganisation of the relations between the different types of perception (external and internal) leads to a somatising psychical disinvestment, receiving a sensory influx from within the body (regressive recorporation). Without manifesting itself as such, its main effect will be to increase the burden of the psychical task (already burdened by the weight of the least psychically invested bodily narcissism confronted with the ego's grandiose fantasies), having to ward off the experience of internal chaos. Each time the capacity of the representative system to deal with symbolic structures is affected, it is compelled to make greater use of projection. Language then becomes the object of a struggle which means it can no longer be conceived, as Freud thought, solely as a restitutive process, but it seems to be the locus of disavowing thought, subverting judgement, and creating another ego – a second ego for the ego – where its reflective capacity, instead of taking shape through its relation to the object, splits itself, dividing the ego not only from itself but from the other ego it has created. Denial is then essentially the negation of affirmation making negation possible, along with the substitution of the ego united by its splitting. The relation to the object is marked by the need to ward it off, making it possible to substitute it – denying its negative hallucination – with the mortal struggle between the two parts of an ego at war with itself and blind to its own division.

The memory-system (and thus the system of object-representations too) is crushed by the weight of a pure present invading all the figures of temporality so that a reserve of traces is never formed which is capable in one way or another of being reunited with the lost object. There is nothing to be found again: that's just how it is ...

Just as the perceptivo-representative 'unchaining' will not leave intact the drive-action equilibrium, paradoxically psychosis erases all consideration of the id as a simple result of the mechanisms we have described as disavowal, splitting and the doubling of the ego to ward off the object. And if the reserve of temporality happens to be lacking, it is the emerging awareness of repetition compulsion which is threatened, not only by unconsciousness which is its usual state, but also by an inaptitude (in the juridical sense) for awareness. This is not through a sense of a lack or inadequacy but through a proclamation of non-qualification rather than disqualification; in other words not so much a lack of suitability as unsuitability, as if the demand for awareness were addressed to the wrong person.

What I have just described in psychosis would not be intelligible without an experience of borderline cases, without it being necessary, however, to adhere to the outmoded idea which conceives of them simply as structures on the borders of psychosis. In the psychical mode of functioning which is specific to these structures we can observe the perpetual movement back and forth between the spheres of representation and perception. Here there is a broadening of the function of negative hallucination which obliges us to formulate its relations with repression more clearly. This leads us to cast our minds back to familiar ideas concerning the defences which are more readily accessible to the experience of the psychoanalytic process.

Repression and Negative Hallucination

We have a sufficiently clear idea already of the mechanisms at work in repression which remains the prototypical form of defence. But repression is employed against the internal processes of drives, affects, and representations, whereas negative hallucination is carried out against perceptions. Whether it is an external or internal perception, we should not confuse representation and perception and it is the role of reality-testing to make the distinction between the two. In this respect we shall see that language poses a particular problem.

What happens when there is a negative hallucination with respect to an external perception? I shall look at things as follows. When a negative hallucination occurs, two scenes unfold almost simultaneously on two different stages. On the one hand between preconscious thought and unconscious representation and, on the other, between preconscious thought and perception. It is this situation which is not understood because what must be avoided above all is the meeting of an unconscious representation and a perception, as if the perception were to acquire the value of a hallucinatory wish-fulfilment. In the internal theatre (of fantasised activity), thought, or preconscious preoccupation is connected with the unconscious representation but the latter is repressed. For example, preconscious thought may express an annoyance or a fear without being more precise than that, or even be accompanied by a conscious representation which is very subdued in comparison with the unconscious representation. But there is a flow of investment in both directions. Against this psychical background, the perception which appears and which is interpreted according to the current state of mind, that is, in function of preconscious preoccupations, crosses these, as it were, and prepares to encounter an unknown psychical phenomenon, just as two trains going at full speed on the same rails are heading for a collision. This time the two trains are the repressed unconscious representation and the conscious perception overwhelming the precarious link between the preconscious representations. This is what gives the perception the value of a hallucinatory wish-fulfilment, but such a fulfilment always carries with it the danger – directly or indirectly – of undermining the subject's narcissistic integrity (threat of castration carried out, of implosion, or of disintegration). As a result the only means of fending it off is cutting off the perception because the drive motion which is at the basis of the unconscious representation cannot be curbed and has got through the cen-sorships. This is especially so in that the unconscious representation becomes incapacitated due to the prohibition against making representation function as a source of thought. On the contrary, it has to be dried up to prevent the meaning of the unconscious representation and its connection with its essential synchronic and diachronic connotations from emerging.

In reality things are not straightforward because the link between uncon-scious representation and perception does not bring together two equivalent psychic forms. It seems therefore that an intense and extremely rapid piece of psychical work is carried out between representations stemming from the central fantasy and its core, as well as between perception and the associative memories it evokes.

It is also noteworthy that negative hallucination is not limited to non-perception but is completed by the unconsciousness of non-perception. Equally, it is possible for the work of disconnection to be completed internally by the displacement–replacement of the unconscious representation onto a related unconscious representation, as in the mechanism of fetishism where the missing perception (of the mother's penis) is covered by that of a piece of clothing near to the sexual organs or by that of another part of the body having some resemblance or close connection with the penis. Of course, the nega-tivisation applies essentially to the encounter between interior and exterior, namely between the unconscious representation and the perception. The neg-ativised perception can give way in the psychical investment to a displaced substitute representation which occupies the subject's mind at this moment, providing rationalisation with the excuse of 'distraction'. It would be more appropriate to speak of '*dystraction*', i.e., traction caused by a difficulty, a state which is deficient when it comes to repressing a psychical event destined to be suppressed or conserved, because the fact that it is part of the repressed, far from shielding the latter, exposes it to danger by making it run the risk of an implosion–explosion. Now such an event would be alarming on several accounts. Dynamically, it goes without saying, owing to the loss of ego organ-isation which leaves it exposed to the risk of chaos. But topographically, as well, (that is, in view of the formal regression) because such an implosion–explosion would inevitably make the ego aware of what it seeks to hide from itself; namely, that its functioning is threatened by its relation to primal fantasies, the meaning, origins and aim of which it is unaware of. Negative hallucina-tion seems therefore to be a radical and extreme defence – even in those cases where it is of short duration – because it carries out a condensation of denials in connection with the sideration of the usual capacities for de-condensation: displacement–substitution, repression–rationalisation, repression–affective reversal, etc. If hallucinatory wish-fulfilment is capable of occupying the space of the internal world, the de-realisation of the latter as a mode of the ego's func-

tioning, accomplished without any trace of its negativising intervention, may
be tempting. And it is in this respect that, from the point of view of the unconscious ego, negative hallucination is indeed the representation of the absence
of representation, as I maintained in *The Fabric of Affects and the Psychoanalytic
Discourse.*[34]

As for the destiny of such a defence mechanism, it is subject to multiple possibilities one of which – but it is neither the most frequent nor the most
inevitable – as in the case of the 'Wolf Man', can give rise to a hallucination
whose destiny is itself subject to a number of factors which will determine the
subject's psychical future.

It is clear that negative hallucination cannot be linked solely to disavowal
or denial, depending on the terminology. The disjunction can probably not
be adequately explained by avoiding the encounter between unconscious representation and perception; the phenomenon no doubt needs to be interpreted
in terms of what Freud designates as 'ideas and judgements which represent
reality in the ego'. There are, in fact, four terms in question: preconscious
thought and perception, each in direct contact, and, further towards preconscious thought, unconscious representation and the non-specular
representation of reality (judgement). Thus in situations which give rise to
negative hallucination, reality then gives unconscious representation a
dangerous pre-eminence which, limiting its appearance in consciousness,
nevertheless deems it absolutely necessary to cut off its links with perception
and strives to disavow the latter. In analysis, we do not often have the opportunity of observing the presence of negative hallucinations although they do
sometimes occur: for example, when the analysand meets his analyst outside
a session, or even when he suddenly spots some detail in the setting which
seems to be new, although in fact it was always there. The importance of these
observations lies less in the content of what leads to them than in the fact that
they invite us to bear in mind the possibility that they may occur in contexts
related to central aspects of the patient's conflictual organisation.

I would like to dwell a moment here on the case of the non-perception of
thoughts through language. I am thinking of those patients whose difficulties
lie on the level of thinking, as Bion has described. For my part, I have tried to
understand the mechanisms involved in blank thought. I think that we would
be able to understand it if we could imagine thinking, not only without images
– without representation – but also without words to perceive what one thinks.
It is in this respect that language is both a representation and a perception; it
represents the relation between things and the relations of thought relations
making it possible for the latter to be perceived. The negative hallucination of
thought also manifests itself in the analytic situation in the inability to express
oneself with words. This is not the silence of an absence of speech but that of
the formation of words as tools for thinking, or of the relation between the

morphology and semantics of words. Words can in this case just about be perceived on a sensory level, but what is lost is the relation of the words to their meaning in accordance with the reference to the unconscious. I am not of course speaking about the unconscious which remains as such, but to that part of it which has already been the subject of an analytic interpretation. At other times, there is evidence that this has been heard, but the patient suddenly seems to be unaware of it again. It is not so much forgotten as treated as if it were something new or something which related to the state which existed prior to any interpretation. In regard to this, there exists in the patient a combination of amnesia (of what was said at the last session or a few minutes before), of aphasia, an inability to speak because words fail, and of agnosia, when the analyst recalls words already spoken by the patient at an earlier time in the analysis, without succeeding in making the patient recognise them. Of course, I am only making use of this terminology, borrowed from psychoneurology, to give an idea of what is happening on a psychical level.

Hallucinatory Negativisation and Unconscious Representation

While we see negative hallucination as a prime example of the work of the negative, we may ask ourselves how it fits into it as a whole? And it is true, as the case of the 'Wolf Man' shows, that it is not always easy to differentiate between an unconscious representation and a hallucinatory negativisation. We cannot just oppose 'representation of the absence of representation' and repression of a representation. Let us take the case of dreams defined by Freud as a deployment of hallucinatory activity in relation to wish-fulfilment, or let us consider it (according to the later definitions of it) as an *attempt* to fulfil a wish. When relating a dream it is frequent for the dreamer to say: 'At this point the dream is unclear and I can no longer see the person I have just been talking about, although I can sense their presence', or again, 'Such and such a person appears but I can't see their facial features.' Should we accept that censorship, whose task it is to disguise meaning, is responsible for this deletion at the heart of representation, when the latter is both omnipresent and when the mechanisms of dream work ensure that the necessary disguises exist? Is there not here a failure of representability and/or a failure of wish-fulfilment, incapable of making use of the disguises at its disposal? What else is there to say other than that this deletion can be understood as a marker of negativity designating, through a lack of disguise and representation, that which, invested by drive motion, exceeds the limits of representative plasticity and no longer seems content to resort to hallucinatory vividness in order to signal its importance. Ordinarily, this hallucinatory vividness gives the dream its feeling of reality, thus attracting attention to what is said during this moment of dreaming, inducing one to look for an interpretation which will make the unconscious fantasy, which is the source of the dream, accessible. Here, the deletion simultaneously sharpens the details and suppresses their existence, as if to draw attention as well to the danger that it is thought to be the cause of this deletion. Which is one way of saying: 'You're dreaming!' In the language of dreams this would be: 'You're not really dreaming about it!', just as in waking life one would say 'You're not really thinking about it!'

Or again, to use analytic language, translating: 'I hadn't thought about it' (which is an admission negatively of the contrary, i.e., 'that is what I was thinking but I shouldn't have been') into the dream dialect by, 'I didn't dream that', reveals that even in dreams, even in the 'fulfilled' reality of the oneiric hallucination, there can be no place for such a thought which has 'come to mind' in this way.

Already in *L'enfant de ça* describing blank psychosis – in which the concept of negative hallucination accounts for thought disorder – J.L. Donnet and I insisted on the difference in patients' discourse between the statement 'I can't remember any more', or 'My memory's failing me', and the seemingly similar statement 'My mind's gone blank.' It might be worth pointing out that Z, the patient who was the subject of our study and who we thought was suffering from thought disorder – which was confirmed by other colleagues who had examined him themselves without our knowing it – did not know how to express, did not possess the words to sustain affects which, moreover, he could hardly name. Here, once again, it was representation which was involved.

It is important therefore to understand the difference between negative hallucination and negativisation at the heart of representation. The negativisation of representation always applies to a representation, a return (of the repressed) or of some mental trait which has already undergone a form of elaboration within the psyche. The only case which might escape this characteristic is the perception of internal sensations and feelings, but we may suppose that it is less these feelings as such which are at stake than the associations which they establish with representations. On the contrary, we have seen with negative hallucination that what is involved is the status of external reality which, as an actualised presence, is shaken and reveals nothing of its resonance with the roots, whose negativisation destroys any possibility of conjecture. The link with the unconscious representations in the violence of the encounter cannot be reduced to a wish-fulfilment, a mode which psychical reality is used to, but can be ascribed to a 'realising' response from reality which indirectly marks the prohibited or impossible status of the wish and thereby increases the potential danger of materialising the primal fantasy.

The question which arises, then, is to know how the perception of thoughts through language is to be understood. For while perception is a mode of being of presence, it always refers to a couple formed with another partner which defines the field in which the problem arises, i.e., there is a gap which is at times unthinkable in its link with hallucination, or problematic in its relation to representation, or again, as we have just seen, has to be reduced by means of the link with unconscious representation. With internal perceptions, this gap is dislocated between two extremes: the first, through internal sensations, concerns the sense of existence through its bodily grounding which adapts poorly to any sort of division or reflection; the second, on the contrary, can only be apprehended in the reflexiveness of language which, in its very manifestation, implies the existence of dual polarities, whether it speaks of the world or of itself, whether it forges links between a speaker and an addressee – sometimes distinct, sometimes confused – or again whether it must face the alternations between presence and absence (Lacan). In the case of psychoanalysis, the dimension of transference has led us to distinguish between transference onto the object and transference onto speech, forming a meeting point for all the issues we have been discussing.[35]

The Change of Paradigm and its Freudian Sources

From the moment psychoanalytic thought was faced with the need to acknowledge the shortcomings of Freudian theory with regard to problems posed by non-neurotic structures and of remedying them, it was not just a new chapter which needed adding to the traditional corpus, but a change of axiological orientation. It went unnoticed by many that the need for this new orientation, which would have to be defined in the light of contemporary experience, had already been sensed by Freud who knew that it would soon be necessary to determine the direction it would take although the length of his own life would not permit him to accomplish this himself. Very briefly: the main preoccupation of psychoanalytic theory was to reveal the unsuspected continent of internal psychical reality, being content to consider external reality – dealt with extensively elsewhere – from the angle of the favour or disfavour accorded to unconscious wishes and to the absolute necessity of taking them into account, Freud having declared cases marked by a repression of reality as unanalysable. We know that this prescription – which was also a proscription – did not prevent some analysts (Freud included) from hitting upon observations of great interest concerning psychical functioning based on investigations of certain psychotic states. Certain disciples disregarded the master's oracles. Many of them followed in the wake of Melanie Klein, a courageous pioneer who no doubt counted on there being better chances of reversibility with children whose continuing growth was supposed to make it possible to get libidinal development moving again along quite ordinary paths. In my view, this approach led to an increase in misunderstanding to the extent that, necessarily, the study of psychotic states in childhood could only accentuate the polarisation of research into the internal world. Now, when we read Freud, we see clearly that while his disinclination for tackling psychotics was not modified in any way, after the 'turning-point of 1920' it was no longer perversion which was opposed to neurosis (as its opposite) but melancholia on the one hand – a pure culture of 'death drives' under which the category of narcissistic neuroses is exclusively subsumed – and, on the other, the psychoses which no longer belonged to the same denomination but continued to be defined by their relation to reality. Furthermore, interest in the perversions did not diminish but there was a change of focus. Indeed, the consideration of pleasure sought after by the component drives in the prevalence of erogenous zones, aims and objects seemed to give precedence to the mystery of the threat of castration being set aside. It was fetishism which now took on a paradigmatic function. It might be helpful to point out that splitting serves as a defence, allowing a link to be made between perversion and psychosis, as the *Outline* of 1938 indicates. Over and beyond that, Freud has a premonition (in the study of the same year) of its central role in the processes of defence. Now the novelty of the discourse introduced in the article 'Fetishism' (1927) which Freud was to pursue until the end of his life, lay in a thoroughly original approach towards perception and the possibilities of denial which were opposed to it, comparing classical repression (henceforth linked to affect) with disavowal (or denial, whose action is directed at perception). This is what analysts did not grasp in reading his work, either because they tried to be faithful to the explicit Freud, consecrated by the psychoanalytic tradition known as 'classical and orthodox', by continuing to link his thought to perversion only, or because they were attracted by the new paths opened up by Melanie Klein, tracking down unfathomable archaisms.

Now what Freud was saying, in fact, was that it was becoming impossible for psychoanalysis to continue along the path which had claimed the interest of his contemporaries, i.e., its revelations of psychopathological forms adjoining normality; henceforth, progress could only come from research into the relationship between psychical reality and external reality. It was not until the impasses of Melanie Klein's thought had become apparent that this message, which had gone unheard at the time, was understood. This was in turn put to the test at the heart of the Kleinian movement by Bion who renewed the Kleinian vision of psychosis, dethroning the archaistic interpretation of unconscious fantasy, replacing it with a new dimension accorded to projective identification – this being closer to the vicissitudes of Freud's drive motions. To this was added the innovation of a theory of thinking (completely absent from Kleinian writings before him) at the basis of psychosis. Winnicott, moreover, who was at first seduced by the Kleinian approach, eventually had to break away from it in order to give the environment its rightful place, its position having been underestimated hitherto. In addition, he enriched it by making allowances for the relation between the internal and external world through the discovery of the intermediate area. These two complementary orientations relativised the assumption of Klein and Isaacs that unconscious fantasy was the equivalent of drive functioning, a hypothesis brought forward during the polemical context of the discussions between the adversaries and partisans of Melanie Klein in the years 1941–45.[36]

Nonetheless, the drift away from Freudian thought would prevent the re-interpretation of it by Hartmann's ego-psychology from gaining much ground in spite of the fact that it enjoyed a certain success. Negative hallucination is evoked, for example, in the works of his disciples Arlow and Brenner, in relation to the psychoanalytic approach to psychoses. M. Mahler alludes to it in passing, in child observation and in connection with autism, but the phenomenon never gave rise to reflections going beyond observable facts. And Lacan was only too happy to play on the short-sightedness of American authors in order to attract his readers to his conception of the ego alienated in its specular identifications – a hypothesis based on the perception of the coupled image of the subject and the other in the mirror, leaving his abstruse theorising on the Real until much later.[37] The late introduction of the tripod Real, Imaginary and Symbolic – RIS – carefully eschewed making a link in any way, as in Freud, between reality and perception. And as the name of Merleau-Ponty cannot be overlooked in evoking the cultural context in which French psychoanalysis developed – *La phénoménologie de la perception* was regularly quoted in any work on hallucination – we shall recall his brief intervention at the Bonneval Colloquium in 1960 in which he expressed his astonishment at seeing language taking up the whole stage without any mention being made of the relation to the world which perception reveals.[38] Let us add for good measure that, on the other hand, the theory of representation has been developed further in French psychoanalysis than elsewhere.

Interest in perception was rekindled in an unexpected way. Generally, the only time psychoanalytic thought came to speak of perception was in relation to conscious errors, following the famous example of Swann's tormented imaginings while watching from the street the lighted window of a certain inaccessible Odette, until he realised that he was looking at the wrong floor. Now the study of certain patients, whose symptoms occur on the somatic stage, provides the analyst who is talking to them with the opportunity of observing a *perceptive hyper-investment* which is quickly seen as the sign of an irregularity in mental functioning attributed to a vacillating permeability of the preconscious.[39] Thus it was no longer the study of the psychoses – in which elaborations on the relation to reality[40] were of limited theoretical interest, merely describing the manifest with psychoanalytic vocabulary and lacking the necessary instruments for laying bare the underlying organisation – which opened up new horizons, but the study of somatic illnesses. It would have been better to follow the path which treated what is perceived not only as the object of a displacement, as is indicated by psychosomatic patients, but probably also as the object of a return to an external world which the subject must cling to. This is because he lacks moorings from which the libidinal reflux can organise lines of defence to cope with the complex products of regression. The psyche appears more clearly in those configurations in which it is endangered; that is, where it finds itself crushed between soma and reality.

A Critique of the Freudian Theory of Perception and the Reference to Representation

One could not help noticing that either the Freudian view of perception had not been sufficiently understood or it lacked something which placed limits on its usefulness. What was without doubt in question was the Freudian postulate of the indefinitely renewed availability of the perceptive surfaces of reception, the need for which was accepted in a situation where there was an exclusive opposition between perception and memory, but which nonetheless contained many obscure points. How then were perceptions and representations to be related, given that the latter are derived from the former? Where, then, was the meeting-point for investments coming from without and those coming from within? Of course, the idea of an interface seemed fairly essential, but was the complexity of these relations compatible with the image of a flat mirror, even if it was endowed with the properties of a two-way mirror? We have been keen to point out the successive corrections which Freud was obliged to make concerning his early ideas that perception provided evidence of a reliable relation to reality.

If we just take the example of visual perception, the source of 80 per cent of perceptive information, how are we to reconcile the idea of its receptivity, which is always ready to take in new data and to link it to consciousness, and the existence of a *visual drive* whose scopic aim is guaranteed by drive motions implying a dynamism necessary for achieving a purpose which goes hand in hand with the search for the object capable of satisfying it, and which is scarcely compatible with the serenity required for a 'faithful' registering of information coming from the external world? And if we have good reason to deplore Freud's destruction of his article on projection, it is also because the lack of it has left us poorly equipped to develop a theory of perception.[41]

We are justified in affirming – I have done so on several occasions – that the reference point of psychoanalysis is representation, a concept which is deployed in several registers, including that of the representations of reality in the psyche. We find ourselves embarrassed on two scores here. For while we are hard pushed to go beyond this summary observation which notes the inescapable character of such a notion, we cannot go much further unless we are able to say what such representations represent, in other words, without establishing a psychoanalytic conception of perception.

It would appear that the solution is easier where representations, corresponding in the internal world to perceptive activity, are concerned. Is the space of consciousness only inhabited by thing-representation, with the verbal complement which is connected with it, or is it not conceivable that the thing thus represented might also be accompanied by what still shows through of its relation to the unconscious thing-representation, by resonating with the preconscious, without the unconscious part being discernible as such? This last aspect can be inferred because language is not confined to its reference to the conscious thing-representation, but also bears the trace *of relations* between conscious and unconscious thing-representations. Better still, by means of affect and beyond it, the drives or their more distant derivatives infiltrate language. In other words, while it is undeniable that the word-representations are related *directly* to conscious thing-representations and cannot entertain relations directly with the unconscious, indirectly they bear the trace, not of unconscious representations alone, *but of the relations between unconscious representations and conscious representations,* the nature of the latter permitting an intricacy with the language of words, even though this dominating mark wavers at times.

Although the theory of perception obliges us to couple it with representations, and preferably conscious representations, it nonetheless implies the potentiality of an indirect infiltration by the unconscious. So the theory of perception is disappointing from the point of view of psychoanalytical research. Its analysis involves introducing parameters which are both more rigid and more disconcerting than the mechanisms discovered by unconscious functioning. One major fact stands out: unlike representation whose properties – whether they concern drives, images, or words – are always liable to fragmentation and then all sorts of operations of combination and re-combinations (with certain elements being suppressed and, of course, the extensive transformation of primitive forms, etc.), *perception, for its part, does not split.* It can be eclipsed – partially or wholly – but not divided up. Perception can be envisaged in terms of different factors including quality (comprising rhythm, intensity, etc.), clarity or confusion, focalisation or diffusion, distinction or fusion, to which can be added the features observable in the configurations of experiences of depersonalisation, projection, denial, negative and positive hallucination, but it neither lends itself to being divided up nor to being combined. There is a 'linearity' which it is difficult to shake off in the analysis of the phenomenon of perception. Before Lacan discovered an unexpected way out, offered by the promotion of linguistics to the rank of a pilot-discipline, he exhausted himself tracking down the forms of the imaginary in the concave and convex interplay of mirrors, engendering the illusions of an inverted vase. They have had little influence on his disciples.[42]

One notable exception was the unexpected encounter with Winnicott who, inspired by reading Lacan's paper 'Le stade du miroir' (1949), put forward the idea of the mother's face having a mirror role. The dilemma perception/representation was thus elegantly transcended by the idea that what the baby sees in the mother's gaze is himself. It was also affirmed that excessive dependence on the impressions perceived in the maternal face created a premature disillusionment prior to the experience of omnipotence which is indispensable to the baby's capacity to create a good subjective object.

Negative Hallucination and Speech

When negative hallucination is not simply an accidental or even isolated phenomenon – when, for instance, the psychical apparatus seems to be caught unawares and it reacts to the unexpected situation in ways which are not customary for it – then it seems that the analytic situation scarcely has the means of identifying such a defence or of understanding in detail how the processes which trigger it work, any more than the consequences that stem from its employment. As we have seen in the case of the 'Wolf Man', it is with subjects whom we suspect demonstrate modes of psychical work which are different from those found in the neuroses that we expect to encounter its expressions. But since it is in relation to reality that these manifestations are most easily identifiable, the analyst is not well-placed to interpret them, particularly as, by a kind of reduplication of the phenomenon – in those cases where the analysand notices, which is not frequent – when it is reported in the session, the fact is treated as trivial and does not arouse the curiosity which generally takes hold of the neurotic subject when he becomes aware of a parapraxis through introspection. In short, with the neurotic subject there is a 'bias of intentionality' which, when it is not very clearly sensed before the cure, is set in motion as soon as it has got under way, for this is the sign by which transference can be apprehended, in all senses of the term. To be sure, the analyst preserves the setting, but in as far as it is amplified by the meaningful potentiality of the subject. The setting is the space-time allotted to the subject for deploying speech which he addresses to the object who is supposed to hear. It is clear that the operation is not without risk when the double understanding of the discourse is insufficiently protected from the dangers to which it is exposed. It seems that negative hallucination then becomes a regular process and not just occasional – in all the cases where reality as a whole (bodily reality and reality of the world) and not only through one or the other of its representatives placed in a symbolic position – is experienced as hostile. This may not be perceived directly, but solely by means of hysterical identification. In any case, the purpose of negative hallucination is to deny the subject's fear of the consequences of his own hostility, in fact of the pleasure that the expression of it would give him if he had the power to exercise it freely. In contradistinction to what occurs in the psychoses, these projections are not due to a desire (foreclosed) placed outside, as is regularly the case in paranoia, the existence of which can be sensed in foreclosed homosexuality. Although we may also suspect this to be a demand lying behind complaints about other people's cruel indifference, it is also a projection of the subject's narcissism, a narcissism which denies the object's existence, found merely to be disappointing, treacherous and unreliable. There is no need to dwell at length on factors we have already emphasised: pregenital fixations, the fragility and vulnerability of the ego's defences which are both rigid and in danger of breaking down, the prevalence of splitting mechanisms and projective identification, a lack of auto-eroticism, the foreclosure of symbolic formation for want of a reference to the paternal law, an absence of capacity for representation, object relations marked by an intolerance of separation, an incapacity to mourn, etc. We place these various descriptions under the heading of processes which are closely related to negative hallucination. The analytic setting – notably when the face-to-face situation places the analytic partners in the field of perception – creates excitation which makes the subject anxious about his insufficient capacity for holding. He fears this will be over-whelmed when the object is no longer there and that he will be deprived of its help, even if, when this help is available it is threatened by a kind of hal-lucinatory realisation (acting) which affects the quality of the transference. Negative hallucination is brought into play by the anxiety provoked by the return of the repressed which is not perceived as such but as a fulfilling actu-alisation. The connotation of restitutive repetition is not recognised in the transference which seems to unfold with the atmosphere of a trauma in full swing. In other words, it is more a question of a return (one-way) of a psychical event needing to be exhausted (rather than repressed), although the means to achieve this are uncertain, faced with an object which is both powerless to cope with the situation and sometimes prompted to contribute, by doubtful inadvertency, to what is involved in the trauma. We therefore have to go much further than this. And since unconscious representation cannot offer the psyche a meaningful potential which can be elaborated, that is, which can be displaced, condensed, etc., and because the latter finds itself, as it were, dogged by the demands of drive motion, the ego finds no other solution than to reverse the course itself of psychic events by situating this point on the nearest surface of what confronts it, i.e., towards speech.

It makes use of speech just as repression makes use of drive motion or its representatives by striving to neutralise it. However, since it cannot bury it – as it would have done with unconscious representation, leaving it free to offer the preconscious only censured, filtered products, in other words, sufficiently purified to be 'thinkable' – the crux of the conflict shifts to the chain of word representations. And it is equally important that negative hallucination cor-responds as closely as possible to the familiar expression 'no one'll be any the wiser' which, if it is to be fully understood, should be taken as meaning 'not seen, not caught', which is tantamount to saying: 'not known, cannot be caught'. Thus it is necessary, while maintaining things as they are, to apply the work of the negative to the perceptive function of thought provided by language, in the hope of stopping the associative flow at the level of word-representations, 'horizontally', if one may put it like that, and to immobilise the relations between representative systems of words, of things, as well as of the body (drive as 'psychical representative') and of reality (judgement of existence) in the direction of depth.

It is clear that in order to apply its action to speech, which is after all the aim, it is the relations which are formed with the body and with reality which are involved. In order to understand this better we must cast our minds back to our hypothesis which requires that we distinguish between the psychical representative of the drive (as the representation of excitations from inside the body reaching the psyche, a delegation which cannot be represented) and object or thing-representation (as a representable representation stemming from perception), the conjunction of the two forming the ideational representative, the famous *Vorstellungs-Repräsentanz*.

> The coaptation of the psychical representative as a bodily demand, but unrepresentable (*infigurable*), the movement of this unrepresentable bodily exigency, coming to invest an earlier trace left by the object which has brought satisfaction constitutes the inaugural moment of thought. And it is this primary binding which is the starting-point for the possibility of analytical work by means of transference as a relation to fixation and displacement.[43]

In other words, the relation word-representation–thing-representation, characteristic of conscious activity, is dependent on such a coaptation because the latter governs the relations of the repressed and determines dynamically, economically and topographically the regime of unconscious representations throughout the entire extent of their domain, and therefore through the preconscious, with what is represented there of the relations between words and things. If, as I maintain, thing-representation is situated between drive and language, we can say equally that word-representation is situated between the objects represented and thought. But while each element of the preceding notions referred to a representational support which was bound up with that of a higher level of organisation, thought offers the particularity of only disposing, at the heart of the psychical apparatus, of the material support of the level which is adjacent to it, i.e., language. Presenting a psychoanalytic view of language would be going beyond the scope of this study, but it is clear that our understanding of the nature of the psychoanalytic process cannot evolve without clarifying a minimum number of ideas.

The Saussurian distinction between speech and language or between message and code indeed seems necessary and indispensable. More recently, H. Atlan has proposed that language be approached from two directions, namely the relations between the brain and language and those of language and thought.[44] However, we cannot overlook the paradox that we are required to use language to know thought, even though the investigation of language can only reveal to us what belongs to language itself, and despite the fact we do not possess any other means of knowing thought than through language. And yet there is more than one reason for believing that thought exists independently of language. The fact remains that Freud's idea, which sees in language the possibility of *perceiving* thought processes, is loaded with consequences. It is less a question of isolating this level from the others than to see it as a continuation of the activity of representability. Listening to the speech of a patient is to 'imaginarise' it (*l'imaginariser*), that is, to carry out an imaginary conversion of speech in order to draw out, not only a representation but also a network of operations raised to this level of intelligibility by referring to what can be represented, starting from a situation which cannot if one continues to adhere to the drive basis of psychical activity. But in turn this representability may make way for operations of another nature which no longer have recourse to what can be represented. What is important to understand is the preservation 'even under different aspects' of investment which permits meaning to be constructed at each stage.

The pair of concepts perceptual identity–thought identity has existed since the earliest days of psychoanalysis. But what becomes of thought identity if it depends on a language-perception of thought? There is no reason to believe that negative hallucination – which we have seen may affect the experience of bodily existence – stops at the gates of language because the latter consists of verbal matter. On the contrary, there is every reason to suppose that language, owing to its relational vocation, may be the preferential target of negative hallucination. Language indeed is, on the one hand, hyper-invested by the very conditions of analysis – analytic speech takes the grief out of language, as we have written elsewhere – and is open, on the other, to the return of the other person's speech. Thus the action of language not only exposes itself by communicating with the other but is exposed to such communication. The source of language is thus endo- and exopsychic, its exercise becomes sensitive to the perception of that which has the same nature as its own thought. It is the interface which is always in danger of being surprised by oneself and by others and so becomes an object of excitation and surveillance, an opportunity to excite the other and elude his watchfulness.

In those structures where the various systems of functioning are the object of confusion and/or splitting, we may, upon identifying these mechanisms and having long attributed them to repression, regard repetition compulsion or the absence of change to be the product of processes which we had hitherto overlooked. The same is true for the non-perception of the identity (of thought) between material produced by the analysand and its interpretation by the analyst. Admittedly, one can always challenge the pertinence or exactness of the interpretation. But there is more to it. On some occasions, reminding the patient of what he has said before – and this cannot date back very far – meets with no recognition on his part. In this case, the non-identity of thought involves first a non-recognition of a perceptual identity which is scarcely open to question. And the analyst would be wrong to think this is simply forgetfulness – that is, resistance through a repetition of repression. I think, in fact, that we should not hesitate to refer here to a negative hallucination of borrowed forms to express the meaning of words which could not be separated from their formulation before they were recalled. There exists a whole graduated series of denials going from the non-recognition of spoken words to the non-comprehension of their meaning and from there to the associations related to this understanding. But apart from this, negative hallucination may involve the affect (connotation of transference) which served as a marker for what was said. It can also direct its potential for denial at the object's presence. Sometimes, too, in a more complex way, the object which is difficult to think about, is not only resistant to representability but presents itself as a presence which cannot be represented, making the excess weight it brings to bear on the subject and the ease with which contact with the latter is lost alternate (and co-exist!).

But why are we speaking here of negative hallucination rather than representation – and its vicissitudes? It might be thought that we were complicating matters unnecessarily if we were not to draw attention to the fact that what needs emphasising here, due to the difficulties connected with the act of thinking, is not so much the domain of psychical activity within the patient as the domain of his relation to that which makes him sensitive to perception, as a phenomenon of actualisation, of 'realisation'. In other words, not so much the re-presentation as a new event to be considered in the absence which enables us see what it refers to, as the presentation of that which, by its very presence, leaves no other alternative but its hallucinatory negativisation.

It is the analyst's task to offer the patient a different approach to the psychical events which are witnessed in the setting, namely to treat them as products to be preserved through transformation, thereby conferring on them the status of transference representations, available for transferring representations. Things will continue in this way until the representation itself can take leave of them, that is to say, to the point where anxiety, rage, impotence, ideas of hate and death, in short negativism can one day find their expression in the formula which we no longer expected to hear. 'No doubt you will think that my intention was to ...' And here, really, the analyst had not thought of it ... or had ceased to think that it could be thought about like that. No doubt he knew, more or less unwittingly, that he would thereby be relieved of his functions by the patient's thought alone, allowing himself to dream of something else.

Review of a Conceptual Development

When I tackled negative hallucination for the first time,[45] I put forward a model of double reversal.[46] In an effort to conceive of a construction based less on the ideational representatives of the drive than on drive investments – today I would say on the psychical representatives of the drive[47] – and on the assumption that a system of functioning exists before repression comes into effect, I assumed that the combination of the turning round upon the self and the reversal into its opposite – the double reversal – created an enclosing circuit, demarcating opposed spaces (internal and external) which could be regarded as a structure providing a frame for psychical space capable of gathering and inscribing representations as well as making them interact. I added that, in addition, there was a need for a mechanism which I called decussation.[48]

> In this reversal by means of decussation it is as if the response expected from the object found itself carried along in this movement in which the extreme positions of the inside and the outside are exchanged in the drive flow. [...] What arises in this way is a circuit which does not have repercussions on the characteristics of the object but on its response which, while preserving the object in its absence, delegates it to the subject, *as if* it were the object which had brought about the realisation. One might see a metaphor at work here.

I continued by comparing the protective shield and repression, stating that

> there is no correspondence, as there is between an inside and an outside, but [...] something between them is crossed so that what is inside may be treated in the same way as that which comes from outside provided that the inside can be perceived as if from the outside, *without their merging*. This clarifies and extends Freud's formula according to which the id is the ego's second external world.

What is lacking therefore in the psychoanalytic theory of perception is the need to include it in a space of reversal[49] which we have described for drive investments by including a part linked to the mother's response, for which we have suggested a figuration which helps one to understand the transit external–internal. Nonetheless, the specific problem of perception still needs to be identified. A few indications should suffice for the time being, but their importance should not be underestimated.

To begin with, it must be remembered that for Freud perception does not come first. What comes first is attributing the object with connotations of pleasure and unpleasure, with the consequences we are familiar with of incorporation and what I have called excorporation.[50] If something is perceived, this is caught in a configuration in which the information conveyed by what is perceived is included in what is transported by the drive motion where the dominant feature is constructed around the modality *contact-movement* whose speciality in touching and kinaesthesia will benefit. Perception stands out from this conglomeration which includes the relational spheres touching–touched, in movement–at standstill, held–released, in symbiosis–in distress, etc., all covered by the contrasting pair pleasure–unpleasure, coupled with the pair which I can only describe very vaguely as 'with–without', a pre-form of the future distinction between presence–absence. These considerations are only important in that they help us to understand what ensues. *Perceiving is not knowing, but re-cognising; re-cognising means following once again the path of a movement defined by its substitutive value for touching which is described as desirable or undesirable, or, failing that, acceptable or unacceptable.*
These points may shed light on the remarks I made in 1967:

The mother is caught in the empty framework of negative hallucination and becomes a containing structure for the subject himself. The subject constructs himself where the nomination of the object has been consecrated in place of its investment.[51]

With this definition I am enlarging considerably the sense of negative hallucination. It is no longer restricted to the more or less regressive register of the manifestations of denial, from the psychopathology of everyday life to hallucinatory confusion. Its basis is no longer internal perception but hallucination in the primary process which Freud sees as being equivalent to perception. This hallucination must not be confused with a representation although there is some justification for doing so. What matters is to distinguish the manifestations of the work of the negative, that is, repression directed at representations or affects, and negative hallucination which is related to the attempt to *create* something perceptible or to thwart what is perceived, even where internal psychical manifestations are concerned. The effect of negative hallucination is to prohibit direct access to representation encouraging the subject to take into account a certain reality which is expressed in the discourse of what can be represented, as an instance of a psychical event to be thought about. The responsibility is not, however, attributed to the vicissitudes of the phenomenon and to what happens to representation, as is the case where the defensive measure has confined itself to the condemnation and/or the distancing of what is conscious (repression). This is why I speak of it as representing the absence of representation, to emphasise its future relation with thought. This is also why it is not surprising that we speak about it by pointing out its effects at the very heart of representation to the extent that, in contradistinction to repression, which only leaves open the possibility of differed knowledge through the return of the repressed, it is in the present that it carries out its informative function by making us aware of how its object 'is blanked out' and leaves a mark by the very manner in which it disappears.

There is no more vivid example of this than the negative hands found on the walls of Neolithic caves. A hand which is drawn never gives the same sensation of its prehensile power and the elusive nature of its grip, of the lure of perception and of the mark which the latter leaves on our body at the point where it perceives.

In this sense, it matters little that the distinction between the supports of negative hallucination sometimes makes us hesitate between perception and representation, for what really matters is to understand that 'the negative hallucination' (of the mother) [...] has made the conditions for representation possible'.[52]

Prospects for Future Research

The review we have just made of these earlier developments leads us to realise that they operate on two fronts. By including the object's 'response' in the constitution of the double reversal, we are considering the overall picture from two points of view: one which strives to apprehend what is usually called 'mental functioning' and the other which implicitly postulates an 'object relation' (even if it is regarded primarily from the angle of primary narcissism). These two approaches echo each other constantly. For, to come back to the containing structure, how are we to imagine its formation without considering what depends on the perceptive sources in the conditions which exist when it is established? The internal context in question cannot be explained solely by negativising the primarily visual representations of the maternal presence, evoked by the mnemic traces of what can be 'looked at' in it, but also by the transformation of non-visual data, tactile and kinaesthetic among others, which provide this closure with the necessary means to 'withstand' and which relates to that in the child which feels (depending on whether we use Winnicott's or Bion's terminology) 'held' or 'contained'. And it is this very impression – or this effect, if you like – which is scarcely 'perceived' in a concrete way which can be represented, but which means that everything which occurs on the psychical scene will be 'held' together, i.e., bound and capable of creating what is binding. Of course, the possibility and even the inevitability of unbinding is included in this binding but comprises the prospect of an eventual rebinding. We can see then how the containing structure is not perceptible as such, but is only perceptible through the productions arising from the setting which remains silent, invisible, and 'imperceptible' in a different way than through a reference to the dimension of latency. Here, then, we are faced with the aporia of the symbolic matrices of thought.

We are bound to say that it is here that the essential justification for the analytic setting lies, i.e., its necessity as well as its function of revealing the internal context which governs what happens in the perceptive and representative spheres. For it is very much in the relation perceived–represented that the whole dimension of what Lacan called the non-specularisable unfurls. This, of course, is nothing other than the act of thinking.

The inside and the outside must be thought about in terms of their relations which are sometimes mutually exclusive, sometimes subject to reciprocal interpenetration, and sometimes only tangential. These are all hypothetical situations enabling us to escape the linearising fatality of the relations which usually link perception and its object. The link which ties the fate of perception to consciousness is equally strong, even in Freud's writings. Now we need only to pause a moment to realise its inadequacy, whether one points to the levels of psychical activity below consciousness (and one thinks here of the 'apperceptions' from Descartes and Leibniz to Husserl) or whether one attempts to integrate perception with the beginnings of understanding. Is this not another way of doing justice to Freud's grouping which covers the field extending from internal sensations to thought processes? It is also no doubt true that modern phenomenology has preferred to structure the question differently by giving preference to the idea of 'appearances' (in consciousness) which does away with the barriers between perception, representations and even hallucinations. Are these terminological distinctions entirely without foundation? Going beyond the criterion of conscious activity, we propose instead to consider the perceptive quality from the angle of 'making present to oneself',[53] which infers a form of existence unrestricted to consciousness, implying a change of state and a plurality of modes of existence, each of which can take over from the other, without linking these to a 'conscious' phenomenon. It should be clear then that Freud's central statement is confirmed and rejected at one and the same time. It is confirmed by the fact that it is indeed the postulation of a latency which is indefinitely renewed so that the presence to oneself can occur in a sufficiently full way to present an exteriority which is definable as such, and rejected by this manifestation which also relates to an interiority, always ready to come and 'join in on the conversation'. 'Presence to oneself' is necessary to explain this transformation which makes it possible to judge what exists, not only because of the dimension of absence which underlies it implicitly and to which it necessarily refers, but also because this 'presentation' convokes the elements which are at play in the elementary forms of knowledge and particularly the division between what is to be known and what makes knowledge possible.[54]

We shall thus be freed from this aspect of immediateness which perceptive experience comes up against in contrast to the discursiveness of understanding. Perception is discursive, just as thought needs to become perceptible to be thought about. And this is no doubt the explanation for the renewed interest in perception – considered from the point of view of investment – whether it be in psychiatry (R. Angelergues) or in psychoanalytic theory (C. and S. Botella).[55]

These directions of enquiry are of great consequence since taking perception into account involves several essential considerations. Certain of these are very familiar and are only mentioned here for the position they have within the overall picture which alone makes them intelligible. Let us recall for memory's sake the findings which concern the distinction ego–non-ego, inside–outside (so eloquently rendered by the Botellas' formula 'only inside, also outside'), subjective–objective, etc. These oppositions underlie what is involved in the theory of the relations perception–representation by implying the questionable precedence of the former over the latter. This is what underlines the link with the insistent materiality of the reference to the object of perception, as opposed to the impalpable evanescence of representation. To these classical notions psychoanalysis has added new properties. First, there is the dominant 'mimetic' characteristic of psychical activity which is expressed in the perceptive–hallucinatory 'equivalence'. Then the negativising property which can modify, transform and even suppress the perception which is liable to arouse unpleasure, and lastly the convertibility not only between the various registers of perception (external–internal, relating to the body or thought) but also between perception and representation. This is the idea we have been developing throughout the preceding pages. When all is said and done, it is '*investment*' which provides the basis for perceptive activity, for it alone explains both the ego's perceptive fascination for the object attracting its activity, because it discovers in it the lack which is met by the object's very existence,[56] and the way in which pain can, to use Freud's expression, 'pull the psychical apparatus away from perception'. This very striking image of 'pulling away' gives us a sense of the importance of the bipolar vision of psychical activity. This is not only shared between the ego and its other (the object, the id, the super-ego), but sees this sharing repeated at the heart of the deepest immediateness which inhabits ego experience, as the reference to 'presence to oneself' implies. The relation to the object indicates, although it is not named as such, the complementary polarity which makes it possible to think about a relation – a specific reflexivity between perceiving and perceived, just as there is between representative and represented. Here we find all the implications involved in the definitions of the psyche provided that we do not confuse the products of the division with representation in the classical sense resulting in a theory of the illusory which can only end by recognising the futility its own approach.

An illusion into which, for example, someone like Winnicott, who defends the idea of the unavoidable paradox which divides and (unites) the subject between subjective object and object objectively perceived, does not fall. Finally, this will enable us to understand the function assigned to language in psychoanalytic treatment which speaks of the thing and of itself at the same time. This is linked to consciousness and its representations and extends – without ever succumbing to its direct influence and always with the help of the detour of the conscious thing-representation – the resonances and harmonies of the latter, or of what can be transmitted through the functioning of such a structure. That is to say representative emanations of the unconscious which enable us to identify – another form of presenting to oneself – the surges coming from the id and even, beyond it, from soma, just as consciousness reproduces in its very functioning a part of reality.

The subject's division is grounded in the diversity characterising the psychical apparatus. Perceptive experience, which seems to be the most undeniable basis of immediateness, does not escape the solipsistic and unitary illusion which underlies its apparent reality. While lacking a clear conception of its constitutive division, it nonetheless has experience, through its negativisation in negative hallucination, of what keeps the subject divided between affirmation and denial, presence and absence, investment and disinvestment.

8

Sublimation: Considered First as a Vicissitude of the Sexual Drive and Then as Being in the Service of the Death Drive

First to possess his books; Remember for without them
He's but a sot, as I am, nor hath not
one spirit to command: they all do hate him
As rootedly as I. Burn but his books.

The Tempest, Act 3, Scene 2, 90–3

In Cézanne's watercolours we can observe that as his work developed he left more and more white space. What does this mean? Is it that the white of the support is used as a colour missing from the palette but discovered on the spot 'in the work-place' ready to form part of the composition? Or is it rather that this white, a real hole in the watercolour or the 'white of the eye' of the painter's vision represents, like a negative hallucination, the representation of the absence of representation? Even if my preferences lean towards this last solution, it is perhaps, nonetheless, a mixture of the two that is involved. It remains true, however, that this white space blends into the whole, losing the privilege of the absence of colour which it denotes, compared with the other multi-coloured marks, and contributes to rendering the dazzling light of the countryside around Aix in mid-summer, the burning heat of natural life and the transparency of the watercolours which may be compared with the finest lace of Flanders.

Aix en Provence, 1990

An Unexamined Vicissitude of the Drive

'The theory of the drives is our mythology': is there any psychoanalyst who is unaware of this formula? It speaks to us and invites contrasting commentaries. Like all mythology, it poses the problem of contradictory statements which

215

we try to bring into a coherent whole. What is true of the theory of the drives can also be said of the particular drive vicissitude of sublimation. The very idea that the drives have a 'destiny' nips in the bud the view that they express themselves directly through a mere transition from the quiescent to the active state. Moreover, the main postulate of the drive, i.e., the *continuous* excitation which impels it, makes us see it as an inexhaustible source exercising its activity, its thrust, without respite. A drive can only cease when its demand is satisfied and at the moment when this satisfaction appeases the ego (a very uncertain moment, for it so happens that as soon as the satisfaction is obtained, desire returns once again). But the most frequent case is where the drive must be transformed and be subjected to a vicissitude. It is from this direction that mythology might surface again.

It will be recollected that Freud names – and the order of nomination is far from being devoid of significance – four vicissitudes: reversal into the opposite, the turning round upon the subject's own self, repression and sublimation. I have brought together the first two under the denomination of *double reversal* by bringing out the idea in Freud's text that these mechanisms took place *before* repression. Today, I would also be inclined to bring together the last two, repression and sublimation, as there seems to be a dialectical link between them. Repression, as its name indicates, pushes the drive derivatives (representatives) back into the depths to the point of creating the impression that what has suffered this fate never existed, whereas sublimation 'preserves while surpassing'; in other words, by means of a kind of settling process or 'volatilisation' (transformation of the solid state into the gaseous state), satisfaction reappears in a disguised and acceptable form, provided it has abandoned its original state, that is to say, has broken off its first ties and makes do with gratifications which are less directly sexual. Can sublimation and spiritualisation be considered as synonyms? I think so, not only in relation to moral purification which is indirectly aimed at here, but also in the sense in which one speaks of the spirit of salt, wood or wine.

One remark needs to be made however: 'Instincts and their Vicissitudes' speaks almost exclusively of the two first modes whose unification I have called the double reversal. *Repression,* dealt with in the following paper in *On Metapsychology,* is given a chapter to itself. Sublimation, for its part, is not made a separate subject of study. We know that Freud, probably unhappy with the result, destroyed his copy, preferring to satisfy our curiosity at a later date. Thus metapsychology was for ever deprived of a study of sublimation as well as projection.

The Insistence of Sublimation

Sublimiert had already appeared under Freud's pen in *Dora*; the idea originally is one of a deviation or diversion[1] in favour of civilisation. If, on an individual level, neurosis is the negative of perversion, collectively, culture is the negative of nature in the sense that the latter may be understood as spontaneously perverse. Against the idea of the noble savage Freud sets that of the polymorphous perverse child; however, this natural perversion is innocent, repression coming into effect as much under the object's influence as from the interior of the subject. We can say that it is the object which will make the subject conscious of his perversity, the latter being practised in the first place 'naturally'. But it is the idea of civilisation which should hold our attention here, for it is present in Freud from the very beginnings, even though he did not possess a theory which would enable him to think it through, something he would only tackle at a later date. It is interesting that it is in connection with a text on hysteria – and therefore potentially on *conversion* – that Freud defines sublimation as a vicissitude of the drive. Freud speaks here of 'revised editions' – no doubt amended and expurgated – and not of 'new impressions'.[2] Transference is considered as a transformed and censured repetition. When civilisation is not cited first, it is art which takes its place. For Freud, there is a metonymical link between art and civilisation. For beauty cannot disavow its connection with *jouissance;* the latter is the result of the transformation of the transition from genital part-object, dispensing limited satisfaction, to the whole body; a bonus of pleasure granted to this beautiful form, aesthetically admirable. The prevalent role of vision may be noted in these early reflections.[3]

From these remarks we can single out the idea of the diversion or deviation, owing to the influence of civilisation, of a drive, sexual in origin, which is required to displace itself when it is transposed into the social field, and to modify itself in consequence, in such a way that it can no longer accomplish its sexual aims in an unrestrained way. Freud would be forced to come back to this thirty years later in *Civilization and its Discontents* although it cannot be said that he met our expectations. In fact, there are two ways of approaching sublimation. The first proceeds (theoretically) in a progressive way, i.e., sublimation is a vicissitude of the drive, one of its vicissitudes, although the weight of cultural influence is such that it is difficult to see how this can be avoided. The second, on the contrary, is inspired by a regressive process: behind the forms of expression valued by culture, one can infer traces of drive activity which collective thinking has rendered invisible.[4] In truth, a synthesis of the two approaches could lead to two conclusions:

1. the drive is *at the origin* of all psychical activities, not only individual but also social;
2. the social activities which are apparently the furthest removed from the drives bear the *trace of their transformations.*

These then are the positions held by Freud if not by all his successors. Sublimation has indeed to be considered in relation to repression: namely, as the outcome of a certain drive quota which has *partially* escaped its action. Repression does not take place just once, as if it were a unique event, but each time there is a return of the repressed liable to 'let through' repressed material. A transformation is therefore necessary to escape the attention of the censors: the displacement onto a non-sexual aim and onto objects of high social value. Let us bear in mind this *negative* definition: a non-sexual aim. Could one go as far as to say *anti-sexual*? I would certainly think so, for Freud mentions particularly art and intellectual curiosity, whereas one also needs to think of the religious cover of many of these activities, at least in the past.

Whether non or anti, the mark of the negative is hardly questionable. As far as the social value is concerned, we are bound to point out that the social dimension which is connected with the 'process of civilisation' is itself subject to ethical pressure which will later come to be known as the super-ego.

The major text on sublimation – not only as a vicissitude of the drive but also as a deviation of this same vicissitude – is *Leonardo da Vinci and a Memory of his Childhood* (1910). The case of the painter makes it possible to study in a special way the relations between art and intellectual inquiry. Alongside the vicissitudes of thought (its sexualisation and inhibition of action), already described as being at the origin of obsessional symptoms, the effects of sublimation allow similar mechanisms in the same field to be discovered. A portion of the libido has escaped repression: 'by being sublimated from the very beginning into curiosity and by becoming attached to the powerful instinct for research as a reinforcement'.[5] Sexuality lays siege to thought, involving itself in the partial *jouissance* of looking, and subjects the latter to an intellectual displacement which ensures the mastery and assurance of knowledge. The object, which was only distanced visually, is dissolved in an exploration which makes one forget the original excitations by which it manifested itself.

It is indeed this idea of sublimation 'from the start' which implies an immediate desexualisation – as if this sacrifice were necessary to save a part of the libido by modifying it. Sexual desire is transformed into a thirst for knowledge. Is it by a common reference to the idea of 'possessing' the object – differently? One speaks of 'having a command' (*posséder*) of one's subject when speaking of an intellectual work. Is it possible that there is a repetition of the regressive movement of the sexual drive flowing back to the opposing pairs: voyeurism–exhibitionism and sadism–masochism? The thirst for knowledge is not unrelated to the couple voyeurism-sadism, epistemophilia taking the place of scopophilia and the desire for mastery that of sadistic domination.

'From the start' makes one think of a kind of drive bivalency which sometimes tips towards libidinal sexual desire, sometimes towards its negative: sublimation.[6] An opposition of this kind already gives us a sense of what is to follow: sublimation–desexualisation is the result of a drive opposed to sexuality. But at the time, in 1910, Freud did not yet suspect its existence, being wholly concerned to situate sublimation within the evolution of the sexual drive. May we object that 'displacement' onto non-sexual aims does not amount to a desexualisation? Freud is not very clear about this before the second topography. He would like to keep sublimation within the context of the vicissitudes of the sexual drive; this may be inferred from his study of Leonardo, when he maintains that the desire for knowledge has inhibited pictorial activity which is undeniably more 'sensual', even though Leonardo claimed it was purely '*cosa mentale*'.

The crux of the issue is to be found in these last remarks. On the one hand sublimation appears to be a vicissitude of the sexual drive, a purified form which has its place among other possible vicissitudes but which remains within the patrimony of Eros, and, on the other, sublimation is the adverse counterpart of Eros which, far from serving its aims, sides with those forces which are antagonistic to its purposes. The paradox cannot easily be overcome and this is the path which Freud's work (the product of his sublimation) will follow.

Reverberations of Sublimation

Let us consider for a moment Stefan Zweig's novella, *Episode in the Early Life of a Privy Councillor D.*[7] On the occasion of his sixtieth birthday and his thirtieth year in the teaching profession, a professor is reflecting on his past while contemplating the *Festschrift*[8] which has been dedicated to him, his work and his life seeming to be of a piece. But only apparently, for there is a secret behind this concerning the decisive influence which had proved to be the creative impetus for his entire intellectual life.

Having little inclination for studies and only being moderately attracted in his youth by philology, which nonetheless later became a daily companion, he began his life as a student in Berlin by giving himself over to the pleasures of the big city which held him much more in their thrall than his studies did. The attraction of women played a large part in the new atmosphere of freedom he enjoyed as a student. One day he received a surprise visit from his father and his bohemian life was exposed, explaining why no marks had been communicated up until then and leaving no doubts as to how the young man spent his time. The time for paternal decisions had come: his stay in Berlin was brought to an end and he was enrolled instead in a small provincial university town with few distractions, particularly as the studies there were strictly supervised. There the local professor ran a seminar where he knew each of his students personally. He even offered to provide the young man with lodgings. Nevertheless, new joys awaited the student. The Master, who was an exceptional teacher, fascinated the young minds asking for nothing more than to be galvanised by his dynamism. He spoke passionately about Shakespeare. The theatre became an arena, a *'circus maximus* in which the wild beasts of feeling attack each other savagely'.[9] In the Elizabethan theatre as it is spoken of by the teacher: 'the tumult of unrestrained human impulses celebrates its impassioned orgy'. Of course, the students lapped up everything which came from the Master's golden mouth. How could they not be enthralled by his words which claimed that 'all spirit issues from blood, all thought from passion, all passion from enthusiasm ...'.[10]

So the former profligate of Berlin was now converted. He took up English literature as if it were a religion. Not only was he his professor's guest but also his voluntary secretary, taking down the dictation of the work his professor had always intended to publish without actually managing to do so. Through force of circumstances the student became almost a son of the family, sharing the couple's meals. Furthermore, they had no heir. Very little attention was paid to the professor's wife whose discretion was exemplary. One day, deciding to take a rest and to enjoy his favourite sport, swimming, he noticed a woman who had the most exciting effect on him. Life seemed to flow back into his veins, his body having become sluggish with the inertia of his studious existence. He followed the woman, caught up with her and accompanied her home, only to realise then that she was no other than the professor's wife whom he never looked at. He shuddered at the idea of being denounced, of losing the love of the 'sublime' (sic) person of the professor who was often solemn and sombre, but above all reserved.

From time to time, this mysterious man would disappear for a few days; no one knew where he went or what he did. He was greatly missed during these absences. Soon work began to take its toll on the young man's health. He would have fallen ill if the young woman had not reminded him of the realities of his youth. So he was buffeted between the love he felt for his professor and the affection of and for the wife. The reader is left in no doubts as to the amorous nature of the student's feelings. One evening, when an important stage seems to have been reached in the work, the professor appeared to be warmer to the student but the latter was evasive, sensing that the wife was watching him closely. And it is at this point that he went down with a fever. Following this failed encounter, the professor disappeared again for a few days while his disciple enjoyed the wife's maternal attention. He decided (disappointed as he was by the teacher's departure) to have a good time – but with very little success. Another day in the country and the knot of the latent romance between student and wife was well and truly tied. This time he learnt that the couple's relations were chaste. The professor returned and the student, full of remorse, wanted to go away. The reader then learns with surprise that the professor has no quarrel with this adultery. Finally the confession comes: the professor is also in love with the student. The suspected homosexuality now comes out. In a moving confession, the professor relates his life-story and his behaviour is now explained. The love which is naturally felt by a teacher for his students was in fact pederasty, a leaning which he indulged during his escapades in order to resist the temptations which his students aroused in him. At the moment of parting, when it was time to say goodbye, the student received a passionate kiss from the Master: 'his lips pressed eagerly against mine nervously and in a kind of trembling convulsion he held me close to his body. It was a kiss unlike any I had ever received from a woman.' [11]

Although today Zweig's story has a ring of desuetude about it in spite of the author's skill and his sense of suspense – in truth, a little too well-worn for our contemporaries – it at least has the merit of raising questions which, while they are treated more casually today, are by no means irrelevant. They retain a measure of truth and are very relevant to the question of sublimation, the failures of which reveal repressed components.

There is a confusion of feelings: between sublimation (for Elizabethan theatre) and sublimated homosexuality (Shakespeare and the professor); between sublimated homosexuality and practised homosexuality (the student and the professor), but also between sublimated heterosexuality (the athletic contest with the young woman) and transgressive heterosexuality (adultery), between unconscious homosexuality and conscious heterosexuality. In each of these aspects we find repression and the part of the drive which eludes or escapes it, i.e., sexuality and its displacements onto non-sexual aims, and lastly desexualisation. Too much sublimation diverts one from life and its pleasures, particularly those of an erotic nature. Without the intervention of the professor's wife, the student would probably have succumbed to illness. But it is also the student's sublimation of his homosexuality towards the professor which saps and torments him, although he does not realise what is happening to him, making us suspect the existence of mental illness. After reading the novel, one is no longer surprised at the affinities which existed between Stefan Zweig and the 'Dear Professor' Sigmund Freud. We should not forget, however, that the author eventually committed suicide, a fact which can only partially be explained by motives of a political order.

'Neg-Sexuality'

It has been pointed out that the content of the ideas relating to sublimation existed before psychoanalysis. Its religious connotation, overtly expressed in certain cases, and its ethical connotation which is expressed in all cases, sets it within the domain of moral purification. Purification and not purgation as in catharsis. Elevation and not trance. What takes leave of the earth, ascends, and what is it striving after? It is the earth which one leaves – and its mud, that of the animal body, its mire and its wallow. It is heaven one implores in prayer in an attempt to join the ethereal powers, the Higher Powers. Does psychoanalysis merely paraphrase ideology? Perhaps the most specific aspect of the psychoanalytic conception resides in the origin of this mechanism. At first sight the problem relating to the post-oedipal phase – in which the intervention of the super-ego plays a major part – is seen to play the decisive role in what might be called this 'conversion' towards the mind. But there is no sublimation without the prior existence of perversion. There can be no sublimation unless the former issue is replaced by a more or less developed social ideology. This indeed leads us to wonder how 'civilising' or simply social values are formed. There is a thread running through Freud's thought which has its origins in the '*Project*', becomes apparent in the *Three Essays on the Theory of Sexuality*, continues up to *Civilization and its Discontents* and finds its culmination in *Moses and Monotheism*. And this thread, which theory created, runs between the primary object, the mother's breast, and what Freud calls progress in the life of the mind, by means of which the father, the intellect, is given pre-eminence. Between these poles comes the super-ego preceded by its unavoidable prolegomenon: the death drive.

Many authors who have written about sublimation have preferred to confine themselves to Freud's early formulations – for example, those set out in *Leonardo*. Some have pushed on as far as *Civilization and its Discontents* without getting involved in the polemic surrounding the final theory of the drives, being content, in order to characterise the effects of civilisation, with the repression of the drives which culture requires. The relations between sublimation and the death drive are rarely commented on in detail. Admittedly, sublimation can be situated comparatively and differentially in relation to other psychoanalytic mechanisms: reaction formation, aim-inhibited drive, but one quickly comes to the conclusion that the problem lies elsewhere. As Jean Laplanche has pointed out, 'in what is sublimated there remains *neither* the object, *nor* even the source of the drive, so that in the end we are supposed to find "sexual energy" alone [...] itself "desexualised", dequalified, put at the service of non-sexual activities'.[12] I would happily qualify sublimation as '*neg-sexuality*', just as one says neg-entropy.

The Function of the Ideal – Super-ego – Sublimation

In a much earlier study,[13] I tackled the problem of desexualisation and its relation to the death drive from the angle of the function of the ideal. It very much seems that as early as Contributions to the Psychology of Love II ('On the Universal Tendency to Debasement in the Sphere of Love', 1912), Freud was beginning to think that the sexual drive is subject to the effect of an *intrinsic* factor which prohibits its full satisfaction. In other words, repression does not explain everything. In his posthumous notes of June 1938 we find a very similar remark. The function of the ideal, on which the super-ego is founded, might be linked to the phenomenon in question. It places more value on the renunciation of drive satisfaction than on satisfaction. There is nothing religious people dread more than the sin of pride; compared with this, transgression is just a weakness which can be overcome quite easily, with the help of guilt. Forgiveness is indispensable here for overcoming, amongst other things, the stubborn determination to consider one's own sins as irremissible. What implacable logic!

The close examination of the question of sublimation in *The Ego and the Id* restores it to the heart of an ensemble marked by a series of transformations. In other words the network comprises narcissism, identification and desexualisation. In the last instance, what all of them have in common is an antagonistic function towards Eros.

If we consider the changes which have occurred since the final theory of the drives, we can notice that the first stage of sublimation initially involves a diversion of sexual aims. We need to make a distinction between diversion of aim (which can take the form of an inhibition) and desexualisation, the latter act involving a modification of the nature of sexuality itself much more than a simple subtraction of properties. Thus in *The Ego and the Id,* in the chapter on the super-ego, it is worth noting that desexualisation is bound up with what one might call the narcissisation of the libido, the libido attached to the object· being transformed into ego-libido. We are dealing then with 'an abandonment – and not simply a diversion – of sexual aims, a desexualisation – a kind of sublimation therefore'.[14] It is therefore clear that in Freud's mind sublimation which is achieved (and not the 'beginning' of it) involves a desexualisation. But Freud asks himself at this point: might not such a transformation result in a defusion of the drives?

For Freud, any decrease in the defusion of the drives results in a liberation of the destructive drives. Thus the paradox is that the apparent 'enrichment' of the ego which benefits from this added supply, linked to the increase of narcissistic libido at the expense of object-libido, is offset by the fact that more space is given to the death drive. So the surprising conclusion is that sublimation is in the service of the antagonist of Eros. A comparison with identification is essential here. Let us recall that the resolution of the little boy's oedipal conflict is achieved by replacing sexual desire for the mother by an identification with the father. Freud calls this a '*modification of the ego which confronts the other contents of the ego as an ego ideal or super-ego*'.[15]

He goes on to stress the way in which the infantile ego strengthens itself through the act of repression by erecting this obstacle within itself. 'It borrowed strength to do this, so to speak, from the father, and this loan was an extraordinarily momentous act.'[16] The work of the negative consists in supporting the energies of counter-investment by borrowing strength from the paternal prohibition thereby making it its own. It is clear here that Freud is making a condensation: initially the strength concerns the power of the father's sanction displaced onto the prohibition which refers to it allusively. The appropriation applies therefore to the father's power of castration which has undergone those transformations which we consider to be the structuring expression of the work of the negative. In the language of Freudian metapsychology, the ego uses the expedient of identification to work against itself in order to carry out a desexualisation. This corresponds to the dimension in man which lends him the image of a 'superior being'. ('The representative of our relation to our parents.'[17]) There is a close relationship between ego ideal and sublimation. *We are even justified in thinking – without it being stated explicitly – that Freud gives for the first time a metapsychological basis for sublimation, seeing it as a result of the effect of the ego ideal and the super-ego.*

The Theoretical Mutation: Sublimation from the Angle of the Death Drive

In the chapter of *The Ego and the Id* devoted to the two classes of drives, Freud is wondering about the relations which connect them (fusion–defusion) and about what governs these relations. On this point, Freud brings together the axes of two major revisions: drive theory and the agencies of the psychical apparatus. In other words, he is considering the relations between the two classes of drives, on the one hand, and the ego, the id, and the super-ego on the other. He includes the way in which the pleasure–unpleasure principle is conceived of in this new context. Moving from the metapsychological to the clinical level, he turns his attention to the relations of love–hate (as expressions of the two classes of drives), seen from the angle of the transformation of one into the other. The most varied clinical configurations are presented (obsessional neurosis, paranoia) in the hope that their investigation may provide a solution for the problems under consideration. What intrigues Freud is the transformation, the mutation of love into hate (especially in paranoia): 'It seems a plausible view that this displaceable and indifferent energy, which is no doubt active both in the ego and in the id, proceeds from the narcissistic store of libido – that is in desexualised Eros.'[18] At this point, Freud again emphasises the object's contingent nature, something he has always maintained due to the fact that it is replaceable, pre-eminence always being given to the drive. The problem may not be quite so simple; we shall have to come back to this.

The essential point does not lie here but comes in what follows. 'If this displaceable energy is desexualised libido, it may also be described as *sublimated* energy; for it would still retain the main purpose of Eros – that of uniting and binding – in so far as it helps towards establishing the unity, or tendency to unity, which is particularly characteristic of the ego.'[19]

Once again it is clear that when one speaks of desexualisation one is speaking of sublimation and also of narcissism, i.e., Ego-ism. The action extends here to thought processes, also an effect of sublimation. Sublimation is carried out by means of the ego's mediation – but an ego which changes its purposes. It renounces the satisfaction of erotic libido, hoping to satisfy itself instead. There is a circularity in Freud's thinking: desexualised libido is sublimated libido; object libido which has become ego libido is desexualised; the libido of the abandoned object-investments becomes libido which is bound in the ego and transformed there into identifications; this transposition into ego libido is accompanied by an abandoning of sexual aims, i.e., desexualisation.

On this point the reasoning is reversed. Whereas a few lines earlier the ego was presented as representing the binding work of Eros, albeit through the mediation of desexualised, sublimated libido, now, by achieving its unity – to the detriment of object investments – it becomes the enemy of Eros. Let us return to the previous quotation again and pursue it further:

> If this displaceable energy is desexualised libido, it may also be described as *sublimated* energy; for it would still retain the main purpose of Eros – that of uniting and binding – in so far as it helps towards establishing the unity, or tendency to unity, which is particularly characteristic of the ego. If thought-processes in the wider sense are to be included among these dis-placements, then the activity of thinking is also supplied from the sublimation of erotic motive forces.
>
> Here we arrive again at the possibility which has already been discussed that sublimation may take place regularly through the mediation of the ego. The other case will be recollected, in which the ego deals with the first object-investments of the id (and certainly with later ones too) by taking over the libido from them into itself and binding it to the alteration of the ego produced by means of identification. The transformation [of erotic libido] into ego-libido of course involves an abandonment of sexual aims, a desexualisation. In any case this throws light upon an important function of the ego in its relation to Eros. By thus getting hold of the libido from the object-investments, setting itself up as sole love-object, and desexual-ising or sublimating the libido of the id, the ego is working in opposition to the purposes of Eros and placing itself at the service of the opposing instinctual impulses.[20]

This reasoning – and I say this without having any sense of exaggerating – is Heraclitean or Hegelian. It proceeds from the extraordinary sense of dialectics which comes quite naturally to Freud (who liked neither Heraclitus nor Hegel). With great ease he conceives of sublimation as coming within the field of Eros, due to its binding action (even desexualised) which helps towards establish-ing unity in the ego. Once this is accomplished, he recalls the case in which object-investments have been abandoned, the ego taking over their libido into itself and dealing with this abandonment by modifying itself through iden-tification (in short, a haunted ego, 'visited', as Alain de Mijolla says). This withdrawal, or this retreat into the ego, corresponding to a desexualisation, results in a unification, a kind of total entity. The ego, thus invested (through identification) with the finery of the object, has desexualised its relations with the latter and, ceasing to love it, sets itself up as its rival. Furthermore, it claims to be superior to the object on account of its desexualisation–sublimation of libido: it promises heaven and lets go of the earthly love in which its life is rooted. By turning away from Eros, it has become the apologue of death, the love (substitutive) of itself not being equivalent to the Eros with which the objects are invested. In other words, the narcissistic connotation has changed here from life narcissism to death narcissism. What Freud means is that the ego's appropriation of the libido has diminished the tensions created by Eros and facilitated libidinal stagnation. We should bear in mind that sublimation is not enough to silence the exigencies of erotic libido.[21] Here, there is not only desexualisation but *enticement* (*leurre*), the sublimated, desexualised ego does not so much give up satisfaction as it claims to be a 'superior' *jouissance*.

It will be recalled that Freud concludes this exposition by extending the activity of the death drive to the state of the organism after orgasm, Eros having been eliminated through the discharge of the satisfaction obtained. The concessions (in the territorial sense) granted to the death drive may well seem exorbitant; does the activity of Eros really just shrink away? For sure, on this point we are faced with Freud at his most speculative; Freud the metaphysician, in spite of himself. But is it really true that it is easy for us to protest in the name of clinical experience, in the hope that we are rallying to his cause? Which of us has not come into contact with one of those extremely narcissistic individuals, cultivated down to the very core of their being, artists of impeccable taste, subtle, well-informed, sharp, with refined judgement, yet nonetheless shut away within the four walls of their egotism, without having any living relationship with a real object? Sometimes they strive to allay suspicion by having harrowing amorous adventures which deceive no one, recovering constantly from their disappointments, rooted in the idealisation of their image which they try to deceive, thanks to the chosen object, thereby traversing the prism of their self-love. The description is so banal that there is scarcely any need to dwell on it further.

Now these caricatures are only caricatures: exaggerations of characteristics which everyone has in them, more or less without realising it. Never, however, has the idea been so compelling that Freud's psychoanalysis *is not a psychology*. One can call it, if one will, a mechanism or physiologism but not a psychologism. In fact, it is a dialectic of the tragic dimension which is grounded in the inexorable character of the human exigency for drive satisfaction and the stratagems which are created by the obstacles it encounters in realising them.

Identification with the Paternal Model: Sublimation, Defusion

Freud's description was not worked out fully. Hence, he comes back to sublimation in the final chapter of *The Ego and the Id*. If reading the foregoing feeds the impression that there is an interplay of forces which move, replace one another, are in conflict or reinforce each other, this is only one of the polarities of Freud's thought. The super-ego is deeply rooted in the id, certainly, but extends its sphere of influence over the whole ego and arises thanks to an identification with the pre-historic father:

> The super-ego arises, as we know, from an identification with the father taken as a model. Every such identification is in the nature of a desexualisation or even of a sublimation. It now seems as though when a transformation of this kind takes place, an instinctual defusion occurs at the same time. After sublimation the erotic component no longer has the power to bind the whole of the destructiveness that was combined with it, and this is released in the form of an inclination to aggression and destruction. This defusion would be the source of the general character of harshness and cruelty exhibited by the ideal – its dictatorial 'Thou shalt'.[22]

Here then is a passage foreshadowing the development which would be followed up for over more than fifteen years, culminating in *Moses and Monotheism*.

These reflections throw light on the nature of the ego. Is it not true that the work ends with a chapter on its dependent relations? There Freud has harsh words for this ego which cannot cope any more; an ego which is me, you, all of us, in the greyness of the everyday world:

> In its position midway between the id and reality, it only too often yields to the temptation to become sycophantic, opportunist and lying, like a politician who sees the truth but wants to keep his place in popular favour.[23]

The miserable wretch is, however, engaged in a task which far exceeds its possibilities. While it seems concerned to ensure its survival in tolerable conditions, by means of a vulgar hedonism, in other respects it is harassed by the sublime:

> Towards the two classes of instincts the ego's attitude is not impartial. Through its work of identification and sublimation it gives the death instincts in the id assistance in gaining control over the libido, but in so doing it runs the risk of becoming the object of the death instincts and of itself perishing. In order to be able to help in this way it has had itself to become filled with

libido; it thus itself becomes the representative of Eros and thenceforward desires to live and to be loved.

But since the ego's work of sublimation results in a defusion of the instincts and a liberation of the aggressive instincts in the super-ego, its struggle against the libido exposes it to the danger of maltreatment and death.[24]

I can affirm that these propositions which seem so abstract, so difficult to translate into the language of ordinary relationships, are indeed the faithful translation – in the language of theory – of situations which are met with in psychoanalytic practice. These relate to structures whose contradictory coherence allows us to discern the tension between a protective sublimation of narcissism which can only be successful at the price of a singular restriction of relationships with others; a sublimation which is open and fertile but which, nonetheless, demands important sacrifices; and a painful, tortured sublimation, always concerned about the outcome of its achievements, never loving enough for the ego, invalidating all positive recognition, whereas it is quick to react to deprecating judgements. This does not prevent whoever it dominates from invoking, if not the malevolence, at least the indifference of others, their lack of concern, their insensibility, leaving the subject to deal with the tortures of self-deprecation. Masochism can also resexualise sublimation in an attempt to seduce the ideal. I would like to be able to find a more convincing explanation which would not involve these pessimistic speculations but I do not know of any which are worth mentioning.

Some Critical Remarks

These remarks, which I admit are rather bewildering, enable us to identify behind the positions which have been put forward a global view which influences the theory in a subterranean way. Where does this subterranean source come from? I shall not be afraid of undermining its postulates by recognising that they may be rooted in Freud's subjective experience. For this exposition inevitably leads us to wonder about its author. How are we to understand such an unusual form of sublimation which involves turning away from sexuality,[25] which makes the ego want to be loved in place of the object? Freud cared more about his work than anything else. This was a source of quarrels with those whom he had successively chosen as his friends. He must have cherished the wild hope that his genius would be recognised through such friendships and that these friends, who were the objects of his affectionate admiration, would thereby acquire a serene objectivity, exempt from all pettiness. Their reactions to him did not only reflect the desire to preserve their self-respect; they disguised their resentment at not being able to pull themselves up to the same level as him. He had to be prepared to do without the advice of others and to be the sole witness and judge of the validity of his ideas. Owing to the severity of his own criticisms, he only became more tormented. And more isolated as well, since he could not count on anyone else, even less so at the end of his work than in its early days. These experiences are so ordinary that I do not see why underlining their subjective aspect should discredit their importance, except for the fact that they affect the judgement of anyone who includes them in a theorisation.

This essential subjective factor is for me, therefore, not a motive for disqualification. And there are other examples which confirm this hypothesis of how the effects of sublimation[26] can involve self-destructive narcissistic regressions. So let us try instead to bring this implicit theory out into the full light of day.

It is necessary to refer to *Beyond the Pleasure Principle* (1920) to understand its significance. Ever since the most fundamental aspect of psychical life was divided between the activity of two classes of drives, the primary task of Eros has been *binding,* which means both holding together the separate elements in order to form greater unities (the organism and, on another level, the ego) and neutralising the unbinding death drive by integrating it – always through binding. Fusion (*la mixtion*) – mixing or mixture, in any case, mixed – becomes a basic priority in order to preserve the dominance of the life drives. What preserves life ... in life is Eros, that is, what Freud called the life or love drives.

It is necessary to listen to the voice of the *erotic* which is inconceivable if the object is not introduced in one way or another. And it is in this respect that the final drive theory rules out the criticism of solipsism which its author has been subject to. For even if erotic libido is eminently displaceable and transformable, everything we have just learnt from Freud's text suggests the contrary. Namely, that the different displacements and transformations are not equivalent to the attachment to primordial objects which, as it were, retains something which is unmovable in the libido and is bound up with it. And this is how the creation of totalities as rivals of the object wanting to captivate all the love for their own benefit carries within it a mortal danger, always more or less tinged with aggression (the ineradicable ambivalence of human desire) as the expression of a paradox. The Eros of life, unmitigated, unamended (i.e., without repression), is unbearable but it is life in all its potency. Conversely, when Eros is transformed, displaced, diverted towards what it itself has contributed to creating so that it is liveable-with, then to the extent that its creations inevitably emerge as life's rivals they will simply pave the way for the death drives. Without proposing a conciliating synthesis, Freud shows us how a compromise can be found. Since alterity is at once an appeal for investment, an opportunity to 'come out' of oneself, the ego's acquisition of an enriching source of pleasure, i.e., a profusion and propensity for a greater capacity to sustain its existence and to make it more worthwhile, nothing can exceed what erotic life implies in terms of surpassing oneself in a process of growth which includes a not-self, another self with whom it wants to come together. But this drive traction, this crossing of limits which all erotic life involves, must then allow both for its own excess which may exceed its limits and for the possibility that the object may initiate erotic activity which does not correspond in its forms, its aims, or in the means it gives itself to achieve them. This is either because the latter fears for its own organisation – owing to the potentialising of its own desires under the influence of what is mobilising it or from influences originating elsewhere – or because of the danger of becoming dependent on the 'good will' of this extraneous origin which seeks to merge with it but hides its aim of dominating the situation totally, or again because this partner's behaviour may vary: it may bring the flow of pleasure abruptly to an end, disturb it for reasons best known to itself – all circumstances which are liable to awaken destructiveness. There is only one solution: to capture death in life, to bind it to the same fate, to construct convergent aims and to develop the nature of their links. However, the constitution of this alloy does not result in any definitive acquisitions which cannot later be called into question. The interest of this acquisition, however, is that it can be interpreted in two ways (with either one of them prevailing according to the circumstances): either it expresses the two aspects (agonist and antagonist) of the desires of one and the same subject, or it may be understood as the relation which links the subject to the other person. A formula which ensures both the necessary separation distinguishing the subject from the object, and the contradictions linked to the desire for their union, always temporary and uncertain. There can be no advance solutions. These can only be found along the way, put to the test, reconsidered in the light of their respective merits; if erotic movement is commended for the safeguard of life values, the discharge in which Eros is exhausted – only momentarily fortunately – is dangerous because, since investment has, as it were, been spent, the terrain is abandoned for a while to the other drive, the death drive, which is deployed in an unrestrained way and without linking. What does this idea correspond to beyond its purely speculative value? Perhaps to the fact that after orgiastic discharge the possibilities of investment are reduced, the temptation of narcissistic regression being very strong.

It is time now to turn to the question of narcissism. We have gone to some length to point out the extent to which it lacks clarity and is frankly embarrassing after the final theory of the drives.[27] On the one hand, Freud never fails to stress the object's contingency – the example of the three tailors and the blacksmith is constantly recalled: one of the three tailors is to be killed in place of the blacksmith who is guilty but irreplaceable in the village. On the other hand, it might be added that if this possibility of replacing one object with another is widespread, and if even this capacity for substitution can extend to the ego itself, which will not hesitate to conceal the investments destined for the object (secondary narcissism), the consequences of such a change (object → narcissistic) are no less perilous. Either the ego reaches the stage where it has to love itself so much that it becomes indifferent to the external world where its objects are located, and it is a withdrawal which is prejudicial for the erotic and psychical economy, or this displacement of the libido onto the ego, compared with object-investments, can only be unsatisfying due to certain limits imposed on the substitutive drive satisfaction; for only the objects can provide the conditions for complete satisfaction and a state of potential frustration is liable to occur. It can be seen, therefore, that what initially is an advantage – the vicariousness offered by substitution – becomes with time a source of weakness which lays it open to uncertain fates. Freud goes further: this diverting of investment – just as one speaks of diverting a legacy – towards the ego, undoes the combination of the two classes of drives. Thus each time the death drive is no longer 'held' by the erotic drives, it becomes free aggression and may therefore attack the erotically invested structure, in this case the ego.

There is therefore an impasse in Freud's position: on the one hand the object is contingent and, on the other, it is not totally and limitlessly so, particularly where its primary forms are concerned. Eros, which can invest anything and everything, is nevertheless, by inclination, led to seek the desired satisfaction with the object's help, auto-eroticism notwithstanding. Let us recollect that in the *Outline*, it is not the sexual drives (sexuality is simply a function of Eros) which Freud designates under the emblem of Eros but the life or *love* drives. Now, whereas the life drives evoke an abstraction which is rather difficult to conceive of, the love drives, while retaining their conceptual status, refer to a common, immediate experience. However, all love involves an object. The ego may be the enticement by which such an operation can be attempted and even achieved, but it is at a very high price and at the risk of neurosis ... narcissistic (in the primary sense of the term). The restriction of the expression to melancholia after 1924 does not invalidate the preceding remark. Whether the risk is of psychosis – through parcelling of the ego under the attacks of destructive drives – or of melancholia – through single splitting into good and bad – in both cases the love which the ego has for itself can avoid neither limitations nor disappointments. The conclusion we shall have to draw from all this is that Freud's position is too self-enclosed. Freud is imprisoned within the limits of the psychical apparatus he has constructed and runs into impasses which are perhaps due to an inadequate conception of the object even when it is considered from the angle of the primacy given to the drive.

The Ideal, Idealisation: Introduction of the Object

Freud designated the ideal as one of the three major functions applied to the different types of materials included in the composition of the various agencies of the psychical apparatus: the function of the ideal is for the super-ego what perception is for the ego and the drive for the id. Moreover, we know that initially Freud did not distinguish much between the ego ideal and the super-ego.

According to a distinction widely accepted in French psychoanalysis, the super-ego is heir to the Oedipus complex, the ego ideal being heir to primary narcissism. However, *idealisation* is supposed to concern the object in contradistinction to sublimation which is a vicissitude of the drive. In an earlier study,[28] I pointed out the numerous links which exist between the sublime and the ideal; each of them echoing the other sometimes to such an extent that the distinction between them is blurred. The sublimated is connected with an ideal object. Desexualising means dematerialising, and dematerialising is synonymous with idealisation. The incorporeal, spiritual, and ideal are closely related. Idealisation presupposes spiritualisation and the latter becomes the model for an ideal.

If these general facts are now applied to psychoanalytic theory, a link can be made between the 'purified' pleasure-ego and the ego ideal. Now the purified pleasure-ego only exists in as far as an object is able to ensure that basic survival needs are met. It is a narcissistic organisation which denies its dependence on the object and may extend this denial to the existence of the object itself, in certain extreme situations.

The development of the Freudian line of thinking reminds us of this attitude. It minimises the object's role repeating the denial of its importance and is only concerned with the secluded alchemy which governs the transformations of the libido and those of the conflict between the two classes of drives. It is understandable that Freud wanted to reassure himself that what he had discovered would neither be unduly minimised nor relativised. It was also important that the theory should not found wanting.

Clinical experience provides us with a precious source of observations. With a subject who presents the characteristics of this narcissistic sublimation, one cannot overlook the role of the imagos – is it not true that identification plays a part in this process? It is not only the paternal super-ego model which is met with here, functioning within the register of prohibition, but also that of the maternal imago seeking to acquire precedence over that of the father. Far from taking over the role of prohibition, the positions which she defends in the name of a higher good allow us to infer, without her knowledge, a paternal transgression in the manner in which, in the circumstances, her own father is invoked to thwart her husband's deficient or even harmful influence. In all innocence, she manages to make him her child, barely older than her own, seeing him, in any case, as a minor. The considerable weight of the mother's ideals which the child has to live up to, for the glory of the mother's deficient narcissism, harnesses the child to this familial task instead of helping him to find his own values. The child's achievements are supposed to make amends for the inadequacies of a father who has disappointed the mother. In fact, the mother's efforts to inculcate the necessity of sublimating facilitates the idealisation of the object which she wishes to incarnate for the child. This leads – through mirroring – to the subject's narcissistic idealisation, the mother relying on the repugnance of drive satisfactions which are thus devalued. 'Bestial' sexuality is therefore the mark of opprobrium with which the father is stigmatised. At least, this is the official version given to the child. Secretly, the latter will find a way which allows him, while apparently doing everything the mother wants, to sabotage her will through mute protest.

Since Melanie Klein, there has been a reassertion of the value of the object's role. We were amazed by Freud's affirmation that sublimation is present 'from the start' or 'from the outset'. With Melanie Klein this reference to origins concerns the object relation. Melanie Klein understands sublimation within the context of reparation during the depressive stage. The emphasis placed on the role of reparation in creation is a constant feature in Kleinian thinking – not only of Klein herself but also of her successors (H. Segal in particular). The creative act is assumed to have been preceded by an intense destructiveness (of a paranoid-schizoid kind). We can see that sublimation is traced back to a very early period, to the first year of life. In fact, when one considers the role Melanie Klein attributes to the idealisation of the breast – which she sees as symmetrical and contrary to the persecution characteristic of the relations of the paranoid-schizoid position, one realises that the nature of the primitive object relation paves the way for the paths of sublimation. It is clear that the Kleinian point of view is far removed from Freud's. Where the latter assumes a desexualisation is at work, Melanie Klein introduces a global binding, which only interests her as reparative re-binding, without having any real consideration for its status vis-à-vis sexuality.

Melanie Klein returns to the case of Leonardo,[29] interpreting it in her own way. Without going into her ideas in detail, let us note the reversal which occurs in this re-evaluation. Whereas Freud postulates a diversion, a turning away of the libido which paves the way for desexualisation, a process which he relates to narcissism, Melanie Klein stresses, on the contrary, the highly developed capacity for identification with objects. In this case it is narcissistic libido which is transformed into object libido, thereby lending itself to sublimation.[30]

I have no doubt stressed the oppositions between Freud and Klein to an excessive degree, for it is true that the relations between ego libido and object libido are more complex than this. Melanie Klein is concerned to reformulate in her own way the exchanges between object libido and ego libido, emphasising the ego's predisposition to attract to itself erotic investment in order to transform it into narcissistic investment (by the formation of symbols), by identifying with erotic objects (nipple, penis and bird's tail in the case of Leonardo[31]). Can we speak of desexualisation here as Freud did? The question is overshadowed by the necessity of underlining the participation of objects in the transition of erotic pleasure to ego interests (moving from the investment of the symbol 'bird's tail' to an interest in its flight which demands that the whole object be taken into account). Once again we come across the idea which is concerned to account for the transition from part to whole. Are we justified in making the hypothesis that such a transition would be accompanied by a desexualisation? The process is presented here from the angle of the other class of drives, i.e., the transition from the unbridled destructiveness of the paranoid-schizoid position to the reparative guilt of the depressive position (striving to achieve the wholeness of the object and to maintain it).

The change of perspective introduced by Melanie Klein led us to consider the role of a dimension which was absent in Freud, that of mourning. From then on, the relations between sublimation and mourning, seen through the process of reparation had to be taken into consideration. But is it absolutely true that this aspect was totally repudiated by Freud? It would seem that the conclusion he comes to at the end of *The Ego and the Id*, identification with the paternal model, implies this. Since Freud does not fail to emphasise that such a model can be found in totemism and that it is the germ of all religions, we cannot allege that he overlooked it.

In fact, the differences cannot be minimised. Melanie Klein works within a strictly ontogenetic perspective: she only takes into account the baby and its mother and operates within the limited framework of the individual development of their relations. The emphasis on the father, which we spoke of earlier, does not only express a straightforward development from the mother to the father; it also involves the transition from the ontogenetic vision to that of phylogenesis which the reference to culture requires us to take into consideration, at least from Freud's perspective. Melanie Klein's *aggiornamento* strives to bring Freud's phylogenetic speculation back within a strictly ontogenetic framework. What the former introduces in the context of a hypothetical murder of the *primitive* father is, in my opinion, taken over and modified by Melanie Klein who retains the hypothesis of the destructive drives applying it to the *first* object: the mother. The role Freud attributes to religion and culture is expressed differently within a developmental vision, i.e., the reparation of the primary object. Where Freud goes beyond the individual perspective in collective psychology (bearing traces of phylogenesis), Melanie Klein does something similar within the context of an individual developmental conception (albeit speculative): transformation of the part object into a whole object and the emergence of reparation as a change in the relational axis. Having strived to avoid – without even saying so expressly – the myths of Freudian mythology concerning the history of the species and the application of its theoretical basis to socio-historical fields, Melanie Klein herself fell into another mythology which brought her scathing criticism. That is, her view of development proved, in spite of considerable support obtained from paediatricians and psychologists, to be unfounded. She was unable to avoid resorting to certain theoretical hypotheses which provoked as many reactions of rejection as Freud received from his most resolute denigrators (for example: the fantasy of the father's penis in the mother's womb whose explanation could only 'reasonably' stem from a phylogenetic theory, given its supposed date of origin). It would be vain to overlook the fact that there is a real difficulty here: the need to account for the constitution of the matrices of individual and collective meanings. Thus one should not be surprised to see Freudian ideas concerning the father, at least their content, reappear in the writings of others whose influence will be no less decisive. This is the successful aspect of Lacan's ideas.

To the extent that the pre-eminence granted to the father results in progress in spirituality, as Freud maintains in *Moses and Monotheism* (1939), it is the 'process of civilisation' itself which is linked up with what Lacan calls the dead father.

Civilisation and Cultural Experience

While it is very difficult to give a metapsychological status to what Freud describes as the process of civilisation and while, in addition, Melanie Klein seems to have shown little interest in the reference to civilisation, Winnicott was to return to this question proposing an unexpected solution. He does not approach the problem from the angle of sublimation, but from the point of view of the status of cultural objects. Attempting to locate cultural experience[32] in psychical topography, Winnicott provides a sanctuary for cultural objects in the intermediate area between external and internal reality, an area which he had already defined as accommodating objects and transitional phenomena. What interests Winnicott is not desexualisation or reparation but the characteristics specific to works of art which cannot be treated suitably according to the criteria of the judgement of existence – they are neither real nor imaginary (in the sense of non-existent).

The problematics of finding–creating are developed here. By this Winnicott is referring to the dilemma relating to that which, because it exists in reality, is simply found in contrast to that which is created by the subject. This is another way of speaking of the object objectively perceived (found) and of the subjective object (created). It can be seen that there is a shift in emphasis towards creation. Winnicott's approach is of interest on several accounts. He gives a specific psychical status to cultural productions in the transitional, intermediate area (between inside and outside), the symbolic field (a place of potential union at the very point where the separation occurred), of paradox (the transitional object both is and is not ... the breast), etc. The question is whether sublimation is a part of this process. What is certain is that the creation of cultural experience and the intermediate area necessitates, beyond the existence of a good internal object – here Winnicott settles his debt towards Melanie Klein – a development which supposes that the object has not been consumed. Drive satisfaction goes hand in hand with the discharge which exhausts tension and the disappearance of the object which is swallowed orally. So there is a 'salvaging' of the object on the periphery, at the very point at which it could disappear. The child who clutches his transitional object tightly or caresses it (a teddybear or a bit of cloth) does not take it into his mouth. This pleasure is not denounced, it is simply entrusted to auto-erotism and its instruments (thumb, index finger, or even index and middle finger) which invest the primitive cavity and maintain the transitional object in the closest proximity but apart. The intermediate area is thus a border area between inside and outside and it can give rise to a vast range of creative possibilities.

There is undoubtedly more than one difference with sublimation for one cannot identify the sublime and the transitional. But what concerns us here is the *creation of a new category of objects,* different from external or internal objects, which, owing to the theoretical construction which is supposed to account for it, makes considerable demands on symbolisation – furthering its elaboration – and enriches the negativity with which transitionality can logically be linked.

The negative was already present in Freudian theory in the form of desexualisation; with Klein, it was implicit in the idea of reparation. Now it takes on the form of paradox, a third dimension, opposing the earlier mutually exclusive oppositions. For the first time in the psychoanalytic debate this thirdness addresses the nature of the mode of existence of sublimated objects.

It might be helpful to point out the meaning of this development. Sexuality was initially considered by psychoanalysis as a source of pleasure. Then, when it was seen that the dimension of pleasure proved to be insufficient, one ventured to speak of love (transformation of sexual drives into life or love drives). Now, the picture must be completed by adding the *creative* dimension. I am not alluding to the link between sexuality and reproduction. It was by dissociating these that psychoanalysis was able to move ahead, drawing attention to the necessity of not confusing genitality and sexuality. I am speaking of the property inherent in psychical sexuality of creating structures and objects which will find their place, their status and their function at the heart of the psychical economy.

The Objectalising Function

The place of the object in Freud's theory is all the more limited in that substitution is its most striking property. However, it might be considered that it is more important than Freud thought. For even if one considers that the process by which objects are interchangeable puts in question the overvaluation which can be seen, for example, in passionate love with the election of a single and irreplaceable object, this eventuality must still be accounted for. There is no lack of candidates for the position of the loved and erotically invested object. They do not have to come from outside since, as we have seen, the ego itself offers itself to the id to be loved by it, instead of by the object whose finery it has taken on by transforming itself through identification. While it is true that 'lovers are alone in the world', the relationship is not 'autistic', which we regard as an enclosed bliss, quasi-circular and self-sufficient.

Furthermore, there are two views which do not fit together well between the object which Freud speaks of in 'Instincts and their Vicissitudes' (1915) and the one he alludes to in 'Mourning and Melancholia'(1917 [1915]).[33]

We have pointed out the close links Klein established between the depressive position and sublimation; in melancholia the ego takes the place of and identifies with the lost object, less by choice than under constraint. It splits in two, one of the two halves taking over the role which its titular has abandoned by disappearing. The melancholic structure is dual in nature and can be expressed through various oppositions:

ego – object
ego – ego, identified with the lost object
ego – super-ego
good object – bad object[34]

The fact that the ego itself, in sublimation just as in melancholia, can transform itself to the point of wanting 'to make an object of itself', leads us to consider that the process by which one object can always be replaced by another is by no means limited to objects designated as such by name. Melanie Klein suggests something similar when she shows how there is a transition from the series of part-objects (nipple – penis – bird's tail) to the interest shown in the flight of the kite. Through the process of sublimation the flight of birds has become an object.

This is what elsewhere[35] I have called the *objectalising function*. We make the hypothesis that the main function of the life or love drives is to establish links with objects and, in order to do this, it is necessary to transform into an object (of the ego), not only that which derives from the relation to primary objects by metonymic extension, but also that which, originally, does not belong to the category of objects – this may be a process or a function. Sublimation allows an activity to acquire object status and to be considered as a possession of the ego. Thus, in sublimation – to return to the case under consideration – it is not just a matter of modifying 'the bird' by desexualisation but of making an object of the drive of investigation (observation of flight). This is an achievement of the objectalising function.

It is clear that an objectalising process which transforms epistemophilia into an object will only succeed in doing so by creating a special category of objects, quite different from those in which erotic investment or identification is involved. But that is the point; since Winnicott our understanding of the field of objects has become more complex. We can no longer be satisfied with dividing objects into external objects and internal objects by opposing their properties. The emergence of transitional objects has considerably enriched psychoanalytic logic: its operations and its products.

What does this new category which assumes there is an objectalising function at work in sublimation correspond to? Thanks to this conception, sublimation ceases to be caught in the dilemma: desexualisation–reparation. Even though the role of the destructive drives can be observed in both cases (due to defusion in Freud, and to the paranoid-schizoid position in Melanie Klein), it remains true that in Freud the object is, to say the least, of secondary importance, whereas it occupies a position of the utmost importance in Klein. The question which we have to resolve is the following: is sublimation an enrichment in the accomplishments of psychical life, a new pleasure which the psychical apparatus is capable of, or does it simply pave the way for the progression of the death drive? Like Melanie Klein but in a different way, Freud opts for a pessimistic view in spite of the consolatory function which both of them attribute to it. Sublimation – like all the effects of civilisation – has an atrophying effect on sexuality. The sacrifice it demands is exorbitant. Are there any compensations? It would seem that not enough consideration is given to the pleasure derived from sublimated activities with too much emphasis being placed on the renunciation which is the price to be paid.

Here we have a strange paradox which claims that analysis demystifies what has been sublimated by showing the price which has to be paid for achieving the sublime whereas, elsewhere, it sees the access to sublimation as being one of the most worthwhile goals of treatment! If sublimation continues to present numerous unresolved enigmas, it may be necessary, before we can hope to clear up the mysteries which continue to puzzle us, to underline a certain number of features which have not always been given the attention they deserve. We may take as an example the idea of *diversion* which is regularly referred to each time Freud mentions sublimation. He certainly intends to distinguish this mechanism from repression. He associates it with the idea of an *attraction*[36] by non-sexual aims.

The originality of Freudian thought has been underestimated here. First of all, it implies the need to recognise the property of the drive not only to exchange sexual aims for non-sexual aims, but above all to exert itself very *far away* from them. Freud speaks moreover of an attraction towards distant aims. The implicit supposition on which this characteristic is based is thus essentially what one might call the 'radiation' of the drive which can be brought into play when a direct link between the thrust and the sexual aim is undesirable. The 'diversion' represents a condensation of the gap between their usual way of relating and the complementary effect of the attraction of that which has been diverted far from its initial aims. However, when one takes into account the context in which Freud makes these remarks, one notices that it concerns the field of vision. Either directly in relation to the scopic drive with the pair voyeurism–exhibitionism, or in the derivation represented by sexual curiosity and epistemophilia in general. There is therefore good reason to think that the sphere of the visible and of the invisible, compared with that of touching, represents a pole which facilitates the substitutions working in favour of diversion–attraction. Later we come across similarities with identification which take into account and develop what we have already emphasised about the opposition of the two types of relations: object relations (at the mother's breast) and relations of identification (with the father of prehistory). We wish to put forward the hypothesis that a distinctive feature of the category of the visible (coupled with the invisible) is to create the conditions of a 'touching-without contact', at a distance, i.e., touching 'metaphorised' (transported–transferred) in such a way that its non-realisation in the context of touching would be compensated by the dynamic of diversion–attraction, mobilising its orientation towards non-sexual aims with the preservation (transformed) of its libidinal investment, without the latter occurring along the lines of drive satisfaction and without this transformation making it lose the quality which continues to link it to the category of drive phenomena.

It cannot be denied – because one is disillusioned at its capacity to prevent the onset of neurosis – that sublimation is not only socially appreciated but is genuinely an innovative source of pleasure. And I do not mean to limit the import of this remark to creative, artistic sublimation; it applies to all the forms of sublimation which creativity implies when processes of psychical transformation are brought into play. Examples abound, however, of exceptional personalities in many fields who have demonstrated a capacity for sublimation far above the ordinary, who have left quite indisputable evidence of the fecundity of their gifts and who, furthermore, have been prey to intolerable conflicts and torturing anxieties. In this case why should we strive towards this goal and congratulate ourselves on it when it is foreseeable in a patient?

In truth, sublimation guarantees nothing, protects one against nothing. It simply permits one to find satisfaction 'differently' in a common sharing of emotions, creating a special realm of 'civilised' relations but which have no power to suppress other forms of much cruder satisfactions. The power of its objectalising function may enable us to be accompanied throughout life by a few loved objects which have the advantage over others of remaining faithful since they can only disappear if we abandon them. We should also distinguish between creative people who are always destined to be unsatisfied with their creations owing to the exigencies of their ideal and art lovers for whom works of art become life companions without their needing themselves to be the authors of them. Perhaps then one should consider sublimation as the work of the negative constantly torn between the psychical, and even physical, forces of life and death. That is, between objectalisation and disobjectalisation.

Sublimation between Reparation and Destruction: *Aurélia*

If there is an example where sublimation seems to display all the factors we have been discussing (desexualisation, reparation, creation, etc.), it is surely that of Gérard Labrunie, known as Nerval. Analysts have already shown interest in his work.[37] One of his works, *Aurélia*, was written soon after his mental breakdowns and shortly before his suicide. The work is subtitled 'Dream and Life' and the very first words are: 'Dream is a second life.'[38] Behind the usual clichés on this theme, I think that Nerval is suggesting that for believers dream is an equivalent, on this earth, of what life in the beyond is supposed to be like when death has taken over from life. Dream anticipates the threat of death and access to the beyond so that one rediscovers, before dying, what has been lost, thus repeating today – the time of present suffering – the loss of a distant past which one thought had been forgotten and overcome. Which in a certain way it is, for instead of through memory, its continuing presence is expressed by an incapacity for living which not only despoils the pleasure of existing of the person who is affected, but takes every opportunity of dragging them down into the mortal abyss where they will disappear for ever, thereby actualising the past more than evoking memories of it. But this outcome must be avoided so that dying may become a reason for hope. Dream which waits upon the threshold of nothingness attracts the subject with an irresistible force in order to block out the attraction of non-being. Literary criticism, focusing exclusively on Nerval's writing, sees it only either as a life having a real existence or as a life which has been created solely through writing, without having much connection with anyone else's. Literature, moreover, is no more concerned with this than it is with the world of pathology, since in fact the work's success delivers it from its dependence on illness. These rationalisations do not carry much weight if one is prepared to take into account a series of splits which were necessary for Nerval but which it is our task to recognise. Dream has two statuses according to his pairing. The first pair unites dream and madness (an issue debated in psychiatry at the time); the second unites dream and poetic imagination. The result for Nerval is to condense – by suppressing the intermediate stages – poetic imagination and delusion, the first transcending the second. One suspects that this uninterrupted continuity between dream and life might be the sign of a pathological process. Nonetheless, the opening of *Aurélia*, even when interpreted from this angle, leads us to understand that the illness is not without reason, nor even illogical. Behind the disconnected forms it takes, owing to delusion, it has all the significant characteristics of dream life. At times Nerval rejects the opinion of doctors (only some of them: certain opinions and certain doctors), whereas at other moments he clearly recognises he is ill. In fact, dreams seem very much to be a kind of geometrical locus in which the pattern of what occurs during sleep is transposed to the reveries of the day before and to delirious hallucinations. Dream gives rise to writing. And writing offers, through the prism of creation, access to what is involved in the dream creation.

There can be no question however of dispossessing *Aurélia* of its quality as a literary work, but it is Nerval himself who rejects the idea that that is all it is. The ambiguity of the status of literary work, the fact that it belongs to the category of the 'transitional', allows us to find in it a mixture of elements in which various approaches meet: the recounting of episodes lived through during the psychotic experience or rather the psychotic experiences merged here into one; recollections, which themselves are comprised of memories mixed with waking dreams constructed *a posteriori;* fantasies, concerning which one cannot tell whether they are related to what has been experienced, or whether they correspond to the necessities of literary fiction or, finally, whether they are the product of an ideology whose origin is difficult to determine in the light of current knowledge or in terms of what gives delusion its substance. At times Nerval seems to be a precursor of President Schreber. It is futile to try to unravel the different threads of this skein: the remarkable nature of the work would be lost in the process. Let us simply say that a good deal of lucidity and 'mental health' was needed to bring to fruition an enterprise which nonetheless gives us a unique insight into the intimacy of the world of mental illness.[39] The written work does not depend, in its relation to reality, only on eye-witness accounts or on a *prise de conscience* either, even if it has a satisfactory outcome. It is an attempt at restitution, as Freud says, or at reparation from Melanie Klein's perspective.

This transitional state allows for the fusion, at the centre of a work, of several identities: firstly, that of the subject who has gone through the psychotic experience; secondly, that of the spectator who can reflect on it with the benefit of distance and hindsight and, thirdly, that of the poet who creates the work of art incorporating the other two in the poetic experience. We should also include a fourth, disguised within the work, which certain elements allow us to identify: that of the doctor. He tries to believe and wants others to believe that he is and has never ceased to be one, seeking thereby to win his father's favour, as much as to compete with him, in order to erase the memory of the latter's disappointment when he gave up his medical studies.[40] Nothing is more pathetic than Gerard's quest to win back the love of a father who remains insensitive to his son's painful feelings of affection just as he seems to have no understanding of what is showing through of his son's deepest self, at a time when there is a real danger of his sinking definitively into alienation. Could one go as far as to say that the father, to whom this work is implicitly addressed, is needed as a witness to this quest which is haunted on every page by the fantasy of being reunited with the lost mother and in which the hope of a permanent reunion with her has to give way to a series of reconciliations and estrangements, marked by as many tragic encounters as sudden separations, each of these moments fading away in turn like the mirage of an evanescent vision. And if one wants to gain a better understanding of the hidden depths of Nerval's relationship with his father, one must turn to his relations with Doctor Blanche. Characterised by a poignant humaneness and moving sincerity, they shed considerable light on his conflicts with the paternal image: a mixture in which provocation, violence, tenderness and regret alternate, with even a touch of homosexual jealousy on the occasion of the doctor's marriage, the poet confessing without any reticence that he felt abandoned. It is clear that *Aurélia* has many things to teach us about the entangled threads of sublimation.

Yet this burst of life which allowed Nerval to 'be cured', was without a tomorrow. *Aurélia* was the end point in this struggle between destruction and creation. After writing this work, illness pursued its course as before. From then on Gérard wandered, with neither hearth nor home and the winter was harsh. On 26 January 1855, three weeks after the publication of the first part of *Aurélia*, he hanged himself in the rue de la Vieille Lanterne. Two days earlier, the last letter he wrote was addressed to his aunt whom he called 'the best of mothers', promising her a place in his Olympus just as he had in her home, 'when I shall have triumphed over everything'. 'Don't wait up for me tonight, for the night will be black and white.'[41]

The following day a letter from Godefroy addressed to the *Préfet de Police* requested the transfer of his body from the mortuary to the Eastern Cemetery 'following the refusal of his family to take care of his inhumation'.[42] The rights of the second instalment of *Aurélia* would pay, in part, for his burial.

Love for the Mother. Love for Women

Gérard had always been a nuisance. As soon as he was born on 22 May 1808, he was put in the care of a nurse near Mortefontaine. His father, a military doctor, was attached to the Rhine army and his wife accompanied him on his duties. He was in charge of a hospital at Glogau in Germany when his wife died there at the age of twenty-five. Gérard was barely thirty months old. His mother, whom he had never known, was to become the object of unfailing affection. On 25 November, 1853, after a severe bout of delirium, he wrote to Doctor Emile Blanche, with whom he had formed a genuine transference, 'if you saw me crying yesterday, do not think it was out of weakness; it is just that I thought we did not understand each other any more. Now, acting the fool is bad enough when one is in one's right mind and it's not on my mother's anniversary that I shall have the courage to do it.'[43]

In the first draft of *Aurélia* which is not as good as the final version, Gérard is in a prison cell (as if in a nurse's care?) when he has a hallucination: 'A woman dressed in black appeared before my bed and it seemed to me her eyes were hollow. Except that I seemed to see tears as brilliant as diamonds pouring forth from the depths of the empty sockets. This woman was for me the spectre of my mother who had died in Silesia.'[44] From the first time it is mentioned, the mother's image has persecutory and idealised traits ('a tutelary angel [...] sparkling eyes [...] an ermine gown [...] a tippet of swansdown').[45] The projection onto her of his own sadness satisfies his desire to see her racked by sorrow over the loss of her son. In the final text, the mother is treated more allegorically, mostly by allusion. By a process of condensation she is combined with Aurélia and Death. Aurélia is based principally on the personality of Jenny Colon, Nerval's only love. Nevertheless, right from the second page there is mention of Dante's Beatrice and Petrarch's Laura. Aurélia is very similar to the anagram of Laura: Gérard's mother's maiden name was Laurent. In both versions of *Aurélia* the circumstances which lead to madness are evocative of Nerval's first attack in 1841 – whereas the major part of the narrative of 1854, thirteen years after, alludes to contemporary episodes. Thus, the different stages of the illness are subject to condensations around certain recurrent themes.

In *Aurélia*, the memory of his mother which is permanently in his thoughts is blended with the more recent events in his relationship with Jenny Colon. The first episode of Nerval's illness followed shortly after his meetings with Jenny Colon had been broken off.[46]

The Story

Aurélia claims to open up the world of dreams – but it takes us above all into the kingdom of the dead. 'A woman I had long loved, and whom I shall call Aurélia, was lost for me.' The loss is followed by the temptation to die – 'later I will explain why I did not choose death.' This love is tinged with a sense of sin. But the choice to go on living obliges Gérard to be detached. 'What madness, I told myself, to go on platonically loving a woman who no longer loves you [...] I have made a Laura [...] out of an ordinary woman of our century.'[47] This superficial lucidity drives him to seek out pleasure which is akin to what mourning mania provokes, that is, a defence against a threatening melancholia which protects the lost object from hate. The displacement onto a substitute love (Marie Pleyel) comes to a sudden end and is resolved amicably. It would seem that these ephemeral reunions with the love object, interrupted by a new separation imposed by a 'pressing obligation', played a part in bringing on the bout of madness. In the story a sinister feminine apparition, 'a woman with a pallid complexion and hollow eyes', conjures ʋ the memory of Aurélia. 'I said to myself: "this must be an omen of her death or mine!" ' This interchangeability is characteristic of primary identification in melancholia. Another apparition which resembles the *Angel of Melancholy* by Dürer haunts his dreams, terrorising him. Is it in order to escape from death as from melancholia that he is tempted to flee '*to the Orient*', as he did after Jenny's death? A star ('My only star is dead') guides his footsteps until the moment of his death. From this moment on Nerval is prey to confusion. As he is dying, he watches for the moment when the soul is supposed to separate from the body, torn between the wish to leave the world and sorrow at having to do so. However, the part of the ego identified with the soul nourishes the hope of finding the object again. In fact mortal hate is idealised; death takes on a different meaning signifying now a definitive reunion with Aurélia.

It is then that a double appears, perhaps a portent of death. During this whole period Gérard seems in fact to be between two deaths: one which has already taken place, the other about to happen. This second death promises a reign of happiness – *la vita nuova* – the second life. He places a talisman (a ring) on his neck at the point where the soul is supposed to exit from the body (a sign of mystical union?). The delusion continues, in the story, in the clinic to which he is taken. Protected by isolation, the magical aspect of the dream-delusion subsides, allowing the emergence of much more familiar content. An old servant whom Gérard calls Marguerite[48] appears in his visions, welcoming him to his maternal uncle's cheerful house. We may assume that there is a repetition here of a serious attack Gérard had when he was small which retrospectively has become part of the fantasy about his mother's death. The displacement of the scene to the family house resembles a family celebration which sees the return of parents who were living far away.[49] The new beginning of this second life enables him to rediscover his lineage with the Edenic family from which he came. Everything is flooded with dazzling light and an atmosphere of innocence. This world of women and children is a painful measure of what Gérard has been taken away from. 'Tears began to well up in me as I remembered a lost paradise.' At this point, Gérard's real childhood and his retrospective idealisation of it, under the protection of divine goodness, are now inseparable in his mind. Another dream enables him to meet up again with women he knew in his childhood. One of them gets up and leads him towards the garden with which she merges before vanishing; Gérard tries in vain to call her back. Soon he notices a bust '*hers*'... And the garden turns into a cemetery. 'The Universe lies in night!' Aurélia came back only to disappear once again.

The text leads us to think that it is the oneiric structure which makes Aurélia evanescent, whereas in fact it is simply an expression of the drive activity which causes erotic drives and destructive drives to alternate, without it being clear whether the ego wants to live or die.

'Besides, she belonged to me far more in her death than in her life.' The apparitions deny the loss. But this illusion is short-lived. For they are destined to see the object disappear again. The suavity of the reincarnations, all bearing the mark of mystical goodness, do not succeed in warding off the anxiety which is threatening the body.

The process of writing is itself integrated with thinking which assumes the power to make beneficent characters appear. But the construction of the text obeys the same alternations which see the interventions of favourable powers impeded by hostile, destructive figures. The success of writing may correspond to what Freud alluded to when he spoke of the *captation*[50] by the ego (in this case its double through writing) of the object's finery, demanding to be loved in its place and provoking a defusion of the drives. Creation is soon followed by a persecution by monsters. The beneficent races are succeeded by the Afrites,[51] eager for power, surrounded by women and slaves. Gérard is their captive. Images of sterility and death invade the story. It is a reign of evil, epidemics and death. 'Everywhere the suffering image of the Eternal Mother kept on languishing, weeping and dying.'[52] Why is this malediction associated with the Orient? Because *a posteriori* in the repentance of melancholia, the pleasures which Gérard experienced after Jenny's death could be the cause of his damnation and nourish his remorse for having survived her.[53] 'I regretted all the more deeply that death had not reunited me with her. But upon reflection, I said to myself that I was unworthy of this. I bitterly reviewed the life I had lived since her death, reproaching myself not for having forgotten her – for this had never been the case – but rather for having profaned her memory by easy loves.'[54]

The ego ideal's reproach for not having observed total abstinence, out of grief for the loved one, later turns into an accusation of having defiled her image. A profanation which calls for repentance. Sublimation and desexualisation work together. Reparation does not contradict this but must be linked to a process of purification in which the idealisation of women underlies the self-reproaches concerning the bad treatment inflicted on the desired object. During his travels in the Orient Gérard is shocked at first by the way in which women are treated. But he quickly gives in to the temptation to make use of them as he wanted. As an after-effect of the delusion, the abandonment by the object (the mother and Jenny both chose to follow another man) brings back the repressed desire to punish it and to treat it with even less respect – satisfying all the sadistic drives, as well as those of control, which avenge the previous disappointment. But this regression to cruelty is severely condemned, and, idealisation, seeking to restore the defiled object, only finds a solution for reconciliation with it in the fantasy of fusion which will seal their deadly union once and for all. Sexual guilt can be sensed behind the struggle between good and evil. This division, this dividing in two, again brings out in the story the *double*, now recognised by Nerval as his 'idealised and aggrandised form'. The reflux onto the ego has enabled the subject to integrate this Manichean duality projected onto the object. One can tell, however, that the work of mourning which is linked to the bad object does not stop there. It also makes the depressive position tip over into the paranoid-schizoid position (that is why he fails, for '*the other*' is hostile towards Gérard). Implicitly, the reader is led to think that this persecution comes from the feeling that the object now belongs to another person. 'Aurélia was no longer mine! ...' there is a fusion in the text between the persecutor – an evil figure – and the rival father to whom the mother belongs.

The story continues with his arrival at a castle where men have stolen the mystery of creation from the gods. Gérard comes across a room being prepared for the marriage of the *double*! With Aurélia, of course. To avoid total defeat, Gérard now invokes magic powers. A shriek rents the air; it is Aurélia's voice. He is woken with a start. But the sense of malediction is the sanction for having attempted to disturb the harmony of the universe. On this note the first part of *Aurélia* comes to an end.

Everything seems to be over, the hero's defeat scarcely allowing us to imagine further developments.

Forgiveness

Gérard's sole concern now is to be reunited with Aurélia – at any price! But we do not know whether he is more likely to find her with the dead or with the living. A funeral procession leads him to the cemetery where several of his relatives are buried.[55] He searches for Aurélia's grave. Her marriage and burial are both connected with loss. He is reminded of how the former was for another person's benefit, which arouses death wishes. Gérard sees Aurélia in the reflection of a mirror at an inn; all he can think about is his marriage while voices are repeating to him '*She is lost!*'[56] In a dream, a woman who had looked after him in his youth reproaches him for having mourned Aurélia more than his parents. Neither writing nor delusion are devoid of logic. The women of Cairo are preferred to the chaste memory of Aurélia; the loss of Aurélia–Jenny is mourned more than that of his mother. In short, only one death deserves to be commemorated: the mother's. One could conclude from this that the amorous quest for other women is an attempt to recover the love which has been lost. On the other hand, the pursuit of these remedies for despair leads to reproaches for insensibility and for finding consolation too quickly for primitive mourning. All these manifestations, which bear the stamp of guilt, concern above all one of its aspects, the super-ego's revelation of its desire to exert sadistic control over the idealised object in order to have it at its mercy and to satisfy its most merciless sexual desires with interchangeable variations of it, thereby fending off any further danger of loss. 'I never knew my mother. She had decided to follow my father into battle, like the wives of the ancient

Germans and had died of fever and exhaustion in a frigid province of Germany; my father was subsequently unable to take charge of my formative years.'[57] The more the text lays stress on the traumatic import of this event of which, as a child, he was the first victim, the more he feels repentant and is condemned by his conscience.

His efforts to make reparation are crushing.[58] Religion is of little help – he begins to entertain suicidal thoughts. The sense that the world is coming to an end, which is a sign of psychotic breakdown, haunts his mind. Even a few adventures do not compensate for the internal struggle he is going through to stay alive. Gérard returns to the neighbourhood of Saint-Eustache where he prays while thinking of his mother. He has a vision of his mother (Marie) while he is sleeping. This appearance is no doubt intended to make him forget the blasphemy uttered a short time before: 'The Virgin is dead and your prayers are useless.'[59] In spite of this pardon, the sense of sin does not leave him, and his ego is assailed by thoughts of suicide. And now comes *The Black Sun*.[60]

The text is full of repetitions. Is it simply that the material he is working on is difficult? There is even an interpretation which sees this as a narrative technique. In fact it may be the only way Gérard has of making us feel that he is inhabited by an iterative force over which he has no control and which obliges his mind to dream rather than granting him this liberty. If the meaning seems to repeat situations which have already been set down in the text, the repetition is there precisely to show that what is really at stake in the work, implicating his very existence, is the irresolute hesitation between the desire to resuscitate the object, in order to internalise it at last, and that of destroying it for ever. It is this indecision which is repeated tirelessly, whereas a parallel fate affects the ego, chained to the object, which is unable to set it definitively either on its path of salvation or on the path of its plunge into the abyss. This vital choice is postponed while the book is being written so that it can be brought to completion. But this is just putting things off until later, for the problem will arise again once the work is finished, the ego being literally 'without work'.

After being hospitalised again and released seven weeks later, the delusional tendency (paranoid-schizoid) gains ascendancy over the depression. However, the delusion is not so much the expression of a projective fragmentation as the formation of a neo-reality which Gérard clings to desperately by attributing to himself the power of restoring universal harmony. So we have come to a point where it is impossible to tell in the text whether the main concern is to record the events which have happened to a person who is increasingly ill, or to create a work of art. Both concur in the tragedy of this solitude exposed to an inexorable psychotic invasion in spite of the intermittent, but increasingly precarious, return of his faith in the protection of maternal divinities. This does not go very far for the story continues with images of women tortured, mutilated, sundered 'as if with the sword'; on other walls there is a bloody assortment of members and heads, but exclusively of women.

Thoughts relating directly to his mother emerge, alternating with apocalyptic images. We are witnesses to the struggle taking place within the ego between being submersed by disorganising elementary forces and the attempt to bring together symbolic figures in order to give the object more reality: 'I am none other than Mary, none other than your mother, none other than the one you have always loved in every shape and manner.'[61] This pathetic attempt to give his mother a form which can be represented, which coincides with the choice of a good object, seems destined to failure. This hope of meeting her – given that he will not be able to recognise her as he has never known her – makes him write a sentence which sums up the current psychical process as well as that of writing. 'At each of your ordeals I have cast off one of the masks that veil my features; soon you will see me as I truly am.'[62] The limpidity of the formulation and the retrospective lucidity about the course of the story suggest there is a close superposition between the author and the narrator which comes together in the person of Nerval. Contrapuntally, the ego, which has set its hopes on this celestial encounter with its idealised object, takes on a Napoleonic identity. There is no doubt that the situation awaits the revelation of the solution which will allow him to find a way out of this impasse. And once again, it is back to the hospital.

Henceforth, the choice to live can only be sustained by resorting to mythical powers conveyed by religions. The struggle of good and evil reaches beyond Gérard's own boundaries to include not only the world in which he lives but the universe of which he is only a tiny fragment. His redemption through his espousal of goodness enables him to include himself at the heart of a system which encompasses various divinities, different religions, under the auspices of the God of all the other gods who is more than the one and only God.

The work finishes with a few pages entitled 'Memorabilia'. These are hymns whose titles are reminiscent of Swedenborg. Aurélia has become 'a great enthusiast' of heavenly visions, 'the heavens opened in all their glory and there I read the word *pardon* written in the blood of Jesus Christ'.[63] Universal harmony is restored. Purification seems at last to have taken place. It is consubstantially linked with the certainty of immortality (of the Virgin mother). No doubt it is a feeling of internal death which Gérard seeks to overcome by restoring life repetitively to the only power which enables him to fend off catastrophes; that is, a distant mother capable of giving him unconditional love, of accepting him as her double.

The Work of the Negative in Sublimation

If I have enlarged upon *Aurélia* it is because it is rare to have such a detailed example of self-observation at one's disposal which takes place on the level both of illness and sublimation. This is seen from two angles: firstly, at the heart of the psychotic process, and, secondly, in the work of writing which transposes it to another level. It would no doubt be an error only to rely on the text of *Aurélia* while forming a judgement on Nerval's illness, the development of the crisis and its resolution. That would be to act as if the author had managed to make us forget his work and had been content to give us his observations of his psychotic crisis. But what are we to think of Nerval's suicide between the publication of the two parts of his story? It is as if the publisher who was giving life to his text had robbed him of his own, draining away what little remained of his soul in order to strip it completely.

If the truth is to be told, no point of view is exempt from criticism where the study of this work is concerned. If we decided to approach it exclusively as a literary text, belonging wholly to the field of fiction and the fantastic, we would feel guilty for pretending not to be aware of the ink of anxiety and *real* sufferings in which the pen recording their characteristics had been dipped. This can be sensed from the very first lines; there is no need to refer to the poet's biographer. To disregard what we know of Nerval's history, of his disappointments in love, of his existence as an orphan, is not to regard oneself as being incorruptible in face of the demands of literature but to yield to the seductions of aestheticism which induce us to enclose writing within an immaterial frame. If, on the other hand, we take everything which is recounted here literally, not only are we letting ourselves be taken in by writing, reduced here to its function of recounting, but we are denying its creative power by confusing what we have read with the work of a psychiatrist. Let us accept the arbitrary nature of the position we are adopting. It is surprising to see the extent to which the literary world confers writing with such high prestige. So much does it consider writing to be the highest accomplishment which a man can achieve that it cannot bring itself, when someone has proved he is able to succeed in this creative area, to believe that he may *really* be vulnerable to a state of anxiety which others would have no difficulty in recognising as a sign of a call for help. From the moment he is in a position to create artistic forms, it is thought that these are the proof that his psychical torment cannot drag him down. It is astonishing to observe how easily the precedent of artists who have given way to madness is erased in our memories or becomes subject to a sterilisation of the imagination. This fact above all arouses the incomprehension of those who, owing to their situation, have in one way or another to take care of or deal with the artist's works. And when, tragically, suicide has not been avoided, it is most often glorified and seen as an act of liberty unrelated to illness. 'The pursuit of the absolute'. Let us bear in mind the gulf separating the significance writing has for the author from the significance it has for us! Although there is much to be gained from situating sublimation in the field which has recently been described as the transitional area, and while it is true that Winnicott has demonstrated convincingly how this enriches the psyche's possibilities as well as the increased vitality of the psyche which can have an effect on its productions, nothing permits us to believe that its use alone is sufficient to protect the subject from psychical catastrophes. And Winnicott himself acknowledged that the setting-up of a good internal object was a prerequisite for establishing the intermediate area of experience. In fact, the transitional field functions as a formation, affected by influences from both the inside and the outside, trying to anchor the ego by interesting it in this kind of production so as to give the deployment of illusion some moorings which can serve as an obstacle and filter against the most impaired defences. Thus, from the point of view of sublimation, Nerval's endeavour cannot be judged either in terms of failure or in terms of success with respect to his conflictual psychical organisation. It has simply been a means of waiting and hoping, while trying to transform dream into delusion, as if to exorcise the pain which it brought with it; and delusion into dream, as if he hoped that, thanks to this appropriation, he would make contact again with himself. It is for us, to whom this sublimation is offered, that *Aurélia* can act as a love object, furthered by the activity of the objectalising function. Moreover, the text puts us in a privileged position to recognise in it the movements of a work of the negative in terms of the mechanisms we have already analysed. In writing then – and through writing – there are sufficiently convincing traces of the resumption of a work of the negative which succeeds in finding its coherence in and through writing.

Writing has the effect, by constructing its own space, of creating its object: the work. More than any other, it requires that we emphasise the transitional status of such a creation. It is impossible to determine a criterion in it which enables us to decide whether it refers to an existing reality – or one which has really existed – or whether the reality in question is a psychical reality drawn exclusively from the author's inner world without his losing control over it. Anyone who came across this story, having no previous knowledge of it, not even knowing who Nerval was, and without the aid of commentaries, would shut the book again without having any means of knowing if there was any relation between Aurélia and a real character or story. But in any case the sense of a ring of truth about what he had read would not escape him. And therein lies the work's success. It is not that Nerval has succeeded in 'rendering' the atmosphere of madness – while managing to come through it – or in winning admiration by imitating it so well that one would swear that that is what it is really like, since we do not know what it consists of, but that he has managed to make the work sufficient unto itself so that the question of its relation to reality simply does not arise.

The fact that we are not obliged to raise such a question does not mean that we must not do so, nor that the attempt to answer it in any way diminishes its interest. For the advantage of such an accomplishment is that we do not have to be content with a transitional dimension which allows the work to be cut up into many parts so that it is seen now from the angle of madness, now from a literary angle. And one cannot get away with saying that all literature is mad, any more than one would think of saying that all madness is literature. Not so long ago one would not have hesitated to praise Gérard's 'clairvoyance' highly and to proclaim that alienation is a superior state to a so-called normal state.[64]

The beauty of the work lies not only in the superb use of language and an unflinching honesty which renounces all concessions to decorum, but also in the stamp which marks the forehead of someone who, having made a descent into hell, managed to come back amongst us for a while, simply to converse with us about it before continuing on his lonely way.

The idea that artistic creation is motivated by the desire for reparation and counters the destructiveness of the psychotic process is illustrated here. The repetition which is characteristic of *Aurélia* might be interpreted less unilaterally. The very fact that one comes across it in the text leads one to wonder if this reproduction on the stage of writing is a pure and simple transcription of what occurs on the stage of delusion. As this is an area where there is a reciprocal interplay of signs it is necessary to nuance somewhat the explanations given. Although Nerval writes in the subtitle of the story that dream is a second life, he does not cease to interpret what has taken hold of his mind as a dream. Not that such a comparison is unfounded; it was made by eminent psychiatrists of the time – but in his case, it takes on a different meaning, owing to the fact that dreams are equally held to be the source of poetic imagination. Hashish dreams serve as a model for invoking psychical mechanisms which are translated by similar manifestations supposed to be a source of delusion as well as of poetry. His attraction to the Orient is probably not unrelated to this. From this point of view, the Nervalian experience, by tracing his delusion back to dreams, aims at helping him find a path towards his artistic transformation as well as his artistic production (by going back to their supposed oneiric sources), thereby enabling him to find meaning in his delusion. We should bear in mind that he wished to be recognised as a doctor. Poetry is his own form of therapy and is undoubtedly superior to that practised by Dr Labrunie, who is obstinately closed to everything concerning the sufferings of the soul.

Nevertheless, when, as is the case here, dreams relate – because of disappointments in love – to the dreamed-of life with the maternal figure whom, he has learnt, has been snatched from this world and is now living in another, the second life acquires a double significance. It is the promise of what is beyond earthly existence, after death, and, at the same time, in this world, it is that which attests for the presence of what is not dead, albeit belonging to the past, and which may, on the contrary, be actualised at any moment, just like something which has not been experienced and is thus ardently desired. The permanence of memory is proof that nothing has disappeared definitively, that nothing can really be dead. The invincible hope of renewing contact with the lost mother, beyond the confines of individual existence, is all the greater in that the latter, no longer being subject to the limitations of life, seems to be omnipresent, waiting for him everywhere, looming up behind whichever character happens to be in his thoughts at the time, radiating like an immaterial and luminous force over the persons touched by Gérard's love.

Sublimation therefore ceases to be merely the expression of the desire to create. The fact that it is constantly connected with delusion, far from enabling the latter to be reintegrated with psychical activity, stimulates the process, exacerbating, as it were, the conflict. It is as if it refused to be pacified by being given poetic expression. Worse still, by being confronted with its limitations, art not only observes its impotence; it has also excited the psyche. The power of creation to provide salvation is not illusory: the large numbers of people who love Nerval's poetry shows that this power exists. But as far as the author is concerned, he paid the highest price for this success which only benefits others. It may be that the demands of the work have robbed the poet of his vital forces for their own gain. It is true that he had no choice. It is in this sense that Freud's strange statement declaring that sublimation is allied with the forces of death finds its justification, even though it went against general opinion, and in spite of the fact that he saw no higher goal for the human mind.

Three days before his death, Gérard handed over the list of his complete works. It simply remained for him to add his signature.

On the manuscript of *El desdichado*, Nerval, who entitled the poem 'Destiny', added five notes to explain certain words.

He wrote line 3 as follows:

'My sole *star* is dead – and my lute constellated'
(...)
and he added:

♁, the sign of the Earth and of the Tomb,[65] above *death*.

I would add this remark: this sign is the inverse of that which denotes the feminine (♀): ♁, Earth, Tomb-*mother*.

The Future of Sublimation

Many psychoanalysts complain about the unsatisfactory character of the theory of sublimation. We have already seen that it is not enough to examine the differences which distinguish it from idealisation and that, on the contrary, it is necessary to emphasise the numerous links uniting the two notions, even though this does not clear up all the difficulties. One might think that, as psychoanalysis – practice and theory – is itself an effect of sublimation, the obscurity surrounding this question could be explained by the fact that sublimation is at the heart of the very process involved in this inquiry. This being the case, it is not clear why these puzzles are difficult to resolve, unless we take into account that the choice we have made to study psychoanalysis comprises an element of negativity which seems to get in the way of a more complete understanding of its nature.

I think it is likely that what clouds our thinking is related to Freud's last theoretical contributions on this subject. These are not the fruit of a lack of reflection. Between the first ideas concerning sublimation, put forward in the *Three Essays* of 1905, and their culmination in *The Ego and the Id,* almost twenty years passed. Few psychoanalysts, in their efforts to advance our understanding in this matter, have been ready to follow Freud's ideas all the way. It is recognised that sublimation is an unavoidable aspect of the psyche and I do not know any analysts who think the notion can be dispensed with. Conclusion: finding it impossible to adhere to Freud's ideas, they have preferred to take short cuts. This is true of Melanie Klein and Jacques Lacan, not to mention others.

Defending the idea of a death drive to account for certain effects of somatic or psychical illness, and even for certain crises that History and psychoanalytic societies periodically act out on the front of the world's stage, might ultimately be acceptable, even if one would prefer another explanation which will eventually be found with the passage of time.

Now, not only has this hope not been fulfilled but we have seen the collapse of alternative theories (like Marxism) which had enjoyed a striking success. Thus our faith in the validity of global systems of ideas has been shaken yet a little further. The position Freud puts forward in *The Ego and the Id* is a radical one and is maintained in *Civilization and its Discontents* in which relatively little attention is given to sublimation and a lot to the possibility that our civilisation, out of breath, might destroy itself. The remarks on sublimation are disappointing, particularly in view of the subject's importance. Nevertheless, Freud appeals to the future of research in metapsychology.[66]

If we follow closely Freud's tortuous train of thought it may suggest possible lines of future research. In *Civilization and its Discontents,* we can see two possible approaches to sublimation. The long note which concludes Chapter IV (it was probably written after the completion of the first draft, during the re-reading of the text) deals with man's animal nature – his neurobiological organisation, as we would say today. It is a development of the idea, already put forward by Freud, which attributes the absence of complete sexual satisfaction to the existence of a factor which is intrinsic to the sexual drive. There are two corollaries to this: the existence of bisexuality which works against the possibility of satisfying all aspects of the sexual constitution, and, a hypothesis which goes deeper, linking this restriction with the assumption of the erect posture provoking an 'organic' repression, affecting sexuality in particular. Sublimation is only mentioned in passing. It is clear that although Freud never wanted to take into account an innate tendency to perfection or to 'elevation', he is seeking an explanation here, in an evolutionary mechanism, for the avoidance of sexual satisfactions in connection with the turning away from sexual aims which sublimation involves. While it cannot be said that Freud's hypothesis has been confirmed by the progress made in neurobiology, this line of thinking should at least be mentioned.

The second line of thought pursued by Freud – once again recorded in a footnote at the end of Chapter II – is to acknowledge the role played by sublimation in work. Freud links the latter with the economics of the libido. For him, work possesses a value 'by no means second to what it enjoys as something indispensable to the *preservation and justification of existence in society'*.[67]

Freud therefore sees sublimation as having an essential function in social organisation which under no circumstances may be considered as a simple extension of human attributes but rather as an inherent characteristic of man's structure. The final explanations, organic repression and social existence, far from being opposed, are implicitly united here in a complementary way.

Well, then, in my opinion it is impossible to confine oneself to an individual or ontogenetic study of sublimation. When we examine how it works we can see that it involves a *remoteness* (of sexual aims) and an *attraction* (towards social aims). The study of these 'attractive' social aims in the relation (hidden) which they maintain with sexual aims opens up an unsuspected perspective which was absent from Freud's explicit comments on sublimation. Freud's heirs, recoiling from the difficulty of the task, have preferred to refrain from going more deeply into the relation between 'remoteness' and 'attraction'. Yet, I am afraid they have no choice since the impasses of the perspective centred on the individual soon prevented any real progress being made with respect to this problem.

The recourse to culture, to the deposits left by thought in History, and the difficulties we have in understanding the meaning of how our lives unfold in the present, when we extend the horizon of our vision to the time in which we live, are there to show that what governs both our natural and cultural organisation is indissociable. But we are faced here with so much obscurity that sometimes we find ourselves torn between opposing explanatory systems. Freud himself could not face these grandiose, crushing speculations. Their persuasive power, however, is merely based on the possibility that they can offer us the figures of thought enabling us to understand the system of links which makes a representable psychical causality intelligible. But this was not something he could envisage. Had he survived – and this is pure speculation

– the last world war, he might have had an inkling of what this chain of inter-
connecting causalities might be. For, to return to this attraction towards social
aims, it would seem that it cannot be adequately explained by referring to the
mere encounter between a subject and the surrounding culture. Now, whether
it is this that is involved or familial vectors whose mediation is necessary if
it is to be intimately integrated with his psyche, the historical dimension carries
particular weight, even if there is no express reference to the historicity which
inhabits it, but merely by its presentation, as if any encounter with the
present, once it goes beyond the field of data immediately affecting an
individual, revealed their temporal dimension, structured by the simplest presentation of facts of this kind to which the individual is exposed. Only this
organisation which has a history, whether it acknowledges it as such or
whether it has to be inferred, can become more than an influence and acquire
a real power of attraction. Freud was probably aware of this but was faced with
the difficulty of harmonising his ideas concerning final causes (postulated by
drive theory) with the exposition of a process which could more easily be
conceived of by the mind. He brought his work to an end with an epistemological mixture of progressive daring and looking over his shoulder in *Moses
and Monotheism* (1939). Here he was no longer concerned with the death or
destructive drives but with promoting an aspect of psychical life with which
he had made us familiar – even though it had taken him a long time to give
it the consistency he wanted – the murder of the father. This has long been
considered a work of capital importance. *Totem and Taboo* (1912–13) made it
clear that Freud placed it at the origin of the foundations of culture. His speculations on the murder of the primitive father and its consequences for the
formation of totemism and religions was not confined to shedding light on
the customs of savages. It was also possible to find remote whiffs of it in the
collective psychology of the time as he would show later. The case of Moses
enabled him to return to it, as if he was trying to fill a gap between the fundamental hypotheses of *Civilization and its Discontents* and the unconscious
organisers, of a historical nature, of contemporary social life. But this return
to a 'theoretical representability' by the application of basic psychoanalytic
ideas to the most structured and the most demanding monotheistic religion
– one might be tempted to link the prohibition to create images with the non-
specularisable dimensions of a theory whose infrastructure is represented by
the drives – could only claim to have consistency by appealing to a phylogenetic transmission applied to culture as a substratum of capacities necessary
for the development of sublimation. Today, while we acknowledge there is a
need to define cultural life by characteristics which go beyond the variety of
its expressions and the aleatory character of its manifestations, we have the
possibility of opting for a solution different from Freud's if the latter proves
unsatisfactory.

In any case, and in keeping with the subject of our inquiry, two conclusions seem indisputable: the first concerns the irreplaceable necessity of sublimation in understanding the human psyche; the second is the impossibility of any theoretical construction whose substance is based on a perspective confined to the individual considered from the developmental point of view as we understand it today.

On the Edge

We know how difficult it is for psychoanalysts to define who they are, either to others or to themselves. As soon as they are questioned about their identity or the nature of their work, one sees them struggling in a state of confusion which suggests that their embarrassment may betray a need to hide something shameful. They are hesitant in describing what they do; they do not like being confined to their role as therapists (although they also protest whenever there is an attempt to call this function into question) and they cannot agree either to being classified as hermeneutists. Contemporary psychoanalytic literature bears witness to the uneasiness of psychoanalysts in situating themselves; none of the clothes which they are invited to put on seem to fit the image which they wish to present of themselves, although they are unable to say exactly what this is.

Yet the analyst is not unaware that those who come to him are moved by a desire for change. They suffer from the effects of a state which seems harmful to them and which can range from a persistent and uncomfortable feeling of unease, making their lives miserable, to the acute feeling of suffering which eats away at them relentlessly, preventing them from enjoying the ordinary things of life which seem to be reserved for others. Even faced with these latter cases, whose increasing frequency has changed the profile of the population frequenting their consulting rooms, analysts are somewhat reluctant to adhere to the standard model of illness. However, very few analysts deny that many psychiatric affections (it is not because these are unamenable to analysis that they hold them to be fundamentally different in nature from the disorders of the patients in their care) indeed belong to a pathological framework. And one would be wrong in thinking that they are inclined to deny it. The truth is otherwise. It resides in the fact that their practice and thinking are such that they cannot recognise themselves in this model of illness, for they do not feel concerned either by the way this is characterised socially (even if they are ready to take the social impact on the patient's condition into account) or by the

way of thinking which explains the symptoms they observe as natural disturbances translated by deviations from biological norms. One might conclude
that it is a consequence of the understanding acquired as a result of the close
relationship they have with their patients, entailing an attitude which is
reluctant to apply anonymous labels to them. Another explanation, which takes
the preceding remark still further, sees the analyst's identification with his
patient as the source of this reluctance. For this identification often leads him
to notice mechanisms in himself which are more or less similar to those
revealed by the analysand through the transference. It is thus not only the
patient whom he protects from the segregation resulting from the state of
illness, but himself as well. Even though these explanations may have some
truth in them, they fall far short of satisfying our curiosity.

For, I firmly believe that this reticence of various kinds and the reactions it
provokes are above all related to the real difficulty in describing what being
an analyst and the nature of analysis are. According to psychoanalysis,
whichever side of the couch one is on, man is conceived of essentially in
relation to the disorder which is intrinsic to the human condition and which,
in certain cases, may develop in such a way that the person who is going
through it has the feeling that the incredibly complicated consequences
resulting from it cannot be solved through the means, opportunities or
situations which he has at his disposal during his life. These can no longer even
play an expedient role which would at least offer the subject, who is prey to a
dereliction which often goes unnoticed by others, a way out making his
existence worthwhile. He could then join the large number of people who, in
spite of the misfortunes which can strike each one of us with greater or lesser
severity, nevertheless still feel life is worth living.

When science is asked what it has to say about it, one finds that it can only
answer within the confines of a grid which falls a long way short of explaining,
even before any sort of response can be envisaged, the very terms in which the
question is set. Is it then not surprising to see it appearing at the centre of this
debate when it has so little to offer? This apparent incongruity can be explained
however by its increasingly explicit claim to be making advances in fields which
hitherto have escaped its influence, merely owing to their complexity. Today,
this no longer deters scientists who may have found the means to bring this
level of complexity down to a relatively simple level. It is both paradoxical and
revealing that whereas the non-human sciences are discovering the need for
a new way of thinking, known as hypercomplexity, certain scientists who are
tackling the field in which this hypercomplexity concerns facts more than
methodology, are only interested in narrowing this down so that they are able
– whatever distortions might follow – to rescue their approach to their subject
from its inadequacies and to mask the shortcomings of their ideas faced with
the tasks, well beyond their capacities, they have assigned themselves, without

due respect for the knowledge accumulated before they intervened. While it is not necessary to adopt the radical position of metaphysical inquiry, it will readily be agreed that there is some cause for disappointment.

At the other extreme, the religions which have the important function of providing an answer to the essential disorder we have been speaking about, tend to be rather restrictive towards the investigative approach which is unsatisfied with ready-made certainties but seeks to penetrate the mysterious enigmas of the essential disorder which dwells within us. The answers provided by dogmas rarely satisfy us nowadays and religious institutions do not look very kindly on the development of curiosity which it considers vain in these areas. Religious institutions of high standing hold that it is not very good for man to err in this uncertainty. And if such inquiry is pursued, it should take place in a context specially designed for it. The churches give way reluctantly to certain mystics, making it clear that they are an exception, and refrain from encouraging us to follow their example. We know, moreover, that secular attempts to take the place of religions – political ideologies – have scarcely been any more favourable to an independence of mind. The illusions they fostered have ended by revealing the deep tears their ideas have inflicted on the truth. Since the relation between psychoanalysis and science is problematic, it would be unforgivable to suggest that psychoanalysis can be inscribed within this filiation. Thus the model of somatic illness, which depends on science, and that of faith, which only recognises the enigmas of the psyche and the causes of the suffering which is connected with them in order to offer solutions which protect against the uncertainties of our knowledge, can under no circumstances serve the same purpose as the research which informs psychoanalytic theory. The relations with philosophy are still more complicated and cannot easily be resolved. Who does not recollect the countless references in Freud's work in which he not only distances himself from philosophy but seems to gibe at the philosophers with a certain pleasure. And yet, it is this same Freud who wrote to W. Fliess: 'As a young man I knew no longing other than for philosophical knowledge, and now I am about to fulfil it as I move from medicine to psychology.'[1] And that is why it is not vain to compare psychoanalytic theory with the questions which philosophy treats of. There was only one other branch of knowledge which Freud showed so much ambivalence towards and that was science. From the beginning, he placed his confidence in it and this would never be retracted. Yet, when he found himself confronted with scientific notions which excluded certain of his hypotheses, he refused to give way. Without wishing to make him say what he himself did not take the trouble to make explicit, we may suppose that the refusal to fall into line with general scientific opinion was an expression of the feeling that the defence of his hypotheses, apparently questioned by science, could be explained by the specific nature of a field of which the latter, as it is usually understood, was unaware. Perhaps this was because it had not yet found a means to explore it – although Freud had discovered this means by his method – or perhaps because, contrary to all expectations, scientists, like every common mortal, are subject to resistance. Lacan developed this point but he believed he had found the conceptual means which would enable us to get round this hurdle. Now, more than ten years after his death, we can measure the extent of his failure.

In short, Freud's ambivalence is positive towards science and negative towards philosophy. Neither of them can satisfy the demands of psychoanalysis. How then did Freud see this science of the psyche? As a scientific philosophy? Surely not. As a philosophical science? Such a discipline does not exist. As a science which deals with questions often studied by philosophy – and for which psychology, taking over from philosophy, has no satisfying solution in his eyes?

Nowadays psychoanalysis is threatened by splits, not only between the different tribes which share Freud's heritage, but also between the contradictory inspirations seeking to overcome its impasses. It is therefore more or less torn between a phenomenological psychology, a developmental psychology, a behaviourist and biological tendency and a group approach. In contrast to these various orientations, one must also mention the importance, due to the seductive effect they have, of fractions attracted by logic or hermeneutics or sub-groups rooted in a philosophical authority which does not always recognise itself as such.

It is therefore not surprising that, in seeking a solid basis for the theorisation of new configurations which psychoanalytic experience requires us to define more closely, we have encountered on our way a philosophical notion, the work of the negative, which we have been able to consider neither as a mere homonymy, nor as the philosophical basis of the phenomena analysis has brought to light. While the links between the philosophical and psychoanalytical approaches still seem obscure, perhaps the future will show us more clearly how these two fields can acknowledge each other mutually on their common border of human temporality.

Thinking about the negative gives us an inkling of the breadth of the field which it covers. One cannot expect it to clarify completely the fields we have just said are unsuited to resolving the problems we have raised. It is merely a more adequate tool for treating our questions. While it cannot provide answers on their behalf, its investigations can perhaps be extended as far as the fringes of science and religion (viewed as a prototype of cultural phenomena).

Thinking about the negative: is such a term not pleonastic? Does not thinking necessarily imply that we are involved in the field of the negative? The consideration of phenomena of thought which it has long neglected is one of the most decisive changes that the development of psychoanalysis has witnessed. Freud seemed to want to avoid 'thinking about it' too much, fearing the return of academic ideas to the body of discoveries which he had managed to extract from the territory of the unknown. But he was to get there imperceptibly, as the last part of his work indicates. A long period of gestation was necessary before it occurred, leading him to wrestle with new problems which in turn raised many interesting issues. In psychoanalysis it is not so much that thought crowns the edifice of the mind as that it has its place within the larger context of the psyche of which it is one of the most differentiated forms. The latter includes it and makes it co-exist alongside elaborations of another kind which, strangely enough, thought can overlook or which it is only ready to take cognisance of providing it can dominate them. The idea of the work of the negative covers both this relative independence of thought within the psyche and the untimely return of its denial vis-à-vis other components whose promiximity it has to tolerate. The various ways in which the work of the negative finds expression invite us to distinguish the configurations in which the functions relating to the psyche's dynamism, its topography, its modes of representation, play their part within the systems communicating to a greater or lesser extent between themselves.

In spite of the theoretical renewal which has resulted from it, it may still be difficult for us to grasp what gives this perspective its unity. This would be to turn up one's nose at what might be called the most essential property of the category of the negative, which is to contest the very idea of unity, for which conflict, division, fusion and defusion, etc., would be substituted.

It is in fact because this conception – linking up with an old philosophical tradition which, however, lacked a corpus going further than merely the process of self-questioning – is also based on a mistrust of appearance, the manifest, consciousness, etc. The attitude we are advocating here is not simply setting ourselves the aim of deepening our knowledge of the nature of what these reveal, but rather leads us to discover an alterity which not only serves as a mirror for them but is also obstinately resistant to attempts to explore it openly. A decisive turning was taken in what one might call the practice of thinking, which required henceforth that the other person be taken into account, which is the basis of the originality of the psychoanalytic position as specified by transference. Today, I think it is clear that agreeing to such an abandonment of sovereignty, without the compensation of any transcendental benefit, was only possible in a situation in which the subject already felt deprived of this sovereignty, but retained sufficient capacities to have the hope of rediscovering something of it. He would be vaguely aware that there was no guarantee of this recuperation coming from 'outside', from what either medicine or religion had to offer him, at a time when authority was already regarded with such suspicion that it was unable to dismantle the secret machine of war represented by psychical suffering.

The consequences of this were numerous and staggered. In turn came the discovery of the unconscious and the observation that the patient resisted knowledge of it, echoing the defences which were partly responsible for his condition and the formation of his symptoms. It was then observed that there could be an absence of symptoms, even though the designation of the foresaid suffering (inhibition, pathological character organisation, anxiety, low spirits, etc.), existed. With a need to find support in propositions of a more general nature we were then led back to transference, i.e., to the surprising discovery of the symmetrical existence of defences and resistances in the analyst who nonetheless adhered consciously and intellectually to the conceptions of psychoanalysis, and finally to the progressive accumulation of cases responding only partially to 'psychoanalytic treatment' which, in certain cases, even reduce the analyst to a state of impotence. His endeavours are destined to failure yet the analysand goes on seeing him although there is no end in sight.

At the same time, the speculative tendency in Freud's thought continually enlarged the range of application of psychoanalysis, as if the double spur of the limited success of treatment and the growing awareness of just how much remained unknown, left this possibility open while waiting for progress in the form of more precise knowledge which would be simpler and less obliged to jump over the shadow of theory. Aided by Freud's personal attributes and his original training, the hypotheses concerning the psyche's foundations presented, when one thinks about it, the paradoxical situation of assuming the existence of a 'biological rock' and of endowing this natural source with speculations smacking of philosophy which Freud however wished to keep at arm's length.

But the essential gain was that a theoretical body of thought was put together, elaborated around a select corpus capable of being examined beyond the limits of philosophical consciousness and subjectivity. Further, it was shown that thinking on the negative was first identified in a field grouping together certain specific aspects (the neuroses) of the human psyche, hitherto considered as aberrant, but which psychoanalytic practice had made it possible to bring back within the realms of common experience. From that point on, it became necessary to investigate further those forms which differ from the primitive core of the neuroses, in the hope that they might shed more light on the lower levels of psychical activity, but which above all had the merit of uncovering the meaning of a use of the negative which was different from what went before. Normality and neurosis not only demonstrate that the fundamental basis of all organisation in its activity of classification, selection and differentiation, rests on the controlled intervention of the negative but that there is always a danger of this relationship sliding towards exclusion and segregation. Once again we come across the normative role of repression and its vicissitudes which give rise to neurosis. But with the drift towards non-neurotic structures, we are faced with a much more enigmatic and disconcerting purpose of the negative. Here, the negative neither separates nor sorts in order to enable the psyche's potentialities to continue to develop, but uses its means to stifle any enrichment of the psyche's capacities as well as its possibilities for displacement. It takes the form of a refusal which is all the more pernicious in that it extends both in breadth and in depth, remaining constantly on guard against any change and is liable to be surprised by anything new. Everything seems to rest on the postulate that leaving the network of links which both protect and imprison it can only result in a violent or torpid, cataclysmic or consuming disintegration. So the results of the research were quite different from those expected. The psyche's foundations retained their mystery! On the other hand, the insurmountable wall which stood in the way of an understanding of the psychoses began to crumble. It was possible to shed light on their functioning once they had developed; however, how they related to normality remained completely opaque. The removal of this obstacle made it possible for the first time to recognise at the core of this behaviour – which from an external point of view was, generally speaking, scarcely more disturbed than that found in neuroses – one of the most remarkable psychical organisations, throwing light on the destructuring experiences of psychosis from which it remained clearly distinct, and without their even being any natural tendency in their direction. We were then able to understand what the 'negativism' which Freud alluded to in the expression 'repression of reality' might mean.

These advances undoubtedly bore fruitful consequences in that they had an influence on the general theory of the normal and pathological psyche. It was necessary to reformulate this with a new emphasis on negativity which offered a better understanding of it, just as the different paths on which it was engaged were elucidated more clearly. When it was put to the use which psychoanalytic experience had for it, negativity soon showed itself to be quite different from the one we were familiar with from the history of philosophy. Nonetheless, even if the new field in which it was being examined had broken all ties with philosophy, it was far from certain that the latter would survive the encounter with it intact, even though it had only been local and transitory.

During the evolution of psychoanalytic concepts and their ambiguous relation to philosophy (in France and in England at any rate) a new formula appeared, owing to Lacan, called 'the subversion of the subject'. It is a very appropriate one. But it makes an inseparable pair with its complement 'and the dialectic of desire' forming the title of one of his articles. Now a question arose concerning the justification for the use of the term 'desire' to qualify what emerged in the analysis of certain patients whose suitability for being analysed was a matter of controversy. This, however, was outweighed by the experience gained from these analyses which acted as a spur to reconsider the postulates and concepts presumed to govern analytic activity. Even by crediting desire with a generic importance, this description seemed inadequate in that it was so poorly adapted to the issue in question, i.e., the way in which these new analysands deployed the chaotic manifestations of their transference.

On the other hand, for some at least, the reference to the negative never ceases to be applicable, and not only for reasons of expedience, for the same term serves to denote an unfortunate vicissitude of the psychoanalytic process. In elaborating the theoretical characteristics of the negative, we have observed that they enable us both to gain a precise idea of how they differ from the neuroses of classical analysis, and to preserve the conceptual coherence of these unusual modes of organisation which deserve to be considered separately. The work is certainly not the same but the reference to the negative is still valid, even if it means that those who feel it is useful to refer to it have to adopt points of view which are sometimes contradictory. At the same time, we may also wonder if the term 'subversion' of the subject is strong enough to express the particular features of these clinical configurations. For while subversion means overthrowing the established order, which is undoubtedly true of the psychoanalytic revolution, the destructive connotation which the word has here is more in the order of a threat than in the realisation of this purpose. It is no longer simply the subject who is subverted by these new forms which have appeared in the analytic field; it is the very nature of subversion which seems to find it difficult to adapt to the order which the unconscious is supposed to want to establish in place of that which bars it from and keeps it out of consciousness.

Freud had sensed that the future of psychoanalysis would eventually oblige it to take into account modes of psychical functioning which were far more remote from usual modes of thought than one suspected.[2] But what is it that we are dealing with, then, if the term 'subversion of the subject' does not give an adequate idea of what these forms of psychical functioning indicate, which are only designated by the term negative therapeutic reaction for lack of something better? It occurs to us in fact that we are dealing with what Nietzsche called, and fervently desired, 'the transvaluation of all values'. And it is indeed our impression that here we are in the presence not only of an upheaval of the principles on which the psyche is grounded, but also of an invalidation which is much more radical than the most nihilistic proclamations, because they take effect in the secrecy of an inviolable intimacy, while appearing to be part of the ordinary play of intersubjectivity. What differentiates them from philosophical nihilism is both the sense that it is useless to seek a rational basis for this mode of experience, and the fact that the subject himself is unaware of the reasons for this axiomatic inversion. In short, whereas subversion can be identified as such because it can only threaten what it recognises, here the trans-valuation leaves no trace of what is to be overthrown because this original layer only appears in a form in which the transformation makes it impossible to know what it may have been like before. In other words, the conflict can no longer be identified because it is hidden by another kind of struggle – explicit, patent and merciless – whose function is to make the initial situation which led to the transvaluation invisible. On the other hand, these modes of thought seem to be a response to a sort of 'intoxication', in the social sense of the word, of intrapsychic communication, precisely because the latter can no longer be inter-preted within a purely 'subjectal' dialectic. Or to be more exact, that subjectivity is no longer exercised in a way which involves the feeling of being colonised by the object who, in these contexts, is less identifiable as a partner in a rela-tionship than as an agent usurping and diverting his operations of thought. As a prior requirement, thought would have to struggle imperatively against the captivating, prying and shamelessly intrusive effect of an extraneous inten-tionality on which it depends through ties of attachment which are uncontrollable and inextricable even if nothing of the original love which created them is visible. Indeed, one cannot get away from the impression that the subject's captivity is the deeply disguised form of the object's capture, just as its alleged powerlessness, owing to the internal control which the object exercises, conceals, as it were, the shadow of the object's all-powerfulness, its 'all-prohibiting' power, reflected in the subject in the guise of 'rejecting everything' which derives its strength from the denigration of the prohibition by mimicking it. This situation is all the more dramatic in that the ego, thereby deprived of the criteria which would define its characteristics and which could assure it that it is in agreement with its own thought, is obliged to position itself, first and foremost, in relation to the object which alone has authority to give it an assignation, before being able to define its position towards its own deployment. The result of this situation is that the inextricable link with the analyst is based on a non-existent transference, since the subject's entire activity is mobilised against the object's enclave which secedes and has not been able to merge into the ego's texture. The said enclave uses subjective activity to maintain a state of belligerence with an object, which itself denies its own unconscious, and makes constant demands on the subject to come and take the place of this unconscious which is thought 'not to exist' in him either. The subject can never again subject himself to (sub-jectum) the deployment of his own subjective production, being obliged to respond to the seductive and persecutory appeals of the said secessionist object. The occasional words addressed to the analyst, when based on a request, are duplicated by an activity which is concerned less to repress than to erase everything which mobilised the psyche to be responsive to the libido. It is now that we witness the confusion between the object and the drive, in the movement which is opposed to any inscription liable to challenge a coded system of postulates which are supposed to ensure the victory of the desubjectivising object. In other words, the two forms of negativity – structuring or disorganising – could be defined respectively as being constitutive of subjectivity, or an expression of the transvaluation giving the right to speak to an object which diverts for its own benefit all the achievements of this subjectivity while leaving the latter with the illusion that it is thinking for itself. The unconscious has been erased, not only to make way for the object but to give a mandate to the negating accomplishments of the unconscious which are not allowed to inhabit it and are aimed at preventing its absolute authority over the subject from being challenged. The contrary would amount to a double murder of the other and of oneself. One might see in this the obscure intuition which led Freud to replace the unconscious with the id, the latter expression not only translating a strangeness more radical with respect to the ego than that denoted by the term unconscious, but carrying out perhaps the condensation, at the heart of this dimension 'outside the ego', of that which brings together what is furthest away from what the subject's consciousness can conceive of and, on the other hand, what relates to an exteriority which, in order to be mediatised by the ego, positions itself paradoxically outside the psychical apparatus (in the external world), colonising it, nonetheless. It can be seen here that we are moving away noticeably from the patients who made the discovery of psychoanalysis and the unconscious possible. And it becomes more understandable that Freud, at a certain point, had to agree to abandon the most novel aspects of his discovery, that is, the reference to the unconscious as a system. We know that many analysts did not accept this sacrifice which they considered to be almost suicidal. Worse still, it was hard to understand his stubborn insistence, come hell or high water, on preserving his 'mythology', i.e., the conviction that the territory of the psyche was to be found nowhere else but in the drives. And in order to save the respectability of psychoanalysis efforts were made to find other hypotheses which were more 'reasonable'.

Psychoanalytic epistemology still has a promising future. It is hoped that this book will have provided a little grist to its mill.

Once again, in order to grasp the immensity of what is involved we must turn to the intuition of the poets; reflection alone is unable to render its richness. For if the negative inhabits the subjective constitution, the avatars of (the) alienating transvaluation must also be considered in relation to other vicissitudes of the negative. This is true of sublimation. With it the dialectic of the drive is not content to withdraw from sexual aims; it feels the attraction, not of an object, but of another world which culture and tradition have succeeded in endowing with its own organisation which forms a bridge thanks to which the 'value' placed on social aims reflects the negativity echoed by primitive sexual aims. This is why, or perhaps it is because of what it has generously given us access to, nothing concerning it is definitively acquired, just as we are owed nothing either for the sacrifices we have made in its name. It may even be that we are still accountable for the pleasures we have drawn from it. What we have tasted, i.e., this new language it has taught us to speak, has become, in retrospect, almost transgressive. Is it not true that it has created in us a mixture of delight, the daughter of sensuality, and bedazzlement, arising from the revelation of what had hitherto remained esoteric but whose force unites us now, and, what's more, can increase as a result of being shared?

Let us appeal to one of the rare people who had the vision to embrace both sides of the path along which he was travelling, poised precariously between culture and the loss of reason. I am referring to Friederich Hölderlin, a friend of Hegel's and a real thinker. In a letter to his brother dated 4 June 1799, five years before he fell victim to the suffering which overwhelmed his mind, he wrote:

Both what is great and small as well as the best and the worst in man arises from one and the same source, and on the whole it is good. Each one accomplishes in his own way, more or less satisfactorily, his mission as a man; namely, to multiply the life of Nature, to accelerate it, to particularise it, to mix it, to separate it and to bind it. One is bound to say that this original instinct which leads us to idealise, accelerate, fashion, develop and perfect Nature scarcely motivates the works of men any longer; what they do, they do out of habit, out of imitation, out of obedience to tradition and as a result of needs created artificially by their ancestors. [...] You will notice, dear brother, that I have just set forth the paradox that the instinct which drives men towards the arts and sciences with all their transformations and varieties, is a genuine service which men render to nature. But we have long been aware that all the diverse currents of human activity flow into the ocean of Nature, just as they take their source in it. For the most part, men make their way blindly, grudgingly, and unwillingly, and show themselves to be ignoble. The role of philosophy, of fine arts and religion, which also originate in this instinct, is to guide them on their way, so that they follow it with their eyes open, with joy and dignity. [...]

Thus philosophy, the arts and religion, these priestesses of Nature, first work their effects on man and only exist for him, and only in as far as they endow man's activity, which has a direct effect on Nature, with nobility, vigour and joy do they in turn have a real and direct effect on Nature. All three of them, but particularly religion, have another effect which is to persuade man, to whom Nature lends itself as the object of his activity, and who is part, as a *powerful motor force,* of its infinite organisation, that he cannot consider himself its master and lord. However great his art and his activity may be, he must bow modestly and piously before this spirit of Nature which he carries within him, which he has about him and which gives him matter and strength. For, however much they have already produced and still can produce, art and the general activity of men can bring nothing living into existence, nor can they create by themselves the primary matter which they transform and fashion; they can develop creative power but the power itself is eternal and not the handiwork of men.[3]

Appendices

1. The Work of the Negative[1] (1986)

Several years ago I proposed to designate as 'the work of the negative' all the psychical operations of which repression is the prototype and which later gave rise to distinct variations such as negation, disavowal and foreclosure. This expression, borrowed from philosophy, no longer owes anything to its Hegelian origins. Moreover, it has been adopted by numerous analysts. Should the work of the negative be related to the ego alone and its mechanisms of defence? One might think so at a first approach. I would maintain on the contrary that the work of the negative extends to the agencies of the psychical apparatus as a whole. In other words, an analysis of it leads us to distinguish the no of the ego, the no of the super-ego and the no of the id. I shall also envisage the effects of the object's response on the constitution of yes–no relations. These problems are not purely theoretical since they raise technical questions about analysability.

In his article on 'Repression' of 1915, Freud, who envisaged two possible vicis-situdes of representation, its disappearance from consciousness when it was conscious or keeping it away from consciousness when it was on the point of becoming conscious, wrote: 'the difference is not important; it amounts to much the same thing as the difference between my ordering an undesirable guest out of my drawing-room (or out of my front hall), and my refusing, after recognising him, to let him cross my threshold at all'. He adds in a note: 'This simile, which is thus applicable to the process of repression, may also be extended to a characteristic of it which has been mentioned earlier: I have merely to add that I must set a permanent guard over the door which I have forbidden this guest to enter, since he would otherwise burst it open.'[2]

The comparison is revealing and comprises several registers. Alongside those aspects we are familiar with, that is, dynamic, topographical and economic (an allusion to the trauma of the door being burst open), its anthropological aspect is particularly striking. Representation is symbolised by the undesirable guest – and repression is a good illustration of the idea of the little man within man – who is subject to other divisions (master of the house and guard), endowed with a power of recognition based on labels (desirable–undesirable) which apply a yes and no logic to them depending on whether they accept or refuse, thus sorting, selecting, orienting like a real Maxwell demon governing particles.

Furthermore, the sorting, discrimination and distribution are unconscious. What determines the access of the unconscious into consciousness is itself unconscious. Does such anthropomorphism owe nothing to the model on which repression is built?

In treatment, what has operated as repression appears in the form of resistance. The fundamental rule of not filtering and of not selecting is transgressed consciously and unconsciously. It implies the lifting of moral and rational censure. Yet, contemporary analytic practice enables us to attribute different meanings to repression:

– Resistance may indicate a fear of being judged, condemned or punished. This can range from the threat of the loss of love to the anxiety of mutilation.

– Resistance opposes the danger of disorganisation through a loss of control of speech and through speech which gives rise to a fear of madness.

– Resistance suggests a fear of annihilation consecutive to an unbinding of predominantly destructive drives.

These three examples, among others, can all be interpreted as the expression of the ego's defensive activity. However, they can also be understood as the expression of a no originating from the super-ego, the ego, and even the id. This last point deserves discussion, the unbinding of the drives opposing the formulation of a desire towards an object which is reduced here to its most undifferentiated state.

Now, all of a sudden, the reasons for repression and resistance can be seen more clearly. They have three aims:

– To control the violence of the drives.

– To organise the ego by establishing links, which presupposes investments of a certain constancy, subject to minimal variations.

– To guarantee the object's love and, secondarily, that of the super-ego.

Repression is therefore inevitable, necessary and indispensable for the structuring of human desire. However, no criterion exists to determine precisely what must be repressed and what can be spared from repression. The result of this is that one always represses too much or too little, just as one resists too well or too badly. The obstacle of the resistances met with in treatment and the analyst's temptation to overcome them, albeit by their analysis, involved a danger of returning to hypnosis. To say to a patient, 'You are resisting!', even in the most subtle way, was not much different from the formula 'You are counter-suggesting' coming from the hypnotist's mouth. Similarly, there is perhaps nothing one can say to a patient presenting a negative therapeutic reaction more traumatising than 'You don't want to change!', whereas he himself has the feeling he cannot do otherwise. In order to avoid this kind of impasse, when Freud was faced with resistance he sometimes resorted to traps. Even if this practice is questionable, we can at least learn certain things from it. He discusses it in his article on 'Negation' (1925). '"What", we ask, "would you consider the most unlikely imaginable thing in that situation? What do you think was furthest from your mind at that time?" If the patient falls into the trap and says what he thinks is most incredible, he almost always makes the right admission.'[3]

In fact Freud is saying to his patient, 'Since your no is opposed to a near yes which you cannot admit consciously, tell me instead what the no is which is furthest from this near yes but inaccessible.' And he concludes by answering that this no which is the furthest away is the near yes which cannot be admitted.

This example brings into play categories of opposing pairs, some of which are explicit, imaginable–unimaginable, believable–unbelievable, near–far; and others implicit, agreeable (in the sense of what can be accepted)–disagreeable, present–past (to the extent that it is a question of obtaining a piece of repressed unconscious material) and no doubt too, good and evil (recognition can be barred by moral disapproval). Thus the opposition yes–no depends on a number of factors distributed throughout the entire psychical apparatus, from the surface to the depths as well as from the oldest to the most recent.

'A negative judgement is the intellectual substitute for repression', says Freud. This intellectual substitute which is linked to desire is the product of a symbolisation by means of language and an economy which saves energy. The no appears to be a label of repression. But before language and repression itself, 'expressed in the language of the oldest drive impulses' (oral), judgement consists in saying 'I would like to eat that' or 'I would like to spit it out.' Thus there is a translation of an ego language which speaks, into an id 'language' which swallows or spits. There is therefore a no of the id which is expressed through the drive motion. Repression is a psychological mechanism; Freud never fails to remind us of it, whereas what is described on the level of the drives of the id is not, at least to his mind. The question which then arises concerns the relation between the psychological mechanism which is connected with speech and the one which is related to another use of the mouth through oral impulses. In other words, do the statements: 'I would like to eat or I would like to spit out' originate from the id or from an archaic primitive ego? If we follow Freud, since the ego differentiates itself from the id, the archaic primitive ego and the id are scarcely discernible.

I would like to dwell a moment on the destiny of these oral impulses. Eating and spitting out involve on the one hand incorporation (of the object) and, on the other, what I have called excorporation, a mechanism which is prior to projective identification, in my view. I spit out or I vomit. Freud uses a verb which is translated by eject. It is generally understood as an action which puts what is inside outside, bringing us back to the boundary between inside–outside. The postulate of this original boundary is based on the existence of an ego reality at the start which is in a position to detect the internal or external origin of excitations. This hypothesis seems to me to be too costly.

The excorporation in which I see the prototype of a no of the id in the forms of 'I am spitting out' or 'I am vomiting', does not imply the existence of an object in the space which receives what is expelled. We may even wonder if the expelled products do not disappear in the process. In any case, the identification of the space seems to me to be prior to that of the objects it might contain. (I am thinking of the noticeably hostile atmosphere in certain delusions before the persecutor is designated). Furthermore, I do not think that we can infer that there is a boundary between inside and outside. All that exists is the idea – if one can put it this way – of expelling as far away as possible. There is no justification for speaking of a 'not ego' at this stage because the ego–not-ego boundary has not been established. It is the consequences of the expulsion which allow it to be established. Expelling what is bad allows for the creation of an internal space in which the ego as an organisation can come into being, setting up an order founded on the formation of links related to experiences of satisfaction. This organisation facilitates recognition of the object as separate in the space of the not-ego as well as the reunion with it.

But even when this recognition and separation have been achieved, the ego itself is obliged periodically to take over from the work of the negative which formerly only concerned the drives. In order to be able to say yes to oneself, one must be able to say no to the object. This work can only be carried out on two conditions, at least:

– that the object continues to take care of the infant's ego by sparing it what is excessively unpleasant;

– that the object takes the place of the undifferentiated space in order to take in what we designated earlier as excorporation and which now deserves to be called projection, by consenting to be experienced as bad while seeking to transform these projections and return them to the infant. (The mother does not have more belief in the baby's badness than in her own.)

In order for the formation of baby's ego to occur, allowing him to say yes to himself, the mother must accept that he can say no to her. And not only in the form of 'you are bad', but also occasionally 'you don't exist'.

This is manifested in analysis not only by hostile projections onto the analyst but also, of course, onto the mother, at a distance – far off – and ultimately by the exclusion of transference.

Excorporation is an illusion, for how can the psyche get rid of what encumbers it? The object's assistance is needed if it is to be possible. Hitherto, we have only taken into account spatial considerations. But temporal considerations play an equally important role, as Winnicott has shown. If the response is immediate, without delay, symbiotic omnipotence sets in, depriving the infant's ego of the possibility to say no to the object and therefore yes to itself.

The idealisation of the maternal object goes hand in hand with the suppression of the subject's own desire. On the other hand, when the delay is too great, it is despair, stamped by the experience of pain, which makes one say no to everything (including oneself). Linking is destroyed, intolerance of frustration is increased and excessive projective identification occurs. The work of the negative takes on the form of a radical exclusion and the negative aspect of relationships (Winnicott) gains the upper hand. This exclusion probably affects even the drive, before there is any question of Freudian *Verwerfung* or Lacanian foreclosure.

It is only when the object's response comes with a sufficient and tolerable delay and in a form which can be assimilated (the mother's capacity for reverie, Bion), that the infant's ego can say to itself 'it's not wonderful, but it's all right'. And it is from this point on that repression can come into effect. Repression is thus carried out on the model of the object's acceptances and refusals. Freud's anthropomorphic comparison cited at the beginning of these reflections is now more understandable. The little man within man is in fact a little mother. What is pleasant or unpleasant for the ego is based on what is accepted or not accepted by the object. The relation to the object has been internalised, the yes and the no have been introjected. Primal repression establishes the boundary between the *Cs.–Pcs.* on the one hand and the *Ucs.* on the other.

These theoretical remarks arise from clinical experience and analytic technique. For it is by means of the latter that the analyst learns to modulate the timing of his interventions and to offer these in a form which is acceptable to the patient. Maintaining distance from the object and evaluating the period of delay which is tolerable go hand in hand. Between the two extremes of successful repression and rejection (foreclosure or *Verwerfung*), the work of the negative can take intermediate paths such as splitting or disavowal in which recognition and denial, yes and no co-exist.

The work of the negative in disavowal cannot simply be characterised by the co-existence of yes and no. For such a co-existence can be conjunctive or disjunctive. When conjunctive, it occurs under the primacy of Eros. The same is true of the transitional object which is and is not the breast or the mother; judgement of existence does not apply to it, any more than it has to be decided if it was created as a subjective object, or found, as an object which is objectively perceived. Regarding spatiality, let us note that it is situated at the intersection of the internal space and the external space in the intermediate area. The intense investment it receives shows that this co-existence is thoroughly positive. When the co-existence is disjunctive, the work of the negative is carried out under the auspices of the destructive drives. This is the case of splitting and disavowal, concerning which, some have claimed that it is difficult to distinguish it from foreclosure. The difference from the earlier case is that instead of bringing about a union, the work of the negative separates and obstructs all choice and positive investment. In this case, it is not yes *and* no, but *neither* yes *nor* no. A well-known example of this is the case of the 'Wolf Man' (who 'won't have it'– that is, castration – which, in spite of his sexual performances, is demonstrated in the analyses that came after those he did with Freud), and his tortuous thought processes, 'He always had at least two opinions on the same subject', said one of his therapists. There is nothing in this case which can be linked with obsessional doubt, but rather to an incapacity to decide if a thing is good or bad (analysis for example) or again, in his choices of identification and his symptoms, whether he is a man or a woman. But in this case the ego, paralysed by ambivalence in its relation to psychical reality as well as material reality, can only accept the co-existence if it can respond with neither a yes nor a no. This response takes its roots in drive life. What is expressed at the level of the ego is simply a reflection of this (what I have called bi-logic). The responses of its objects have doubtless only aggravated the situation. They have been marked neither by a capacity to receive its destructive projections by returning them in an acceptable form nor by the decision to confront it, on another level, with a structuring 'no'. They have preferred to play the role of a prosthesis upholding the disavowal of castration, right to the end. As far as we know at least. Yet the example of the 'Wolf Man' is not unique. Many analysands presenting a negative therapeutic reaction reveal in the transference that the agonising struggle between yes and no is a vitiation of the work of the negative. What they show us in fact is that the refusal to choose, the refusal to believe, the refusal to invest is nothing other than the refusal to live.

2. Negative Hallucination (1977)

Let us consider two examples taken from Freud. They concern a psychotic structure without hallucinatory clinical phenomena, but have the advantage of allowing us to compare an isolated hallucination and a central dream in the same subject. You will have guessed that I am alluding to the 'Wolf Man', to his hallucination of the severed finger and to his wolf dream. Concerning the hallucination of the severed finger, the 'Wolf Man' recounts: 'I was playing in the garden near my nurse, and was carving with my pocket-knife in the bark of one of the walnut trees that come into my dream as well.[4] Suddenly, *to my unspeakable horror*, I noticed that I had cut through the little finger of my (right or left?) hand, so that it was only hanging on by its skin. I felt no pain, but great fear. I did not venture to say anything to my nurse, who was only a few paces distant, but I sank down on the nearest seat and sat there *incapable of casting another glance at my finger*. At last I calmed down, took a look at the finger, and saw that it was entirely uninjured.' Freud interprets this event by comparing it with the experience of Tancred as told by Tasso, and relates the hallucinatory wound to the mother's haemorrhages which are evocative of castration.

But immediately afterwards, he links the origin of the hallucination to a story that a female relation of his had been born with six toes and that the extra one had immediately been chopped off with an axe.

If we analyse this fragment, many associations will come to mind. First, the interpolation of a false recollection, the cutting of the tree, which belongs to another context 'hallucinatorily falsified'. This false recollection fills a void. For what the young child was doing and thinking at that moment, we cannot know and so this is the first blank. Be that as it may, this false recollection forms a bridge between the memory of the hallucination of the severed finger and the walnut trees in the wolf dream. Then, in a state of inexpressible terror, comes the hallucination of the severed finger. Now what is remarkable in this hallucination *is not the sight of blood – there is no question of that – but the void which separates the finger from the hand so that it was only attached by a fragment.* No pain, but fear: the feeling of pain is replaced by that of fear. A moment of silence follows, then a collapse, and an incapacity to cast the slightest glance at the finger ... Finally, there is a return of normal perception and feeling, along with a state of calm. The origin of the event shows us that the *one too few* which threatens the hand finds its source in the *one extra*, the relation's sixth toe which was chopped off with an axe, an instrument used for felling trees. Here we come across an enigma relating to the drawing of the dream in which five wolves are represented, whereas the account of the dream mentions six or seven (six or seven: one extra, in fact two in relation to the drawing, whereas compared with the dream the drawing represents one too few, at least). *The hallucination of the severed finger is preceded by the negative hallucination of the extra finger hidden in the hallucinatory content, the latter simply positivises, on the basis of this negative hallucination, an amputation which has already been carried out in on the level of thought.* The traces of it are: the void which separates the finger from the hand, the absence of pain, the silence, the state of collapse and above all the inability to look.[5]

Now let us turn to the dream. The fairy tale forms a bridge between them. I shall not expand further on this dream which has already been analysed at length by generations of psychoanalysts following Freud. I shall simply cite the opening sentence: 'I dreamt that it was night and that I was lying in my bed.' This is a strange thing: the wolf man dreams that it is night, that is to say that he is dreaming; in his dream he sees the dark night: the invisible. And Freud interprets, not without reason, 'it was night' as a deformation of 'I had been asleep.' This means the dream, obeying the conditions of representability, *imagines* – in the strict sense of the word – the unimaginable, *the non-imaginable in sleep.* The imaginary world of dream imagines the image of blackness where there is an absence of any image. Hence the interpretation of the opening of the window as representing the sleeper waking up: 'Suddenly I woke up *of my own accord*' (my italics). The wolf dream is therefore a dream within the dream, an imaginary dream within the dream of the unimaginable. Then the walnut tree appears with its seven white wolves. For Freud the colour white alludes to the whiteness of the seven goats in the fairy tale which is echoed by the white of his parents' bedclothes and underclothes. This interpretation is undoubtedly right but it calls for a theoretical commentary.

Bertram Lewin has made us aware of the existence of the dream screen and blank dreams. In his opinion, the dream screen is a visual representation of the sleeper's wish to sleep which is empty, blank, without stimulation. He interprets these blank dreams as a repetition of the fulfilment of the wish to sleep – let us bear in mind that this is the dreamer's ultimate desire according to Freud – in its full form, to fall into a deep sleep after being fed. He believes that we are dealing with a relatively uniform experience, with a physiological basis comparable to a reflex, which is completely independent of the structure of the ego; consequently, any idea which suggests that the baby is defending itself against something is out of place. We might wish to discuss with B. Lewin whether the representation of the blank is necessarily related to the after-image of the breast; in any case, what is fundamental is the representation of the absence of representation which deep sleep implies.

These remarks thus lead me to insist on the *constituting structure of negative hallucination*, or to be more exact, *on its containing function of representation*. Negative hallucination is not a pathological phenomenon. It is not the absence of representation as is suggested by the absence of the image in the mirror, but the *representation of the absence of representation*. Negative hallucination is the theoretical concept which is the precondition for any theory of representation, whether it is dreams or hallucination which is concerned. Undoubtedly dreams and hallucination cannot be superimposed. Negative hallucination is their common matrix. In psychosis, hallucination has to be related not only to wish-fulfilment but to *wishful thoughts*, as I argued with J.L. Donnet in *L'enfant de ça* where we described *blank psychosis* as a fundamental[6] psychotic kernel. I can only refer readers to it. I would simply point out that structured thought is only established in discontinuity and this structuring discontinuity involves, in the spaces, the blank which constitutes any chain of thought. In psychosis, this blank is materialised by the *blank thought* whose empty space is urgently filled by hallucination, occupying the space with drive offshoots.

Let us take another well-known example: President Schreber. Fortunately, we have access both to Freud's work and its unabridged source, The President's *Memoirs*. Freud rightly notes the often repeated observation, one should say the leitmotif, of the *Memoirs* which is the withdrawal of divine rays which Schreber attracts in an almost magnetic way by his supernatural powers of attraction. But what he then describes in great despair is the emptiness which he feels. 'Every time that my intellectual activities ceased, God jumped to the conclusion that my mental faculties were extinct and that the destruction of my understanding (the idiocy), for which He was hoping, had actually set in, and that a withdrawal had now become possible.'[7] It is necessary to follow Schreber's developments in order to see how in fact he carries out an inversion of psychical events: the withdrawal of the divine rays is the repetition of the emptiness which precedes the hallucinatory phenomenon, an emptiness which is replaced by a supernatural erotic power. This calls for a detailed analysis which I will undertake on another occasion. But reading the *Memoirs* has other surprises in store for us. There has been a constant tendency to confuse – and this continues to be the case – two kinds of data: the first relate to *chaos* to which Schreber's delusion attempts to restore the Order of Things through healing; the second concern the nothingness of which chaos is never more than *the least imaginable evil*, albeit at the sacrifice of thought. *It is of this nothingness that negative hallucination is the sign and positive hallucination the symptom. The voluptuousness of the soul is nothing other than the ghost of the soul-murder condemning it to narcissism by pushing it to homosexuality, as a temptation to meet up again with the same, who is lost.* With regard to paranoid psychoses Freud says, 'Paranoia decomposes just as hysteria condenses.'[8] One might add: hallucination decomposes whereas dreams condense. What this division of hallucination amounts to is the positivising of negative hallucination which transforms the zero into two, short-circuiting the subject's unity, albeit illusory. Nothing, not even God, who is responsible for the world's unity, can escape division into two according to Schreber. And when at the end of the *Memoirs* he seems only to be one, it is so that Schreber can affirm that henceforth God, the saviour, cannot do without him. The hallucinations are the creations – in the strict sense of the word – the children of Schreber's mind. Generation is found both in Schreber's semantics as well as in his syntax. Negative hallucination is its precondition.

Freud understands this well and writes:

> The distinctive character of paranoia (or of dementia paranoides) must be sought for elsewhere [than in the paternal complex] – namely, in the particular form assumed by the symptoms; and we shall expect to find that this is determined, not by the nature of the complexes themselves, but by the mechanism by which the symptoms are formed or by which repression is brought about.[9]

In the end, his analysis leads him to posit an ultimate stage in the various propositions relating to delusion – concerning which linguistic conclusions have been drawn which go beyond the bounds of our subject here) – 'I do not love at all – I do not love anyone' for which Freud substitutes 'I love only myself.' But this last statement is only a minimal step back from the earlier one, which is the basis of negative hallucination. Thus projection is simply the reaction against chaos to which the threat of nothingness is subordinated. That is, the abolition of the inside makes room for the return of what is outside.

Yet we would scarcely be justified in allotting negative hallucination with the essential function we have attributed to it without evidence to substantiate it. This proof is difficult to provide since the psychical phenomenon we are talking about originates in what is negativised and therefore not easily accessible to examination. Nonetheless, the strangest aspect of these negativising phenomena is that they generally manage to represent themselves in the form of discreet signs. The rays are obliged to go to Schreber because their 'thoughts are lacking'.[10] It is indeed this projection of emptiness requiring to be filled which underlies the state of bliss. But we have to consider the representation even of this constitutive blank which materialises against the background on which all figures appear. So, when Schreber finds himself prey to the 'frightening miracles' by which he is persecuted, he counter-attacks by becoming in turn the agent of similar miracles: 'I can even provoke the frightening miracles or something very like it: if I put my hand in front of a white surface, perhaps the white-painted door of my room or the white glazing of the stove, I can see very peculiar distortions of shadows obviously caused by certain changes in the light rays of the sun.' And he adds, protesting, not without reason, 'I am quite certain that these phenomena are not only my subjective sensations ("hallucinations" in the sense of Kraepelin's psychiatry), as with every frightening miracle my attention is particularly drawn to it by directing my gaze (turning my eyes).'[11]

Thus Schreber sees himself in turn as a psychiatrist, correcting Kraepelin. We could almost be taken in if we were not careful. For although he is quite right to distinguish the production of his frightening miracles from 'visual hallucinations', since he recognises himself to be the agent of this visual production and not subjected to its effects, he risks leading us astray by directing our attention, just as he directs his gaze, to the positivity of the phenomenon, to the form rather than its background. For it is thanks to this 'white surface' that the phenomenon can occur, this screen whose existence we are unaware of. At the cinema, the film makes us forget that without it there would be nothing for us to see. What is projected, then, is not the figures of the imaginary world as psychoanalysis has long believed, i.e., fantasies, but *processes*. To be more exact, these imaginary figures are mimes and figures of thought. Freud had caught a glimpse of this, but only a glimpse, when he wrote at the end of his study, 'Since I neither fear the criticism of others nor shrink from criticising myself, I have no motive for avoiding the mention of a similarity which may possibly damage our libido theory in the estimation of many of my readers. Schreber's "rays of God", which are made up of a condensation of the sun's rays, of nerve-fibres, and of spermatozoa, *are in reality nothing else than a concrete representation and projection outwards of libidinal investments; and they thus lend his delusions a striking conformity with our theory.'*[12]

Thus the function of hallucination which divides the mind is to condense external perceptions (sun rays), bodily representations (nerve-fibres) and sexual productions (spermatozoa), that is to say, to give a hallucinated representation in the positive form of the negative hallucination of thought. This being so, the delirious patient and the analyst cease to be radically different from each other; the first represents what the other has to content himself with thinking abstractly. Each of them makes use of the negative in his own way; the delirious patient positivises it, the analyst negativises it a second time in order to represent not thought, but meaning. A bridge thrown between the two allows them to meet mid-way, i.e., the dream which is projected onto the blank screen of sleep.

3. Seminar on the Work of the Negative (1988)

Compared with Freud's work, the great innovation in modern psychoanalysis is undeniably the role of the object and the ideas which have been elaborated in connection with it. Although Freud did indeed think that there was a problem involving the object and negativity, in mourning, for example, he did not go much further than that. What I mean is, with many patients we have the feeling that not all the psychical activity elaborated in them, whether normal or pathological, can be considered as being determined by the interplay of the drives alone, and that in this work of elaboration the object is a factor of interference which plays a part in the constitution of subjectivity through its unusual effects. Let me explain myself. Just as an analytic setting which fulfils its function should not draw attention to itself, which Donnet has called burying the setting, I would say, in the same way, that the object, which is absolutely necessary for the elaboration of psychical structure, should remain very much in the background. Its role as a constituent of psychical structure should be forgotten about; it exists in the shape of illusion which is not con-stitutive of psychical structure but presents itself as being different from it, as an object of attraction or repulsion. But when the object cannot be forgotten, there is a sort of 'perversion' of this function of the object; not perversion in the sense of a perversion of the drives, but perversion in the sense of *something which deviates, which goes wrong in its function as object, which in any case involves being fallible.* This is where the subversion of the subject – Lacan's formula – is a response to the object. That is why Winnicott speaks of the good enough mother, necessarily fallible, necessarily making mistakes, necessarily failing to adapt or to be adequate. *The intrinsic factor of the object is paradoxical: the object is there to stimulate, to awaken the drive and at the same time to contain it.* And it is equally there to give the individual the essential and important notion that it is necessary to accept the idea that *there is more than one object.* The rest is self-evident. Because if there is more than one object, uniting two objects on the principle of their mutual attraction becomes a vain goal when it is pursued for its own sake. I think I understand what is known as separation anxiety: it is the result of what has actually occurred within the subject, i.e., an intolerable intrusion. This is when the object is excessively present owing to the very fact of its lack. We then meet with a sort of coalescence between the object and the drive and instead of making the drive more tolerable, on the contrary, the object makes it even more intolerable. Without any solution, with no compromise. It would be abusive to speak here of desire, or even of nostalgia. Paradoxically, the object's excessive presence does not give rise to representation but to all kinds of extra-representative effects, e.g., acting out, perverse behaviour, toxicomania, sudden onsets of depression, moments of delirium, psychosomatic crises, etc. It is quite obvious that under these conditions transference is very disturbed. These problems were first discussed around 1920 by Rank and Ferenczi on the development of psychoanalysis. The question then arose of the choice between different theories in psychoanalytic technique. Put somewhat simplistically, the theory of object relations, implicit since Abraham, actualised by Ferenczi, and finally made explicit by M. Klein, following Fairbairn, became a sort of alternative, supposedly more appropriate than the old Freudian theory of representations and affects. It was a mistake which in my opinion was soon bound to provoke reactions and it is not simply a coincidence if Marty, who was very close to Bouvet who tried to promote a personal view of object relations, later developed a different point of view, and even, to some extent, an opposing one, by insisting on *mental functioning*. If you do not differentiate this object relationship, if you do not filter it, if you do not decant it, if you do not analyse it in terms of psychical functioning, you have gained nothing from the exchange. Object relations theory was founded on an empiricism arising from the questionable notion that this theory was not the result of speculation but was based on transference experience. *Object relation means the relationship to the analyst as an object of transference; the supposition being that this object relationship is paradigmatic of childhood object relations.* Now Freud's article, 'Remembering, Repeating and Working-Through' (1914) seems to me to argue against a naively positive notion of transference and to call for a consideration of the negative and its work.

Negation is the conception of the symbol. What do I mean by that? *I mean that the whole work of analysis consists in leading the subject to recognise himself as a result of being recognised by you.* What is this, other than a reversal of negativity? What is desire? What is this crucial first experience of Freud which is called *hallucinatory wish-fulfilment? It is the movement which consists in going back over the traces of earlier experience, when the object is not there, in order to repeat it.* Melanie Klein does away with hallucinatory wish-fulfilment putting in its place either an idealisation of the good object or anxieties of annihilation, persecutory anxieties accompanied by an experience of annihilation attributed, through projection, to the bad object. As soon as one accepts the dichotomy between good and bad, the question of negation arises. Two parameters are involved: the parameter of good or bad, judgement of attribution, and the parameter of real or imaginary, judgement of existence. You have before your eyes two forms of the negative: that which is bad and that which does not exist. What is bad is what must be spat out. It can come either from the ego, from my prohibited drives, sexual or aggressive, or from the object, that is to say, from that which works towards or against the aim of my drives, my prohibitions, which depend on the object's drive towards me. We can understand the interest of the model of the double limit.[13] Apart from the mechanisms described by Freud in 'Negation', there are others which need to be considered: I can either aggress the object or deny its existence. Either I deny the object's existence or, in certain cases, I consider that it is the effect of its own hostile drives towards me which provokes my reaction. Let me remind you of what Freud says in 'Negation': 'thinking possesses the capacity to bring before the mind once more something that has once been perceived, by reproducing it as a presentation without the external object having still to be there'.[14] 'Without the external object having still to be there.' The theory of representation may relate to what exists but is not there, or to what does not exist but which I have created. As far as the representation of objects in reality is concerned, Freud says it is not a question of *finding* an object but of *refinding* an object. When we refer to what does not exist we are speaking of the presentation concerning the fantasy object, that is, an object I have invented. However, on the basis of this two-fold reference to what is bad and to what does not exist, we can see the necessity for symbolisation, which was understood very differently by Lacan and Winnicott respectively.

The work of the negative in its destructive form in analysis is met with in everything which we call, without always knowing what we are talking about, attacks on the setting. I say, 'without knowing what we are talking about', because what we call attacks on the setting are exemplified by the situation in which the patient says to you, 'I cannot talk.' Whether he says it or not, that is what it means. 'You see, I cannot talk and you, you can't force me to talk', a female patient said to me. Since it was like that, I said to myself, 'she cannot talk, so I don't see where we are going', and then she added: 'You see, you want to force me to choose between being and not being, desiring and not desiring, but me, I want both, I want both one and the other, and when I have one and I have recovered the other, that is still not enough because I am afraid I've lost the first.' It is here that we see what the work of the negative is in its structural form; it is in talking, in the activity of speaking, obviously not in the sense of Lacan's conception of speech, but of speech as *negativity in relation to the drive.* I am quoting here from memory: '*You would like me to choose between life, that is, between life and death, and nothing; and me, I want both, I mean nothing and the rest. You would like me to choose between being there and not being there, and me, I want both at the same time, not to be there when I am there and to be there nonetheless; I don't want contradiction, I want neither one thing nor the other and sometimes, that is not enough, so I want one thing and the other. Choosing always means losing.'* It is not a coincidence if you have also asked me to speak about primary anality.[15] Of course, here we are dealing with the dialectics of expulsion. Another patient said to me: 'I cannot say where I am, I can only say where I am not, but I cannot say that I had thought of that much; speaking is dropping poisoned bombs.' All this leads me from a clinical point of view to the experience of emptiness, to the neuroses of emptiness, in which one encounters a kind of mixture of disinvestment, of unacceptable destructivity, of fusion with the object, and of identification with an object destroyed by separation. Confusion between the desire imposed by the other and the refusal which one is obliged, which one feels obliged, to enact. Because the provocation of this desire by the other comes from the field vacated by the subject's desire. The subject can only bring such a desire into play in the form of negating the object, or by reducing the other to serving as an object of projection, for the expulsion of the unacceptable part of oneself, reduced to emptiness by the control exercised over the object.

All this can quite easily happen, occasionally, without the object and become the theatre of a drama in which the subject alone incarnates the different characters, without there being any scenario to reveal the content of these events. A female patient takes an hour, after a long period of work, to decide to go and see an exhibition. She hesitates for a long while, and then finally decides; she chooses her exhibition, goes out through the door and then cannot take a step further. She goes back into her apartment and cries all afternoon.

All this calls for a new discussion on the end of the article on 'Negation' when Freud explains the meaning of the words of a patient who says 'I didn't think that.' It is the mark, the undeniable proof that your interpretation was exactly right and is still true today. If we take this line of thinking a bit further and apply it to the stereotyped phrases of patients which look like phrases that everyone uses, such as: 'I don't know, I don't understand, I've forgotten ...', we must put them back into their context and see what function they have in relation to the material at the very moment when it was said. *Unconsciousness does not do away with psychical work.* Patients think that in saying, 'I've forgotten', 'I don't know', 'I don't understand', they have managed to evacuate the psychical work. This is how this kind of negativity is very different from 'I didn't think that'.

The conjunction of the two aspects of the negative is on the one hand what limits the possible and on the other hand what destroys it. What limits the possible can be conceived of in relation to the idea of the impossible, prohibited as impossible. In this impossibility, the rebellion of the mind extends infinitely the domain of the possible in order to suppress the notion, the very meaning of what is prohibited. The negative in the sense of limiting the possible makes the impossible exist in a different way. It is important that it does not restrict itself to realising it differently; the impossible is represented in transgression. Whereas, in the other sense, what destroys the possible is the structure which considers the possibility of the possible which is accomplished. It may be said that all psychical functioning develops two kinds of data: one related to the relationship which the subject maintains with the world outside him; the other related to himself. He himself is not a mere reduplication, but he is liable to reveal another external world within him which is similar and different from the first. It is this 'self' which is the major unknown entity. Psychoanalysis finds the negative at the very roots of his existence because its theory rests on an excess of positivity. This is due to drive functioning which the subject can only come to terms with by nega- tivising it or through the activity of defence mechanisms by making drive activity compatible with the demands of cultural life, itself the result of a negation of natural life.

It is indeed the binary structure which governs relations, for it offers the pos- sibility of complementarity and precludes the self-sufficiency of one term from providing a solution. Everything resides therefore in the structuring or destruc- turing value of the lack which puts in question the capacity which is correlative to it and transforms the relation fullness–lack into one of centring–decenter- ing. The axial components of this binarity comprise masculine–feminine bisexuality and the drive dualism of love–hate. This double binarity is contained by the fundamental relationship ego–other; no ego is self-sufficient and no ego can completely satisfy the other, no other can be a substitute for the ego, and no other can completely satisfy the ego. The problem of the ego concerns the constitution of a centre as a basic nucleus investing the other without however withdrawing investment from itself and without coinciding with this centre. As for the other, he will always remain other, that is, different in his essence, having his own centre which can be invested as such by his own ego. However, there is neither a possibility of lasting fusion between the two centres, nor of separation which would give each one its liberty. Only the centres remain separated, but this does not however prevent there being alternating movements of reunion, more or less fusional, and of separation, more or less incomplete. Such oscillations allow for the function of lack, the condition of progressive movement and of the decentralising use of metaphor. But nothing comes of these alternations. That is to say that the opposing movements which inform them do not lead to any binding. Nothing is generated, as if, para- doxically, each moment was sufficient unto itself. The notion of centre is correlative to that of limit: there can be no nucleus without an ego, but no ego without a centre. No centre without decentring. Language is a complete system lacking nothing.

4. Primary Anality (1993)

It is difficult to bring together into a coherent whole the distinctive features of primary anality. This description is based on observations drawn from an insufficient number of cases and, as such, runs the risk of mixing general and significant features with singular characteristics which are more or less idiosyncratic. Without launching into theory prematurely, let me say, nonetheless, that the following outline deserves the denomination *primary* anality because the aspects which I shall be singling out have scarcely any resemblance with those we usually come across in studies devoted to anality. These usually deal with its secondary, later forms. In the description which follows, the anal tonality differs from classical anality in the fact that the fixation appears to be marked by narcissism in a prevalent manner. As for the object relation, this only tallies very imperfectly with what is usually understood on the subject of anality, as we shall see.

The narcissism of these subjects is bruised; it is in pieces. The narcissistic wound whose origin goes back, of course, to childhood, has barely healed. The wound is always liable to reopen for the slightest reason. It seems literally untreatable; any approach which is too direct provokes acute mental pain. There is often mention in this context of disturbed ego boundaries and there is certainly no lack of evidence to suggest that behind the appearances of normal social functioning, the ego suffers the consequences of a chaotic narcissistic economy of the most precarious kind, without established boundaries. Hence the feeling we have that the patients concerned have been 'flayed alive'. Patients speak of their psychical envelopes in terms of an outer layer which, once it has fallen away, leaves a dermis exposed to all kinds of aggression. The result of this distinctive characteristic of the 'ego-skin' (Anzieu) is paradoxically a rigid structure. This can give an impression of firmness when in fact, as we know, what is involved is obstinacy. All conflict easily veers towards a stubborn attitude which is incomprehensible for those around as well as sometimes for the analyst himself. Of course, this lack of flexibility is often seen as a virtue, a loyalty to moral principles which cannot be compromised. In fact, *anal narcissism* gives these subjects an internal axis, a genuinely invisible prosthesis, which is only maintained by *the unconscious erotisation of any conflictual situation affecting narcissism*. Life itself provides an appreciable contingent of circumstances which the subject can make use of in this way. Very often, in fact, in most cases, a lucid examination shows that the subject is within his rights but that he feeds the wound caused by the wrong he has suffered, attaching a degree of importance to it which many others, more concerned for their peace of mind, would not have given to the same situation, with the result that it loses significance and is soon forgotten. However, opposition is vital for these subjects; it enables them to get a better sense of their identity which can only be established through this difference acquired through fighting. When this is externalised, it gives the ego the opportunity to feel alive. This is of course evocative of paranoia but here there is no real feeling of persecution, simply the conviction that one is scarcely made for reality as it is. These patients are, moreover, perfectly capable of perceiving it without the deformation that paranoiacs subject it to. Situations of conflict are also an opportunity to repeat the parental trauma caused by their belittling judgement. Instead of giving the support one would expect when faced with the everyday challenges of life all they could say was: 'You're not up to it!' After that, each new confrontation serves to reinforce this psychical backbone which was acquired through realising a task experienced as a challenge to be met. It can be seen that what passes for strength of will or tenacity is in fact founded on a deficiency – and counters the temptation of masochistic submission. Although I continue to think that the term paranoia would be improper here, we should nonetheless notice the intensity of the *intermittent projective functioning* in which the patient relives with the analyst the feeling he has already had with the primary object. 'You changed the position of the furniture purposely to see how I would react', 'You're saying that to trouble me', etc. Here, we are concerned with a register in which narcissism and object relation are intertwined – this will enable us to understand better one characteristic of these patients: *falling back on thought as an inalienable possession.* Faced with the internal harassment by parental imagos and their direct or indirect representatives in the external world, there is one refuge which constitutes the last isolate, an inviolable shelter against enemy intrusions, and that is thought. In fact, these patients say *my* thought and speak of it as if it were a possession in which their individuality takes refuge. It is a last recourse which, if it falls into the hands of others, makes the subject disappear himself. Hence the strong possessive aspect of this intellectual narcissism which is supposed to be a defence against the 'de-individuating' possessiveness of objects. 'That's something that can't be taken away from me!' Thought has become a bastion in which subjectivity as a whole has found its last source of protection before surrendering. Without reaching these extremes, one can notice in those circumstances which are less overtly conflictual, an affirmation of singularity (more than originality). 'I want to do things my own way', is accompanied by a feeling that other people are a hindrance to this.

By making what would doubtless be a very schematic short-circuit, one might imagine that *thought has taken the place of the primitive anal object* or, to be more precise, that if the anal object is destined in the end to be evacuated and lost, thought may have survived this evacuation. Admittedly, between the concrete anal object and abstract thought, there are many intermediaries: the psychical representative of the anal drive is caught in the contradiction of holding back/pushing or of retaining/evacuating, or again of feeling the faeces are its property or offering them as a gift etc., the ideational representative of the object, the representative of the fantasy object etc. But just as we are led to make a distinction between faeces and anal mucous, as between content and container, we can also imagine the bipartition between the various psychical forms which we have just mentioned and the thoughts which inhabit them. It would be as if the subject was clinging to the sense of ownership which he experienced towards what he feels is a part of his 'belly' (his intestines) to console himself for the loss of what it contained and which he notices he has been deprived of 'against his will'.

This fierce defence of subjective territory can be explained by a permanent feeling of being impinged on by others. So much so that the paradox is that solitude, which is usually experienced as an object desert, is ultimately sought after to the extent that it may signify the suppression of the invaders and thus access to a burrow where one no longer has to fear the abuses of power of other people who violate the freedom of those around them.

It is now time to deal with the second aspect, i.e., object-relations, of the psychical structure of primary anality. Here, too, the relationship is full of contradictions. Moreover, at the basis of this mode of relating to the object, there is the affirmation of a right to a contradiction of choices. 'I don't want to choose; I want this and the opposite.' Needless to say, in these conditions we are talking about something very different from what is usually called ambivalence. In effect, love easily takes on the shape of hate and hate is the sign of an attachment that nothing can undo. *Hate seals a pact of eternal fidelity to the primary object*; the latter may be replaced by others which, nonetheless, do not efface its memory in spite of appearances to the contrary. One then expects to see the subject getting involved in sadomasochistic relationships, but in fact these do not have the intensity that one finds elsewhere, since his relationships to external objects are fragile. They hardly ever last and the rupture condemns the subject to a return to solitude, that is, to the internal primary objects which, for their part, remain unchanged. They are permanently the theatre of a sadomasochistic relationship based on a power struggle. But in transference the relationship is often, I repeat, paradoxical. On the one hand there is a grasping after the object and, on the other, during long periods, this relationship takes a parasitic turn. Sessions are dreary, empty and stagnant. And yet the patient would not miss one for anything in the world. He protests at the analyst's slightest absence and makes him pay dearly for the interruption when he returns. The patient realises, moreover, that he is himself the agent of the sterility of the sessions, but he says he cannot do otherwise; that is, invest the analyst as an object. And it is the analyst who experiences (instead of the patient) very acute feelings of aggressivity due to boredom and to the sense that the work is useless, although he is ready to admit that in fact the patient cannot do otherwise. Sometimes the analyst has the distinct impression that *this anal opposition stems from an unconscious negativism where it is more important to say no to the object than yes to oneself.* Unconscious negativism, we have said, is not perceived as such by the subject, but nonetheless reminds the analyst of the connection between the present situation and certain memories recounted by the patient. 'I would have preferred to die rather than to give in and confess.'

This kind of obstinacy in communication co-exists with its opposite: a fusional relationship in which the subject communicates secretly and internally – aided by an uninterrupted interior discourse outside the session – with an entirely good object. This is the only way to bear the frustrations imposed either by its absence or by the conflicts engendered by contact with it when it is present.

What place is there for sexuality in this way of relating to the object? Generally speaking the sexual life of these subjects is poor and we may justly be surprised by the way they seem to tolerate abstinence. Admittedly, there is some reason to think that their character difficulties are aggravated as a result. But on the other hand they do not seem to suffer from it, or at least do not complain about it, and the exacerbation of their character disturbances does not seem to be directly related to the absence of sexual satisfaction. However, their reserve with respect to sexuality often leaves us ignorant of what they feel about it. More often than not, the feeling of humiliation which accompanies any talk of sexual desire dries up any vague desire there may be to speak about it. Their self-image is not very differentiated sexually – often they claim the neuter gender, that is, the feeling of being neither a man nor a woman. It is not so much psychical hermaphroditism or androgyny we are dealing with as asexual identity. The sexual member is contingent; neither castration anxiety, properly speaking, nor obvious penis envy is noticeable.

On the other hand, experience shows that the sexual desires which appear to be drastically repressed are in fact not really absent. They may occasionally manifest themselves. But generally speaking they are like frozen assets, quite secondary to a need for love with which they do not have simple relations. It would be simplifying the situation to think that the need for love dictates repression. On the contrary, *sexuality frees itself easily when love (shared) is found.* It then seems to be experienced without any major conflict. It really seems as if *because the prerequisite condition for the assumption of sexuality, i.e., love, is lacking, sexual desire as such no longer existed.* The object is more problematic as a love object than as a prohibited sexual object and this leads to renunciation or even asceticism which are much more easily accepted than the danger of being disinvested by the object.

The rejection of one's self-image can go as far as negative hallucination in front of the mirror. In order to be accepted, one's self-image needs to be mediated by another person's gaze; the confrontation with one's own image is cruel. As appearance cannot be corrected and representation is attacked, only a recreation of the subject's image by productions which are his own creation are acceptable. Sublimation thus bears the stamp of the anal seal.

This is why *objects are often chosen as narcissistic doubles.* An intellectual work involves one's self-image; the accomplishment of a creative piece of work is clearly perceived as a double of oneself in an almost concrete way. It must, of course, be perfect, without error. We see that the attempt to describe a typical style of relating to the object brings us back to narcissism. For, in fact, as the self-image has barely developed or is unappeased by self-hate, *the subject can only define himself through the image of himself which is reflected by others.* 'If only I knew what you thought of me, then I could see myself in relation to that.' Taken to extremes, defences other than repression, or splitting, can in certain traumatic, painful circumstances, take on a massive character forcing the subject to *deny the object's existence and even his own.* There is nothing here resembling a philosophical doubt but rather it suggests an extreme measure taken to counter suicidal despair. 'You don't exist' or even 'I don't exist' can become the ultimate positions adopted by the ego against the weight exerted by the object, either because of its demands or because of the weaknesses resulting from its various failings. Here we are on the threshold of a denial of reality which may raise fears of the subject's toppling over into psychosis but *it is not a real repression of reality.* The subject has indeed entered a process of negotiations with the real (*le réel*), a permanent source of traumatisms, but these constitute a compromise with reality to ensure a minimum survival, enabling him to cling desperately to life and the harshness of the real. If the subject seems to attach little importance to this as well as to the object as intercessor, it is in the form of a denial which is similar to spitting: 'I know you exist, but I have to convince myself that you don't in order to pre-empt the power that your actions can have over me.' Here, as well, the world seems to be split in two: on the one hand, there is the domain of reality from which one must expect nothing if one is not to be disappointed and, on the other, the realm of fantasy in which everything is possible because nothing can really happen and so consequently cannot inflict any disappointment.

The complement of this denial of the object's existence is a confusion of identity with it: 'You got angry and that was a relief for me because it is as if it was me who had got angry.' There is more than a projection here: a real transporting of oneself into the other, an effect of the other person's image in which the subject recognises, as belonging to himself, what he cannot accept when he looks at himself and sees himself alone. Hence the painful feeling of difference which also arises when the object differs from the subject through a non-co-incidence and non-reciprocity of the affects which it feels. We can deduce from this that *primary anality is connected with the end of symbiotic omnipotence.* The object is no longer one with whom communication is established in a mode of perfect harmony, uninterrupted continuity, of a mutual correspondence of desires and satisfactions which nothing can disturb. A sense of difference has emerged obliging the subject to deal with incomprehension, the non-coincidence of desires, changing moods and the object's inconstancy. This is an ordeal which can lead to black anger, impotent rage and even sometimes the parcelling of the subject, especially if the crisis is accompanied by the feeling that the object has been lost through destruction.

What occurs next is not a process of mourning with a desire for reparation but an accentuation of distress which confirms that the world (the object) is bad, cruel and that the subject's acts can receive no recognition giving him the right to a recognised existence. In fact, *it is the subject who does not recognise the object's right to be different and who feels in turn distressed at not being recognised himself.* However, fusional regression has not disappeared entirely; it may persist in the shape of *psychic 'niches'*. This term is particularly appropriate in that it concerns the creation of spaces of solitude where, once again, the subject has the impression of being able to escape the effect of objects which always prove disappointing. 'My bed is the only place where I feel good. There, I have the impression at last of being left alone.'

All these factors which are more coherent than one would at first think when they manifest their characteristics in a transference relationship are extremely difficult to bear for the analyst who is sorely tested in the counter-transference. *Counter-transference cannot escape the necessity of reflecting the problematics of the subject, as in a mirror.* The analyst feels compassion for the subject but equally succumbs to what Winnicott rightly called hate in the counter-transference. The desire to help the patient comes up against the obstinacy of his non-communication which periodically makes the analyst feel he wants to end a relationship which is felt to be fixed, sterile and parasitic, but the subject's distress is so considerable that the analyst finally tells himself that an interruption would be an insurmountable trauma. When the relationship is continued, the analyst would do well to abandon all hope, and simply to concern himself with withstanding, resisting the patient's destructive and self-destructive attacks. Once again Winnicott comes to mind with his article on 'The Use of an Object' (1968) in which he shows, perhaps with exaggerated optimism, how the analyst who can survive the patient's repeated destructive attacks, ends up being useful to him by helping him tolerate himself through understanding what he is.

It is often particularly trying for the analyst to notice that the patient's unconscious communication, when it becomes understandable, is not experienced as a fortunate event enabling him to have access to a psyche which is otherwise defended excessively and quite irrationally, but as something escaping his control which wounds him because it marks a failure of his mastery. *Mastery is moreover less in question than ascendancy.* This is experienced as if the patient had in fact given way to an involuntary loss of control (sphincteral), thus offering against his will the product of his bowels to a mother who is abandoning (she no longer carries him), authoritarian (imposing bowel-training and immobilisation on the pot), sadistic (enjoying the submission of her offspring) and inquisitive (about the abdominal content and the pleasure derived from its retention). The development of this relationship leads to the introjection of a rigorous super-ego which pays for the merciless criticism of the actions and productions of others by the perfectionist censorship of its own productions to the point of sterilising any form of personal realisation.

These patients have great difficulty in deciding that they want to develop, that is, to grow, because growing means accepting the dynamic of change in objects (in reality) and thus submitting to it – especially as the fear of adopting a less negative attitude involves the risk that the patient will lapse into fusional regression which, by its very anachronism, is likely to give rise to new, intolerable disappointments. What is worse, changes sometimes occur, translated by appreciable improvements in social life, resulting in a lessening of conflicts in everyday life. This change brings hardly any satisfaction since, for the subject, it only concerns the surface of things and does not change anything which really matters to him, i.e., the realisation of his deep narcissistic aims concerning which the analyst is felt to be ineffective; this is more important even than seeking happiness with an object. More than mere patience is needed to tolerate this slow evolution and the disappointing judgement about what the analytic relationship has achieved in the way of change. It is very understandable that often the analyst throws in the towel whatever it may cost him. And the cost to the patient is even greater.

But for those who have had the tenacity to maintain the relationship in spite of the ordeals it entails, a mutative change sometimes occurs which allows for some satisfaction to be taken in the work achieved, without however expecting miracles from the therapeutic relationship which would be too redolent of those fostered by the patient's idealisation of himself.

This hypothetical construction far from exhausts the distinctive characteristics which we have outlined in our descriptive chapter. For what seems most remarkable to us is the feeling of being crushed and the feeling of impotence in the face of conflicts which characterise the subject's relations with other people in the most diverse circumstances: in the spheres of work, love and the family, and particularly in regard to the realisation of tasks where these subjects are the only ones involved and experience an obstinate resistance to achieving what they have to do. In other words, while the external conflicts reveal an object relationship which is immediately perceptible, the difficulty in accomplishing tasks which depend only on oneself reveals that the core of the problem lies in the internalisation of the conflict with an imago representing the primary object. The advantage of this second type of conflict is to get rid of all the rationalisations surrounding the conflicts involving other people. But this is also what is most difficult to understand for we have very little information owing to the fact that censorship is so strong; that is to say, the unconscious desire for oppositional retention is extremely powerful because it is the basis of a demarcation of identity between the temptation towards fusional regression and the destruction of the other as the only proof of self-affirmation.

The corollary of this inhibition is that thought processes seem to be paralysed, taken over by a *blank* which nothing will fill, compelling the subject to stand still, to mark time without there being any solution. If one tries to go further in the description of mental functioning at these times, one finds nothing which sheds light on this sterilisation of representative psychical activity, which in the most severe cases seems to border on psychical emptiness. When, however, the subject wants to gain understanding of what is happening to him by telling the analyst how he experiences what he is going through, one discovers the existence of an introject of the primary object which is nothing more than a totally abstract form of it and simply has the effect of preventing narcissistic pleasure from feeling it is alive, active and progressing. For the analyst it becomes difficult to untangle, in this state, what belongs to the introjection of the primary object or to the internalised projection which he is the object of. One might then indulge in speculations on the relations container–contained or between part object–whole object, as if one was dealing with a subject-turd, the prisoner of a constrictive mucous mother or, if paralysis dominates, it is due to a petrified subject (unconscious) who strives to immobilise, to retain, to keep a mother who comes and goes, attending to her affairs, thinking about something else, neglecting her child.

These different scenarios which come to life in transference are not contradictory. They reveal the high degree of complexity, resisting univocality, of these structures which I felt were worthy of an original description, owing to their difference from the figures which have been familiar to us since Freud's first description of the anal character.

Notes

Translator's Note

1. Green, A., 'On negative capability, a critical review of W.R. Bion's *Attention and Interpretation*', *International Journal of Psychoanalysis*, 1973, **54**, pp. 115–19.
2. Masud Khan in the preface to Winnicott's *Through Paediatrics to Psychoanalysis* (1958) p. X1, Karnac Books, 1992.
3. Russ, J. (1991) *Dictionary of Philosophy*, p. 336, Bordas, Paris.
4. 'consciousness is what it is not'.

An Introduction to the Negative

1. Three recent publications bear witness to this. In 1987, there was Jean Guillaumin's *Entre blessure et cicatrice. Le destin du négatif dans la psychanalyse*, Champ Vallon. Then, in 1988, under Jean Guillaumin's supervision, *Pouvoirs du négatif dans la psychanalyse et la culture*, Dunod, with contributions by Y. Bonnefoy, C. David, J. Chasseguet-Smirgel, J. Cournut, M. Gaguchi, R. Kaes, M.T. Neyraut-Sutterman, M. de M'Uzan and, in 1989, *Le négatif et ses modalités*, under the supervision of Missenard, with contributions by G. Rosolato, J. Guillaumin, J. Kristeva, Y. Gutierrez, J.J. Baranès, R. Kaes, R. Roussillon, R. Moury. Jean Guillaumin's name is associated with all three publications. The first is exclusively his own; he supervised the second and collaborated in the third which focuses particularly on group phenomena. If we examine these works closely, we notice that the negative in psychoanalysis is most often approached indirectly. Other recent studies on this subject are: B. Rosenberg, 'Sur la négation' in *Cahiers du centre de psychanalyse et de psychothérapie*, 1981, no. **2**, pp. 3–54; J.-B. Pontalis, *Perdre de vue* (especially I, 6) Gallimard, 1988; G. Rosolato 'La psychanalyse au négatif' in *Topiques*, 1977, no. **18**, pp. 11–29; B. Penot, *Figures du déni*, Dunod, 1989.
2. Hyppolite, J., 'Commentaire sur la *Verneinung* de Freud', in *La Psychanalyse*, vol. I.
3. 'Le travail du négatif', in *Revue française de psychanalyse*, 1986, no. **I** (a paper given at the XLVe Congress for French-speaking psychoanalysts from Latin countries, May 1985), see Appendix I.
4. 'La double limite', in *Nouvelle Revue de Psychanalyse*, 1982, reprinted in *La folie privée*, Gallimard, 1991.
5. Bonnafe, L., Ey, H., Lacan, J. and Rouart, J. (1950) *Le problème de la psychogénèse des névroses et des psychoses*, Desclée de Brouwer.
6. Cf. Jacques Lacan, *Ecrits*, Le Seuil, 1966 (first publication 1954), [*Ecrits: A Selection*, transl. A. Sheridan, Routledge, 1977]. Elsewhere we have made a critique of the Lacanian interpretation of the Freudian development in two studies, 'Répétition, différence, réplication' (*Revue française de psychanalyse*, 1972) and 'Le langage dans la psychanalyse' (*Langages*, Belles Lettres, 1984).
7. Henry Ey, who animated the post-war debates in French psychiatry, had a nostalgia for the great controversies which agitated psychiatry in the nineteenth century. The

meetings which he organised at Bonneval for almost fifteen years count among the richest periods of this discipline, before the return of a summary thinking which used the discoveries of chemotherapy as a pretext for attempting to absolve psychiatrists from the duty of thinking.

8. For further information on Borromean knots see *An Introductory Dictionary of Lacanian Psychoanalysis*, pp. 18–20, by Dylan Evans, Routledge, 1996 [transl. note].

9. This was recently attempted by Juranville, A. (1984) in *Lacan et la philosophie*, PUF.

10. See *The Letters of Sigmund Freud to Eluard Silberstein, 1871–1881*, Karnac Books, 1992.

11. Let it be noted that it dates from a period when Marxist theory enjoyed a certain favour in the intellectual world to which Lacan belonged. Georges Bataille comes to mind here.

12. *SE*: idea or presentation. See translator's note at the beginning of the book.

13. Cf. Alain Gibeault, 'Jugement et négation. De la théorie du jugement chez Kant et Freud', *Cahiers du Centre de Psychanalyse et de Psychothérapie*, 1981, no. **2**, pp. 91–132. It is possible that received ideas on the philosophical sources of Freud's thought, i.e., the thought of Kant, which is undeniable, and that of Schopenhauer, nearer to his own time and lending itself to a comparison due to an immediately noticeable resemblance – have helped to obscure the relation of psychoanalytic thought to Hegel's ideas, all the more so in that Freud clearly differentiated himself from them.

14. A central Lacanian concept closely related to knowledge (*connaissance*) borrowed from Hegel: the sense is of 'a failure to recognise', a mis-appraisal, an ignorance of consciousness about itself [transl. note].

15. His personal notes, recently published under the title of *Cogitations* (Karnac Books, 1992), show even more clearly than in his books the presence of thinking on the negative which he develops to the point of drawing a parallel between mathematical reasoning and dream work. See our review of the book in the *International Journal of Psychoanalysis*, 1992, **73**, pp. 585–9.

16. Bion, W.R. (1959) 'Attacks on Linking' in *Second Thoughts*, Karnac Books, 1987.

17. It is well-known that the *coup de Jarnac* consists in directing a surprise attack on the Achilles' tendon which is severed sharply, thus immobilising the adversary.

18. Cf. André Green, 'On negative capability, a critical review of W.R. Bion's, *Attention and Interpretation*', *International Journal of Psychoanalysis*, 1973, **54**, pp. 115–19.

19. Freud, S. (1924)[1923] 'Neurosis and Psychosis', *SE*, **19**: 153.

20. Green, A. (1986) Hogarth. French title: *La Folie privée*, Gallimard [transl. note].

21. Searles, H. 'Driving the Other Person Crazy' in *Collected Papers on Schizophrenia and Related Subjects*, Karnac Books, 1993, and *Countertransference and Related Subjects: Selected Papers*, Karnac Books, 1979.

22. Marty, P. (1976) *Les mouvements individuels de vie et de mort*, Paris, Payot; *L'ordre psychosomatique*, Paris, Payot, 1980.

23. Fr: *motions pulsionnelles*; G: *Triebregungen* [transl. note].

24. In accordance with the author's preferences and to reflect the general usage in French psychoanalysis as well as recent American writings, the term death drive has been preferred to the *SE* translation of Freud's *Todestrieb as* death instinct and is also used in the title of Chapter 4 of this book [transl. note].

25. This term, created by the author, cannot be understood without reference to the objectalising function. It refers not only to the withdrawal (sometimes radical) of investment from objects but also to attacks on the objectalising process. This is developed more fully in Chapter 4. See translator's note at the beginning of this book.

1 Aspects of the Negative

1. *'pour-autrui'* [transl. note].
2. Lacanian term. Generally *le réel* is opposed to *l'imaginaire*. In a personal communication the author stated that *le réel* is *'ce qui ne peut pas ne pas etre.* Imagination can distort everything. With the real you cannot pretend it never happened.' For a further discussion of this term see Dylan Evans' *An Introductory Dictionary of Lacanian Psychoanalysis*, Routledge, 1996 [transl. note].
3. *'l'ayant été n'étant plus'* [transl. note].
4. During his comments on my paper presented to the New York Psychoanalytic Society on 5 April 1988, F. Baudry analysed the terms of this debate. Cf. 'Negation and its vicissitudes', *Contemporary Psychoanalysis*, 1989, **25**, pp. 501–8.
5. Culioli, A., 'La négation, marqueurs et operations', *Recherches Sémiologiques*, 1988, no. **5–6**, pp. 17–38. Reprinted in *Pour une linguistique de l'énonciation*, Ophrys, 1990 [transl. note: the quotations which follow are my translation].
6. *Loc. cit.*, p. 22.
7. *Ibid.*
8. *Loc. cit.*, p. 27.
9. *Loc. cit.*, p. 38.

2 Hegel and Freud

1. Hegel, G.W.F. (1807), transl. A.V. Miller, p. 19 (1977) Oxford University Press.
2. Hyppolite, Jean (1946) *Genèse et structure de la Phénomenologie de l'Esprit*, p. 18, Aubier, Paris [transl. A.W.].
3. *Ibid.*, p. 68.
4. *Ibid.*, p. 63.
5. Hegel, G.W.F., *op. cit.*, p. 10.
6. *Ibid.*, p. 264.
7. Here, we find again the familiar figures of the Lacanian concepts *'a'* and *'grand Autre'*. In Hegel the Other of self-consciousness has a capital, a privilege Lacan reserves for the *grand Autre*.
8. Serves in French as a translation for Heidegger's *das Seiende:* it refers to what is; concrete being [transl. note].
9. The title of an autobiographical study by André Gide: transl. Bussy (1950) as *'If It Die ...'* .
10. According to Lacan *'jouissance* is suffering' (S7, 184). Briefly, it refers to the pleasure the subject derives from pain, from his symptoms, for example. For a fuller discussion, see *An Introductory Dictionary of Lacanian Psychoanalysis* by Dylan Evans, 1996, Routledge [transl. note].

3 Traces of the Negative

1. Freud, S., *New Introductory Lectures on Psychoanalysis, SE,* **22**: 73.
2. Green, A. (1986) *On Private Madness*, Hogarth, London (*La folie privée* (1990) Gallimard, Paris.)
3. Freud, S. (1900) *The Interpretation of Dreams, SE,* **5**: 566.
4. The sentence is highlighted with italics by Freud in *Three Essays on the Theory of Sexuality, SE,* **7**: 163.
5. Guillaumin, J. (1987) *Entre blessure et cicatrice*, éd. Champ Vallon, p. 171.

6. Guttières-Green, L., 'Problématique du transfer douloureux', *Revue française de psychanalyse*, **2**/1990, pp. 407–519.
7. Abraham, N. and Torok, M. (1978) *L'écorce et le noyau*, Aubier-Flammarion, Paris.
8. Freud, S., *Group Psychology and the Analysis of the Ego*, SE, **18**: 105.
9. Freud, S., *The Ego and the Id*, Chapter 3, *SE*, **19**.
10. See *Narcissisme de vie. narcissisme de mort*, Minuit, Paris 1983.
11. In English in the original.

4 The Death Drive

1. Note 1998. Psychoanalysts have not devoted the slightest consideration to the description of *apoptosis*, a death programming mechanism in cells in any ageing or pathological process.
2. In connection with melancholia, Freud contrasts strong fixation (oral) with weak investment of the object (*Mourning and Melancholia*).

5 Masochism(s) and Narcissism

1. The French reads: *'le moi sera plus ou moins "pulsionnalisé" dans son fonctionnement propre ...'* [transl. note].
2. Rosenberg, B. (1991) 'Masochisme mortifère, masochisme guardien de la vie', *Paris Psychoanalytic Society Monograph*, PUF.
3. Freud, S. (1930) *Civilization and its Discontents*, SE, **21**: 123.
4. *Ibid.*, p. 129.
5. Freud, S. (1915) 'Instincts and their Vicissitudes', *SE*, **14**: 138.
6. *Ibid.*, p. 129.
7. *Ibid.*, p. 126.
8. Green, A., 'Pulsion de mort, narcissisme négatif, fonction désobjectalisante'. Cf. Chapter 4.
9. Fenichel, O. (1928) 'The clinical aspect of the need for punishment', *International Journal of Psychoanalysis*, **3**, pp. 47–70.
10. Bergler, E. (1949) *The Basic Neurosis. Oral Regression and Psychic Masochism*, New York, Grune & Stratton.
11. Riviere, J. (1936) 'A contribution to the analysis of the negative therapeutic reaction', *International Journal of Psychoanalysis*, **17**, pp. 304–20.
12. Rosenfeld, H. (1971) 'A clinical approach to the psychoanalytic theory of life and death instincts', *International Journal of Psychoanalysis*, **52**.
13. de M'Uzan, M. (1972) 'Un cas de masochisme pervers', in *La sexualité perverse*, Payot.
14. Green, A. (1982) 'Après coup l'archaique' in *La folie privée* (1990), Gallimard.
15. The French here is: *d'avoir capté l'objet*. The verb *capter* has the sense both of captivating and capturing. Lacan used the neologism *captation* to refer to the imaginary effects of the specular image. See D. Evans' *An Introductory Dictionary of Lacanian Psychoanalysis*, p. 20, Routledge, 1996 [transl. note].

6 Splitting

1. I have commented on the issues involved here and of their repercussions for post-Freudian thought in the preface of *On Private Madness*.
2. Freud, S. (1927) 'Fetishism', *SE*, **21**: 149.
3. Freud, S. (1938) 'Splitting of the Ego in the Process of Defence', *SE*, **23**: 273. We do not find the same hesitation when Freud deals with the same problem elsewhere:

'the facts of this splitting of the ego, which we have just described, are neither so new nor so strange as they may at first appear' (*An Outline of Psychoanalysis*, 1938, *SE*, **23**: 204). I do not think that its dating, earlier or later, is sufficient to remove the contradiction. I am more inclined to believe Freud oscillated between two frames of mind.

4. We know how rich the semantic importance of fetishism is. It is sufficient to mention its place in anthropology and the function Marx gave to it in political economy. The range of implications it raises in analysis is no less vast: by relocating its relation to perversion, it was possible to link its function to the organisation of phobia as well as to the intermediate zone of transitional phenomena. It is thus sometimes considered as a semantic concentration leading to the delimitation of an object possessing specific characteristics, and sometimes as the expression of a creative symbolisation of a reflexive field. So its association with psychosis is not fortuitous. Freud ends his article on 'Neurosis and Psychosis' of 1924 with some remarks concerning the role of fantasy in the creation of the neo-reality and, foreshadowing Winnicott, points out the importance of play and symbolisation. Unfortunately, although Winnicott develops them theoretically to a high level, he dissociates them from sexuality.

5. In point of fact several stages need to be distinguished. First, the constitution of the new platform in two steps: the latest theory of the drives and the second topography (1919–23) resulting in the reorganisation of the theoretical field, then (from 1923 to 1926) a collection of short articles as a follow-up to the Oedipus complex, infantile sexuality, interwoven with others on masochism, the relations between neurosis and psychosis, and the general functioning of the psychical apparatus – negation and magic pad – the need for which is explained by the imprecise nature of the new theory. This intercalary period gives rise to a new modification concerning the theory of anxiety (1926), the third and last stage before the new development of fetishism, which inaugurates the final phase.

6. Cf. the remarks on 'transvaluation' further on.

7. In 1924, Freud expressed a contrary opinion in an article on 'The Loss of Reality in Neurosis and Psychosis', where he maintains that neurosis does not disavow reality, or very little; just enough to transform that reality, without loss of it, that is, in short, without ... disavowal.

8. This was what was expected – although it did not take place – of Anna Freud's work (supervised by her father?), *The Ego and the Mechanisms of Defence* (1936). It was a bit of an anti-climax. Instead of the expected watershed – disavowal is quite simply absent from Anna Freud's work – a compilation of defensive modalities none of which raise problems comparable with the richness and fecundity of disavowal and splitting. In spite of a certain amount of resistance, Melanie Klein's thinking, which included the latter while putting it to other uses, did not meet with any real obstacles. Now, in *Inhibitions, Symptoms and Anxiety* (1925) Freud developed his own thinking on the relations between the paradigm of repression and the old concept of defence by means of a detailed analysis of the psychic functioning of certain neuroses like obsessional neurosis. The theoretical position of repression is not very clear here, compared with the defences of this neurosis which stand out clearly from it.

9. In 'Analysis Terminable or Interminable', concerning the normal ego, or, one more or less similar to a psychotic's.

10. The rule is dictated by the super-ego, established by the ego. This is how it differs. The norm is the recognition of the super-ego; it does not emanate from it directly.

11. The fact that he wrote, just a few months apart, two articles on a subject which does not concern the problems raised by his practice could be an indication of this.

12. This did not however permit the theoretical advantage this remark offered to be pushed further and certainly, today, few analysts accept that the perversions represent simple fixations of infantile sexuality, free from repression and without the ego playing its part. But this argument confuses what is essential and what is not. The separation of the two domains of sexuality and the ego remains justified, the domain of the perversions remains – in spite of certain attacks – a category which possesses enough special characteristics to justify being preserved.

13. Expression borrowed from Pascal.

14. It is necessary to recall that his ideas on adaptation were forged in Europe before the war and so, *a fortiori,* before he went to America in 1941.

15. This was really the proof of the immense richness of this small discovery of Freud's with its considerable advantages concerning the 'inconsistencies, eccentricities and follies of men'. Far from considering them as relics, as *'fueros'* according to Freud's comparison, it is better to anchor them to a passionate core which reacts immediately to everything which it experiences as a threat to its narcissism. Now, through its own evolution and that of its recent history, this is exactly what psychoanalysis has become for culture, i.e., a narcissistic threat. Those who are interested by it are only prepared to approach it by trying to protect their narcissism by means of all kinds of manoeuvres in which they are themselves taken in, sometimes by the vision which they choose to have of it. It is then used for perpetuating a voluntary servitude as a result of maintaining illusions hoping for an infusion of charisma which feeds more than it analyses persecutory projections. Or again, it is seen to become the object of doping for those who conceive of its transmission in this way, with the idea that the most suspect manoeuvres surrounding its practice, justified by the most specious arguments, are supposed to be in the service of an ideal which the others are said to have sold in exchange for social recognition. As a last recourse there remains negation: 'Who? Us? But who do you mean? They are jealous of us, they resent us. Because we are young, beautiful ... and modern.'

16. Of whom I myself was one.

17. It is with such a purpose in mind that I have formulated my hypotheses on the dis-objectalising function and negative narcissism.

18. Cf. *On Private Madness*, Chapter 1.

19. French: *une pulsionnalisation de ses défenses* [transl. note].

20. See 'The Borderline Concept' in *On Private Madness*.

21. Cf. André Green (1990), 'Le complexe de castration', *Que sais-je?* PUF.

22. Political segregation is not part of this series precisely because it only occurs in the struggle for its own suppression.

23. In describing this type of transference relationship as fetishist we fall a long way short of the truth, since the choice of the fetish has the virtue of having found a solution for anxiety. The choice of an object in this case scarcely poses a problem of availability or, to be more exact, it means the erotic excitement it procures can be regulated, even when allowing for the unexpected.

24. A neologism in French adopted by Lacan to refer to the imaginary effects of the specular image. The term conveys the ambiguous nature of the power of the image

which is both captivating, seductive and imprisoning. See Dylan Evans' *Introductory Dictionary of Lacanian Psychoanalysis*, Routledge, 1996 [transl. note].

25. This term was created by the author to gather together a number of terms pertaining to the subject in contemporary psychoanalysis which all have a common basis (I, ego, self, etc.) forming a symmetrical pair with the already existing French term *objectal* [transl. note].

26. Donnet, J.-L., and Green, A. (1973) *L'enfant de ça*, Paris: Minuit.

27. I do not moreover see any difficulty in making use of what is best in this research as a source of knowledge external to psychoanalysis, without any direct relation to it, and without any privilege with respect to other fields which are a source for psychoanalytic reflection.

28. Unorthodox work.

29. Green, A. (1991) 'De la tierceité' in *La Psychanalyse: questions pour demain*, Monographies de la Société psychanalytique de Paris.

7 The Work of the Negative

1. Loeb Classical Library (1936), translated by W.S. Hett, Harvard University Press.

2. Breuer, J. and Freud, S. (1895) *Studies on Hysteria, SE*, **2**: 26. Breuer does not give the same meaning to the phenomenon, emphasising its characteristic of absence [author's note].

3. Cf. Couvreur, C., 'L'illusion d'absence, hallucination négative et hallucinatoire négatif', Duparc, F., 'Nouveaux développements sur l'hallucination négative et la représentation', Conference at the Paris Psychoanalytic Society. These two studies which are based on my earlier publications will be made use of here. See the *Revue française de psychanalyse*, 1992: **1**, pp. 85–100 and pp. 101–21.

4. Cf. *Draft K. the Neuroses of Defence SE.*, **1**: 220–9 and 'Further Remarks on the Neuro-Psychoses of Defence', *SE*, **3**: 159–74.

5. 'Further Remarks' *SE*, **3**: 162.

6. Freud, S. (1910) 'Psychoanalytic Notes on an Autobiographical Account of a Case of Paranoia (Dementia Paranoides)', *SE*, **12**: p. 14.

7. *Loc. cit.*, p. 69. We know that this 'later' never came as Freud destroyed the study of projection which was to appear in his *Papers on Metapsychology*, without coming back to the subject to study it in depth.

8. 'A Project for a Scientific Psychology', *SE*, **1**: 319.

9. The possibility of an investment of desire producing a hallucination provides Freud with his first intuition about the nature of a primary process.

10. It has been amply explored and developed in the studies of S. and C. Botella and especially in 'La problématique de la regression formelle de la pensée et de l'hallu-cinatoire' in *La psychanalyse: questions pour demain*, Monographies de la Revue française de psychanalyse, 1990.

11. Freud, S., *SE*, **14**: 230.

12. *Loc. cit.*, p. 232. If reality-testing is considered as the third crucial experience alongside those introduced in the 'Project', satisfaction and pain, it is clear that negative hallucination is located between pain and reality.

13. 'Such a withdrawal may be put on a par with the processes of repression', *loc. cit.*, p. 234.

14. The quotation marks are Freud's.

15. *New Introductory Lectures on Psychoanalysis,* Lecture 31. 'Dissection of the Personality' *SE*, **22**: 75.

16. Freud, S., *SE*, **19**: 183–7.
17. Freud, S. (1927) 'Fetishism' *SE*, **21**: 153.
18. *Ibid.*
19. Cf. Ey, H., *Etudes psychiatriques*, vol. II, Etude no. 16, Desclée de Brouwer, 1950, pp. 427–51.
20. McDougall, J. (1986) *Theatres of the Mind*, Free Association Books, London, see especially Chapters 5 and 7.
21. 'Further Remarks on the Neuro-Psychoses of Defence', *SE*, **3**: 184–5.
22. 'L'hallucination negative', *L'Evolution psychiatrique*, 1977, **42**: pp. 645–6. Cf. *infra* appendix 2. Actually, it was not the first time that I 'had attacked' – to use Freud's expression – the question. I had already expressed my views in 'L'objet a de J. Lacan, sa logique et la théorie freudienne', *Cahiers pour l'analyse*, no. **3**, le Seuil, 1965, and I had proposed a model for it in 'Le narcissism primaire structure ou état', published in 1966–7 and included in *Narcissisme de vie, narcissisme de mort*, éditions de Minuit, 1983.
23. Freud, S. (1918) 'From the History of an Infantile Neurosis', *SE*, **17**: 85.
24. In the reflections on the relations between 'Shitting on God' and 'Shitting something for God', *ibid.*, p. 83.
25. An association which concerns an extra toe and which appears in the context of another story (*déjà raconté*); is this a reduplication of disavowal?
26. Green, A. 'Travail psychique et travail de la pensée', in the *Revue française de psychanalyse*, 1982, XLVI, pp. 419–30.
27. My italics. 'L'hallucination negative', *L'Evolution psychiatrique*, 1977, t. XLII, p. 650, see *infra*, appendix 2.
28. *Moses and Monotheism, SE*, **23**: 3.
29. Janin, C. 'L'empiètement psychique: un problème de clinique et de technique psychanalytique', monograph in *La Revue Française Psychanalytique: La psychanalyse, questions pour demain* pp. 151–60, PUF, 1990.
30. The title of a book by H. Hecaen and J. de Ajuriaguerra.
31. Gregory, R.L. and Wallace, J.G. in *La fonction du regard*, éditions INSERM.
32. *New Introductory Lectures on Psychoanalysis*, Lecture 29 *SE*, **22**: p. 16.
33. *les choses laissées 'en plan'* [transl. note].
34. Translated by A. Sheridan (1999), Routledge. Original title *Le discours vivant* (1973), PUF, Paris.
35. Green, A. (1984) 'Le langage dans la psychanalyse', in *Langages*, Les Belles Lettres.
36. Cf. *The Freud-Klein Controversies 1941–1945*, edited by Pearl King and Ricardo Steiner, Tavistock Routledge, London, 1991.
37. Cf. Lacan, J. (1936) 'Au-delà du principe de réalité' in *Ecrits*, Le Seuil, 1966, pp. 73ff.
38. *L'Inconscient*, Bonneval Colloquium of 1960, published under the direction of Henri Ey and Desclée de Brouwer, 1965, p. 143.
39. Marty, P., de M'Uzan, M., David, C. (1963) *L'investigation psychosomatique*, PUF.
40. We cannot overlook here Henry Ey's monumental *Traité des Hallucinations*, Masson, 1973, the crowning achievement of his work and the sum of knowledge of his era.
41. We have put forward a model – based on hypothetical inferences – for the origins of the perceptive function in our study 'Méconnaissance de l'Inconscient' in *L'Inconscient et la science*, edited by R. Dorey, Dunod, 1991. We wish to refer the reader to it.
42. See in the *Ecrits* the remarks on D. Lagache's paper.

43. Green, A., 'Pulsions, psyché, langage, pensée' in *Revue française de psychanalyse*, 1988, p. 493. See also, 'La représentation de chose entre pulsion et langage', *Psychanalyse à l'université*, 1987, no. **12**, pp. 357–72.
44. Atlan, H., 'L'émergence du nouveau et du sens' in *L'auto-organisation*, under the supervision of P. Dumonchel and J.P. Dupuy, Le Seuil, 1983.
45. This was shortly after I had emphasised its importance during one of Lacan's seminars on 21 December 1965, cf. 'L'objet a de Jacques Lacan, sa logique et la theorie freudienne; convergences et interrogations ' in *Cahiers pour l'analyse*, no. **3**, Le Seuil.
46. Cf. *Narcissisme de vie, narcissisme de mort*, Minuit, 1982, pp. 117ff. Original publication 1966–67. This vicissitude of the work of the negative gives me a chance to point out that I used a similar expression (negative moment) for the first time in 1960 in the discussion of the report by J. Laplanche and S. Leclaire on The Unconscious at the Bonneval Conference of 1960; Cf. *L'inconscient, loc. cit.*
47. See Green, A., 'La réprésentation de chose entre pulsion et langage', in *Psychanalyse à l'université*, 1987.
48. From the Latin *decussare*, 'divide in a cross shape' (*The Concise Oxford Dictionary*) [transl. note].
49. A study by Guy Lavallée, 'la bouche contenante et subjectivante de la vision' postulates a comparable process based on the view of introjection and projection (personal communication).
50. Cf. Green, A., 'Projection' in *On Private Madness*, Hogarth, 1986.
51. Le Narcissisme primaire: structure ou état. Taken up again in *Narcissisme de vie, narcissisme de mort, loc. cit.*
52. *Loc. cit.*, p. 127.
53. French: 'rendre présent à soi' [transl. note].
54. Cf. Green, A., 'Méconnaissance de l'Inconscient' in *L'Inconscient et la science*.
55. That the former made a long detour through psychoneurology before returning to psychiatry lends even more weight to his approach. And the fact that the latter strive to understand what underlies the concept of *representability (figurabilité)* as a 'figure' which is common to representation and perception should be noted.
56. Botella, C. and S., 'La regression formelle de la pensée et l'hallucinatoire', Monograph in *La Revue française de psychanalyse: La psychanalyse: questions pour demain*, PUF, 1990. Botella, S. 'Le statut métapsychologique de la perception et l'irreprésentabilité', *Revue française de psychanalyse*, 1992, vol. LVI. Papers given at the day of study on January 17, 1991 organised by the Centre R. de Saussure in Geneva. Personal Communication. 'The perceiving subject is for ever affected by the failure of the hallucinatory solution, by the mark of his own existence in the lost object of satisfaction.'

8 Sublimation

1. 'Fragment of an Analysis of a Case of Hysteria', *SE*, **7**: 50.
2. *Loc. cit.*, p. 116.
3. *Cosmos* signifies beautiful, as N. Nicolaïdis has reminded me.
4. This is the approach taken by Laplanche and Pontalis in their *Vocabulaire de la Psychanalyse*.
5. *Leonardo da Vinci and a Memory of his Childhood, SE*, **11**: 80.
6. Laplanche, J. (1980) *Problématiques* **III**, p. 111, PUF, upholds a similar point of view.
7. In *Conflicts,* a collection of stories translated from the German by Eden & Cedar Paul, London, Allen & Unwin, 1928. Original title: 'Verwirrung der Gefühle: Private

Aufzeichnungen des Geheimrates R. v. D.' in *Verwirrung der Gefühle* (1927), Fischer Taschenbuch Verlag (1984). Translated into French by Hella and Bournac as *La Confusion des Sentiments* (1948), Stock, Paris. The French title of the story bears more relationship to sublimation than the English title. The translation here is mine based on the German. It is interesting that certain homoerotic passages at the end of the story have been censored in the English edition of 1928 [transl. note].

8. A commemorative publication [transl. note].
9. *Verwirrung der Gefühle*, p. 196.
10. *Ibid.*, p. 198.
11. *Ibid.*, p. 278 [transl. note: this scene does not appear in the English translation and appears to have been censored].
12. *Loc. cit.*, p. 122, author's italics. This double *neither* points to the power of the work of the negative in this case.
13. 'Le narcissisme primaire: structure ou état', published for the first time in 1966–67 and taken up again in *Narcissisme de vie, narcissisme de mort*.
14. 'If we choose, we may recognise in this diversion of aim a beginning of the *sublimation* of the sexual instincts', *Group Psychology and the Analysis of the Ego, SE*, **18**: 139.
15. *The Ego and the Id, SE*, **19**: 34.
16. *Ibid.*, p. 36.
17. *Ibid.*, p. 36.
18. *Ibid.*, p. 44.
19. *Ibid.*, p. 45.
20. *Ibid.*, pp. 45–6.
21. 'The repressed instinct never ceases to strive for complete satisfaction, which would consist in the repetition of a primary experience of satisfaction. No substitutive or reactive formations and no sublimations will suffice to remove the repressed instinct's persisting tension; and it is the difference in amount between the pleasure of satisfaction which is *demanded* and that which is actually achieved that provides the driving factor which will permit of no halting at any position attained, but, in the poet's words, "*presses ever forward unsubdued*" (Mephisto in *Faust*, Act 1, Scene 4). Freud, S. (1920g) *Beyond the Pleasure Principle, SE*, **18**: 42.
22. *The Ego and the Id*, pp. 54–5.
23. *Ibid.*, p. 56.
24. *Ibid.*, p. 56.
25. One even thinks of the ligature of the deferents – Steinach operation – which Freud decided to undergo voluntarily, thinking it would have a positive influence on the course of his cancer.
26. Green, A., 'Une variante de la position phallique-narcissique, considérée plus particulièrement sous l'angle du jeu et des fonctions de l'activité fantasmatique dans la création littéraire en regard de la sublimation et de l'idéal du moi', *Revue française de psychanalyse*, 1963.
27. Cf. *Narcissisme de vie, narcissisme de mort*, 1983. Freud may have neglected the case of a discharge comparable to the orgasm, at the level of the ego, comprising the same dangers. This hypothesis could be applied to drugs and other forms of toxicomania.
28. 'L'idéal: mesure ou démesure' (1983) in *La Folie privée*, Gallimard, 1990 [transl. note: this article is not included in *On Private Madness*].
29. See M. Klein, 'Early Analysis' (1923) in *Love, Guilt and Reparation and Other Works 1921–1945*, Virago, 1988.

30. *Ibid.*, p. 87.

31. For a different interpretation of the question of his childhood memory, see our study *Révélations de l'inachèvement, Léonard de Vinci*, Flammarion, 1992.

32. Winnicott, D.W. (1971) *Playing and Reality*, Routledge, 1991.

33. Cf. our discussion in 'La pulsion et l'objet', preface to B. Brusset's study *La relation d'objet*, Le Centurion, 1989.

34. There is no equivalence between the different terms placed on the same side of the hyphen.

35. 'Death Drive, Negative Narcissism, Disobjectalising Function', Chapter 4 of this volume.

36. Cf. Freud, S., *Three Essays on the Theory of Sexuality* (1905), *SE*, **7**.

37. Kristeva, J., *Soleil Noir*, Gallimard, to confine ourselves to one of the most recent studies. (*Black Sun: Depression and Melancholia*, London, Karnac Books, 1992.)

38. *Aurélia*, Pléiade, I, p. 359, Paris, Gallimard. Henceforth the quotations and references to this edition will simply indicate the relevant page. [Transl. note: I have referred where possible to *Gerard de Nerval's Selected Writings*, Penguin Classics, 1999 (tr. Richard Sieburth), which I have abbreviated as *SW* in the notes. Where this is not indicated the translation is mine.]

39. With the exception perhaps of *L'ombilic des limbes* by d'A. Artaud, but in this case acute psychosis is not involved.

40. Nerval wrote to his father on 2 December 1853: 'I am engaged in writing down and recording all the impressions occasioned by my illness. This will be a study not without utility for first-hand observation and science. I have never felt such ease in my powers of analysis and description. I hope you will agree with me' (Pléiade p. 1117; *Selected Writings*, p. 338). The contradictory aspects of Nerval's opinions on his mental states and the writings which deal with them depend on whom he is addressing. Here he is speaking to his father, a doctor – a few months before, Gérard wrote to his father (complaining about his silence), relating certain episodes of his last attack and mentioning his efforts to have his medical competence recognised by those around him: 'I cannot persuade anybody here that I am something of a doctor myself [...]. But the only point I want to make is that, having complemented my partial medical studies with philosophical observation and first-hand experience [... here Gérard uses his experience of the plague and rabies as an argument] I have some right to offer my opinion and to call myself a *hakim* [Arabic for doctor]' (*SW*, p. 336). Letter to Dr Labrunie, dated 21 October 1853 (the second today), probably written in a state of mental agitation provoked by worries about his father's servant. He had learnt of the latter's death between the two letters. A few days before this, on 12 October, he had showed signs of a severe state of delirium. Following the attack of 1853, Gérard left on a long journey to Germany. During this trip he visited Glogau, where his mother had died – but he makes no mention of it in his correspondence even though he wrote regularly to his father. There is no doubt that Gérard was in the same state of mind when he began writing *Aurélia*, after his stay in 1854 in the Passy clinic. He left prematurely having enlisted the help of his friends in the Société des Gens de Lettres. The letters he wrote after leaving the clinic show that it is likely that the psychotic episode was not over. Again we see, although in a less pronounced manner (but this means that he is now on the other side, 'Initiate and vestal') that he wished to have his views on his condition recognised, against the opinion of doctors (Letter of 24 October 1854, *loc. cit.*, p. 1187; *SW* p. 342). During this period, Gérard stepped up his assurances towards his father and warmly

expressed his affection. He wrote to him for the last time on 2 November 1854, about three months before his suicide. This last letter hints of a coming meeting. Did it take place? If so, what happened? One is led to surmise that there was a rupture of relations since his remains were abandoned by the family and received by the Société des Gens de Lettres.

41. Pléiade p. 1197; *SW*, p. 343.
42. *Loc. cit.*, p. 1119.
43. *Loc. cit.*, p. 1108. I only intend to recall a very limited number of biographical facts whose purpose is simply to accompany my remarks.
44. *Loc. cit.*, p. 420; *SW*, p. 320. Following this he sees three impaled children, one of whom appeared to be himself.
45. *SW*, p. 320.
46. Let us retrace rapidly the chronology of this relationship. The poet is thought to have met the singer in 1833. She accelerated the squandering of his grandparents' heritage by his excessive spending aimed at conquering her. In 1836, while Gérard was in Belgium, his mother's and his grandmother's bodies were transferred from the Montmartre cemetery to the 'clos de Nerval' at Mortefontaine. It was in the following year that Gérard's passion for Jenny began, and was at first mutual, it seems. During the years '37 and '38, the letters to Jenny Colon reveal the masochistic tone of this love. And we can already read: 'Dying, good heavens! Why does this idea constantly come back to me, as if only my death would be equivalent to the happiness you promise! Death! Yet this word does not fill my thoughts with darkness: it appears crowned with pale roses like at the end of a feast; I have sometimes dreamed that it lay in waiting for me smiling at the bedside of a woman I loved, not in the evening but in the morning after the joy, after the ecstasy, and that it said to me: Come on, young man! You have spent your night as others spend their day! Come and sleep now, come and rest in my arms; I am not beautiful but I am good and helpful, and I do not give pleasure but eternal peace' (p. 758). In fact, Gérard associates this image with that of a woman who looked like Jenny and with whom he spent the night in Naples, having to scarper at dawn before the return of the girl's regular lover, an officer of the King's guard. In 1837, Jenny left Gérard to marry a flautist who gave her numerous children. In December 1840, through the mediation of Marie Pleyel, he saw Jenny again in Brussels. On 21 or 22 February he had his first bout of madness which required his internment. Gérard had already been through depressive bouts without needing to be hospitalised. This time, it meant the *maison de santé* in the rue Picpus. He was ill until the end of November. On 5 June 1842, Jenny died, exhausted from numerous pregnancies and the demands of her profession. At the end of the year, Gérard left for the Orient.
47. *SW*, pp. 265–6.
48. This is Jenny Colon's real name. The dream takes place on the banks of the Rhine (one of his father's favourite spots).
49. Nerval's father only returned to France at the end of 1812. Gérard lived with him until 1834.
50. 'Seductive appropriation' (see note 15 to Chapter 5 and note 23 to Chapter 6) [transl. note].
51. An Arabic term meaning spirits; the allusion to the Orient is clear.
52. *SW*, p. 283.
53. Cf. Letter to Th. Gautier of 2 May 1843, p. 934, even if disillusionment was not far off.

54. *SW*, p. 285. Cf. Pléiade p. 934, 'Fonfride is quite decent. He has bought an Indian slave (an intimate detail follows) [...] You can have as many other women as you like. You get married *à la copte* or *à la grecque*, and it's far less expensive than buying women; as a companion was boorish enough to do. They are brought up according to the customs of the harem, and they have to be served, it's tiring.' 'O women! With you everything is different: I was happy, pleased with everything.' *Voyage en Orient*, 'Les femmes du Caire', Pléiade II, p. 183.
55. Including his mother and his grandmother.
56. Pléiade p. 391; *SW*, p. 295.
57. *Loc. cit.*, p. 393; *SW*, p. 297.
58. 'The burden of reparations to be made was crushing, especially given my incapacitation.' *Loc. cit.*, p. 395; *SW*, p. 299.
59. *Loc. cit.*, p. 396.
60. In fact the sun disappears (*loc. cit.*, p. 397); an occurrence which F. Duparc connects with a negative hallucination. At the same time the stars go in.
61. *Loc. cit.*, p. 329; *SW*, p. 303.
62. *SW*, p. 303.
63. *Loc. cit.*, p. 410; *SW*, p. 313.
64. In spite of the fact that André Breton dabbled for a while in psychiatry and flirted with the unconscious, *L'amour fou* is not *Aurélia*. [Transl. note: Breton's *L'amour fou* was translated as *Mad love* by Mary Ann Caws, Lincoln: University of Nebraska Press, 1987.]
65. *Loc. cit.*, p. 1220.
66. Cf. Freud, S., in *Civilization and its Discontents, SE*, **21**: 59.
67. *SE*, **21**: 80. The italics are mine.

On the Edge

1. Letter from S. Freud to W. Fliess, dated 2 April 1896. Freud, S. *The Complete Letters to Wilhelm Fliess 1887–1904* (translated and edited by J.M. Masson), p. 180, London, Karnac Books. It is worth pointing out that this letter, while it mentions explicitly that Freud was distancing himself from medicine, refers implicitly to the failure of his 'Project for a Scientific Psychology'.
2. Cf. Green, A., *La Folie privée*, Chapter 1.
3. Hölderlin, F., *Sämtliche Werke und Briefe*, vol. 3, Frankfurt am main: Deutscher klassiker Vlg, 1992 [transl. A. Weller].

Appendices

1. Due to a lack of space I am obliged to put forward only one argument the justifications for which necessitate a more lengthy treatment. I propose to come back to this on another occasion.
2. *SE*, **14**: 153.
3. Freud, S. (1925) 'Negation', *SE*, **19**: 233.
4. Here, Freud inserts a note: 'Cf. "The occurrence in Dreams of Material from Fairy Tales". In telling the story again on a later occasion he made the following correction: "I don't believe I was cutting the tree. That was a confusion with another recollection, which must also have been hallucinatorily falsified, of having made a cut in a tree with my knife and of *blood* having come out of the tree."' *SE*, **17**: 85.
5. Here I would like to add a personal observation. A patient suffering from infantile asthma which resulted in strengthening a repression of infantile amnesia, spent

endless nights suffering during which she would scrutinise the deserted landscape and the starry sky waiting for daybreak which would bring relief. She had no memory of her parents' bedroom which was adjacent to the one where she spent her sleepless nights. During her analysis with me, she told me the following: one morning, seeing that her young son looked worried, she asked him what was troubling him. The child then told her that he had spent a sleepless night because he had had a terrible nightmare. He had dreamed that his head only remained attached to his body by a bit of skin. He had woken up in horror and, gripped by the powerful effect of this dream, he had spent the rest of the night awake, immobilised, for fear that his head might be separated from his body completely. Hence the worried look he still had in the morning. The event was quickly forgotten during the following day. But as a result of the dream, the mother had a skin allergy on her chest.

6. Donnet, J.L. and Green, A. (1973) *L'enfant de ça*, Minuit, Paris.
7. *SE*, **12**: 25.
8. *Ibid.*, p. 49.
9. *Ibid.*, p. 59.
10. *Memoirs of my Nervous Illness*, p. 207 (transl. Macalpine and Hunter), Dawson, London, 1955.
11. *Ibid.*, p. 190.
12. *SE*, **12**: 78. My italics.
13. Cf. 'La double limite' (1982) in *La folie privée*, 1990 [only in the French edition: transl. note].
14. *SE*, **19**: 237.
15. See Appendix 4.

References of Publication

The contents of this book have not been published before with the exception of two contributions, unabridged: 'The Death Drive, Negative Narcissism, Disobjectalising Function', appeared in *La Pulsion de mort*, Green *et al.*, PUF, 1986, pp. 49–59. The First Symposium of the European Federation of Psychoanalysis, Marseille, 1984.

The second, in the appendices, 'The Work of the Negative', was published in the *Revue française de psychanalyse*, 1986, 1, pp. 489–93, in the proceedings of the XLV Congress of French Speaking Psychoanalysts from Latin Countries where it was presented.

Furthermore, appendix 2 includes part of an earlier article: 'L'hallucination négative. Note pour un addendum à un Traité des hallucinations', *L'Evolution psychiatrique*, t. XLII, fasc.III/2, numéro spéciale, 1977.

Appendix 3 is the transcription of a seminar given in 1988 at the Paris Psychoanalytic Institute.

Appendix 4 is an extract from an article of the Paris Psychoanalytic Society Monograph on Obsessional Neurosis: 'L'analité primaire dans la relation anale', PUF, 1993.

The chapter 'Masochism(s) and Narcissism in Analytic Failures' was presented in Munich and Bern.

Finally, 'The Work of the Negative and Hallucinatory Activity' was the subject of a series of conferences in Zurich, Buenos Aires, Bordeaux, Tel Aviv and Paris.

Index

Index compiled by Sue Carlton